Official *TOEFL iBT*® Te

Using the DV

The test questions on this DVD-ROM are from actual *TOEFL iBT*® tests. However, the screens and delivery formats are not identical to the actual test. When you take the actual *TOEFL iBT*® test, you may notice some variations in how the questions are presented to you on screen.

Installation

Insert the DVD-ROM into your computer. Go to the DVD drive and select the file labeled **Audio** to copy and save the audio tracks to your device for use in working through the **book** tests. On a PC computer, select the file labeled **Setup** to be guided through a short series of screens. At the end of the process, the program of electronic practice tests will be installed on your computer. On a Mac® computer, the DVD-ROM will automatically display its contents. To install the computer practice tests, drag the program icon to the **Applications** folder.

Main Menu

When you launch the program, this screen appears:

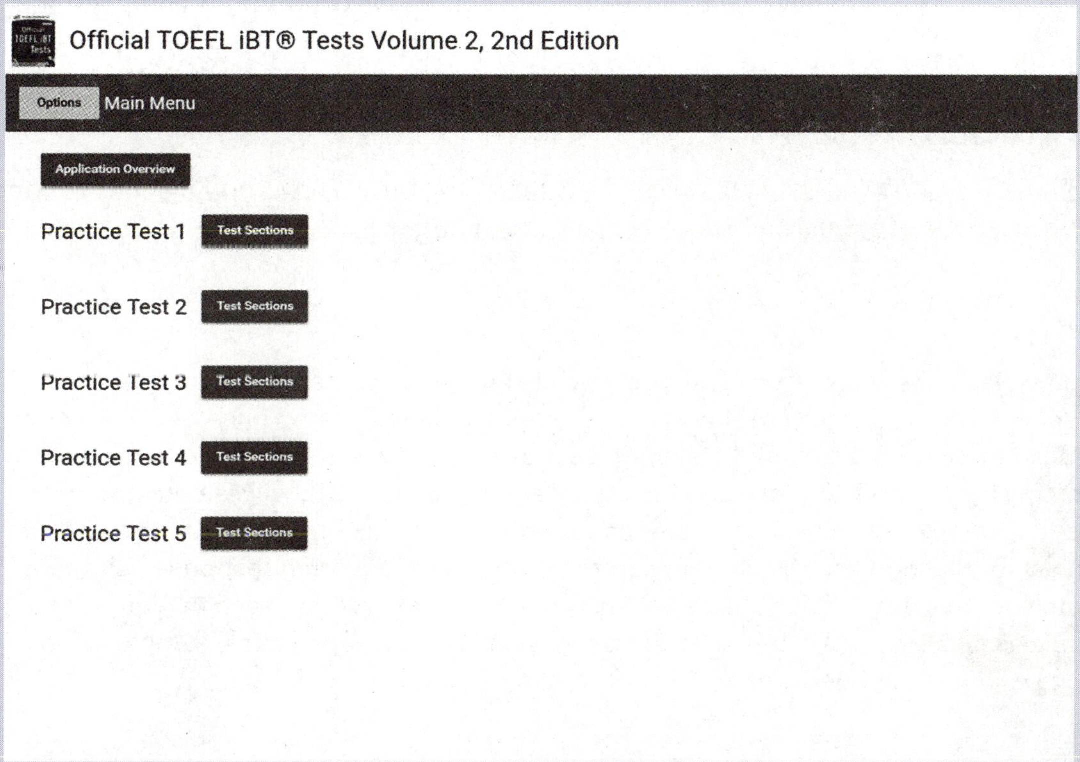

Taking *TOEFL iBT*® Tests on Your Computer

From the **Main Menu**, choose Test 1, 2, 3, 4, or 5. Then select the test section you wish to take: **Reading, Listening, Speaking**, or **Writing**. Note that you can take each section more than once.

When you open a test section, you will first see the instructions for that section. A timer on the screen shows how many minutes and seconds you have left for that section. You can hide the timer if you find it distracting.

If you must take a break during the test, select **Main Menu** at the top of the screen. This will take you back to the main menu. When you are ready to resume, open the test section again, and select the Continue button. Your work will not be lost, and when you resume, you will begin exactly where you left off. The timer clock will stop while you are on your break and will restart immediately when you resume the test. Try not to take breaks too often, because on the actual test, the clock keeps running even if you leave the room on a break.

Answering Questions

To answer the questions in the Reading and Listening sections, click on the corresponding answer oval or follow the instructions given. For some questions, you will need to select more than one answer choice. Once you select your answer(s), the **Next** button is enabled. Click on it to move forward to the next question. For the Reading section, you can move back to review your answer choice by clicking on the **Previous** button.

For the Speaking section, you should record your response to each question into a recording device after you hear the instruction telling you to begin speaking. Stop recording once the response time expires.

For the Writing section, write your response to each question in the space provided in the time allowed.

When all the questions in a section have been answered, select the **Next** button to complete the section.

Playing Audio Tracks

In the Listening, Speaking, and Writing sections, you will listen to audio tracks. Audio controls are available at the bottom of the screen. At the end of a track, select **Next** button to start answering questions.

Your Performance

On the **Main Menu**, select a section of any test you have taken. You will get information on when you completed the section and your score for the Reading and Listening sections only. Select **Review Section**. For each question in the Reading and Listening sections, you will see the correct answer and the rationale explaining why the answer is correct. For the Speaking section, you will see the important points for each question, sample responses, and rater comments on the responses. Follow the instructions for listening to sample responses. Use the important points, sample writing responses and rater comments to evaluate your performance on the Speaking Section. For the Writing section, you will see the topic notes, sample essays, and rater comments on the essays. Use the topic notes, sample essays, and rater comments to evaluate your performance on the Writing section.

Working Through the Tests in the Book

You may choose to work with the tests printed in the book rather than with the tests on the DVD-ROM. If so, you will still need to listen to the audio tracks. From your copied and saved Audio folder, you can select the audio tracks by number as they are numbered in the book. As you work through the tests in the book, you will be told when to play each audio track. Each time you need to play a track, you will see the following symbol: 🎧. Click on the number of the track as instructed in the book.

托福考试

官方真题集 2

Official TOEFL iBT® Tests

Volume 2

SECOND EDITION

• 美国教育考试服务中心 编著

群言出版社
QUNYAN PRESS
· 北京 ·

图书在版编目(CIP)数据

托福考试官方真题集. 2 = Official TOEFL iBT Tests Volume 2: Second Edition / 美国教育考试服务中心编著. —北京：群言出版社，2018（2019.5重印）
ISBN 978-7-5193-0468-3

Ⅰ. ①托… Ⅱ. ①美… Ⅲ. ①TOEFL—习题集 Ⅳ. ①H310.41-44

中国版本图书馆CIP数据核字（2018）第248835号

版权登记：图字01—2018—7819号

Educational Testing Service
Official TOEFL iBT Tests Volume 2, Second Edition
ISBN 978-1-260-44099-7

责任编辑： 孙平平
封面设计： 大愚设计+李　倩

出版发行： 群言出版社
地　　址： 北京市东城区东厂胡同北巷1号（100006）
网　　址： www.qypublish.com（官网书城）
电子信箱： dywh@xdf.cn　qunyancbs@126.com
联系电话： 010-62418641　65267783　65263836
经　　销： 全国新华书店

印　　刷： 廊坊十环印刷有限公司
版　　次： 2018年12月第1版　2019年5月第2次印刷
开　　本： 889mm×1194mm　1/16
印　　张： 29.25
字　　数： 545千字
书　　号： ISBN 978-7-5193-0468-3
定　　价： 128.00元

Contents

Introduction

About the TOEFL iBT® Test

托福考试测试考生应用与理解英语的能力，等同于在大学课堂上读、听、说、写英语的水平。目前，全球130多个国家中的10,000多所大学、政府行政部门以及其他机构将托福成绩作为录取标准之一，托福也因此成为世界上应用范围最为广泛的英语考试。

托福考试由阅读、听力、口语和写作四部分测试组成。每部分测试中的题目均考查考生英语读、听、说、写的水平。另外，还考查考生综合运用这些语言技能的能力，因此有些测试题目可能会要求考生综合使用自己的语言技能。例如，考生可能先阅读一篇文章或者听一个讲座，然后写出或者讲出刚才获取的内容。下面是对每个测试部分的简要介绍，包括各部分测试的内容及其所包含的题型。

Reading Section

阅读部分测试考生理解英文学术文章的能力。该部分中的文章均节选自大学程度的教科书及类似的学术材料。

考生要正确回答每道题目，并不需要具备任何与文章所谈主题相关的背景知识。回答问题所需的全部信息都可以在文章中找到。阅读题目考查考生寻找和理解基本信息、进行推断以及通过阅读获取信息的能力。

下表是阅读部分的题型及其说明：

细节题	该题型要求考生识别出文章中明确阐述的事实信息。
排除题	该题型要求考生将正确的信息与不正确的信息或者文章中没有提到的信息区别开来。
推论题	该题型考查文章中暗示但没有明确阐述的信息。
修辞目的题	该题型考查文章中某条特定信息的修辞功能。这种题型考查为什么作者在文章中提到或者涉及某条特定的信息。
词汇题	该题型要求考生确认某单词或短语在文章中的具体含义。

指代题	该题型考查考生确认文章中提到的观点与指代该观点的语言表述之间关系的能力。例如，文章中提到了一种观点，另一个句子可能将其指代为“该观点（This idea）”。问题可能会问“该观点（This idea）”指的是什么。
简化句子题	该题型要求考生选出与文章中某个句子意思基本相同的句子。
插入句子题	该题型要求考生将题目中给出的一个新句子插入文章中最适合的位置。
文章总结题	该题型考查考生辨识文章主要观点的能力，要求考生能够将主要观点从次要观点或者文中没有提及的观点中辨别出来。要选出正确的答案，考生既要理解文中哪些信息相对重要，又要能够辨别出哪些答案综合了文中的主要观点。
填表题	该题型要求考生分别挑选出属于表格所列类别的答案选项，表格中通常包含两到三个类别。考生需要对文章中的主要观点或者要点进行正确地组织或者分类。

Listening Section

听力部分考查考生理解英语对话和学术讲座的能力。

考生将听到两段对话。一段对话发生在教授的办公室，可能包括对学术材料或者课程要求的讨论。另一段对话发生在大学校园，包括与大学生活相关的非学术性内容的讨论。每段对话之后都有五个问题。

考生还将听到四个不同话题的讲座。在其中的两个讲座中只有教授讲话。在另外两个讲座中，学生会参与讨论；教授可能会就所讨论的话题向学生提出问题，或者教授回答学生的提问。每个讲座之后有六个问题。

每段对话和讲座只能听一遍。播放每段对话或讲座时，电脑屏幕上会有显示说话人的背景图片。有的对话和讲座还包含其他视图，比如展示了技术词汇或者特殊名称的黑板。

下表是听力部分的题型及其说明：

基本理解题	该类题型考查对话或者讲座的主要观点或主要目的，或者考查其中讨论的重要细节。
整合信息题	该类题型要求考生能够确定对话或者讲座信息的组织脉络，能够将所讨论的信息要点联系起来，或者能够根据讨论的信息要点进行推论。
情景理解题	该类题型要求考生能够确认讲话者在说某句话或者提出某个问题时的目的，或者能够确认讲话者的态度、观点或确信的程度。

大部分听力题是多选一的单选题，有些问题是有一个以上正确答案的多选题。考生可能还会遇到对流程步骤进行排序的题目，在方格中勾选合适答案的题目，或者重听对话或讲座中的某一段再进行作答的题目。

Speaking Section

口语部分考查考生用英语谈论各种话题的能力。

对于每个问题，考生需要在很短的时间内准备答案。准备时间结束后，在问题给定时间内尽可能全面地回答问题。对于本书中的测试题，考生应该使用录音设备录下自己的答案。通过这样的方式，考生可以重听自己的答案并与参考答案和评分标准进行比对。

在口语部分第一题中，考生需要谈论一个熟悉的话题，比如一个自己认识的人、一个喜欢去的地方、一件重要的物品，或者一次愉快的活动。考生应该根据自己的个人经历或者自己熟悉的内容进行回答。

在口语部分第二题中，考生需要就一个熟悉的话题给出自己的观点。考生需要阐述自己的观点并解释持有此种观点的理由。

在口语部分第三题中，考生首先需要阅读一篇短文，接着听一段相同话题的对话或阅读对话稿。然后，就这两部分内容被提问。考生需要结合短文和对话中的适当信息，针对问题提供完整的答案。考官会根据考生能否清晰、连贯地表达，以及能否准确地传达短文和对话中的信息，对考生的回答进行评分。

在口语部分第四题中，考生首先需要阅读一篇学术性主题的短文，接着听一个相同话题的讲座或者阅读讲座稿。然后，就这两部分内容被提问。考官会根据考生能否清晰、连贯地表达，以及能否整合并传达短文和讲座的关键信息，对考生的回答进行评分。

在口语部分第五题中，考生会听到一段与校园相关的对话或者阅读对话稿。考官会根据考生能否简要总结对话中描述的问题，能否从对话中选择自己认可的解决方案并表述清楚，以及能否就自己所做的选择给出理由，对考生的回答进行评分。

在口语部分第六题中，考生会听到讲座的部分内容或者阅读讲座稿。之后，考官会就此内容进行提问。考官会根据考生能否清晰、连贯地表达，以及能否准确地传达讲座信息，对考生的回答进行评分。

口语回答将根据三个重要层面的表现进行打分：信息传达、语言应用，以及话题展开。当考官给考生评分时，他们会同时从这三个方面进行考虑。没有哪个方面的权重会高于另外一个方面。

Writing Section

写作部分考查考生用英语写作进行学术交流的能力。

在写作部分第一题中，考生首先会阅读一篇文章，接着听讲座或者阅读讲座稿。然后，考生就所读文章和讲座有何关系进行回答。考生应尽量使用文章和讲座中的信息全面作答。本题不要求考生表达个人观点。开始写作时，考生可能需要再次浏览阅读文章。通常，有效的回答应是一篇150~225字的作文。考官会根据考生写作的质量、内容的完整性和准确性予以评分。

在写作部分第二题中，考生需要写一篇作文，陈述、解释并支持自己对某一问题的看法。通常，一篇有效的作文至少要包含300字。考官会根据考生的写作质量对作文予以评分，包括考生观点的展开、作文的组织结构，以及表达观点时运用语言的能力与准确度。

How to Use This Book/DVD Set

本书有助于考生准备托福考试。书中包含五套完整的托福实考题目。全部考试题目均为全球考生在各考点做过的托福考题，不过个别题目与实考题目呈现的方式略有区别。

考生可以通过以下两种方式来做本书的测试题：

- 在书中，使用钢笔或铅笔标出答案或写出回答。当考生看到页面上印有耳机图标时，即表示这里需要听录音。听力部分的所有音频文件都通过随书所附的DVD-ROM提供。在光盘主界面中，点击Audio Tracks即可看到已编号的音频列表。根据书中指示，点击相应音频即可。

- 使用电脑DVD-ROM中的互动版测试题。按照本书第一页“Using the DVD-ROM”的指示进行。点击你所选择的答案，或者按照指示输入书面回答。对于需要听录音回答的问题，问题出现在屏幕上时，录音会自动播放。

本书附录B中有音频部分的文本内容。如果考生无法获取音频文件，但是可以接触到英语发音准确的人，则可以请这些人为自己大声地朗读出文本内容。听文本内容要比自己朗读的效果更佳。别人朗读文本时，考生需要同时参看配图。

在使用印刷版的测试题时，每个音频文件只能听一遍。考生可以像在实际考试中一样，边听录音边做笔记，并使用笔记帮助自己回答问题。

Answers

每套测试题之后都附有相应题目的答案。

阅读和听力部分会提供答案。

口语和写作部分没有标准答案。答案部分提供了如何取得高分的策略。考生还可以使用附录A中的评分标准评估自己的答案。

对于口语部分，如果考生使用录音设备录音，可以将其与答案部分的指导说明以及评分标准进行对比。

在使用DVD-ROM中的电脑版测试时，根据屏幕上的指示查看阅读和听力部分的答案，以及口语和写作部分的评分标准。

Rubrics

评分标准用来指导评分者（即考官）评估考生口语和写作部分的答案。附录A中提供了托福考试四个测试部分的评分标准。

口语分数是对回答能否很好地传达考生想法的整体性判断。对于独立口语问题（第1–2题）和综合口语问题（第3–6题），**信息传达（delivery）**和**语言运用（language use）**是评分者评分时考虑的两个关键因素。**话题展开（topic development）**是第三个关键因素。对于独立口语问题，话题展开要求具备的特点是，答案内容的完整性及整体的连贯性。对于综合口语问题，话题展开要求具备的特点是，答案内容的准确度和全面性，以及整体的连贯性。

写作分数同样是对作文能否很好地传达考生意图的整体性判断。对于综合写作问题（第1题）和独立写作问题（第2题），**写作质量（quality of the writing）**是评分者评分时考虑的关键因素。高质量作文的特点是组织结构好，以及语法和词汇运用得恰当、准确。对于独立写作问题，高质量作文还要求能有效地突出主题和任务，并且能很好地展开阐述。**内容的全面性和准确性（completeness and accuracy of the content）**是评分者评分时考虑的另一个关键因素。全面、准确的答案要呈现出讲座和文章的相关要点，展示各个要点之间的关系，涵盖支持性细节内容，不要涉及讲座和文章中没有提及的信息。

More Official Resources

为了帮助考生准备托福考试，ETS提供了多种官方学习资源，包括：

- 《托福考试官方指南：第5版》（*The Official Guide to the TOEFL® Test, Fifth Edition*）
- 托福在线练习（TOEFL® Practice Online）
- "Inside the TOEFL® Test"视频（"Inside the TOEFL® Test" Videos）
- 托福备考（*TOEFL® Test Preparation: The Insider's Guide (MOOC)*）
- *TOEFL GO!* 官方App

有关这些学习资源及更多信息，以及注册托福考试，请访问*www.toeflgoanywhere.org*。

TOEFL iBT Test 1

READING

This section measures your ability to understand academic passages in English.

There are three passages in the section. Give yourself 20 minutes to read each passage and answer the questions about it. The entire section will take 60 minutes to complete.

You may look back at a passage when answering the questions. You can skip questions and go back to them later as long as there is time remaining.

Directions: Read the passage. Then answer the questions. Give yourself 20 minutes to complete this practice set.

COLONIZING THE AMERICAS VIA THE NORTHWEST COAST

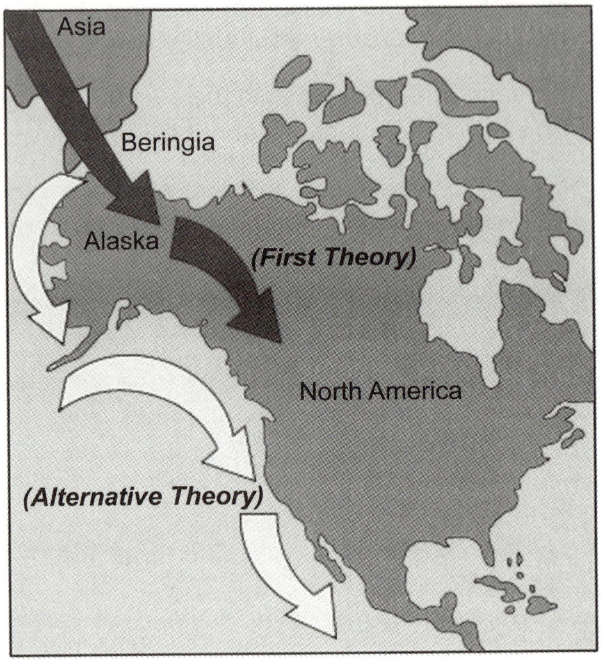

It has long been accepted that the Americas were colonized by a migration of peoples from Asia slowly traveling across a land bridge called Beringia (now the Bering Strait between northeastern Asia and Alaska) during the last Ice Age. The first water craft theory about this migration was that around 11,000–12,000 years ago there was an ice-free corridor stretching from eastern Beringia to the areas of North America south of the great northern glaciers. It was this midcontinental corridor between two massive ice sheets—the Laurentide to the east and the Cordilleran to the west—that enabled the southward migration. But belief in this ice-free corridor began to crumble when paleoecologist Glen MacDonald demonstrated that some of the most important radiocarbon dates used to support the existence of an ice-free corridor were incorrect. He persuasively argued that such an ice-free corridor did not exist until much later, when the continental ice began its final retreat.

Support is growing for the alternative theory that people using watercraft, possibly skin boats, moved southward from Beringia along the Gulf of Alaska and then southward along the Northwest Coast of North America possibly as early as 16,000 years ago. This route would have enabled humans to enter southern areas of the Americas prior to the melting of the continental glaciers. Until the early 1970s, most archaeologists did not consider the coast a possible migration route into the Americas because geologists originally believed that during the last Ice Age the entire Northwest Coast was covered by glacial ice. It had been assumed that the ice extended westward from the Alaskan/Canadian mountains to the very edge of the continental shelf—the flat, submerged part of the continent that extends into the ocean. This would have created a barrier of ice extending from the Alaska Peninsula, through the Gulf of Alaska and southward along the Northwest Coast of North America to what is today the state of Washington.

The most influential proponent of the coastal migration route has been Canadian archaeologist Knut Fladmark. He theorized that with the use of watercraft, people gradually colonized unglaciated refuges and areas along the continental shelf exposed by the lower sea level. Fladmark's hypothesis received additional support from the fact that the greatest diversity in Native American languages occurs along the west coast of the Americas, suggesting that this region has been settled the longest.

More recent geologic studies documented deglaciation and the existence of ice-free areas throughout major coastal areas of British Columbia, Canada, by 13,000 years ago. Research now indicates that sizable areas of southeastern Alaska along the inner continental shelf were not covered by ice toward the end of the last Ice Age. One study suggests that except for a 250-mile coastal area between southwestern British Columbia and Washington State, the Northwest Coast of North America was largely free of ice by approximately 16,000 years ago. Vast areas along the coast may have been deglaciated beginning around 16,000 years ago, possibly providing a coastal corridor for the movement of plants, animals, and humans sometime between 13,000 and 14,000 years ago.

The coastal hypothesis has gained increasing support in recent years because the remains of large land animals, such as caribou and brown bears, have been found in southeastern Alaska dating between 10,000 and 12,500 years ago. This is the time period in which most scientists formerly believed the area to be inhospitable for humans. It has been suggested that if the environment were capable of supporting breeding populations of bears, there would have been enough food resources to support humans. Fladmark and others believe that the first human colonization of America occurred by boat along the Northwest Coast during the very late Ice Age, possibly as early as 14,000 years ago. The most recent geologic evidence indicates that it may have been possible for people to colonize ice-free regions along the continental shelf that were still exposed by the lower sea level between 13,000 and 14,000 years ago.

The coastal hypothesis suggests an economy based on marine mammal hunting, saltwater fishing, shellfish gathering, and the use of watercraft. Because of the barrier of ice to the east, the Pacific Ocean to the west, and populated areas to the north, there may have been a greater impetus for people to move in a southerly direction.

Directions: Now answer the questions.

PARAGRAPH 1

It has long been accepted that the Americas were colonized by a migration of peoples from Asia, slowly traveling across a land bridge called Beringia (now the Bering Strait between northeastern Asia and Alaska) during the last Ice Age. The first water craft theory about this migration was that around 11,000–12,000 years ago there was an ice-free corridor stretching from eastern Beringia to the areas of North America south of the great northern glaciers. It was this midcontinental corridor between two massive ice sheets—the Laurentide to the east and the Cordilleran to the west—that enabled the southward migration. But belief in this ice-free corridor began to crumble when paleoecologist Glen MacDonald demonstrated that some of the most important radiocarbon dates used to support the existence of an ice-free corridor were incorrect. He persuasively argued that such an ice-free corridor did not exist until much later, when the continental ice began its final retreat.

1. According to paragraph 1, the theory that people first migrated to the Americas by way of an ice-free corridor was seriously called into question by

Ⓐ paleoecologist Glen MacDonald's argument that the original migration occurred much later than had previously been believed
Ⓑ the demonstration that certain previously accepted radiocarbon dates were incorrect
Ⓒ evidence that the continental ice began its final retreat much later than had previously been believed
Ⓓ research showing that the ice-free corridor was not as long lasting as had been widely assumed

2. The word "persuasively" in the passage is closest in meaning to

Ⓐ aggressively
Ⓑ inflexibly
Ⓒ convincingly
Ⓓ carefully

PARAGRAPH 2

Support is growing for the alternative theory that people using watercraft, possibly skin boats, moved southward from Beringia along the Gulf of Alaska and then southward along the Northwest Coast of North America possibly as early as 16,000 years ago. This route would have enabled humans to enter southern areas of the Americas prior to the melting of the continental glaciers. Until the early 1970s, most archaeologists did not consider the coast a possible migration route into the Americas because geologists originally believed that during the last Ice Age the entire Northwest Coast was covered by glacial ice. It had been assumed that the ice extended westward from the Alaskan/Canadian mountains to the very edge of the continental shelf—the flat, submerged part of the continent that extends into the ocean. This would have created a barrier of ice extending from the Alaska Peninsula, through the Gulf of Alaska and southward along the Northwest Coast of North America to what is today the state of Washington.

3. Paragraph 2 begins by presenting a theory and then goes on to

Ⓐ discuss why the theory was rapidly accepted but then rejected
Ⓑ present the evidence on which the theory was based
Ⓒ cite evidence that now shows that the theory is incorrect
Ⓓ explain why the theory was not initially considered plausible

4. The phrase "prior to" is closest in meaning to

Ⓐ before
Ⓑ immediately after
Ⓒ during
Ⓓ in spite of

5. Paragraph 2 supports the idea that, before the 1970s, most archaeologists held which of the following views about the earliest people to reach the Americas?

Ⓐ They could not have sailed directly from Beringia to Alaska and then southward because, it was thought, glacial ice covered the entire coastal region.
Ⓑ They were not aware that the climate would continue to become milder.
Ⓒ They would have had no interest in migrating southward from Beringia until after the continental glaciers had begun to melt.
Ⓓ They lacked the navigational skills and appropriate boats needed for long-distance trips.

PARAGRAPH 3

The most influential proponent of the coastal migration route has been Canadian archaeologist Knut Fladmark. He theorized that with the use of watercraft, people gradually colonized unglaciated refuges and areas along the continental shelf exposed by the lower sea level. Fladmark's hypothesis received additional support from the fact that the greatest diversity in Native American languages occurs along the west coast of the Americas, suggesting that this region has been settled the longest.

6. Which of the sentences below best expresses the essential information in the highlighted sentence in the passage? Incorrect choices change the meaning in important ways or leave out essential information.

Ⓐ Because this region has been settled the longest, it also displays the greatest diversity in Native American languages.
Ⓑ Fladmark's hypothesis states that the west coast of the Americas has been settled longer than any other region.
Ⓒ The fact that the greatest diversity of Native American languages occurs along the west coast of the Americas lends strength to Fladmark's hypothesis.
Ⓓ According to Fladmark, Native American languages have survived the longest along the west coast of the Americas.

PARAGRAPH 4

More recent geologic studies documented deglaciation and the existence of ice-free areas throughout the major coastal areas of British Columbia, Canada, by 13,000 years ago. Research now indicates that sizable areas of southeastern Alaska along the inner continental shelf were not covered by ice toward the end of the last Ice Age. One study suggests that except for a 250 mile coastal area between southwestern British Columbia and Washington State, the Northwest Coast of North America was largely free of ice by approximately 16,000 years ago. Vast areas along the coast may have been deglaciated beginning around 16,000 years ago, possibly providing a coastal corridor for the movement of plants, animals, and humans sometime between 13,000 and 14,000 years ago.

7. The author's purpose in paragraph 4 is to

Ⓐ indicate that a number of recent geologic studies seem to provide support for the coastal hypothesis
Ⓑ indicate that coastal and inland migrations may have happened simultaneously
Ⓒ explain why humans may have reached America's northwest coast before animals and plants did
Ⓓ show that the coastal hypothesis may explain how people first reached Alaska but it cannot explain how people reached areas like modern British Columbia and Washington State

8. The word "Vast" in the passage is closest in meaning to

Ⓐ Frozen
Ⓑ Various
Ⓒ Isolated
Ⓓ Huge

PARAGRAPH 5

The coastal hypothesis has gained increasing support in recent years because the remains of large land animals, such as caribou and brown bears, have been found in southeastern Alaska dating between 10,000 and 12,500 years ago. This is the time period in which most scientists formerly believed the area to be inhospitable for humans. It has been suggested that if the environment were capable of supporting breeding populations of bears, there would have been enough food resources to support humans. Fladmark and others believe that the first human colonization of America occurred by boat along the Northwest Coast during the very late Ice Age, possibly as early as 14,000 years ago. The most recent geologic evidence indicates that it may have been possible for people to colonize ice-free regions along the continental shelf that were still exposed by the lower sea level between 13,000 and 14,000 years ago.

9. According to paragraph 5, the discovery of the remains of large land animals supports the coastal hypothesis by providing evidence that

Ⓐ humans were changing their hunting techniques to adapt to coastal rather than inland environments
Ⓑ animals had migrated from the inland to the coasts, an indication that a midcontinental ice-free corridor was actually implausible
Ⓒ humans probably would have been able to find enough resources along the coastal corridor
Ⓓ the continental shelf was still exposed by lower sea levels during the period when the southward migration of people began

10. The word "inhospitable" in the passage is closest in meaning to

Ⓐ not familiar
Ⓑ not suitable
Ⓒ not dangerous
Ⓓ not reachable

11. According to paragraph 5, the most recent geologic research provides support for a first colonization of America dating as far back as

Ⓐ 16,000 years ago
Ⓑ 14,000 years ago
Ⓒ 12,500 years ago
Ⓓ 10,000 years ago

PARAGRAPH 6

The coastal hypothesis suggests an economy based on marine mammal hunting, saltwater fishing, shellfish gathering, and the use of watercraft. Because of the barrier of ice to the east, the Pacific Ocean to the west, and populated areas to the north, there may have been a greater impetus for people to move in a southerly direction.

12. The word "impetus" in the passage is closest in meaning to

Ⓐ chance
Ⓑ protection
Ⓒ possibility
Ⓓ incentive

PARAGRAPH 1

It has long been accepted that the Americas were colonized by a migration of peoples from Asia slowly traveling across a land bridge called Beringia (now the Bering Strait between northeastern Asia and Alaska) during the last Ice Age. **(A)** The first water craft theory about this migration was that around 11,000–12,000 years ago there was an ice-free corridor stretching from eastern Beringia to the areas of North America south of the great northern glaciers. It was this midcontinental corridor between two massive ice sheets—the Laurentide to the east and the Cordilleran to the west—that enabled the southward migration. **(B)** But belief in this ice-free corridor began to crumble when paleoecologist Glen MacDonald demonstrated that some of the most important radio-carbon dates used to support the existence of an ice-free corridor were incorrect. **(C)** He persuasively argued that such an ice-free corridor did not exist until much later, when the continental ice began its final retreat. **(D)**

13. **Directions:** Look at the part of the passage that is displayed above. The letters **(A)**, **(B)**, **(C)**, and **(D)** indicate where the following sentence could be added.

Moreover, other evidence suggests that even if an ice-free corridor did exist, it would have lacked the resources needed for human colonization.

Where would the sentence best fit?

Ⓐ Choice A
Ⓑ Choice B
Ⓒ Choice C
Ⓓ Choice D

14. **Directions:** An introductory sentence for a brief summary of the passage is provided below. Complete the summary by selecting the THREE answer choices that express the most important ideas in the passage. Some sentences do not belong in the summary because they express ideas that are not presented in the passage or are minor ideas in the passage.

Write your answer choices in the spaces where they belong. You can either write the letter of your answer choice or you can copy the sentence.

Recent evidence favors a rival to the long-standing theory that the Americas were colonized 11,000–12,000 years ago by people migrating south from Beringia along a midcontinental ice-free corridor.

-
-
-

Answer Choices

A Evidence that an ice-free corridor between two ice sheets developed when the continental ice first began to melt came primarily from radiocarbon dating.

B There is growing support for the theory that migration took place much earlier, by sea, following a coastal route along Alaska and down the northwest coast.

C Recent geologic evidence indicates that contrary to what had been believed, substantial areas along the coast were free of ice as early as 16,000 years ago.

D Research now indicates that the parts of the inner continental shelf that remained covered with ice were colonized by a variety of early human groups well adapted to living in extremely cold environments.

E There is evidence suggesting that areas along the coast may have contained enough food resources between 13,000 and 14,000 years ago to have made human colonization possible.

F Even though the northern part of the continent allowed for a more varied economy, several early human groups quickly moved south.

Directions: Read the passage. Then answer the questions. Give yourself 20 minutes to complete this practice set.

REFLECTION IN TEACHING

Teachers, it is thought, benefit from the practice of reflection, the conscious act of thinking deeply about and carefully examining the interactions and events within their own classrooms. Educators T. Wildman and J. Niles (1987) describe a scheme for developing reflective practice in experienced teachers. This was justified by the view that reflective practice could help teachers to feel more intellectually involved in their role and work in teaching and enable them to cope with the paucity of scientific fact and the uncertainty of knowledge in the discipline of teaching.

Wildman and Niles were particularly interested in investigating the conditions under which reflection might flourish—a subject on which there is little guidance in the literature. They designed an experimental strategy for a group of teachers in Virginia and worked with 40 practicing teachers over several years. They were concerned that many would be "drawn to these new, refreshing conceptions of teaching only to find that the void between the abstractions and the realities of teacher reflection is too great to bridge. Reflection on a complex task such as teaching is not easy." The teachers were taken through a program of talking about teaching events, moving on to reflecting about specific issues in a supported, and later an independent, manner.

Wildman and Niles observed that systematic reflection on teaching required a sound ability to understand classroom events in an objective manner. They describe the initial understanding in the teachers with whom they were working as being "utilitarian . . . and not rich or detailed enough to drive systematic reflection." Teachers rarely have the time or opportunities to view their own or the teaching of others in an objective manner. Further observation revealed the tendency of teachers to evaluate events rather than review the contributory factors in a considered manner by, in effect, standing outside the situation.

Helping this group of teachers to revise their thinking about classroom events became central. This process took time and patience and effective trainers. The researchers estimate that the initial training of the teachers to view events objectively took between 20 and 30 hours, with the same number of hours again being required to practice the skills of reflection.

Wildman and Niles identify three principles that facilitate reflective practice in a teaching situation. The first is support from administrators in an education system, enabling teachers to understand the requirements of reflective practice and how it relates to teaching students. The second is the availability of sufficient time and space. The teachers in the program described how they found it difficult to put aside the immediate demands of others in order to give themselves the time they needed to develop their reflective skills. The third is the development of a collaborative environment with support from other teachers. Support and encouragement were also required to help teachers in the program cope with aspects of their professional life with which they were not comfortable. Wildman and Niles make a summary comment: "Perhaps the most important thing we learned is the idea of the teacher-as-reflective-practitioner will not happen simply because it is a good or even compelling idea."

The work of Wildman and Niles suggests the importance of recognizing some of the difficulties of instituting reflective practice. Others have noted this, making a similar point about the teaching profession's cultural inhibitions about reflective practice. Zeichner and Liston (1987) point out the inconsistency between the role of the teacher as a (reflective) professional decision maker and the more usual role of the teacher as a technician, putting into practice the ideas of others. More basic than the cultural issues is the matter of motivation. Becoming a reflective practitioner requires extra work (Jaworski, 1993) and has only vaguely defined goals with, perhaps, little initially perceivable reward and the threat of vulnerability. Few have directly questioned what might lead a teacher to want to become reflective. Apparently, the most obvious reason for teachers to work toward reflective practice is that teacher educators think it is a good thing. There appear to be many unexplored matters about the motivation to reflect—for example, the value of externally motivated reflection as opposed to that of teachers who might reflect by habit.

Directions: Now answer the questions.

PARAGRAPH 1

Teachers, it is thought, benefit from the practice of reflection, the conscious act of thinking deeply about and carefully examining the interactions and events within their own classrooms. Educators T. Wildman and J. Niles (1987) describe a scheme for developing reflective practice in experienced teachers. This was justified by the view that reflective practice could help teachers to feel more intellectually involved in their role and work in teaching and enable them to cope with the paucity of scientific fact and the uncertainty of knowledge in the discipline of teaching.

15. The word "justified" in the passage is closest in meaning to

Ⓐ supported
Ⓑ shaped
Ⓒ stimulated
Ⓓ suggested

16. According to paragraph 1, it was believed that reflection could help teachers

Ⓐ understand intellectual principles of teaching
Ⓑ strengthen their intellectual connection to their work
Ⓒ use scientific fact to improve discipline and teaching
Ⓓ adopt a more disciplined approach to teaching

PARAGRAPH 2

Wildman and Niles were particularly interested in investigating the conditions under which reflection might flourish—a subject on which there is little guidance in the literature. They designed an experimental strategy for a group of teachers in Virginia and worked with 40 practicing teachers over several years. They were concerned that many would be "drawn to these new, refreshing conceptions of teaching only to find that the void between the abstractions and the realities of teacher reflection is too great to bridge. Reflection on a complex task such as teaching is not easy." The teachers were taken through a program of talking about teaching events, moving on to reflecting about specific issues in a supported, and later an independent, manner.

17. The word "flourish" in the passage is closest in meaning to

Ⓐ continue
Ⓑ occur
Ⓒ succeed
Ⓓ apply

18. All of the following are mentioned about the experimental strategy described in paragraph 2 EXCEPT:

Ⓐ It was designed so that teachers would eventually reflect without help from others.
Ⓑ It was used by a group of teachers over a period of years.
Ⓒ It involved having teachers take part in discussions of classroom events.
Ⓓ It involved having teachers record in writing their reflections about teaching.

19. According to paragraph 2, Wildman and Niles worried that the teachers they were working with might feel that

Ⓐ the number of teachers involved in their program was too large
Ⓑ the concepts of teacher reflection were so abstract that they could not be applied
Ⓒ the ideas involved in reflection were actually not new and refreshing
Ⓓ several years would be needed to acquire the habit of reflecting on their teaching

PARAGRAPH 3

Wildman and Niles observed that systematic reflection on teaching required a sound ability to understand classroom events in an objective manner. They describe the initial understanding in the teachers with whom they were working as being "utilitarian . . . and not rich or detailed enough to drive systematic reflection." Teachers rarely have the time or opportunities to view their own or the teaching of others in an objective manner. Further observation revealed the tendency of teachers to evaluate events rather than review the contributory factors in a considered manner by, in effect, standing outside the situation.

20. The word "objective" in the passage is closest in meaning to

Ⓐ unbiased
Ⓑ positive
Ⓒ systematic
Ⓓ thorough

21. According to paragraph 3, what did the teachers working with Wildman and Niles often fail to do when they attempted to practice reflection?

Ⓐ Correctly calculate the amount of time needed for reflection
Ⓑ Provide sufficiently detailed descriptions of the methods they used to help them reflect
Ⓒ Examine thoughtfully the possible causes of events in their classrooms
Ⓓ Establish realistic goals for themselves in practicing reflection

PARAGRAPH 4

Helping this group of teachers to revise their thinking about classroom events became central. This process took time and patience and effective trainers. The researchers estimate that the initial training of the teachers to view events objectively took between 20 and 30 hours, with the same number of hours again being required to practice the skills of reflection.

22. How is paragraph 4 related to other aspects of the discussion of reflection in the passage?

Ⓐ It describes and comments on steps taken to overcome problems identified earlier in the passage.
Ⓑ It challenges the earlier claim that teachers rarely have the time to think about their own or others' teaching.
Ⓒ It identifies advantages gained by teachers who followed the training program described earlier in the passage.
Ⓓ It explains the process used to define the principles discussed later in the passage.

PARAGRAPH 5

Wildman and Niles identify three principles that facilitate reflective practice in a teaching situation. The first is support from administrators in an education system, enabling teachers to understand the requirements of reflective practice and how it relates to teaching students. The second is the availability of sufficient time and space. The teachers in the program described how they found it difficult to put aside the immediate demands of others in order to give themselves the time they needed to develop their reflective skills. The third is the development of a collaborative environment with support from other teachers. Support and encouragement were also required to help teachers in the program cope with aspects of their professional life with which they were not comfortable. Wildman and Niles make a summary comment: "Perhaps the most important thing we learned is the idea of the teacher-as-reflective-practitioner will not happen simply because it is a good or even compelling idea."

23. It can be inferred from paragraph 5 that the teachers working with Wildman and Niles held which of the following beliefs concerning reflection?

Ⓐ Reflection is such a good idea that it is likely to gain the support of others.
Ⓑ Administrators tend to be stronger supporters of reflection than teachers are.
Ⓒ Teachers will become more comfortable with the process of reflection if they receive help from administrators.
Ⓓ Teachers can afford to engage in reflection only after other needs have been met.

24. The word "compelling" in the passage is closest in meaning to

Ⓐ commonly held
Ⓑ persuasive
Ⓒ original
Ⓓ practical

PARAGRAPH 6

The work of Wildman and Niles suggests the importance of recognizing some of the difficulties of instituting reflective practice. Others have noted this, making a similar point about the teaching profession's cultural inhibitions about reflective practice. Zeichner and Liston (1987) point out the inconsistency between the role of the teacher as a (reflective) professional decision maker and the more usual role of the teacher as a technician, putting into practice the ideas of others. More basic than the cultural issues is the matter of motivation. Becoming a reflective practitioner requires extra work (Jaworski, 1993) and has only vaguely defined goals with, perhaps, little initially perceivable reward and the threat of vulnerability. Few have directly questioned what might lead a teacher to want to become reflective. Apparently, the most obvious reason for teachers to work toward reflective practice is that teacher educators think it is a good thing. There appear to be many unexplored matters about the motivation to reflect—for example, the value of externally motivated reflection as opposed to that of teachers who might reflect by habit.

25. According to paragraph 6, teachers may be discouraged from reflecting because

Ⓐ it is not generally supported by teacher educators
Ⓑ the benefits of reflection may not be apparent immediately
Ⓒ it is impossible to teach and reflect on one's teaching at the same time
Ⓓ they have often failed in their attempts to become reflective practitioners

26. Which of the sentences below best expresses the essential information in the highlighted sentence in the passage? Incorrect choices change the meaning in important ways or leave out essential information.

Ⓐ The practice of being reflective is no longer simply a habit among teachers but something that is externally motivated.
Ⓑ Most teachers need to explore ways to form the habit of reflection even when no external motivation exists.
Ⓒ Many aspects of the motivation to reflect have not been studied, including the comparative benefits of externally motivated and habitual reflection among teachers.
Ⓓ There has not been enough exploration of why teachers practice reflection as a habit with or without external motivation.

PARAGRAPHS 4 & 5

Helping this group of teachers to revise their thinking about classroom events became central. **(A)** This process took time and patience and effective trainers. **(B)** The researchers estimate that the initial training of the teachers to view events objectively took between 20 and 30 hours, with the same number of hours again being required to practice the skills of reflection.

(C) Wildman and Niles identify three principles that facilitate reflective practice in a teaching situation. **(D)** The first is support from administrators in an education system, enabling teachers to understand the requirements of reflective practice and how it relates to teaching students. The second is the availability of sufficient time and space. The teachers in the program described how they found it difficult to put aside the immediate demands of others in order to give themselves the time they needed to develop their reflective skills. The third is the development of a collaborative environment with support from other teachers. Support and encouragement were also required to help teachers in the program cope with aspects of their professional life with which they were not comfortable. Wildman and Niles make a summary comment: "Perhaps the most important thing we learned is the idea of the teacher-as-reflective-practitioner will not happen simply because it is a good or even compelling idea."

27. **Directions:** Look at the part of the passage that is displayed above. The letters **(A)**, **(B)**, **(C)**, and **(D)** indicate where the following sentence could be added.

    However, changing teachers' thinking about reflection will not succeed unless there is support for reflection in the teaching environment.

    Where would the sentence best fit?

    Ⓐ Choice A
    Ⓑ Choice B
    Ⓒ Choice C
    Ⓓ Choice D

28. **Directions:** An introductory sentence for a brief summary of the passage is provided below. Complete the summary by selecting the THREE answer choices that express the most important ideas in the passage. Some sentences do not belong in the summary because they express ideas that are not presented in the passage or are minor ideas in the passage.

    Write your answer choices in the spaces where they belong. You can either write the letter of your answer choice or you can copy the sentence.

    Wildman and Niles have conducted research on reflection in teaching.

    -
    -
    -

Answer Choices

[A] Through their work with Virginia teachers, Wildman and Niles proved conclusively that reflection, though difficult, benefits both teachers and students.

[B] Wildman and Niles found that considerable training and practice are required to understand classroom events and develop the skills involved in reflection.

[C] Wildman and Niles identified three principles that teachers can use to help themselves cope with problems that may arise as a result of reflection.

[D] Wildman and Niles concluded that teachers need sufficient resources as well as the cooperation and encouragement of others to practice reflection.

[E] There are numerous obstacles to implementing reflection in schools and insufficient understanding of why teachers might want to reflect.

[F] Whether teachers can overcome the difficulties involved in reflection may depend on the nature and intensity of their motivation to reflect.

Directions: Read the passage. Then answer the questions. Give yourself 20 minutes to complete this practice set.

THE ARRIVAL OF PLANT LIFE IN HAWAII

When the Hawaiian Islands emerged from the sea as volcanoes, starting about five million years ago, they were far removed from other landmasses. Then, as blazing sunshine alternated with drenching rains, the harsh, barren surfaces of the black rocks slowly began to soften. Winds brought a variety of life-forms.

Spores light enough to float on the breezes were carried thousands of miles from more ancient lands and deposited at random across the bare mountain flanks. A few of these spores found a toehold on the dark, forbidding rocks and grew and began to work their transformation upon the land. Lichens were probably the first successful flora. These are not single individual plants; each one is a symbiotic combination of an alga and a fungus. The algae capture the Sun's energy by photosynthesis and store it in organic molecules. The fungi absorb moisture and mineral salts from the rocks, passing these on in waste products that nourish algae. It is significant that the earliest living things that built communities on these islands are examples of symbiosis, a phenomenon that depends upon the close cooperation of two or more forms of life and a principle that is very important in island communities.

Lichens helped to speed the decomposition of the hard rock surfaces, preparing a soft bed of soil that was abundantly supplied with minerals that had been carried in the molten rock from the bowels of Earth. Now, other forms of life could take hold: ferns and mosses (two of the most ancient types of land plants) that flourish even in rock crevices. These plants propagate by producing spores—tiny fertilized cells that contain all the instructions for making a new plant—but the spores are unprotected by any outer coating and carry no supply of nutrient. Vast numbers of them fall on the ground beneath the mother plants. Sometimes they are carried farther afield by water or by wind. But only those few spores that settle down in very favorable locations can start new life; the vast majority fall on barren ground. By force of sheer numbers, however, the mosses and ferns reached Hawaii, survived, and multiplied. Some species developed great size, becoming tree ferns that even now grow in the Hawaiian forests.

Many millions of years after ferns evolved (but long before the Hawaiian Islands were born from the sea), another kind of flora evolved on Earth: the seed-bearing plants. This was a wonderful biological invention. The seed has an outer coating that surrounds the genetic material of the new plant, and inside this covering is a concentrated supply of nutrients. Thus, the seed's chances of survival are greatly enhanced over those of the naked spore. One type of seed-bearing plant, the angiosperm, includes all forms of blooming vegetation. In the angiosperm the seeds are wrapped in an additional layer of covering. Some of these coats are hard—like the shell of a nut—for extra protection. Some are soft and tempting, like a peach or a cherry. In some angiosperms the seeds are equipped with gossamer wings, like the dandelion and milkweed seeds. These new characteristics offered better ways for the seeds to move to new habitats. They could travel through the air, float in water, and lie dormant for many months.

Plants with large, buoyant seeds—like coconuts—drift on ocean currents and are washed up on the shores. Remarkably resistant to the vicissitudes of ocean travel, they can survive prolonged immersion in saltwater. When they come to rest on warm beaches and the conditions are favorable, the seed coats soften. Nourished by their imported supply of nutrients, the young plants push out their roots and establish their place in the sun.

By means of these seeds, plants spread more widely to new locations, even to isolated islands like the Hawaiian archipelago, which lies more than 2,000 miles west of California and 3,500 miles east of Japan. The seeds of grasses, flowers, and blooming trees made the long trips to these islands. (Grasses are simple forms of angiosperms that bear their encapsulated seeds on long stalks.) In a surprisingly short time, angiosperms filled many of the land areas on Hawaii that had been bare.

Directions: Now answer the questions.

PARAGRAPH 2

Spores light enough to float on the breezes were carried thousands of miles from more ancient lands and deposited at random across the bare mountain flanks. A few of these spores found a toehold on the dark, forbidding rocks and grew and began to work their transformation upon the land. Lichens were probably the first successful flora. These are not single individual plants; each one is a symbiotic combination of an alga and a fungus. The algae capture the Sun's energy by photosynthesis and store it in organic molecules. The fungi absorb moisture and mineral salts from the rocks, passing these on in waste products that nourish algae. It is significant that the earliest living things that built communities on these islands are examples of symbiosis, a phenomenon that depends upon the close cooperation of two or more forms of life and a principle that is very important in island communities.

29. The phrase "at random" in the passage is closest in meaning to

Ⓐ finally
Ⓑ over a long period of time
Ⓒ successfully
Ⓓ without a definite pattern

30. Which of the sentences below best expresses the essential information in the highlighted sentence in the passage? Incorrect choices change the meaning in important ways or leave out essential information.

Ⓐ Some of the earliest important examples of symbiosis—the close cooperation of two or more living things—occur in island communities.
Ⓑ Symbiosis—the close cooperation of pairs or small groups of living organisms—is especially important in these island environments.
Ⓒ The first organisms on these islands worked together closely in a relationship known as symbiosis, which is particularly important on islands.
Ⓓ It is significant to note that organisms in the beginning stages of the development of island life cannot survive without close cooperation.

31. It can be inferred from paragraph 2 that the fungi in lichens benefit from their symbiotic relationship with algae in what way?

Ⓐ The algae help the fungi meet some of their energy needs.
Ⓑ The algae protect the fungi from the Sun's radiation.
Ⓒ The algae provide the fungi with greater space for absorbing water.
Ⓓ The fungi produce less waste in the presence of algae.

PARAGRAPH 3

Lichens helped to speed the decomposition of the hard rock surfaces, preparing a soft bed of soil that was abundantly supplied with minerals that had been carried in the molten rock from the bowels of Earth. Now, other forms of life could take hold: ferns and mosses (two of the most ancient types of land plants) that flourish even in rock crevices. These plants propagate by producing spores—tiny fertilized cells that contain all the instructions for making a new plant—but the spores are unprotected by any outer coating and carry no supply of nutrient. Vast numbers of them fall on the ground beneath the mother plants. Sometimes they are carried farther afield by water or by wind. But only those few spores that settle down in very favorable locations can start new life; the vast majority fall on barren ground. By force of sheer numbers, however, the mosses and ferns reached Hawaii, survived, and multiplied. Some species developed great size, becoming tree ferns that even now grow in the Hawaiian forests.

32. The word "abundantly" in the passage is closest in meaning to

Ⓐ occasionally
Ⓑ plentifully
Ⓒ usefully
Ⓓ fortunately

33. The word "propagate" in the passage is closest in meaning to

Ⓐ multiply
Ⓑ emerge
Ⓒ live
Ⓓ evolve

34. According to paragraph 3, what was the relationship between lichens and ferns in the development of plant life on Hawaii?

Ⓐ Ferns were able to grow because lichens created suitable soil.
Ⓑ The decomposition of ferns produced minerals that were used by lichens.
Ⓒ Lichens and ferns competed to grow in the same rocky environments.
Ⓓ Lichens and ferns were typically found together in volcanic areas.

PARAGRAPH 4

Many millions of years after ferns evolved (but long before the Hawaiian Islands were born from the sea), another kind of flora evolved on Earth: the seed-bearing plants. This was a wonderful biological invention. The seed has an outer coating that surrounds the genetic material of the new plant, and inside this covering is a concentrated supply of nutrients. Thus, the seed's chances of survival are greatly enhanced over those of the naked spore. One type of seed-bearing plant, the angiosperm, includes all forms of blooming vegetation. In the angiosperm the seeds are wrapped in an additional layer of covering. Some of these coats are hard—like the shell of a nut—for extra protection. Some are soft and tempting, like a peach or a cherry. In some angiosperms the seeds are equipped with gossamer wings, like the dandelion and milkweed seeds. These new characteristics offered better ways for the seeds to move to new habitats. They could travel through the air, float in water, and lie dormant for many months.

35. The word "This" in the passage refers to

Ⓐ the spread of ferns and mosses in Hawaii
Ⓑ the creation of the Hawaiian Islands
Ⓒ the evolution of ferns
Ⓓ the development of plants that produce seeds

36. Why does the author mention "a nut," "a peach," and "a cherry"?

Ⓐ To indicate that some seeds are less likely to survive than others
Ⓑ To point out that many angiosperms can be eaten
Ⓒ To provide examples of blooming plants
Ⓓ To illustrate the variety of coverings among angiosperm seeds

37. The word "dormant" in the passage is closest in meaning to

Ⓐ hidden
Ⓑ inactive
Ⓒ underground
Ⓓ preserved

38. According to paragraph 4, why do seeds have a greater chance of survival than spores do? To receive credit, you must select TWO answer choices.

[A] Seeds need less water to grow into a mature plant than spores do.
[B] Seeds do not need to rely on outside sources of nutrients.
[C] Seeds are better protected from environmental dangers than spores are.
[D] Seeds are heavier than spores and are therefore more likely to take root and grow.

PARAGRAPH 5

Plants with large, buoyant seeds—like coconuts—drift on ocean currents and are washed up on the shores. Remarkably resistant to the vicissitudes of ocean travel, they can survive prolonged immersion in saltwater. When they come to rest on warm beaches and the conditions are favorable, the seed coats soften. Nourished by their imported supply of nutrients, the young plants push out their roots and establish their place in the sun.

39. According to paragraph 5, a major reason that coconuts can establish themselves in distant locations is that their seeds can

Ⓐ survive long exposure to heat on island beaches
Ⓑ float and survive for long periods in ocean water
Ⓒ use saltwater for maintenance and growth
Ⓓ maintain hard, protective coats even after growing roots

PARAGRAPHS 1 2 3 4 5 & 6

When the Hawaiian Islands emerged from the sea as volcanoes, starting about five million years ago, they were far removed from other landmasses. Then, as blazing sunshine alternated with drenching rains, the harsh, barren surfaces of the black rocks slowly began to soften. Winds brought a variety of life-forms.

Spores light enough to float on the breezes were carried thousands of miles from more ancient lands and deposited at random across the bare mountain flanks. A few of these spores found a toehold on the dark, forbidding rocks and grew and began to work their transformation upon the land. Lichens were probably the first successful flora. These are not single individual plants; each one is a symbiotic combination of an alga and a fungus. The algae capture the Sun's energy by photosynthesis and store it in organic molecules. The fungi absorb moisture and mineral salts from the rocks, passing these on in waste products that nourish algae. It is significant that the earliest living things that built communities on these islands are examples of symbiosis, a phenomenon that depends upon the close cooperation of two or more forms of life and a principle that is very important in island communities.

Lichens helped to speed the decomposition of the hard rock surfaces, preparing a soft bed of soil that was abundantly supplied with minerals that had been carried in the molten rock from the bowels of Earth. Now, other forms of life could take hold: ferns and mosses (two of the most ancient types of land plants) that flourish even in rock crevices. These plants propagate by producing spores—tiny fertilized cells that contain all the instructions for making a new plant—but the spores are unprotected by any outer coating and carry no supply of nutrient. Vast numbers of them fall on the ground beneath the mother plants. Sometimes they are carried farther afield by water or by wind. But only those few spores that settle down in very favorable locations can start new life; the vast majority fall on barren ground. By force of sheer numbers, however, the mosses and ferns reached Hawaii, survived, and multiplied. Some species developed great size, becoming tree ferns that even now grow in the Hawaiian forests.

Many millions of years after ferns evolved (but long before the Hawaiian Islands were born from the sea), another kind of flora evolved on Earth: the seed-bearing plants. This was a wonderful biological invention. The seed has an outer coating that surrounds the genetic material of the new plant, and inside this covering is a concentrated supply of nutrients. Thus, the seed's chances of survival are greatly enhanced over those of the naked spore. One type of seed-bearing plant, the angiosperm, includes all forms of blooming vegetation. In the angiosperm the seeds are wrapped in an additional layer of covering. Some of these coats are hard—like the shell of a nut—for extra protection. Some are soft and tempting, like a peach or a cherry. In some angiosperms the seeds are equipped with gossamer wings, like the dandelion and milkweed seeds. These new characteristics offered better ways for the seeds to move to new habitats. They could travel through the air, float in water, and lie dormant for many months.

Plants with large, buoyant seeds—like coconuts—drift on ocean currents and are washed up on the shores. Remarkably resistant to the vicissitudes of ocean travel, they can survive prolonged immersion in saltwater. When they come to rest on warm beaches and the conditions are favorable, the seed coats soften. Nourished by their imported supply of nutrients, the young plants push out their roots and establish their place in the sun.

By means of these seeds, plants spread more widely to new locations, even to isolated islands like the Hawaiian archipelago, which lies more than 2,000 miles west of California and 3,500 miles east of Japan. The seeds of grasses, flowers, and blooming trees made the long trips to these islands. (Grasses are simple forms of angiosperms that bear their encapsulated seeds on long stalks.) In a surprisingly short time, angiosperms filled many of the land areas on Hawaii that had been bare.

40. According to the passage, which of the following characteristics do spores and seeds have in common?

Ⓐ They may be surrounded by several layers of covering.
Ⓑ They are produced by flowering plants.
Ⓒ They may be spread by wind.
Ⓓ They are able to grow in barren soils.

PARAGRAPH 3

Lichens helped to speed the decomposition of the hard rock surfaces, preparing a soft bed of soil that was abundantly supplied with minerals that had been carried in the molten rock from the bowels of Earth. Now, other forms of life could take hold: ferns and mosses (two of the most ancient types of land plants) that flourish even in rock crevices. **(A)** These plants propagate by producing spores—tiny fertilized cells that contain all the instructions for making a new plant—but the spores are unprotected by any outer coating and carry no supply of nutrient. **(B)** Vast numbers of them fall on the ground beneath the mother plants. **(C)** Sometimes they are carried farther afield by water or by wind. **(D)** But only those few spores that settle down in very favorable locations can start new life; the vast majority fall on barren ground. By force of sheer numbers, however, the mosses and ferns reached Hawaii, survived, and multiplied. Some species developed great size, becoming tree ferns that even now grow in the Hawaiian forests.

41. **Directions:** Look at the part of the passage that is displayed above. The letters **(A)**, **(B)**, **(C)**, and **(D)** indicate where the following sentence could be added.

So since the chances of survival for any individual spore are small, the plants have to produce many spores in order to propagate.

Where would the sentence best fit?

Ⓐ Choice A
Ⓑ Choice B
Ⓒ Choice C
Ⓓ Choice D

42. **Directions:** An introductory sentence for a brief summary of the passage is provided below. Complete the summary by selecting the THREE answer choices that express the most important ideas in the passage. Some sentences do not belong in the summary because they express ideas that are not presented in the passage or are minor ideas in the passage.

Write your answer choices in the spaces where they belong. You can either write the letter of your answer choice or you can copy the sentence.

After the formation of the Hawaiian Islands, much time passed before conditions were suitable for plant life.

•

•

•

Answer Choices

[A] Algae are classified as symbiotic because they produce energy through the process of photosynthesis.

[B] The first successful plants on Hawaii were probably lichens, which consist of algae and fungi living in a symbiotic relationship.

[C] Lichens helped create favorable conditions for the growth of spore-producing plants such as ferns and mosses.

[D] Seed-bearing plants evolved much later than spore-producing plants, but both types of plants had evolved well before the formation of the Hawaiian islands.

[E] Unlike spores, seeds must move to new habitats in order to have a strong chance of survival and growth.

[F] Seed-bearing plants arrived and spread quickly in Hawaii, thanks to characteristics that increased their seeds' ability to survive and to move to different areas.

LISTENING

This section measures your ability to understand conversations and lectures in English.

Listen to each conversation and lecture only one time. After each conversation and lecture, you will answer some questions about it. Answer each question based on what is stated or implied by the speakers.

You may take notes while you listen and use your notes to help you answer the questions. Your notes will not be scored.

Answer each question before moving on. Do not return to previous questions.

It will take about 60 minutes to listen to the conversations and lectures and answer the questions about them.

Directions: Listen to Track 1.

Directions: Now answer the questions.

1. Why does the woman go to see the professor?

   Ⓐ To get advice on the topic of a term paper
   Ⓑ To discuss different types of food packaging
   Ⓒ To find out if the university will offer courses in food packaging
   Ⓓ To ask about jobs in the food industry

2. Why does the professor mention his previous jobs?

   Ⓐ To explain why the woman should study physics, math, and chemistry
   Ⓑ To recommend that the woman get a summer job on a fishing boat
   Ⓒ To point out that industry jobs can lead to a teaching career
   Ⓓ To confirm an assumption the woman made about finding a job

3. The woman mentions a research study of milk packaging. What was the finding of the study?

   Ⓐ Plastic containers may change the flavor of milk.
   Ⓑ Light may negatively affect the quality of milk.
   Ⓒ People prefer to buy milk in see-through containers.
   Ⓓ Opaque containers are effective in protecting milk from bacteria.

4. What does the professor imply about the dairy in Chelsea?

   Ⓐ It has plans to start bottling milk in opaque containers.
   Ⓑ Some of its employees attended the university.
   Ⓒ Employees there might be able to provide useful information.
   Ⓓ He worked there before joining the university faculty.

5. Listen to Track 2.

Ⓐ She has read conflicting information.
Ⓑ She has been too busy to begin her research.
Ⓒ The topic she is researching is too broad.
Ⓓ The information she needs is not available.

Directions: Listen to Track 3.

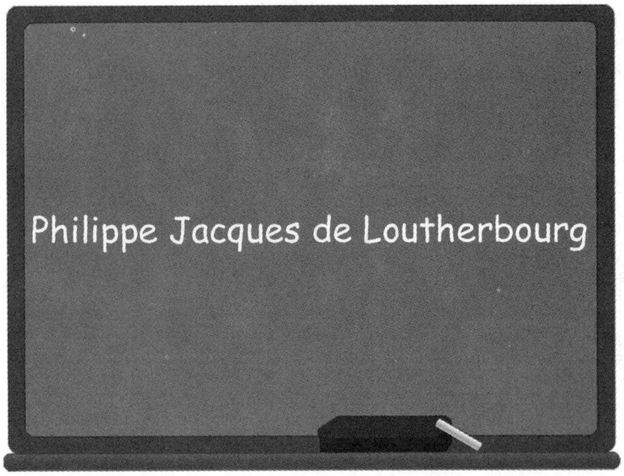

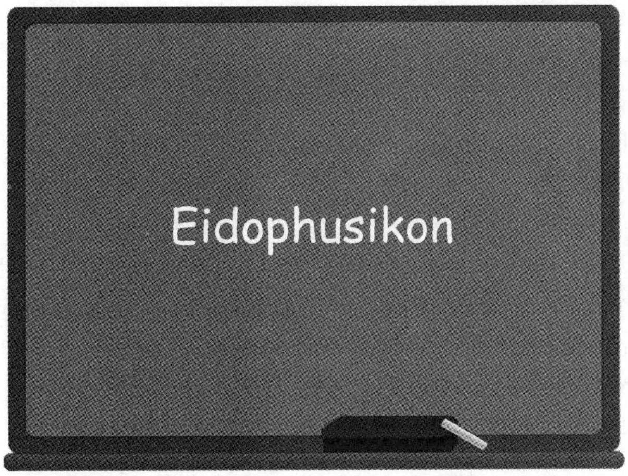

Directions: Now answer the questions.

6. What does the professor mainly discuss?

   Ⓐ The history of set design in English theater
   Ⓑ A French painter's innovations in set design
   Ⓒ A kind of play popular in eighteenth-century English theater
   Ⓓ A leading playwright of the eighteenth century

7. According to the professor, how did Loutherbourg create a feeling of greater depth on the stage? *Choose 2 answers.*

   [A] He enlarged the stage area.
   [B] He used mainly dark colors in the painted backgrounds.
   [C] He carefully spaced separate pieces of scenery.
   [D] He used three-dimensional objects in his sets.

8. What can be inferred about theatergoers in late eighteenth-century England?

   Ⓐ They did not accept Loutherbourg's set designs at first.
   Ⓑ They were accustomed to sitting in dark theaters.
   Ⓒ Most of them attended the theater mainly to see popular actors.
   Ⓓ Some of them used the theater as a substitute for travel.

9. What is the professor's opinion about the relationship between English landscape painters and Loutherbourg?

   Ⓐ He thinks English landscape painters were unfair in their criticism of Loutherbourg's work.
   Ⓑ He thinks Loutherbourg's relationship with English landscape painters was less important than most experts think.
   Ⓒ He thinks Loutherbourg and the English landscape painters probably influenced each other.
   Ⓓ He thinks English landscape painters helped Loutherbourg's work gain in popularity.

10. What are two notable features of the Eidophusikon? *Choose 2 answers.*

    [A] It was identical to the Drury Lane Theatre.
    [B] It did not make use of actors.
    [C] It used paintings made by Gainsborough.
    [D] It had a small stage.

11. Why does the professor mention a storm that passed over Loutherbourg's home?

    (A) To demonstrate the authenticity of Loutherbourg's sound effects
    (B) To provide context in a discussion about lighting effects
    (C) To mention one of the problems the Eidophusikon faced
    (D) To explain how Loutherbourg got an idea for a theater set

Directions: Listen to Track 4.

microbes

Directions: Now answer the questions.

12. What is the lecture mainly about?

Ⓐ Factors involved in the increased growth of shrubs in Arctic Alaska
Ⓑ How temperature increases might be affecting the permafrost in Arctic Alaska
Ⓒ Why nutrient production of microbes in the soil in Arctic Alaska is declining
Ⓓ Reasons that grasslands are turning into tundra in Arctic Alaska

13. According to the professor, what are two features of shrubs that allow them to grow well in Arctic regions? *Choose 2 answers.*

[A] They have roots that can penetrate permafrost.
[B] Their height allows them to absorb more sunlight.
[C] They absorb nutrients from the soil efficiently.
[D] They have a shallow root system.

14. What is one reason for the increase in shrub growth in Arctic Alaska?

Ⓐ Decreases in grass and moss growth have altered the balance of nutrients in the soil.
Ⓑ Increases in ground temperature have led to increased microbial activity.
Ⓒ Increases in average winter temperatures have made permafrost permeable to water.
Ⓓ Increases in snowfall have provided more water for shrubs.

15. Why are nutrients in the soil NOT carried away by spring runoff?

Ⓐ The roots of shrubs prevent nutrient-filled soil from being washed away.
Ⓑ Most nutrients are not in the area of the soil most affected by runoff.
Ⓒ Most nutrients remain frozen in the permafrost when spring runoff is at its peak.
Ⓓ Most nutrients have been absorbed by vegetation before the runoff period begins.

16. Why does the professor mention shrub expansion into other environments, such as semiarid grasslands?

    Ⓐ To suggest that new shrubland may not convert back to tundra
    Ⓑ To explain how shrubland can expand in a warm climate
    Ⓒ To cite a similarity between the types of shrubs in semiarid grassland and tundra environments
    Ⓓ To explain how a biological loop can cause shrub expansion

17. Listen to Track 5.

    Ⓐ The information she gave is important enough to be repeated.
    Ⓑ Climate scientists are asking the wrong questions.
    Ⓒ The phenomenon she is describing is more complex than it appears.
    Ⓓ Students should be able to solve the puzzle easily.

Directions: Listen to Track 6.

Directions: Now answer the questions.

18. What are the speakers mainly discussing?

Ⓐ A book that the man is trying to find in the library
Ⓑ A book that the man already returned to the library
Ⓒ A book that the man is using to write his senior thesis
Ⓓ A book that the man lent to his sociology professor

19. What does the woman offer to do for the man?

Ⓐ Let the man know when a book he needs is returned to the library
Ⓑ Photocopy a chapter of a book for him
Ⓒ Ask a professor to return a book the man needs
Ⓓ Find a copy of a book for him at another library

20. What is the woman trying to explain when she mentions students who have lost their borrowing privileges?

Ⓐ Why the man should not photocopy part of the book
Ⓑ The reasons for one of the library's policies
Ⓒ What will happen if the man does not return the book
Ⓓ The reason the man has to fill out a form

21. How does the man probably feel at the end of the conversation?

Ⓐ Annoyed that he has to pay a fine on the book
Ⓑ Upset that he will lose his library privileges
Ⓒ Glad that he can keep the book for two more weeks
Ⓓ Appreciative that the woman is helping him

22. Listen to Track 7.

Ⓐ To make sure she understands what the man's problem is
Ⓑ To encourage the man to return the book to the library soon
Ⓒ To check whether the man has already returned the book
Ⓓ To explain to the man a change in the library's policies

Directions: Listen to Track 8.

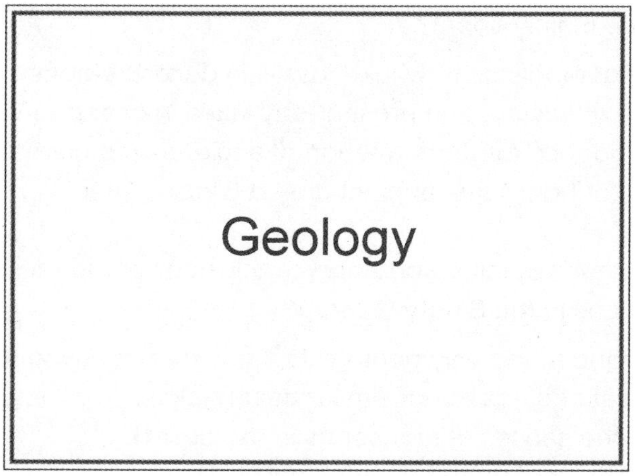

Directions: Now answer the questions.

23. What is the lecture mainly about?

    Ⓐ Reasons that geologists study lake fossils in desert regions
    Ⓑ A comparison of ancient and present-day lakes in desert environments
    Ⓒ Geological evidence for the formation of ancient sand dunes
    Ⓓ A hypothesis for how some ancient desert lakes formed

24. What is the professor's opinion about the conclusions of the recent study of the limestone formations in the Empty Quarter?

    Ⓐ They have changed the way geologists study desert environments.
    Ⓑ They contradict findings about similar desert lakes.
    Ⓒ They explain the causes of monsoons in the desert.
    Ⓓ They need to be confirmed by additional studies.

25. According to the professor, what feature of the sand dunes made the formation of the lakes possible?

    Ⓐ The degree of slope of the sides of the dunes
    Ⓑ The presence of clay and silt particles in the dunes
    Ⓒ The position of the dunes relative to the wind and rain
    Ⓓ The narrowness of the valleys between the dunes

26. How is it possible to determine in which rainy period a lake was formed? *Choose 2 answers.*

    [A] By examining the location of the lake bed
    [B] By measuring the amount of sand covering the lake bed
    [C] By examining the color of the limestone formation
    [D] By identifying the types of fossils found in the limestone

27. What does the professor imply about the lack of water buffalo and hippopotamus fossils in the more recent lakes?

    Ⓐ The level of water in the lakes was not sufficient for these animals.
    Ⓑ The bottoms of the lakes were too sandy for these animals to stand in.
    Ⓒ The location of the lakes made them too difficult for these animals to reach.
    Ⓓ The vegetation near the lakes did not attract these animals.

28. What possible explanation does the professor give for the apparent absence of fish in the most ancient lakes?

    Ⓐ The presence of predators
    Ⓑ Lack of appropriate food
    Ⓒ Lack of suitable water
    Ⓓ Extreme desert temperatures

Directions: Listen to Track 9.

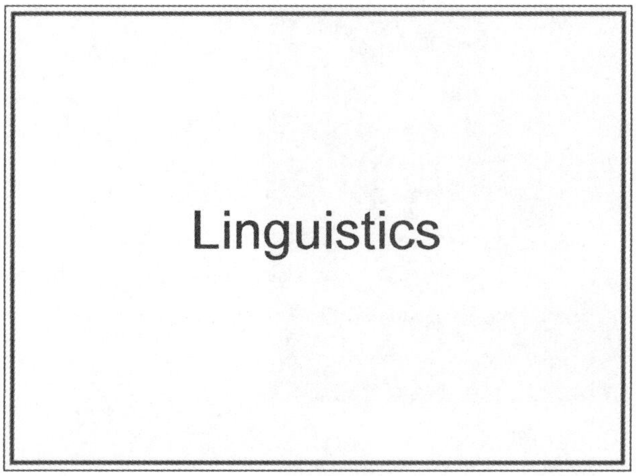

Directions: Now answer the questions.

29. What does the professor mainly discuss?

    Ⓐ The findings of a study on prairie dog communication
    Ⓑ The way that mammals learn to make warning cries
    Ⓒ Features that distinguish language from animal communication systems
    Ⓓ Various types of signals used by animals to communicate with each other

30. Why does the student mention a research project she studied in a biology class?

    Ⓐ To point out similarities in the behavior of rodents and monkeys
    Ⓑ To explain how she first became interested in animal communication
    Ⓒ To introduce an instance of an animal species that might have language
    Ⓓ To show how she applied her knowledge of linguistics in another course

31. What is the professor's opinion of a recent study of prairie dogs?

Ⓐ She finds the study interesting but is not convinced that prairie dogs can communicate.
Ⓑ She thinks that some claims made by the researchers are not supported by their findings.
Ⓒ She sees the study as proof that mammals other than humans possess a form of language.
Ⓓ She thinks the researchers misinterpreted the high-pitched barks as warning signals.

32. What does the professor say about the individual units that make up human languages?

Ⓐ They can be combined to create an infinite number of new messages.
Ⓑ They are not capable of being reproduced by members of any other species.
Ⓒ They function in the same way as the signals all animals use to communicate.
Ⓓ They are acquired instinctively without having to be learned.

33. The professor uses the sentence, "Move the large coyote fast," in order to illustrate two features of language. What are they? *Choose 2 answers.*

[A] Displacement
[B] Learnability
[C] Productivity
[D] Discreteness

34. Listen to Track 10.

Ⓐ To see if anyone knows the answer to the student's question
Ⓑ To suggest that the student is using the wrong terminology
Ⓒ To express frustration because she has already answered a similar question
Ⓓ To determine whether she has been speaking clearly enough

SPEAKING

This section measures your ability to speak in English about a variety of topics.

There are six questions in this section. For each question, you will be given a short time to prepare your response. When the preparation time is up, answer the question as completely as possible in the time indicated for that question. You should record your responses so that you can review them later and compare them with the answer key and scoring rubrics.

Directions: You will now be asked to speak about a familiar topic. Give yourself 15 seconds to prepare your response. Then record yourself speaking for 45 seconds.

1. Listen to Track 11.

> Talk about an important experience that you recently had. Describe what happened and explain why it was important to you.
>
> **Preparation Time: 15 seconds**
> **Response Time: 45 seconds**

Directions: You will now be asked to give your opinion about a familiar topic. Give yourself 15 seconds to prepare your response. Then record yourself speaking for 45 seconds.

2. Listen to Track 12.

> Some people think that family members are the most important influence on young adults. Others believe that friends are the most important influence. Which do you agree with? Explain why.
>
> **Preparation Time: 15 seconds**
> **Response Time: 45 seconds**

Directions: You will now read a short passage and listen to a conversation on the same topic. You will then be asked a question about them. After you hear the question, give yourself 30 seconds to prepare your response. Then record yourself speaking for 60 seconds.

Listen to Track 13.

Reading Time: 45 seconds

Required Work Experience

The business studies department at State University will now require all students enrolled in its program to complete one semester of work experience in a local corporation or small business. It is felt that students will benefit from this work experience by developing leadership and organizational skills that would not normally be learned in a classroom or campus setting. Furthermore, the relationships that students establish with the company that they work for may help them to secure permanent employment with that company once they have completed the program and graduated.

Listen to Track 14.

3. The woman expresses her opinion of the university's new policy. State her opinion and explain the reasons she gives for holding that opinion.

Preparation Time: 30 seconds
Response Time: 60 seconds

Directions: You will now read a short passage and listen to a lecture on the same topic. You will then be asked a question about them. After you hear the question, give yourself 30 seconds to prepare your response. Then record yourself speaking for 60 seconds.

Listen to Track 15.

Reading Time: 50 seconds

The Establishing Shot

Film directors use different types of camera shots for specific purposes. An establishing shot is an image shown briefly at the beginning of a scene, usually taken from far away, that is used to provide context for the rest of the scene. One purpose of the establishing shot is to communicate background information to the viewer, such as the setting—where and when the rest of the scene will occur. It also establishes the mood or feeling of the scene. Due to the context that the establishing shot provides, the characters and events that are shown next are better understood by the viewer.

Listen to Track 16.

4. Using the professor's example, explain what an establishing shot is and how it is used.

Preparation Time: 30 seconds
Response Time: 60 seconds

Directions: You will now listen to part of a conversation. You will then be asked a question about it. After you hear the question, give yourself 20 seconds to prepare your response. Then record yourself speaking for 60 seconds.

Listen to Track 17.

5. Briefly summarize the problem the speakers are discussing. Then state which solution you would recommend. Explain the reasons for your recommendation.

Preparation Time: 20 seconds
Response Time: 60 seconds

Directions: You will now listen to part of a lecture. You will then be asked a question about it. After you hear the question, give yourself 20 seconds to prepare your response. Then record yourself speaking for 60 seconds.

Listen to Track 18.

6. Using points from the lecture, explain how the passion plant and the potato plant defend themselves from insects.

Preparation Time: 20 seconds
Response Time: 60 seconds

WRITING

This section measures your ability to write in English to communicate in an academic environment.

There are two writing questions in this section.

For question 1, you will read a passage and listen to a lecture about the same topic. You may take notes while you read and listen. Then you will write a response to a question based on what you have read and heard. You may look back at the passage when answering the question. You may use your notes to help you answer the question. You have 20 minutes to plan and write your response.

For question 2, you will write an essay based on your own knowledge and experience. You have 30 minutes to plan and complete your essay.

Directions: Give yourself 3 minutes to read the passage.

Reading Time: 3 minutes

Archaeologists have recently found a fossil of a 150-million-year-old mammal known as *Repenomamus robustus* (*R. robustus*). Interestingly, the mammal's stomach contained the remains of a psittacosaur dinosaur. Some researchers have therefore suggested that *R. robustus* was an active hunter of dinosaurs. However, a closer analysis has made the hypothesis that *R. robustus* was an active hunter unlikely. It was probably just a scavenger that sometimes fed on dinosaur eggs containing unhatched dinosaurs.

First, *R. robustus*, like most mammals living 150 million years ago, was small—only about the size of a domestic cat. It was much smaller than psittacosaurs, which were almost two meters tall when full grown. Given this size difference, it is unlikely that *R. robustus* would have been able to successfully hunt psittacosaurs or similar dinosaurs.

Second, the legs of *R. robustus* appear much more suited for scavenging than hunting: they were short and positioned somewhat to the side rather than directly underneath the animal. These features suggest that *R. robustus* did not chase after prey. Psittacosaurs—the type of dinosaur found in the stomach of *R. robustus*—were fast moving. It is unlikely that they would have been caught by such short-legged animals.

Third, the dinosaur bones inside the stomach of the *R. robustus* provide no evidence to support the idea that the dinosaur had been actively hunted. When an animal has been hunted and eaten by another animal, there are usually teeth marks on the bones of the animal that was eaten. But the bones of the psittacosaur inside the *R. robustus* stomach do not have teeth marks. This suggests that *R. robustus* found an unguarded dinosaur nest with eggs and simply swallowed an egg with the small psittacosaur still inside the eggshell.

Listen to Track 19.

Directions: You have 20 minutes to plan and write your response. Your response will be judged on the basis of the quality of your writing and on how well your response presents the points in the lecture and their relationship to the reading passage. Typically, an effective response will be 150 to 225 words.

Listen to Track 20.

Response Time: 20 minutes

1. Summarize the points made in the lecture, being sure to explain how they respond to the specific points made in the reading passage.

Directions: Read the question below. You have 30 minutes to plan, write, and revise your essay. Typically, an effective response will contain a minimum of 300 words.

Response Time: 30 minutes

2. Do you agree or disagree with the following statement?

   Technology has made children less creative than they were in the past.

   Use specific reasons and examples to support your answer.

ANSWERS

Reading Section

1. B
2. C
3. D
4. A
5. A
6. C
7. A
8. D
9. C
10. B
11. B
12. D
13. D
14. B, C, E
15. A
16. B
17. C
18. D
19. B
20. A
21. C
22. A
23. D
24. B
25. B
26. C
27. C
28. B, D, E
29. D
30. C
31. A
32. B
33. A
34. A
35. D
36. D
37. B
38. B, C
39. B
40. C
41. B
42. B, C, F

Listening Section

1. A
2. D
3. B
4. C
5. C
6. B
7. C, D
8. D
9. C
10. B, D
11. A
12. A
13. C, D
14. B
15. B
16. A
17. C
18. C
19. B
20. C
21. D
22. A
23. D
24. D
25. B
26. A, D
27. A
28. C
29. C
30. C
31. B
32. A
33. C, D
34. B

Speaking Section

Prompts, Important Points, and Sample Responses with Rater Comments

Use the sample Independent and Integrated Speaking Rubrics in Appendix A to see how responses are scored. The raters who listen to your responses will analyze them in three general categories. These categories are Delivery, Language Use, and Topic Development. All three categories have equal importance.

This section includes important points that should be covered when answering each question. All of these points must be present in a response in order for it to receive the highest score in the Topic Development category. These important points are guides to the kind of information raters expect to hear in a high-level response.

This section also refers to sample responses, which can be found on the accompanying DVD. Some responses were scored at the highest level, while others were not. The responses are followed by comments from certified ETS raters.

Question 1

Prompt

Talk about an important experience that you recently had. Describe what happened and explain why it was important to you.

Important Points

In this question, you should describe a recent experience and explain why it was important. After briefly describing the experience, you should explain its importance by giving specific reasons. Reasons such as, "I learned to appreciate life" or "It changed my way of thinking" are overly general and lack the specificity needed for full credit in topic development. You should also explain <u>how</u> you learned to appreciate life or <u>how</u> it changed your way of thinking. For example, "This experience taught me to appreciate life. Before, I was spending all my time working, usually alone, and I wasn't happy. But after this happened, I realized that it was more important to spend time with my friends. So now I see my old friends more, and I'm more relaxed and enjoy life more."

High-level Response: Listen to Track 21.

Rater Comments

This is a fully developed response to the question. She describes her experience studying abroad in Spain and gives a few examples of the importance of the experience (learning a new language, new culture, and so on.); she also gives a longer explanation to describe the experience of living alone for the first time. Although she doesn't provide a lot of support for the importance of the event, she does mention several things such as learning a new language and living in a different culture for which the importance is implicit. She doesn't sound like a native English speaker, and there are occasional mispronunciations, but her speech is clear throughout and she uses correct, precise language and vocabulary to describe the topic.

Mid-level Response: Listen to Track 22.

Rater Comments

The speaker gives a specific recent experience—her brother's car accident—but does not develop it fully with specific reasons. She also does not specifically discuss why it was important to her. General statements, such as, "We practically had to do everything ourselves" are not supported with specific details. Too often the speaker is not precise in what she says. Her statement, "I think we all learned about it" is vague. For example, she does not make clear what the pronoun "it" refers to. Therefore, listeners are not sure what the speaker means. A lack of precise vocabulary and grammar prevent this speaker from fully developing her ideas. Her pronunciation is clear in general, but there are some hesitations that cause problems for listeners.

Question 2

Prompt

Some people think that family members are the most important influence on young adults. Others believe that friends are the most important influence. Which do you agree with? Explain why.

Important Points

In this question, you need to say whether you think family members or friends are the most important influence on young adults. Then you must explain why this is your preference. You should try to explain it fully; you should not just give a list of reasons. Instead, you should try to pick one or two reasons and explain your opinion in more detail. Add examples when appropriate. If you think family members are the most important influence, for example, you could explain by discussing reasons such as the amount of time young adults spend with family versus friends, which gives family members more opportunities to influence them.

Sometimes test-takers would like to choose both options, saying, for example, that one might be more true in some circumstances and the other true in different circumstances. This approach is acceptable; however, it is difficult to then fully explain your opinion if you choose both options, and it might lower your score if you don't finish or don't sufficiently support both choices during your response time. Only very fluent speakers should use the approach of choosing both options.

High-level Response: Listen to Track 23.

Rater Comments

The speaker states her view that both family members and friends influence young adults depending on the stage of life they're in, and then supports this view fully by describing the stages of life when family and when friends have an influence. She provides examples of when family members are more influential and when friends are, and discusses the importance of friends when you're separated from your family, such as when you're away at college. Her pronunciation is clear and she does not need to pause to think of how to say her ideas in English. Sometimes her vocabulary choices are not perfect—for example, she says "*how you wear*" instead of "how you dress," but these errors are minor and the listener can still easily understand her ideas.

Low-level Response: Listen to Track 24.

Rater Comments

The speaker's pronunciation of individual words is fairly clear, but he pauses and hesitates often to think of the next word to say. His hesitations cause him to run out of time before he can finish what he would like to say. This shows that he still needs to improve his fluency in English. Also, while he states which view he agrees with—that friends are the most important influence—he does not develop this idea with much detail. He says "*they spend much of their time with their friends,*" but he doesn't explain why this causes friends to have more influence, possibly because he lacks the vocabulary to talk more about it. Instead, he simply repeats that friends are the most important influence.

Question 3

Prompt

The woman expresses her opinion of the university's new policy. State her opinion and explain the reasons she gives for holding that opinion.

Important Points

When answering this question, it is important to include information from both the reading passage and the conversation between students. You should indicate that the woman disagrees with the business studies department's new policy, which requires students in the business department to spend one semester working in a local corporation or small business. You should also explain the two reasons she gives for disagreeing with this policy: she doesn't think students will actually develop leadership and/or organizational skills at the jobs they would have to work, since they would be doing basic tasks that won't be meaningful; and she doesn't think that this experience will help students find permanent jobs in the future, since many other universities have similar programs and so there will be too much competition with other students.

High-level Response: Listen to Track 25.

Rater Comments

This speaker clearly states the woman's opinion of the policy ("*The woman believe that this policy is not a positive move*"), a brief explanation of the policy, and the two reasons why she disagrees with the policy. The speaker makes a few very minor agreement errors ("*the woman believe*"; "*the abundance of university who*"; "*offered to student*"), but these do not prevent listeners from understanding what the speaker is communicating. The speaker has very clear pronunciation and speaks at an even pace, making use of appropriate pauses and intonation. He is also able to use advanced vocabulary and grammatical structures effectively ("*she believes that job that would be offered to student would be really low-level and low-responsibility jobs which will not allow them to grow into and develop the qualities of leadership*"; "*contrary to what the policy says*").

Low-level Response: Listen to Track 26.

Rater Comments

This speaker addresses the question, but does not provide a complete answer, and her response is overall somewhat difficult to follow. She states the woman's opinion, but does not explain what the woman is disagreeing with, since she only makes a vague reference to the policy "*Girl says, say, say that uh recruiting proposed by university is not a good uh, um, uh, a good statement*". While she does use some sophisticated vocabulary ("*particular skills*," "*permanent employment*"), she does not fully explain her ideas. For example, when she says, "*he didn't give any particular skills in leadership or organization*," she does not make it clear that she is talking about the woman's brother or his job experience, and how that relates to the new policy. Her pronunciation is clear, but her control of grammar is weak, which makes it difficult to understand her meaning: "*when the student um attain graduation, have to compete with older students . . . so there's no any. . . .*"

Question 4

Prompt

Using the professor's example, explain what an establishing shot is and how it is used.

Important Points

In this item, you should explain that in a movie or film, an establishing shot is used at the beginning of a scene to provide context, such as place, time, and mood. The shot in the professor's example showed a detective's office in a city in the past (1940s), so the viewer knows that the rest of the scene takes place in the city in the 1940s. The shot in the example is filmed with darkness, rain, and shadows that give it a gloomy or mysterious feeling, so the viewer knows that the events which follow will be dark and mysterious. A high-level response will communicate in a coherent and organized way the purpose of the establishing shot (to let viewers know where and when the scene is taking place and to set a mood) and explain how the establishing shot in the professor's example carries out this purpose.

High-level Response: Listen to Track 27.

Rater Comments

The speaker clearly describes what an establishing shot is: "*shown at the beginning of the movie, it gives like a sense of what the feeling is like in the movie.*" The professor's example is described accurately, with all important points included and connected clearly to the concept ("*it describes the movie beforehand, so he could tell that the movie was in the 1940s*"). The speaker uses sophisticated language fluently ("*by that he could tell that the movie was going to have a dark setting*"). The speaker pauses several times to organize her thoughts, but the pauses are located at natural places and do not seriously interrupt the response. Although the speaker is rushed at the end, she remains understandable and successfully includes all points.

Low-level Response: Listen to Track 28.

Rater Comments

The speaker does manage to express the central idea of the establishing shot and partially describe the shot used in the professor's example. However, he does not have very strong control of grammar or vocabulary, often resulting in vague ("*gives some example using lights, or we are in an office, some very old office*") or confusing statements ("*that the director's, like, that the people concern about it*"). Although the speaker connects the example to the concept, important parts of the example are left out (that the scene gave a gloomy and mysterious feeling, that it showed a city). The speaker's unclear pronunciation also requires the listener to work hard to understand his speech. Several important words cannot be understood at all, leaving the listener to guess at their meaning.

Question 5

Prompt

Briefly summarize the problem the speakers are discussing. Then state which solution you would recommend. Explain the reasons for your recommendation.

Important Points

For this task, the prompt asks you to briefly summarize the problem being discussed (the woman has a problem in her house with the water—the pipes broke—and she needs a place to stay temporarily) and recommend *one* of the solutions. It is important to note that taking time to summarize both solutions is not a requirement of the task. Summarizing the problem, however, is required. You should also offer reasons and support for why you prefer one solution over the other. If you prefer the second solution, for example, you may say that it is worth spending the extra money on a hotel since getting good grades on her exams should be her priority as a student.

High-level Response: Listen to Track 29.

Rater Comments

This response is well-organized and easy to understand. The speaker explains the woman's problem quickly and clearly. Even though it is not required of the task, she briefly mentions what the two solutions from the conversation are before choosing the second solution (staying in a hotel) and defending her choice with reasons. The response is not perfect—the speaker says the woman should *"rent a small hotel"* instead of a hotel *room*, and she pauses at times and repeats some phrases. However, her pronunciation is easy to follow and she uses advanced grammatical structures to express her opinion, like when she says that the woman *"wouldn't have to worry about noise and inconveniencing other people"* if she stayed in a hotel.

Mid-level Response: Listen to Track 30.

Rater Comments

The speaker makes a clear choice of solution and gives some reasons for that choice. It's clear from her response that she understands what the woman's problem is; however, to improve on this response she could have begun by summarizing the problem explicitly before recommending a solution. The speaker is not able to convey the reasons for her recommendation very clearly or with precise language. For example, when trying to explain that the woman needs to stay in a hotel so that she can focus on studying for exams, she says, *"and . . . two weeks is an amount of time, and by the time she's going to have her midterm exams, which is very important to get . . ."* The listener has to make an effort here to understand what the speaker is trying to say. Her frequent pauses and some repetitions of certain words and phrases also require enough listener effort to place this response in the mid-level.

Question 6

Prompt

Using points from the lecture, explain how the passion plant and the potato plant defend themselves from insects.

Important Points

For this task, you should use the examples from the lecture to explain how plants defend themselves from insects. You should explain that plants can use both physical and chemical defenses. The passion plant uses a physical defense. This plant has spiky hairs on its leaves which prevent insects from landing on the plant and eating the leaves. The potato plant, on the other hand uses a chemical defense. This plant releases a chemical through its leaves when an insect eats it. The chemical makes the insect feel full, so it stops eating the plant.

High-level Response: Listen to Track 31.

Rater Comments

The speaker gives a well-organized, clear response and is able to summarize all of the important information from the lecture. He jumps immediately into a summary of the examples, but he shows a clear connection between the two examples to the main concept. Consider his sentence: *"On the other side, potato plants uses chemical features to prevent being eaten by insects."* Though there are some grammatical errors in this sentence, he uses a transitional phrase *"on the other side,"* and he stresses the word *"chemical"* to emphasize the contrast between the two examples. He does speak very quickly at times, but he shows that he is able to communicate without too many pauses and searching for words. He makes occasional pronunciation errors but has the ability to correct himself. For instance, he describes the chemical defenses that the potato plant uses *"to prevent being eaten."* At first, "being eaten" is pronounced incorrectly, but he quickly corrects his pronunciation and continues with the response.

Mid-level Response: Listen to Track 32.

Rater Comments

This speaker is able to convey all of the important points from the lecture, but her response takes some effort to understand. She pauses frequently, searching for words. She clearly understood and is able to explain both examples, but her vocabulary is sometimes vague (*"the potato plant has some, like, chemical things"*) or inaccurate. For instance, in the first point about the passion plant, she describes the spikes *"which* prevent him *from the insect"* instead of "which *protect it* from the insect." Her pronunciation is mostly easy to understand, but she does make a few mistakes that confuse her meaning. For example, while describing the chemical defenses of the potato plant, she says that *"the insect doesn't feel hungry,"* but her pronunciation of "hungry" sounds more like "angry."

Writing Section

Prompts, Topic Notes, and Sample Responses with Rater Comments

Use the sample Integrated and Independent Writing Rubrics in Appendix A to see how responses are scored.

This section includes topic notes that are guides to the kind of information raters expect to read in a high-level response.

This section also refers to sample responses, which can be found on the accompanying DVD. These responses were scored at the highest level. The responses are followed by comments from certified ETS raters.

Question 1

Prompt

Summarize the points made in the lecture, being sure to explain how they respond to the specific points made in the reading passage.

Topic Notes

The reading discusses three reasons to believe that a small mammal, R. robustus, could not have been an active hunter (perhaps it was a scavenger that sometimes fed on unhatched eggs of the psitticosaur dinosaur), but the lecturer presents reasons why each of these three reasons are unconvincing.

Point made in the reading	Corresponding point from the lecture
R. robustus was smaller than psitticosaurs. So given their size, R. robustus was not likely to be a successful hunter of psitticosaurs or similar dinosaurs.	R. robustus was too small to hunt adult psitticosaurs, but it could have hunted baby psitticosaurs or other similarly sized dinosaurs—prey that was smaller than or had less mass than R. robustus.
R. robustus would not have been able to move fast enough to catch prey because it had short legs positioned to the side.	There is a modern day mammal, the Tasmanian Devil, that has the same leg features as R. Robustus but can achieve speeds fast enough to make it an effective predator.
The lack of teeth marks on the bones found in the stomach of R. robustus indicates it was not an active hunter (and that it probably just swallowed a dinosaur egg whole).	R. robustus probably swallowed its prey whole or in large pieces; R. robustus had no marks on its back teeth, which were probably not used for chewing.

Responses with scores of 4 and 5 typically discuss all three points in the table.

Sample Response

The lecture completely refutes the reading passage. The professor use the following points to indicate that R. robustus could have been actively hunting baby psittacosaur and similar sized baby dinosaurs.

First, although R. robustus was small, it was much bigger than baby psittacosaurs dinosaur, more than twice in size. This means R. robustus was big enough to hunt baby psittacosaurs.

Second, even though R. robustus had short legs and they were positioned somewhat to the side, these features are not sufficient indications that R. robustus could not run as fast enough to be successful predator. The professor pointed out that Tasmanian Devil, a morden-day successful predator whose legs share similar "disadvantages", can run as fast as 50 KM/H and is an active and very successful hunter today. So its possible R. robustus could run just as fast and therefore be as successful in hunting.

Last but not the least, lack of teeth marks on the dinosaur bones is not enough evidence to support conclusion that the dinosaur was not actively hunted. Studies of fossil records show that though R. robustus had powerful jaws but also, it did not use its back-teeth for chewing because its back teeth had no wear and tear. So we can also guess that R. robustus could had swallowed the baby dinosaur whole and therefore not leaving any teeth marks.

Rater Comments

This response earns a score of 5. Grammatical errors are few and minor. This response clearly conveys the three main points from the lecture and shows how those points challenge the information from the three points in the reading passage. Note that the response does not discuss the dinosaur egg to get the point across as to why the bones of the prey did not contain teeth marks; although this would have been helpful, it could be argued that this is not essential information for conveying the point clearly. Therefore, even though this last sentence is not quite as clear as the rest of this response, holistically, it still conveys all of the relevant information with sufficient clarity to rate a score of 5.

Question 2

Prompt

Do you agree or disagree with the following statement?

Technology has made children less creative than they were in the past.

Use specific reasons and examples to support your answer.

Topic Notes

This topic asks you whether you believe technology has negatively affected children's creativity over time. Successful responses can agree with the statement, disagree with the statement, or show the merits of both positions. No matter which position you take, it is important to support your opinion with details and examples.

If you agree with the statement and believe that technology stifles children's creativity, you might support that by explaining how the computer keeps kids in the home and away from other kids; the ability to deploy communication skills in face-to-face situations, suffers as a consequence, and this in turn hinders the development of creativity. You might argue that children who experience the world by being out in it rather than being online all the time can use their imagination to create their own games or put on performances; however, this has become very rare these days because with the advancement of technology, most forms of entertainment that kids are interested in are ready-made. You could even extend the argument to say that this is becoming a problem with modern life in general: most problems have been solved, so no special thinking or creativity by anyone—whether it be adults or kids—is needed these days to deal with new situations or problems.

If you disagree with the statement, you might point out and develop the ways in which technology stimulates the imagination. Rather than stifling creativity, technology allows kids to engage in such creative endeavors as producing their own blogs and websites, or designing clever and interesting new games and apps for computers or phones. More resources and viewpoints than ever before are now within reach of most people, including children, because technology has provided us with new ways to access such a wealth of information; this exposure can lead to enhanced creativity. In a response that explores reasons for disagreeing with the statement, you might come to the conclusion that the meaning of creativity itself has shifted over time.

Sample Response

Technology is today part of the everyday life; we are surrounded it by it and can't live without it. But despite all the good things that derive from technology, I strongly agree that there are some ways that technology causes children to think less.

For one thing, there is almost no information that cannot be found on the internet. When it comes to reading, many high school students agree to refer to "notes" sites instead of reading a complete book assigned by their teachers. These sites usually map out the important stories, passages, and characters for the student. This destroys creativity by not allowing the student to understand the story on his or her own and discover the true personal meanings of the assignment. An activity such as reading is suppose to question one's intellect and challenge one's thinking but with these sites available, kids now rely on the information given and fail to appreciate and grow that is the purpose of reading many books.

During other activities encountered in school, such as projects, children now tend to rely on the internet to come up with ideas. I have observed this many times. When a creative assignment is given by the teacher, instead of brainstorming ideas together, children just hop on a computer and search for ideas on the internet. It's one thing to use the internet as a tool as oppose to using it incessantly and not letting your imagination and creativity take charge.

Other forms of technology such as video games and TV has a great impact on using up time that used to be devoted to imagination and creative activities. Before TV and computer, children invented their world just on their own using their fantasy when building things with blocks or being outdoors in the nature. They used simple things for constructing adventures and had great ideas for new games together or alone. This means they learn to be creative and also self-determined and self-conscious. Nowaday, how can they learn these skills when passively watching TV or doing what the computer says?

In summary, there is a lot about technology that takes away from chances for children to be creative and develop creative skills.

Rater Comments

This 5-level response mainly presents examples of how technology has reduced opportunities to be creative and develop creative skills. The writer first discusses the existence of book summaries and interpretive notes on Web sites, and explains how students use this information instead of actually reading books assigned at school; this results in students not being able to read well or form their own creative interpretations of what they are reading. In the third paragraph the writer talks about students getting ideas for projects from Web sites instead of interacting with other students to creatively brainstorm ideas together. And in the fourth paragraph the writer explains that what used to be time for creative fantasizing or inventing playtime activities has now been replaced by time watching TV or following instructions on the computer. This response is well-organized and unified, and gives ample support for the writer's point of view. Grammatical errors are very minor and a variety of complex structures are used.

TOEFL iBT Test 2

READING

This section measures your ability to understand academic passages in English.

There are three passages in the section. Give yourself 20 minutes to read each passage and answer the questions about it. The entire section will take 60 minutes to complete.

You may look back at a passage when answering the questions. You can skip questions and go back to them later as long as there is time remaining.

Directions: Read the passage. Then answer the questions. Give yourself 20 minutes to complete this practice set.

CHINESE POTTERY

China has one of the world's oldest continuous civilizations—despite invasions and occasional foreign rule. A country as vast as China with so long-lasting a civilization has a complex social and visual history, within which pottery and porcelain play a major role.

The function and status of ceramics in China varied from dynasty to dynasty, so they may be utilitarian, burial, trade, collectors', or even ritual objects, according to their quality and the era in which they were made. The ceramics fall into three broad types—earthenware, stoneware, and porcelain—for vessels, architectural items such as roof tiles, and modeled objects and figures. In addition, there was an important group of sculptures made for religious use, the majority of which were produced in earthenware.

The earliest ceramics were fired to earthenware temperatures, but as early as the fifteenth century B.C., high-temperature stonewares were being made with glazed surfaces. During the Six Dynasties period (A.D. 265–589), kilns[1] in north China were producing high-fired ceramics of good quality. Whitewares produced in Hebei and Henan provinces from the seventh to the tenth centuries evolved into the highly prized porcelains of the Song dynasty (A.D. 960–1279), long regarded as one of the high points in the history of China's ceramic industry. The tradition of religious sculpture extends over most historical periods but is less clearly delineated than that of stonewares or porcelains, for it embraces the old custom of earthenware burial ceramics with later religious images and architectural ornament. Ceramic products also include lead-glazed tomb models of the Han dynasty, three-color lead-glazed vessels and figures of the Tang dynasty, and Ming three-color temple ornaments, in which the motifs were outlined in a raised trail of slip[2], as well as the many burial ceramics produced in imitation of vessels made in materials of higher intrinsic value.

Trade between the West and the settled and prosperous Chinese dynasties introduced new forms and different technologies. One of the most far-reaching examples is the impact of the fine ninth-century A.D. Chinese porcelain wares imported into the Arab world. So admired were these pieces that they encouraged the development of earthenware made in imitation of porcelain and instigated research into the method of their manufacture. From the Middle East the Chinese acquired a blue pigment—a purified form of cobalt oxide unobtainable at that time in China—that contained only a low level of manganese. Cobalt ores found in China have a high manganese content, which produces a more muted blue-gray color. In the seventeenth century, the trading activities of the Dutch East India Company resulted in vast quantities of decorated Chinese porcelain being brought to Europe, which stimulated and influenced the work of a wide variety of wares, notably Delft. The Chinese themselves adapted many specific vessel forms from the West, such as bottles with long spouts, and designed a range of decorative patterns especially for the European market.

Just as painted designs on Greek pots may seem today to be purely decorative, whereas in fact they were carefully and precisely worked out so that at the time, their meaning was clear, so it is with Chinese pots. To twentieth-century eyes, Chinese pottery may appear merely decorative, yet to the Chinese the form of each object and its adornment had meaning and significance. The dragon represented the emperor, and the phoenix, the empress; the pomegranate indicated fertility, and a pair of fish, happiness; mandarin ducks stood for wedded bliss; the pine tree, peach, and crane are emblems of long life; and fish leaping from waves indicated success in the civil service examinations. Only when European decorative themes were introduced did these meanings become obscured or even lost.

From early times pots were used in both religious and secular contexts. The imperial court commissioned work and in the Yuan dynasty (A.D. 1279–1368) an imperial ceramic factory was established at Jingdezhen. Pots played an important part in some religious ceremonies. Long and often lyrical descriptions of the different types of ware exist that assist in classifying pots, although these sometimes confuse an already large and complicated picture.

kilns[1]: enclosed ovens used to heat and harden clay objects
slip[2]: a mixture of clay and water used to decorate pottery

Directions: Now answer the questions.

PARAGRAPH 2

The function and status of ceramics in China varied from dynasty to dynasty, so they may be utilitarian, burial, trade, collectors', or even ritual objects, according to their quality and the era in which they were made. The ceramics fall into three broad types—earthenware, stoneware, and porcelain—for vessels, architectural items such as roof tiles, and modeled objects and figures. In addition, there was an important group of sculptures made for religious use, the majority of which were produced in earthenware.

1. The word "status" in the passage is closest in meaning to

Ⓐ origin
Ⓑ importance
Ⓒ quality
Ⓓ design

2. According to paragraph 2, which of the following is true of Chinese ceramics?

Ⓐ The function of ceramics remained the same from dynasty to dynasty.
Ⓑ The use of ceramics as trade objects is better documented than the use of ceramics as ritual objects.
Ⓒ There was little variation in quality for any type of ceramics over time.
Ⓓ Some religious sculptures were made using the earthenware type of ceramics.

PARAGRAPH 3

The earliest ceramics were fired to earthenware temperatures, but as early as the fifteenth century B.C., high-temperature stonewares were being made with glazed surfaces. During the Six Dynasties period (A.D. 265–589), kilns in north China were producing high-fired ceramics of good quality. Whitewares produced in Hebei and Henan provinces from the seventh to the tenth centuries evolved into the highly prized porcelains of the Song dynasty (A.D. 960–1279), long regarded as one of the high points in the history of China's ceramic industry. The tradition of religious sculpture extends over most historical periods but is less clearly delineated than that of stonewares or porcelains, for it embraces the old custom of earthenware burial ceramics with later religious images and architectural ornament. Ceramic products also include lead-glazed tomb models of the Han dynasty, three-color lead-glazed vessels and figures of the Tang dynasty, and Ming three-color temple ornaments, in which the motifs were outlined in a raised trail of slip, as well as the many burial ceramics produced in imitation of vessels made in materials of higher intrinsic value.

3. The word "evolved" in the passage is closest in meaning to

Ⓐ divided
Ⓑ extended
Ⓒ developed
Ⓓ vanished

4. Which of the sentences below best expresses the essential information in the highlighted sentence in the passage? Incorrect choices change the meaning in important ways or leave out essential information.

Ⓐ While stonewares and porcelains are found throughout most historical periods, religious sculpture is limited to the ancient period.
Ⓑ Religious sculpture was created in most periods, but its history is less clear than that of stonewares or porcelains because some old forms continued to be used even when new ones were developed.
Ⓒ While stonewares and porcelains changed throughout history, religious sculpture remained uniform in form and use.
Ⓓ The historical development of religious sculpture is relatively unclear because religious sculptures sometimes resemble earthenware architectural ornaments.

5. Paragraph 3 supports all of the following concerning the history of the ceramic industry in China EXCEPT:

Ⓐ The earliest high-fired ceramics were of poor quality.
Ⓑ Ceramics produced during the Tang and Ming dynasties sometimes incorporated multiple colors.
Ⓒ Earthenware ceramics were produced in China before stonewares were.
Ⓓ The Song dynasty period was notable for the production of high-quality porcelain ceramics.

PARAGRAPH 4

Trade between the West and the settled and prosperous Chinese dynasties introduced new forms and different technologies. One of the most far-reaching examples is the impact of the fine ninth-century A.D. Chinese porcelain wares imported into the Arab world. So admired were these pieces that they encouraged the development of earthenware made in imitation of porcelain and instigated research into the method of their manufacture. From the Middle East the Chinese acquired a blue pigment—a purified form of cobalt oxide unobtainable at that time in China—that contained only a low level of manganese. Cobalt ores found in China have a high manganese content, which produces a more muted blue-gray color. In the seventeenth century, the trading activities of the Dutch East India Company resulted in vast quantities of decorated Chinese porcelain being brought to Europe, which stimulated and influenced the work of a wide variety of wares, notably Delft. The Chinese themselves adapted many specific vessel forms from the West, such as bottles with long spouts, and designed a range of decorative patterns especially for the European market.

6. The word "instigated" in the passage is closest in meaning to

Ⓐ improved
Ⓑ investigated
Ⓒ narrowed
Ⓓ caused

7. According to paragraph 4, one consequence of the trade of Chinese ceramics was

Ⓐ the transfer of a distinctive blue pigment from China to the Middle East
Ⓑ an immediate change from earthenware production to porcelain production in European countries
Ⓒ Chinese production of wares made for the European market
Ⓓ a decreased number of porcelain vessels available on the European market

PARAGRAPH 5

Just as painted designs on Greek pots may seem today to be purely decorative, whereas in fact they were carefully and precisely worked out so that at the time, their meaning was clear, so it is with Chinese pots. To twentieth-century eyes, Chinese pottery may appear merely decorative, yet to the Chinese the form of each object and its adornment had meaning and significance. The dragon represented the emperor, and the phoenix, the empress; the pomegranate indicated fertility, and a pair of fish, happiness; mandarin ducks stood for wedded bliss; the pine tree, peach, and crane are emblems of long life; and fish leaping from waves indicated success in the civil service examinations. Only when European decorative themes were introduced did these meanings become obscured or even lost.

8. The word "whereas" in the passage is closest in meaning to

Ⓐ while
Ⓑ previously
Ⓒ surprisingly
Ⓓ because

9. In paragraph 5, the author compares the designs on Chinese pots to those on Greek pots in order to

   (A) emphasize that while Chinese pots were decorative, Greek pots were functional
   (B) argue that the designs on Chinese pots had specific meanings and were not just decorative
   (C) argue that twentieth-century scholars are better able to understand these designs than were ancient scholars
   (D) explain how scholars have identified the meaning of specific images on Chinese pots

10. Which of the following is mentioned in paragraph 5 as being symbolically represented on Chinese ceramics?

    (A) Chinese rulers
    (B) love of homeland
    (C) loyalty to friends
    (D) success in trade

11. Paragraph 5 suggests which of the following about the decorations on Chinese pottery?

    (A) They had more importance for aristocrats than for ordinary citizens.
    (B) Their significance may have remained clear had the Chinese not come under foreign influence.
    (C) They contain some of the same images that appear on Greek pots.
    (D) Their significance is now as clear to twentieth-century observers as it was to the early Chinese.

PARAGRAPH 6

From early times pots were used in both religious and secular contexts. The imperial court commissioned work and in the Yuan dynasty (A.D. 1279–1368) an imperial ceramic factory was established at Jingdezhen. Pots played an important part in some religious ceremonies. Long and often lyrical descriptions of the different types of ware exist that assist in classifying pots, although these sometimes confuse an already large and complicated picture.

12. The word "these" in the passage refers to

    (A) religious ceremonies
    (B) descriptions
    (C) types of ware
    (D) pots

PARAGRAPH 4

Trade between the West and the settled and prosperous Chinese dynasties introduced new forms and different technologies. One of the most far-reaching examples is the impact of the fine ninth-century A.D. Chinese porcelain wares imported into the Arab world. **(A)** So admired were these pieces that they encouraged the development of earthenware made in imitation of porcelain and instigated research into the method of their manufacture. **(B)** From the Middle East the Chinese acquired a blue pigment—a purified form of cobalt oxide unobtainable at that time in China—that contained only a low level of manganese. Cobalt ores found in China have a high manganese content, which produces a more muted blue-gray color. **(C)** In the seventeenth century, the trading activities of the Dutch East India Company resulted in vast quantities of decorated Chinese porcelain being brought to Europe, which stimulated and influenced the work of a wide variety of wares, notably Delft. **(D)** The Chinese themselves adapted many specific vessel forms from the West, such as bottles with long spouts, and designed a range of decorative patterns especially for the European market.

13. **Directions:** Look at the part of the passage that is displayed above. The letters **(A)**, **(B)**, **(C)**, and **(D)** indicate where the following sentence could be added.

Foreign trade was also responsible for certain innovations in coloring.

Where would the sentence best fit?

Ⓐ Choice A
Ⓑ Choice B
Ⓒ Choice C
Ⓓ Choice D

14. **Directions:** An introductory sentence for a brief summary of the passage is provided below. Complete the summary by selecting the THREE answer choices that express the most important ideas in the passage. Some sentences do not belong in the summary because they express ideas that are not presented in the passage or are minor ideas in the passage.

Write your answer choices in the spaces where they belong. You can either write the letter of your answer choice or you can copy the sentence.

Ceramics have been produced in China for a very long time.

-
-
-

Answer Choices

[A] The Chinese produced earthenware, stoneware, and porcelain pottery, and they used their ceramics for a variety of utilitarian, architectural, and ceremonial purposes.

[B] The shape and decoration of ceramics produced for religious use in China were influenced by Chinese ceramics produced for export.

[C] As a result of trade relations, Chinese ceramic production changed, and Chinese ceramics influenced the ceramic production of other countries.

[D] Chinese burial ceramics have the longest and most varied history of production and were frequently decorated with written texts that help scholars date them.

[E] Before China had contact with the West, the meaning of various designs used to decorate Chinese ceramics was well understood.

[F] Ceramics made in imperial factories were used in both religious and non-religious contexts.

Directions: Read the passage. Then answer the questions. Give yourself 20 minutes to complete this practice set.

VARIATIONS IN THE CLIMATE

One of the most difficult aspects of deciding whether current climatic events reveal evidence of the impact of human activities is that it is hard to get a measure of what constitutes the natural variability of the climate. We know that over the past millennia the climate has undergone major changes without any significant human intervention. We also know that the global climate system is immensely complicated and that everything is in some way connected, and so the system is capable of fluctuating in unexpected ways. We need therefore to know how much the climate can vary of its own accord in order to interpret with confidence the extent to which recent changes are natural as opposed to being the result of human activities.

Instrumental records do not go back far enough to provide us with reliable measurements of global climatic variability on timescales longer than a century. What we do know is that as we include longer time intervals, the record shows increasing evidence of slow swings in climate between different regimes. To build up a better picture of fluctuations appreciably further back in time requires us to use proxy records.

Over long periods of time, substances whose physical and chemical properties change with the ambient climate at the time can be deposited in a systematic way to provide a continuous record of changes in those properties over time, sometimes for hundreds or thousands of years. Generally, the layering occurs on an annual basis, hence the observed changes in the records can be dated. Information on temperature, rainfall, and other aspects of the climate that can be inferred from the systematic changes in properties is usually referred to as proxy data. Proxy temperature records have been reconstructed from ice core drilled out of the central Greenland ice cap, calcite shells embedded in layered lake sediments in Western Europe, ocean floor sediment cores from the tropical Atlantic Ocean, ice cores from Peruvian glaciers, and ice cores from eastern Antarctica. While these records provide broadly consistent indications that temperature variations can occur on a global scale, there are nonetheless some intriguing differences, which suggest that the pattern of temperature variations in regional climates can also differ significantly from each other.

What the proxy records make abundantly clear is that there have been significant natural changes in the climate over timescales longer than a few thousand years. Equally striking, however, is the relative stability of the climate in the past 10,000 years (the Holocene period).

To the extent that the coverage of the global climate from these records can provide a measure of its true variability, it should at least indicate how all the natural causes of climate change have combined. These include the chaotic fluctuations of the atmosphere, the slower but equally erratic behavior of the oceans, changes in the land surfaces, and the extent of ice and snow. Also included will be any variations that have arisen from volcanic activity, solar activity, and, possibly, human activities.

One way to estimate how all the various processes leading to climate variability will combine is by using computer models of the global climate. They can do only so much to represent the full complexity of the global climate and hence may give only limited information about natural variability. Studies suggest that to date the variability in computer simulations is considerably smaller than in data obtained from the proxy records.

In addition to the internal variability of the global climate system itself, there is the added factor of external influences, such as volcanoes and solar activity. There is a growing body of opinion that both these physical variations have a measurable impact on the climate. Thus we need to be able to include these in our deliberations. Some current analyses conclude that volcanoes and solar activity explain quite a considerable amount of the observed variability in the period from the seventeenth to the early twentieth centuries, but that they cannot be invoked to explain the rapid warming in recent decades.

Directions: Now answer the questions.

PARAGRAPH 1

One of the most difficult aspects of deciding whether current climatic events reveal evidence of the impact of human activities is that it is hard to get a measure of what constitutes the natural variability of the climate. We know that over the past millennia the climate has undergone major changes without any significant human intervention. We also know that the global climate system is immensely complicated and that everything is in some way connected, and so the system is capable of fluctuating in unexpected ways. We need therefore to know how much the climate can vary of its own accord in order to interpret with confidence the extent to which recent changes are natural as opposed to being the result of human activities.

15. According to paragraph 1, which of the following must we find out in order to determine the impact of human activities upon climate?

Ⓐ The major changes in climate over the past millennia
Ⓑ The degree to which the climate varies naturally
Ⓒ The best method for measuring climatic change
Ⓓ The millennium when humans began to interfere with the climate

PARAGRAPH 2

Instrumental records do not go back far enough to provide us with reliable measurements of global climatic variability on timescales longer than a century. What we do know is that as we include longer time intervals, the record shows increasing evidence of slow swings in climate between different regimes. To build up a better picture of fluctuations appreciably further back in time requires us to use proxy records.

16. According to paragraph 2, an advantage of proxy records over instrumental records is that

Ⓐ they are more reliable measures of climatic variability in the past century
Ⓑ they provide more accurate measures of local temperatures
Ⓒ they provide information on climate fluctuations further back in time
Ⓓ they reveal information about the human impact on the climate

PARAGRAPH 3

Over long periods of time, substances whose physical and chemical properties change with the ambient climate at the time can be deposited in a systematic way to provide a continuous record of changes in those properties over time, sometimes for hundreds or thousands of years. Generally, the layering occurs on an annual basis, hence the observed changes in the records can be dated. Information on temperature, rainfall, and other aspects of the climate that can be inferred from the systematic changes in properties is usually referred to as proxy data. Proxy temperature records have been reconstructed from ice core drilled out of the central Greenland ice cap, calcite shells embedded in layered lake sediments in Western Europe, ocean floor sediment cores from the tropical Atlantic Ocean, ice cores from Peruvian glaciers, and ice cores from eastern Antarctica. While these records provide broadly consistent indications that temperature variations can occur on a global scale, there are nonetheless some intriguing differences, which suggest that the pattern of temperature variations in regional climates can also differ significantly from each other.

17. Which of the sentences below best expresses the essential information in the highlighted sentence in the passage? Incorrect choices change the meaning in important ways or leave out essential information.

Ⓐ Because physical and chemical properties of substances are unchanging, they are useful records of climate fluctuations over time.
Ⓑ For hundreds or thousands of years, people have been observing changes in the chemical and physical properties of substances in order to infer climate change.
Ⓒ Because it takes long periods of time for the climate to change, systematic changes in the properties of substances are difficult to observe.
Ⓓ Changes in systematically deposited substances that are affected by climate can indicate climate variations over time.

18. According to paragraph 3, scientists are able to reconstruct proxy temperature records by

Ⓐ studying regional differences in temperature variations
Ⓑ studying and dating changes in the properties of substances
Ⓒ observing changes in present-day climate conditions
Ⓓ inferring past climate shifts from observations of current climatic changes

PARAGRAPH 4

What the proxy records make abundantly clear is that there have been significant natural changes in the climate over timescales longer than a few thousand years. Equally striking, however, is the relative stability of the climate in the past 10,000 years (the Holocene period).

19. The word "striking" in the passage is closest in meaning to

Ⓐ noticeable
Ⓑ confusing
Ⓒ true
Ⓓ unlikely

PARAGRAPHS 3 & 4

Over long periods of time, substances whose physical and chemical properties change with the ambient climate at the time can be deposited in a systematic way to provide a continuous record of changes in those properties over time, sometimes for hundreds or thousands of years. Generally, the layering occurs on an annual basis, hence the observed changes in the records can be dated. Information on temperature, rainfall, and other aspects of the climate that can be inferred from the systematic changes in properties is usually referred to as proxy data. Proxy temperature records have been reconstructed from ice core drilled out of the central Greenland ice cap, calcite shells embedded in layered lake sediments in Western Europe, ocean floor sediment cores from the tropical Atlantic Ocean, ice cores from Peruvian glaciers, and ice cores from eastern Antarctica. While these records provide broadly consistent indications that temperature variations can occur on a global scale, there are nonetheless some intriguing differences, which suggest that the pattern of temperature variations in regional climates can also differ significantly from each other.

What the proxy records make abundantly clear is that there have been significant natural changes in the climate over timescales longer than a few thousand years. Equally striking, however, is the relative stability of the climate in the past 10,000 years (the Holocene period).

20. According to paragraphs 3 and 4, proxy data have suggested all of the following about the climate EXCEPT:

Ⓐ Regional climates may change over time.
Ⓑ The climate has changed very little in the past 10,000 years.
Ⓒ Global temperatures vary more than regional temperatures.
Ⓓ Important natural changes in climate have occurred over large timescales.

PARAGRAPH 5

To the extent that the coverage of the global climate from these records can provide a measure of its true variability, it should at least indicate how all the natural causes of climate change have combined. These include the chaotic fluctuations of the atmosphere, the slower but equally erratic behavior of the oceans, changes in the land surfaces, and the extent of ice and snow. Also included will be any variations that have arisen from volcanic activity, solar activity, and, possibly, human activities.

21. The word "erratic" in the passage is closest in meaning to

Ⓐ dramatic
Ⓑ important
Ⓒ unpredictable
Ⓓ common

22. All of the following are mentioned in paragraph 5 as natural causes of climate change EXCEPT

Ⓐ atmospheric changes
Ⓑ the slow movement of landmasses
Ⓒ fluctuations in the amount of ice and snow
Ⓓ changes in ocean activity

PARAGRAPH 6

One way to estimate how all the various processes leading to climate variability will combine is by using computer models of the global climate. They can do only so much to represent the full complexity of the global climate and hence may give only limited information about natural variability. Studies suggest that to date the variability in computer simulations is considerably smaller than in data obtained from the proxy records.

23. According to paragraph 6, which of the following is true of computer models of the global climate?

Ⓐ The information they produce is still limited.
Ⓑ They are currently most useful in understanding past climatic behaviors.
Ⓒ They allow researchers to interpret the data obtained from proxy records.
Ⓓ They do not provide information about regional climates.

PARAGRAPH 7

In addition to the internal variability of the global climate system itself, there is the added factor of external influences, such as volcanoes and solar activity. There is a growing body of opinion that both these physical variations have a measurable impact on the climate. Thus we need to be able to include these in our deliberations. Some current analyses conclude that volcanoes and solar activity explain quite a considerable amount of the observed variability in the period from the seventeenth to the early twentieth centuries, but that they cannot be invoked to explain the rapid warming in recent decades.

24. The word "deliberations" in the passage is closest in meaning to

Ⓐ records
Ⓑ discussions
Ⓒ results
Ⓓ variations

25. The word "invoked" in the passage is closest in meaning to

Ⓐ demonstrated
Ⓑ called upon
Ⓒ supported
Ⓓ expected

26. What is the author's purpose in presenting the information in paragraph 7?

Ⓐ To compare the influence of volcanoes and solar activity on climate variability with the influence of factors external to the global climate system
Ⓑ To indicate that there are other types of influences on climate variability in addition to those previously discussed
Ⓒ To explain how external influences on climate variability differ from internal influences
Ⓓ To argue that the rapid warming of Earth in recent decades cannot be explained

PARAGRAPH 7

In addition to the internal variability of the global climate system itself, there is the added factor of external influences, such as volcanoes and solar activity. **(A)** There is a growing body of opinion that both these physical variations have a measurable impact on the climate. **(B)** Thus we need to be able to include these in our deliberations. **(C)** Some current analyses conclude that volcanoes and solar activity explain quite a considerable amount of the observed variability in the period from the seventeenth to the early twentieth centuries, but that they cannot be invoked to explain the rapid warming in recent decades. **(D)**

27. **Directions:** Look at the part of the passage that is displayed above. The letters **(A)**, **(B)**, **(C)**, and **(D)** indicate where the following sentence could be added.

    Indeed, the contribution of volcanoes and solar activity would more likely have been to actually reduce the rate of warming slightly.

    Where would the sentence best fit?

    Ⓐ Choice A
    Ⓑ Choice B
    Ⓒ Choice C
    Ⓓ Choice D

28. **Directions:** An introductory sentence for a brief summary of the passage is provided below. Complete the summary by selecting the THREE answer choices that express the most important ideas in the passage. Some sentences do not belong in the summary because they express ideas that are not presented in the passage or are minor ideas in the passage.

    Write your answer choices in the spaces where they belong. You can either write the letter of your answer choice or you can copy the sentence.

    A number of different and complex factors influence changes in the global climate over long periods of time.

    •
    •
    •

Answer Choices

A In the absence of instrumental records, proxy data allow scientists to infer information about past climates.

B Scientists see a consistent pattern in the global temperature variations that have occurred in the past.

C Computer models are used to estimate how the different causes of climate variability combine to account for the climate variability that occurs.

D Scientists have successfully separated natural climate variation from changes related to human activities.

E Scientists believe that activities outside the global climate system, such as volcanoes and solar activity, may have significant effects on the system.

F Scientists have concluded that human activity accounts for the rapid global warming in recent decades.

Directions: Read the passage. Then answer the questions. Give yourself 20 minutes to complete this practice set.

SEVENTEENTH-CENTURY EUROPEAN ECONOMIC GROWTH

In the late sixteenth century and into the seventeenth, Europe continued the growth that had lifted it out of the relatively less prosperous medieval period (from the mid 400s to the late 1400s). Among the key factors behind this growth were increased agricultural productivity and an expansion of trade.

Populations cannot grow unless the rural economy can produce enough additional food to feed more people. During the sixteenth century, farmers brought more land into cultivation at the expense of forests and fens (low-lying wetlands). Dutch land reclamation in the Netherlands in the sixteenth and seventeenth centuries provides the most spectacular example of the expansion of farmland: the Dutch reclaimed more than 36,000 acres from 1590 to 1615 alone.

Much of the potential for European economic development lay in what at first glance would seem to have been only sleepy villages. Such villages, however, generally lay in regions of relatively advanced agricultural production, permitting not only the survival of peasants but also the accumulation of an agricultural surplus for investment. They had access to urban merchants, markets, and trade routes.

Increased agricultural production in turn facilitated rural industry, an intrinsic part of the expansion of industry. Woolens and textile manufacturers, in particular, utilized rural cottage (in-home) production, which took advantage of cheap and plentiful rural labor. In the German states, the ravages of the Thirty Years' War (1618–1648) further moved textile production into the countryside. Members of poor peasant families spun or wove cloth and linens at home for scant remuneration in an attempt to supplement meager family income.

More extended trading networks also helped develop Europe's economy in this period. English and Dutch ships carrying rye from the Baltic states reached Spain and Portugal. Population growth generated an expansion of small-scale manufacturing, particularly of handicrafts, textiles, and metal production in England, Flanders, parts of northern Italy, the southwestern German states, and parts of Spain. Only iron smelting and mining required marshaling a significant amount of capital (wealth invested to create more wealth).

The development of banking and other financial services contributed to the expansion of trade. By the middle of the sixteenth century, financiers and traders commonly accepted bills of exchange in place of gold or silver for other goods. Bills of exchange, which had their origins in medieval Italy, were promissory notes (written promises to pay a specified amount of money by a certain date) that could be sold to third parties. In this way, they provided credit. At mid-century, an Antwerp financier only slightly exaggerated when he claimed, "One can no more trade without bills of exchange than sail without water." Merchants no longer had to carry gold and silver over long, dangerous journeys. An Amsterdam merchant purchasing soap from a merchant in Marseille could go to an exchanger and pay the exchanger the equivalent sum in guilders, the Dutch currency. The exchanger would then send a bill of exchange to a colleague in Marseille, authorizing the colleague to pay the Marseille merchant in the merchant's own currency after the actual exchange of goods had taken place.

Bills of exchange contributed to the development of banks, as exchangers began to provide loans. Not until the eighteenth century, however, did such banks as the Bank of Amsterdam and the Bank of England begin to provide capital for business investment. Their principal function was to provide funds for the state.

The rapid expansion in international trade also benefitted from an infusion of capital, stemming largely from gold and silver brought by Spanish vessels from the Americas. This capital financed the production of goods, storage, trade, and even credit across Europe and overseas. Moreover, an increased credit supply was generated by investments and loans by bankers and wealthy merchants to states and by joint-stock partnerships– an English innovation (the first major company began in 1600). Unlike short-term financial cooperation between investors for a single commercial undertaking, joint-stock companies provided permanent funding of capital by drawing on the investments of merchants and other investors who purchased shares in the company.

Directions: Now answer the questions.

PARAGRAPH 1

In the late sixteenth century and into the seventeenth, Europe continued the growth that had lifted it out of the relatively less prosperous medieval period (from the mid 400s to the late 1400s). Among the key factors behind this growth were increased agricultural productivity and an expansion of trade.

29. According to paragraph 1, what was true of Europe during the medieval period?

Ⓐ Agricultural productivity declined.
Ⓑ There was relatively little economic growth.
Ⓒ The general level of prosperity declined.
Ⓓ Foreign trade began to play an important role in the economy.

30. The word "key" in the passage is closest in meaning to

Ⓐ historical
Ⓑ many
Ⓒ important
Ⓓ hidden

PARAGRAPH 2

Populations cannot grow unless the rural economy can produce enough additional food to feed more people. During the sixteenth century, farmers brought more land into cultivation at the expense of forests and fens (low-lying wetlands). Dutch land reclamation in the Netherlands in the sixteenth and seventeenth centuries provides the most spectacular example of the expansion of farmland: the Dutch reclaimed more than 36,000 acres from 1590 to 1615 alone.

31. According to paragraph 2, one effect of the desire to increase food production was that

Ⓐ land was cultivated in a different way
Ⓑ more farmers were needed
Ⓒ the rural economy was weakened
Ⓓ forests and wetlands were used for farming

PARAGRAPH 3

Much of the potential for European economic development lay in what at first glance would seem to have been only sleepy villages. Such villages, however, generally lay in regions of relatively advanced agricultural production, permitting not only the survival of peasants but also the accumulation of an agricultural surplus for investment. They had access to urban merchants, markets, and trade routes.

32. According to paragraph 3, what was one reason villages had such great economic potential?

Ⓐ Villages were located in regions where agricultural production was relatively advanced.
Ⓑ Villages were relatively small in population and size compared with urban areas.
Ⓒ Some village inhabitants made investments in industrial development.
Ⓓ Village inhabitants established markets within their villages.

PARAGRAPH 4

Increased agricultural production in turn facilitated rural industry, an intrinsic part of the expansion of industry. Woolens and textile manufacturers, in particular, utilized rural cottage (in-home) production, which took advantage of cheap and plentiful rural labor. In the German states, the ravages of the Thirty Years' War (1618–1648) further moved textile production into the countryside. Members of poor peasant families spun or wove cloth and linens at home for scant remuneration in an attempt to supplement meager family income.

33. Paragraph 4 supports the idea that increased agricultural production was important for the expansion of industry primarily because it

Ⓐ increased the number of available workers in rural areas
Ⓑ provided new types of raw materials for use by industry
Ⓒ resulted in an improvement in the health of the rural cottage workers used by manufacturers
Ⓓ helped repair some of the ravages of the Thirty Years' War

34. The word "meager" in the passage is closest in meaning to

Ⓐ very necessary
Ⓑ very low
Ⓒ traditional
Ⓓ primary

PARAGRAPH 5

More extended trading networks also helped develop Europe's economy in this period. English and Dutch ships carrying rye from the Baltic states reached Spain and Portugal. Population growth generated an expansion of small-scale manufacturing, particularly of handicrafts, textiles, and metal production in England, Flanders, parts of northern Italy, the southwestern German states, and parts of Spain. Only iron smelting and mining required marshaling a significant amount of capital (wealth invested to create more wealth).

35. Why does the author mention that "English and Dutch ships carrying rye from the Baltic states reached Spain and Portugal"?

Ⓐ To suggest that England and the Netherlands were the two most important trading nations in seventeenth-century Europe
Ⓑ To suggest how extensive trading relations were
Ⓒ To contrast the importance of agricultural products with manufactured products
Ⓓ To argue that shipping introduced a range of new products

PARAGRAPH 6

The development of banking and other financial services contributed to the expansion of trade. By the middle of the sixteenth century, financiers and traders commonly accepted bills of exchange in place of gold or silver for other goods. Bills of exchange, which had their origins in medieval Italy, were promissory notes (written promises to pay a specified amount of money by a certain date) that could be sold to third parties. In this way, they provided credit. At mid-century, an Antwerp financier only slightly exaggerated when he claimed, "One can no more trade without bills of exchange than sail without water." Merchants no longer had to carry gold and silver over long, dangerous journeys. An Amsterdam merchant purchasing soap from a merchant in Marseille could go to an exchanger and pay the exchanger the equivalent sum in guilders, the Dutch currency. The exchanger would then send a bill of exchange to a colleague in Marseille, authorizing the colleague to pay the Marseille merchant in the merchant's own currency after the actual exchange of goods had taken place.

36. By including the quotation in paragraph 6 by the financier from Antwerp, the author is emphasizing that

Ⓐ sailing was an important aspect of the economy
Ⓑ Increasing the number of water routes made trade possible
Ⓒ bills of exchange were necessary for successful trading
Ⓓ financiers often exaggerated the need for bills of exchange

37. According to paragraph 6, merchants were able to avoid the risk of carrying large amounts of gold and silver by

Ⓐ using third parties in Marseille to buy goods for them
Ⓑ doing all their business by using Dutch currency
Ⓒ paying for their purchases through bills of exchange
Ⓓ waiting to pay for goods until the goods had been delivered

PARAGRAPH 7

Bills of exchange contributed to the development of banks, as exchangers began to provide loans. Not until the eighteenth century, however, did such banks as the Bank of Amsterdam and the Bank of England begin to provide capital for business investment. Their principal function was to provide funds for the state.

38. According to paragraph 7, until the eighteenth century, it was the principal function of which of the following to provide funds for the state?

Ⓐ Bills of exchange
Ⓑ Exchangers who took loans
Ⓒ Banks
Ⓓ Business investment

PARAGRAPH 8

The rapid expansion in international trade also benefitted from an infusion of capital, stemming largely from gold and silver brought by Spanish vessels from the Americas. This capital financed the production of goods, storage, trade, and even credit across Europe and overseas. Moreover, an increased credit supply was generated by investments and loans by bankers and wealthy merchants to states and by joint-stock partnerships–an English innovation (the first major company began in 1600). Unlike short-term financial cooperation between investors for a single commercial undertaking, joint-stock companies provided permanent funding of capital by drawing on the investments of merchants and other investors who purchased shares in the company.

39. The phrase "an English innovation" in the passage is closest in meaning to

Ⓐ a new development introduced by the English
Ⓑ an arrangement found only in England
Ⓒ a type of agreement negotiated in English
Ⓓ a type of partnership based on English law

40. According to paragraph 8, each of the following was a source of funds used to finance economic expansion EXCEPT

Ⓐ groups of investors engaged in short-term financial cooperation
Ⓑ the state
Ⓒ wealthy merchants
Ⓓ joint-stock companies

PARAGRAPH 6

The development of banking and other financial services contributed to the expansion of trade. By the middle of the sixteenth century, financiers and traders commonly accepted bills of exchange in place of gold or silver for other goods. Bills of exchange, which had their origins in medieval Italy, were promissory notes (written promises to pay a specified amount of money by a certain date) that could be sold to third parties. In this way, they provided credit. **(A)** At mid-century, an Antwerp financier only slightly exaggerated when he claimed, "One can no more trade without bills of exchange than sail without water." **(B)** Merchants no longer had to carry gold and silver over long, dangerous journeys. **(C)** An Amsterdam merchant purchasing soap from a merchant in Marseille could go to an exchanger and pay the exchanger the equivalent sum in guilders, the Dutch currency. **(D)** The exchanger would then send a bill of exchange to a colleague in Marseille, authorizing the colleague to pay the Marseille merchant in the merchant's own currency after the actual exchange of goods had taken place.

41. **Directions:** Look at the part of the passage that is displayed above. The letters **(A)**, **(B)**, **(C)**, and **(D)** indicate where the following sentence could be added.

They could also avoid having to identify and assess the value of a wide variety of coins issued in many different places.

Where would the sentence best fit?

Ⓐ Choice A
Ⓑ Choice B
Ⓒ Choice C
Ⓓ Choice D

42. **Directions:** An introductory sentence for a brief summary of the passage is provided below. Complete the summary by selecting the THREE answer choices that express the most important ideas in the passage. Some sentences do not belong in the summary because they express ideas that are not presented in the passage or are minor ideas in the passage.

Write your answer choices in the spaces where they belong. You can either write the letter of your answer choice or you can copy the sentence.

In late sixteenth- and early seventeenth-century Europe, increased agricultural production and the expansion of trade were important in economic growth.

•

•

•

Answer Choices

[A] Bringing more land under cultivation produced enough food to create surpluses for trade and investment as well as for supporting the larger populations that led to the growth of rural industry.

[B] Most rural villages established an arrangement with a nearby urban center that enabled villagers to take advantage of urban markets to sell any handicrafts they produced.

[C] Increases in population and the expansion of trade led to increased manufacturing, much of it small-scale in character but some requiring significant capital investment.

[D] The expansion of trade was facilitated by developments in banking and financial services and benefitted from the huge influx of capital in the form of gold and silver from the Americas.

[E] Bills of exchange were invented in medieval Italy but became less important as banks began to provide loans for merchants.

[F] Increased capital was required for the production of goods, for storage, for trade, and for the provision of credit throughout Europe as well as in more distant markets overseas.

LISTENING

This section measures your ability to understand conversations and lectures in English.

Listen to each conversation and lecture only one time. After each conversation and lecture, you will answer some questions about it. Answer each question based on what is stated or implied by the speakers.

You may take notes while you listen and use your notes to help you answer the questions. Your notes will not be scored.

Answer each question before moving on. Do not return to previous questions.

It will take about 60 minutes to listen to the conversations and lectures and answer the questions about them.

Directions: Listen to Track 33.

Directions: Now answer the questions.

1. Why does the student go to see the professor?

Ⓐ To discuss the latest trends in photography shows
Ⓑ To find out why some of her work was not selected for a show
Ⓒ To discuss how to get her photographs exhibited
Ⓓ To find out about a student photography show on campus

2. According to the professor, what is the best way to create work that is likely to be chosen for a show?

Ⓐ By taking photographs that fit with current trends
Ⓑ By following one's own artistic views
Ⓒ By consulting experienced photographers
Ⓓ By learning what gallery owners are interested in

3. What does the professor imply about photography created outside of the classroom?

Ⓐ It is usually technically stronger than work created for a class.
Ⓑ It tends to be more interesting than class work.
Ⓒ It faces increased pressure to be trendy.
Ⓓ It is more likely to be exhibited than is work created for a class.

4. According to the professor, what are two ways young photographers can market their work? *Choose 2 answers.*

[A] Share examples of their work with others
[B] Hire a professional agent to sell their work
[C] Display their work in places other than galleries
[D] Ask a professor to recommend their work to gallery owners

5. Listen to Track 34.

Ⓐ To ask the professor to reevaluate her work
Ⓑ To indicate that she understands the importance of sharing her work
Ⓒ To show that she disagrees with the professor's opinion
Ⓓ To suggest that her work has met the professor's criteria

Directions: Listen to Track 35.

Marine Biology

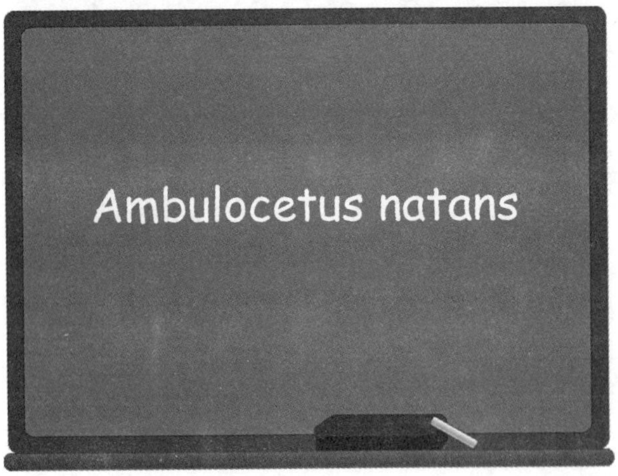

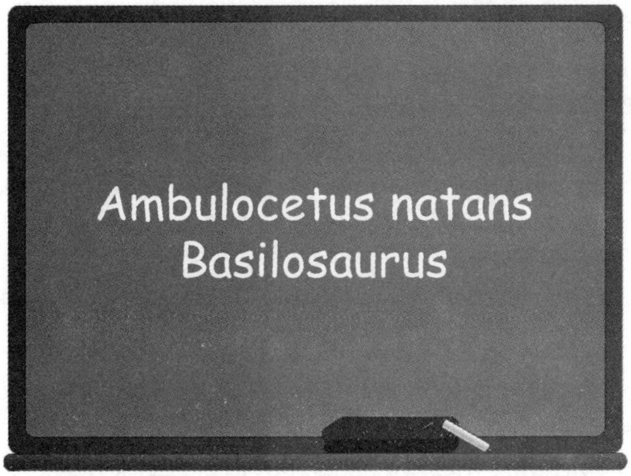

Note: The lecture you just listened to provides one professor's interpretation of evidence related to the evolution of whales. You might be interested to know that the evolution of whales is still being studied, and as new evidence becomes available, alternative interpretations may be more accurate.

Directions: Now answer the questions.

6. What is the lecture mainly about?

   Ⓐ Recent fossil evidence connecting whales and the hippopotamus
   Ⓑ Difficulties in determining the evolutionary history of whales
   Ⓒ Similarities among ancient ancestors of whales
   Ⓓ Similarities between whales and other modern-day animals

7. According to the professor, what three aspects of the Ambulocetus fossil make Ambulocetus a likely bridge between land mammals and sea mammals? *Choose 3 answers.*

   [A] It had an elongated skeletal structure.
   [B] It strongly resembled a modern hippopotamus.
   [C] It had an unusually long and thin tail for a whale.
   [D] It had limbs that could have been used for walking.
   [E] Its skull had ear bones characteristic of land mammals.

8. According to the professor, what does the discovery of Ambulocetus mean to researchers?

   Ⓐ It fills a gap in the fossil evidence for whale evolution.
   Ⓑ It has become less significant since the discovery of Basilosaurus.
   Ⓒ It calls into doubt the theory that whales evolved from land mammals.
   Ⓓ It suggests that whales evolved more recently than was previously believed.

9. What evidence suggests that whales are descendants of the hippopotamus?

Ⓐ Similarities between hippopotamus fossils and the Ambulocetus fossil
Ⓑ Similarities in the genes of hippopotamuses and whales
Ⓒ Similarities in the habitats of modern hippopotamuses and ancient whales
Ⓓ Similarities in the skeletal structures of modern hippopotamuses and ancient whales

10. What is the professor's opinion about recent genetic studies relating to whale evolution?

Ⓐ They solve a long-standing mystery involving fossil evidence.
Ⓑ They contain significant errors.
Ⓒ They present evidence that conflicts with fossil evidence.
Ⓓ The findings of the various studies should not have surprised researchers.

11. What does DNA evidence indicate about relationships among whales?

Ⓐ All modern whales descend from sperm whales.
Ⓑ Differences among toothed whales are less significant that was previously thought.
Ⓒ Not all toothed whales are closely related.
Ⓓ Sperm whales are more closely related to killer whales than was previously thought.

Directions: Listen to Track 36.

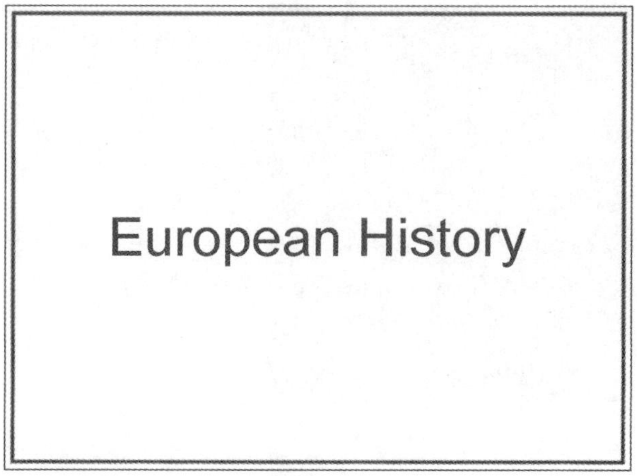

Directions: Now answer the questions.

12. What is the main purpose of the lecture?
    - Ⓐ To describe the trade in food crops between Europe and the Americas
    - Ⓑ To describe the introduction of American food crops to Europeans
    - Ⓒ To describe the influence of American food crops on traditional European dishes
    - Ⓓ To describe the difficulties of growing American food crops in European climates

13. What does the professor imply about certain plants in the nightshade family?
    - Ⓐ They grow best in Mediterranean climates.
    - Ⓑ Their leaves are high in nutritional value.
    - Ⓒ They were mistakenly believed to be related to potatoes.
    - Ⓓ They are dangerous when eaten by human beings.

14. What does the professor imply about Thomas Jefferson's attitude toward tomatoes?

    Ⓐ It was typical of his unconventional way of thinking.
    Ⓑ It helped to advance his political career.
    Ⓒ It changed the eating habits of North Americans.
    Ⓓ It helped to make tomatoes popular in Europe.

15. According to the professor, what was the long-term effect of the introduction of American corn and potatoes to Europe?

    Ⓐ It had a negative effect on the nutritional intake of people living near the Mediterranean Sea.
    Ⓑ It contributed to a shift in the balance of power from southern Europe to northern Europe.
    Ⓒ It encouraged the development of new types of cuisine in southern Europe.
    Ⓓ It led to the failure of many native European grain crops.

16. According to the professor, what is one of the reasons why potatoes became popular in Ireland?

    Ⓐ Potatoes were more nourishing than native Irish food crops.
    Ⓑ Potatoes grew better at higher altitudes than native Irish crops.
    Ⓒ Political leaders in Ireland encouraged the cultivation of potatoes.
    Ⓓ People in Ireland were not aware that potatoes are members of the nightshade family.

17. Listen to Track 37.

    Ⓐ She expects the student to provide an answer to her question.
    Ⓑ She is surprised by the student's question.
    Ⓒ She thinks that she knows what the student was going to ask.
    Ⓓ She expects other students in the class to express their opinions.

Directions: Listen to Track 38.

Directions: Now answer the questions.

18. Why does the student go to the bookstore?
    - Ⓐ To purchase a book by Jane Bowles
    - Ⓑ To find out which books he needs for a course
    - Ⓒ To return a book that was originally assigned for a course
    - Ⓓ To find out how to order a book for a course

19. What is the store's policy about giving refunds on books? *Choose 2 answers.*
    - [A] Books that are not for a specific course will receive a store credit instead of a refund.
    - [B] Course textbooks can be returned for a full refund early in the school semester.
    - [C] All books must be returned within two weeks to be eligible for a full refund.
    - [D] Only books that are in new condition will get a full refund.

20. Why is the professor not going to discuss the book by Jane Bowles in the class?
    - Ⓐ There is not enough time left in the semester.
    - Ⓑ Not all of the students were able to get a copy of the book.
    - Ⓒ The professor miscalculated the difficulty level of the book.
    - Ⓓ The book was not on the course syllabus.

21. What does the woman imply about the book written by Jane Bowles?
    - Ⓐ It is worth reading.
    - Ⓑ It focuses on a serious topic.
    - Ⓒ She is not familiar with it.
    - Ⓓ She read it for a literature class.

22. Listen to Track 39.

Ⓐ He thinks the store's policy is too strict.
Ⓑ He is happy that the woman has agreed to his request.
Ⓒ He is surprised at the woman's suggestion.
Ⓓ He is annoyed that he needs to give the woman more information.

Directions: Listen to Track 40.

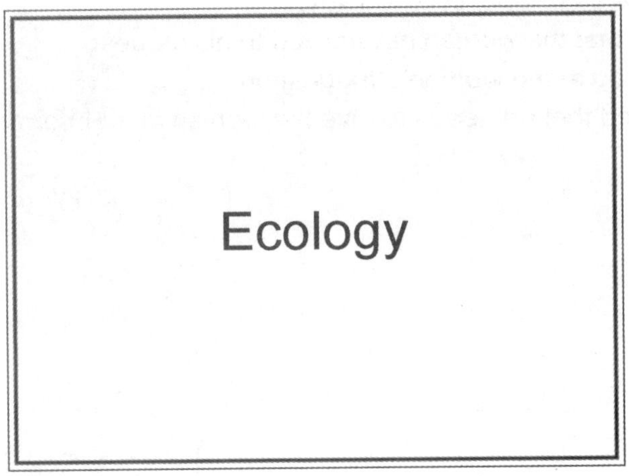

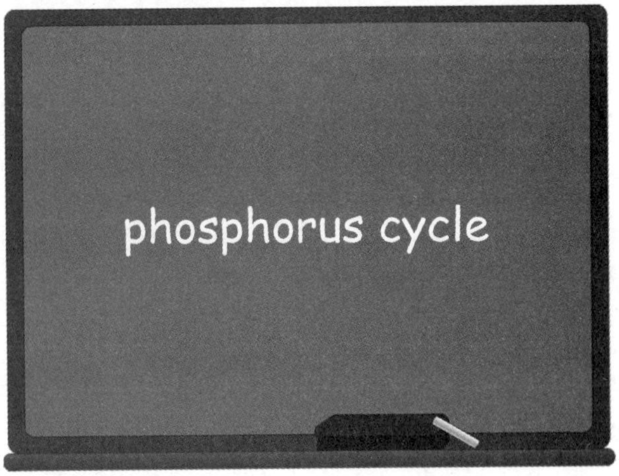

Directions: Now answer the questions.

23. What is the main purpose of the lecture?

    Ⓐ To discuss environmental phenomena that have changed the phosphorus cycle
    Ⓑ To illustrate how interrupting the phosphorus cycle can affect the environment
    Ⓒ To describe how phosphorus ends up in the atmosphere
    Ⓓ To explain how phosphorus gets recycled in the environment

24. Which human activities that influence the phosphorus cycle does the professor mention? *Choose 2 answers.*

    [A] Fishing
    [B] Building dams on rivers
    [C] Polluting the oceans
    [D] Making and using fertilizer

25. Why does the professor discuss underwater volcanoes?

    Ⓐ To describe the location of most of the phosphorus on Earth
    Ⓑ To point out the difficulty of studying the phosphorus cycle
    Ⓒ To describe a step in the phosphorus cycle
    Ⓓ To illustrate the differences between two phases in the phosphorus cycle

26. What can be inferred about the professor's view on phosphorus getting washed into rivers?

    Ⓐ She is unconcerned because phosphorus is a beneficial nutrient.
    Ⓑ She is concerned about the quantity of phosphorus entering the waterways.
    Ⓒ She thinks that the amount of research conducted on the topic is excessive.
    Ⓓ She is frustrated that most of her students are unaware of the phenomenon.

27. What comparison does the professor make involving phosphorus and nitrogen?

Ⓐ Sediment on the ocean floor contains more nitrogen than phosphorus.
Ⓑ The atmosphere contains more nitrogen than phosphorus.
Ⓒ Nitrogen requires more time to get recycled than phosphorus does.
Ⓓ Phosphorus is more important than nitrogen to the development of fish.

28. Listen to Track 41.

Ⓐ She realizes that the students are struggling with the concept.
Ⓑ She is surprised that the student knew the answer to her question.
Ⓒ She thinks that the answer to the question is obvious.
Ⓓ She thinks that this phase of the cycle has an unusual name.

Directions: Listen to Track 42.

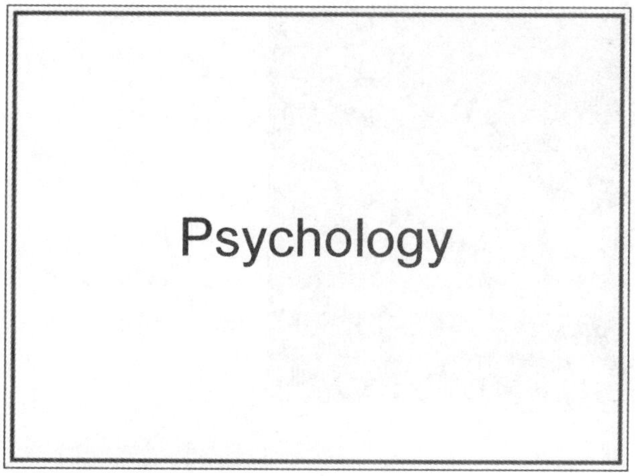

Directions: Now answer the questions.

29. What is the main purpose of the lecture?

Ⓐ To discuss possible explanations for childhood amnesia
Ⓑ To describe key features of childhood amnesia
Ⓒ To explain methods of testing memory in children of different ages
Ⓓ To discuss why the ability to recall memories diminishes as a person ages

30. Why does the professor ask students about their earliest memories?

Ⓐ To help students relate to the topic she is about to discuss
Ⓑ To establish that people vary in the time of their earliest memory
Ⓒ To introduce the connection between language and memory
Ⓓ To point out a common theme in the earliest memories of most people

31. What does the professor imply about some of the explanations for childhood amnesia that she describes?

Ⓐ They can never be proved or disproved.
Ⓑ They were formed without proper evidence.
Ⓒ They explain only certain types of childhood amnesia.
Ⓓ They are contradicted by her own research.

32. The professor mentions some commonly held explanations for childhood amnesia. Indicate whether each of the following is one of the explanations she mentions.
Put a check (✓) in the correct boxes.

	Yes	No
Early memories are repressed.		
Young children have few experiences to remember.		
Young children are unable to form memories.		
Children lose memories at a faster rate than adults.		
Young children do not make an effort to remember events.		

33. How was recall tested in children without language ability?

Ⓐ By recording children's responses to familiar faces
Ⓑ By observing children's reactions to a repeated series of actions
Ⓒ By having children imitate each other's actions
Ⓓ By having children imitate an ordered sequence of actions

34. The professor mentions a study in the 1980s that tested memory in children under age 3. What did the researchers conclude from this study?

Ⓐ Young children do not develop the capacity for recall until after age 3.
Ⓑ Piaget's theory linking language development to memory was incorrect.
Ⓒ Young children typically remember events for about nine months.
Ⓓ The formation of memories is dependent upon language development.

SPEAKING

This section measures your ability to speak in English about a variety of topics.

There are six questions in this section. For each question, you will be given a short time to prepare your response. When the preparation time is up, answer the question as completely as possible in the time indicated for that question. You should record your responses so that you can review them later and compare them with the answer key and scoring rubrics.

Directions: You will now be asked to speak about a familiar topic. Give yourself 15 seconds to prepare your response. Then record yourself speaking for 45 seconds.

1. Listen to Track 43.

Talk about a time when you accomplished something you did not think you could do. What did you accomplish? Why did you think you could not do it?

Preparation Time: 15 seconds
Response Time: 45 seconds

Directions: You will now be asked to give your opinion about a familiar topic. Give yourself 15 seconds to prepare your response. Then record yourself speaking for 45 seconds.

2. Listen to Track 44.

Do you agree or disagree with the following statement? Use details and examples to explain your answer.

All children should be required to learn a second language in school.

Preparation Time: 15 seconds
Response Time: 45 seconds

Directions: You will now read a short passage and listen to a conversation on the same topic. You will then be asked a question about them. After you hear the question, give yourself 30 seconds to prepare your response. Then record yourself speaking for 60 seconds.

Listen to Track 45.

Reading Time: 45 seconds

Student Art Display

The university is currently considering possible locations on campus for displaying paintings and other artwork by students. I think the lobby at the entrance to the student center would be a great location. Since many students pass through the student center every day, artwork displayed in the lobby would be viewed by hundreds of people. Also, because the whole front of the building is made of glass windows, the lobby is filled with natural light. This makes it perfect for displaying artwork, which should have plenty of light to be seen and appreciated.

Listen to Track 46.

3. Briefly summarize the proposal in the student's letter. Then state the woman's opinion about the proposal and explain the reasons she gives for holding that opinion.

Preparation Time: 30 seconds

Response Time: 60 seconds

Directions: You will now read a short passage and listen to a lecture on the same topic. You will then be asked a question about them. After you hear the question, give yourself 30 seconds to prepare your response. Then record yourself speaking for 60 seconds.

Listen to Track 47.

Reading Time: 50 seconds

Entertainment Merchandising

An effective, widely used marketing practice in the entertainment industry is entertainment merchandising. Entertainment merchandising is a form of marketing in which the brand or image from one product is also used to sell another. The practice of entertainment merchandising often occurs in connection with movies and television shows, especially those associated with children. For example, the success of a popular children's television show may result in the marketing of toys that are designed to look like characters in the show. Or the situation may be reversed when a children's television show is written to include characters that are based on already-popular toys.

Listen to Track 48.

4. Using the examples from the lecture, explain the concept of entertainment merchandising.

Preparation Time: 30 seconds
Response Time: 60 seconds

Directions: You will now listen to part of a conversation. You will then be asked a question about it. After you hear the question, give yourself 20 seconds to prepare your response. Then record yourself speaking for 60 seconds.

Listen to Track 49.

5. Briefly summarize the woman's problem. Then state which solution you would recommend. Explain the reasons for your recommendation.

Preparation Time: 20 seconds
Response Time: 60 seconds

Directions: You will now listen to part of a lecture. You will then be asked a question about it. After you hear the question, give yourself 20 seconds to prepare your response. Then record yourself speaking for 60 seconds.

Listen to Track 50.

6. Using the points from the lecture, explain why researchers think that babies may feel empathy.

Preparation Time: 20 seconds
Response Time: 60 seconds

WRITING

This section measures your ability to write in English to communicate in an academic environment.

There are two writing questions in this section.

For question 1, you will read a passage and listen to a lecture about the same topic. You may take notes while you read and listen. Then you will write a response to a question based on what you have read and heard. You may look back at the passage when answering the question. You may use your notes to help you answer the question. You have 20 minutes to plan and write your response.

For question 2, you will write an essay based on your own knowledge and experience. You have 30 minutes to plan and complete your essay.

Directions: Give yourself 3 minutes to read the passage.

Reading Time: 3 minutes

The sea otter is a small mammal that lives in waters along the western coast of North America from California to Alaska. When some sea otter populations off the Alaskan coast started rapidly declining a few years ago, it caused much concern because sea otters play an important ecological role in the coastal ecosystem. Experts started investigating the cause of the decline and quickly realized that there were two possible explanations: environmental pollution or attacks by predators. Initially, the pollution hypothesis seemed the more likely of the two.

The first reason why pollution seemed the more likely cause was that there were known sources of it along the Alaskan coast, such as oil rigs and other sources of industrial chemical pollution. Water samples from the area revealed increased levels of chemicals that could decrease the otters' resistance to life-threatening infections and thus could indirectly cause their deaths.

Second, other sea mammals such as seals and sea lions along the Alaskan coast were also declining, indicating that whatever had endangered the otters was affecting other sea mammals as well. This fact again pointed to environmental pollution, since it usually affects the entire ecosystem rather than a single species. Only widely occurring predators, such as the orca (a large predatory whale), could have the same effect, but orcas prefer to hunt much larger prey, such as other whales.

Third, scientists believed that the pollution hypothesis could also explain the uneven pattern of otter decline: at some Alaskan locations the otter populations declined greatly, while at others they remained stable. Some experts explained these observations by suggesting that ocean currents or other environmental factors may have created uneven concentrations of pollutants along the coast.

Listen to Track 51.

Directions: You have 20 minutes to plan and write your response. Your response will be judged on the basis of the quality of your writing and on how well your response presents the points in the lecture and their relationship to the reading passage. Typically, an effective response will be 150 to 225 words.

Listen to Track 52.

Response Time: 20 minutes

1. Summarize the points made in the lecture, being sure to explain how they respond to the specific points made in the reading passage.

Directions: Read the question below. You have 30 minutes to plan, write, and revise your essay. Typically, an effective response will contain a minimum of 300 words.

Response Time: 30 minutes

2. Do you agree or disagree with the following statement?

   Playing computer games is a waste of time. Children should not be allowed to play them.

   Use specific reasons and examples to support your answer.

ANSWERS

Reading Section

1. B
2. D
3. C
4. B
5. A
6. D
7. C
8. A
9. B
10. A
11. B
12. B
13. B
14. A, C, E
15. B
16. C
17. D
18. B
19. A
20. C
21. C
22. B
23. A
24. B
25. B
26. B
27. D
28. A, C, E
29. B
30. C
31. D
32. A
33. A
34. B
35. B
36. C
37. C
38. C
39. A
40. B
41. C
42. A, C, D

Listening Section

1. C
2. B
3. C
4. A, C
5. D
6. B
7. A, C, D
8. A
9. B
10. C
11. C
12. B
13. D
14. A
15. B
16. A
17. C
18. C
19. B, D
20. A
21. A
22. C
23. D
24. A, D
25. C
26. B
27. B
28. C
29. A
30. A
31. B
32.

	Yes	No
Early memories are repressed.	✓	
Young children have few experiences to remember.		✓
Young children are unable to form memories.	✓	
Children lose memories at a faster rate than adults.	✓	
Young children do not make an effort to remember events.		✓

33. D
34. B

Speaking Section

Prompts, Important Points, and Sample Responses with Rater Comments

Use the sample Independent and Integrated Speaking Rubrics in Appendix A to see how responses are scored. The raters who listen to your responses will analyze them in three general categories. These categories are Delivery, Language Use, and Topic Development. All three categories have equal importance.

This section includes important points that should be covered when answering each question. All of these points must be present in a response in order for it to receive the highest score in the Topic Development category. These important points are guides to the kind of information raters expect to hear in a high-level response.

This section also refers to sample responses, which can be found on the accompanying DVD. Some responses were scored at the highest level, which others were not. The responses are followed by comments from certified ETS raters.

Question 1

Prompt

Talk about a time when you accomplished something you did not think you could do. What did you accomplish? Why did you think you could not do it?

Important Points

When answering this question, you could talk about topics such as an award you received or an activity you completed successfully. Describe the activity or award and then explain why you believed it would not be possible. You may choose to talk about any type of accomplishment, major or minor. You will be evaluated on your ability to describe the event or activity and fully explain the reasons you thought you would not be successful at it or the reasons you were surprised by your success.

High-level Response: Listen to Track 53.

Rater Comments

The speaker clearly explains what the accomplishment was (transitioning from dentistry into banking) and why he thought he wouldn't be able to do it (he lacked knowledge, he had insecurity). Although this is not specifically required by the prompt, he explained how he overcame the obstacles, through additional training and rehearsing. His ideas are well connected and easy to follow: "*When I had to change my profession from dentistry to banking I thought I would not be able to sell any banking product because I lacked the knowledge of... but I....*" He also uses intonation and pauses effectively, pausing or using emphasis in ways that help the listener understand the structure and tone of the sentences. Although he makes occasional errors in grammar ("*I thought I will not be able to...*") or usage ("*I tried to put down everything I learned*"), in general he is able to use complex structures ("*because I lacked the knowledge of the more senior banking associates*", "*when I had to change my profession from dentistry to banking*") with ease and accuracy.

Mid-level Response: Listen to Track 54.

Rater Comments

The speaker communicates the accomplishment (doing well on a test) and why he thought he wouldn't be able to do it (he doesn't have self-confidence), but his response is not as detailed or well organized as high-level responses. The description of the accomplishment is rather vague ("*a very good thing, which is a challenge... consisting on a test*"), and his explanation of why he thought he wouldn't be able to accomplish the task is limited and somewhat repetitive. The speaker is not able to successfully use more complex grammar and sophisticated vocabulary to elaborate on his ideas. Grammatical errors and incorrect word choice also cause slight misunderstandings at times. To score at a higher level, the speaker would need to clearly explain what the test was and why exactly he wasn't confident he would do well on this particular test.

Question 2

Prompt

Do you agree or disagree with the following statement? Use details and examples to explain your answer.

All children should be required to learn a second language in school.

Important Points

When you answer this question, you should take a stance and state whether you agree or disagree that all children should be required to learn a second language in school. In order to support your opinion, you should provide at least one specific reason why children should or shouldn't be required to learn a second language, along with information to elaborate on and explain that reason. It is acceptable to talk about more than one reason for agreeing or disagreeing with the statement, but you should not simply provide a list of reasons without any explanation of them.

High-level Response: Listen to Track 55.

Rater Comments

In this response, the speaker states that she agrees with the statement, and although she doesn't explicitly say what the statement is, she implicitly refers to it throughout her response ("*let's say, if children don't know English, all degrees now required um a second language*" and "*so I believe Eng—like a second language it's a benefit and it's a plus for kids*"). She supports her agreement with the statement by explaining specific scenarios in which children would benefit from being required to learn a second language in school; she uses the example of English and the job market, saying that most degrees and jobs now require English, and also talks about how English will help kids communicate when they travel. Although her speech is not always smooth (she says "*um*" and hesitates somewhat frequently) and she makes some small grammatical errors ("*general speaking*"; "*all degrees now required*"; "*can able to communicate*"), it is still easy for the listener to understand her.

Mid-level Response: Listen to Track 56.

Rater Comments

In this response, the speaker states his agreement with the statement but does not provide full support for his opinion. Rather than choosing one or two reasons and explaining them in detail (using a personal experience, hypothetical situation, etc.), he lists many different and somewhat vague reasons but does not provide explanations for them: "*because it helps really to uh thinks about other stuff*"; "*you're just smarter and you can just have better job*"; "*it's really hard to learn second language.*" The speaker has mostly clear pronunciation and uses some sophisticated grammatical structures ("*not only the language but also other cultures*"), but his vague explanations make it somewhat difficult for a listener to follow his response.

Question 3

Prompt

Briefly summarize the proposal in the student's letter. Then state the woman's opinion about the proposal and explain the reasons she gives for holding that opinion.

Important Points

When answering this question, it is important to include information from both the reading passage and the conversation between students. Begin by summarizing the student's proposal, which is that the lobby of the student center should be selected as the location for a student art display. Then indicate the woman's opinion of the proposal and why she feels that way. In this item, you would say that the woman disagrees that the lobby is a good place for the art displays. She says that because there are so many people passing through the lobby, it will make it difficult to view the artwork. Also, the natural light in the lobby is sometimes too bright or too dark for viewing artwork (and it is better to have controlled electric light).

High-level Response: Listen to Track 57.

Rater Comments

The speaker accurately and effectively covers all the important points. She explains the proposal clearly and efficiently, and covers the woman's opinion about the natural light with great detail. She does a particularly good job of organizing her response. For example, after she summarizes the letter-writer's proposal, she says "*these last two points are actually exactly the points the woman is criticizing . . .*" before continuing on to the woman's opinion, and this transition makes her ideas easy to follow. She does not talk as much about how crowding in the lobby makes the artwork difficult to view, but she does mention it in sufficient detail. She has a wide vocabulary range, and is able to summarize ideas in her own words, such as saying "*the light is dependent on the weather*" to summarize the woman's point about natural light. Her pronunciation, pacing, and intonation are also clear and effective, so it is not difficult for listeners to understand her.

Low-level Response: Listen to Track 58.

Rater Comments

The speaker's response contains relevant points, such as using a lobby to display art work, the fact that the woman doesn't agree, and an explanation for why she doesn't agree. He makes some factual errors, however, such as claiming the newspaper itself is recommending the new location for the artwork. Most importantly, the response contains some major grammar problems that make it difficult to understand. For example, the speaker says *"the one who is going to just appreciate art work will be know it,"* which does not make much sense. Sometimes the speaker's pronunciation of individual words is difficult to understand as well, such as the word "proposal."

Question 4

Prompt

Using the examples from the lecture, explain the concept of entertainment merchandising.

Important Points

For this task, the prompt asks you to use the examples from the lecture to explain the concept described in the reading. You should begin your response by briefly explaining entertainment merchandising (a type of marketing where a popular brand or image of one product is used to sell another product). For the first example from the lecture, you could begin by mentioning that entertainment merchandising often occurs when children's toys are created based on popular characters in a television program or movie. For example, the professor and his friends bought Action-hero toys because they liked the Action-hero TV show. For the second example from the lecture, you could explain that entertainment merchandising can also work in a reverse way from the first example—sometimes TV shows or movies become popular because they are based on well-known children's toys. For instance, the professor's daughter enjoys playing with a doll named Rosa. So, when a TV show about Rosa is created, she and her friends begin watching it.

High-level Response: Listen to Track 59.

Rater Comments

At the beginning, the speaker's explanation of the concept is a little unclear (*"brand or images are used to sell"*). However, her summary of the examples shows that she fully understood how the lecture relates to the reading. She does not confuse any details, remembering that Action-hero was first a television show and then a toy but that the Rosa doll was first a toy and then a television show. Her pronunciation is easy to understand, and she speaks without pausing or hesitating. She uses complex sentences (*"And then, they create a television show which has the doll Rosa as the main character"*) and shows a good range of vocabulary.

Mid-level Response: Listen to Track 60.

Rater Comments

The speaker mostly does a good job of explaining all the main points of the reading and the lecture. Her first sentence, explaining the concept of entertainment merchandising, is very clear. Her explanation of the Action-hero example is also good, but she has significant difficulty explaining the example of the Rosa doll. For example, she says, *"after she was bought from all the kids' society,"* which is unclear. It can be inferred from the rest of the response that she understands the basic ideas in the lecture, but parts of her response are a little confusing. Overall, her pronunciation is clear and she speaks fluently. She has some minor grammatical errors, but she is still easy to understand.

Question 5

Prompt

Briefly summarize the woman's problem. Then state which solution you would recommend. Explain the reasons for your recommendation.

Important Points

For this task, the prompt asks you to briefly summarize the problem being discussed. In this item the problem is that the woman, because of a power failure, cannot use her computer to finish a term paper that is due tomorrow. The prompt then asks you to recommend one of the solutions and the reason for your solution. Taking time to summarize both solutions is not a requirement of the task and doing so may cause you to run out of time before stating your solution and the reason for your solution. You need to offer reasons and support for why you prefer one solution over the other. For example, if you prefer the first solution of writing the paper in the library, you could say that it would be quiet and easy to concentrate in the library. Another strategy is to provide reasons against the other solution. You could say you recommend going to the library because you know the professor will not give an extension and it would be a waste of time to ask him. If you choose to recommend the other solution, you would of course need to provide suitable reasons and support also.

High-level Response: Listen to Track 61.

Rater Comments

The speech in the response is clear and fluid, with few problems in pronunciation or intonation. The speaker's language use is also good and he demonstrates knowledge of a wide range of structures and vocabulary. The content is also organized well. He starts with a brief summary of the problem and includes a short summary of both solutions. He also chooses to include the drawback for the solution he doesn't choose (that the professor said he would not give extensions), which strengthens his argument. He includes good support for his solution, which is mainly an argument against the other solution: *"She would be gambling thinking that the professor might agree to extend the period."* He also uses appropriate transitional words and phrases, such as "*in my opinion*," which clearly show the progression of his ideas. He also provides a nice summary phrase at the end to conclude his response: *"so it is better for her to go to the library."*

Mid-level Response: Listen to Track 62.

Rater Comments

The speaker's pronunciation of individual words is good. The pace of the response is fluid, also, though at times it seems rushed. A larger problem is his imprecise language use throughout; as a result, his ideas are unclear and confusing to the listener. In his summary of the problem, for example, he says *"There is electricity . . . (unclear) and one of the student doesn't know how to do."* The speaker does not adequately complete the task because he does not provide a clear solution. He does say that he thinks one of the options is a bad idea, which is not the same as stating a clear preference of solution and providing clear reasons. His language is also unclear when he says that the second option is a bad idea: *"People shouldn't waste their time and work harder every day to avoid such problems like electricity."*

Question 6

Prompt

Using the points from the lecture, explain why researchers think that babies may feel empathy.

Important Points

In this item, your summary of the key ideas from the lecture should include that researchers believe that babies are capable of feeling empathy. They think this because they did an experiment where a baby listened to other babies crying. The baby cried when he heard the other babies crying (which is what they expected). However, when the researchers played the baby a tape of his own crying, he didn't cry. This told researchers that noise wasn't the cause of the crying. Rather, it suggested that the baby cried because he felt empathy or concern for the other babies.

High-level Response: Listen to Track 63.

Rater Comments

The speaker gives a clear summary of the lecture, starting with a statement of what researchers believed until now and then explaining what was found in the experiment. She doesn't say explicitly that the researchers played a recording or tape of babies crying, and she also mispronounces the word *"experiment."* These are minor errors, however, and do not prevent the listener from understanding what happened in the experiment. One of the speaker's particular strengths is that she places emphasis on certain words to help communicate the difference between the two parts of the experiment ("*. . . it's not the actual* noise *that triggers the baby's reflex to cry, but actually an emotional* feeling").

Mid-level Response: Listen to Track 64.

Rater Comments

In this response, the speaker gives a basic summary of both parts of the experiment. Her pronunciation is also quite clear. However, she hesitates often while searching for words to describe what happened in the experiment. These pauses and the limits in her vocabulary prevent her from making the final connection and explaining *why* the results of the experiment led researchers to believe that babies feel empathy. The point isn't, as the speaker says, that babies can "differentiate" between their own cries and those of other babies. The point is that the baby only cried when he heard the other babies cry, which made researchers think that *noise* wasn't an issue, but rather that he felt concern for the other babies. Overall, the response is slightly confusing to the listener because of these missing pieces and lack of organization.

Writing Section

Prompts, Topic Notes, and Sample Responses with Rater Comments

Use the sample Integrated and Independent Writing Rubrics in Appendix A to see how responses are scored.

This section includes topic notes that are guides to the kind of information raters expect to read in a high-level response.

This section also refers to sample responses, which can be found on the accompanying DVD. These responses were scored at the highest level. The responses are followed by comments from certified ETS raters.

Question 1

Prompt

Summarize the points made in the lecture, being sure to explain how they respond to the specific points made in the reading passage.

Topic Notes

The reading discusses three reasons to believe it is because of pollution that there has been a decline of sea otters off of Alaska and California, while the lecture discusses why predation, especially by orcas, is a better explanation of the evidence presented in the reading.

Point made in the reading	Corresponding point from the lecture
The passage argues that increased levels of pollution detected along the Alaskan coast could cause the deaths of sea otters by making them vulnerable to infections.	No dead sea otters have been found washed up on shore; this weakens the pollution theory but supports the predator theory, since the predators would eat the otters as they caught them, leaving no remains.
The decline of other sea mammals (seals and sea lions) points to a systemic cause such as pollution; the orca, a predator that could conceivably hunt several sea mammal species, is not the likely cause because it prefers larger prey such as whales.	Since the population of whales that orcas prefer to hunt has declined, orcas started hunting smaller prey, such as otters, as well as seals and sea lions.
The decline of sea otter populations is greater in some locations than in others, which again seems consistent with the pollution theory since varying concentrations of pollutants could account for such an uneven pattern.	The uneven pattern of sea otter decline can be explained by the fact that some locations where sea otters live are accessible to orcas and some are not; the accessible areas experience decline, while the populations in the inaccessible areas remain steady.

Responses with scores of 4 and 5 typically discuss all three points in the table with good accuracy.

Sample Response

The topic discussed here is the investigation of the causes of the disappearance of the sea otter, which is a small mammal that lives in waters along the western coast of North America from California to Alaska. The woman in the lecture argues that the cause of their disappearance is the presence of the predators, especially orcas, and not pollution as the reading says.

Firstly, she argues that one of the proofs of their being attacked by the predators is the fact that no one can find any dead sea otters. If the cause was the pollution, many dead sea otters would be found along the shores. In addition, a predator will immediately eat its prey so this is why no dead sea otters were found.

Secondly, the woman in the lecture argues there is another explanation than pollution why smaller sea mammals are all disappearing. She says that, since the whales tend to disappear because of the humans hunting them, the orcas had to adapt their food habits to the sea conditions and as a result they have started eating the smaller sea animals available among them sea otters being included.

Thirdly, she argues that the orcas cannot access the shallow locations. This is why there are some areas where the sea otters are numerous. It's not because of uneven concentrations of pollutants.

Rater Comments

This response earns a score of 5. The response clearly conveys the three points from the lecture showing why predation by orcas is a better explanation than pollution for why no remains of the sea otters are found, for why a number of small animals including the sea otter started declining at the same time, and for why sea otter decline seems to have occurred to a lesser extent or not at all in some places, and to a greater extent in others. Grammatical errors are few and minor.

Question 2

Prompt

Do you agree or disagree with the following statement?

Playing computer games is a waste of time. Children should not be allowed to play them.

Use specific reasons and examples to support your answer.

Topic Notes

This topic asks you whether children should be banned from playing computer games. Successful responses can agree with the statement, disagree with the statement, or show the merits of both positions. No matter which position you take, it is important to support your opinion with details and examples.

If you agree with the statement, you might discuss why alternative activities, for example, playing physical games and getting exercise, are better for children rather than sitting at a computer or you might talk about social skills that can be obtained only by interacting face-to-face with other children. You could also talk about negative aspects of some computer games, such as addiction to game playing or the violence depicted in some games, and how some might worry about fantasy transferring to real life.

On the other side, you might want to argue that games are a positive way to train children to analyze events and organize their reactions. For example, computer games can be good for learning logic and practicing certain academic or athletic skills. Skill at computer games can also be a source of pride for children who might not be recognized for their achievements at school or on sports teams.

Sample Response

I disagree with statement that children should not be allowed to play computer games; it is not a waste of time. Lots of new skills and ideas can be developed through games and children should be encouraged to play games throughout their life. These days computer games can really enhance learning, help the development of manual and physical skills and even promote bonding people together.

I see computer games as new tools of learning for children. With development of computer games industry, more and more games are focused on mental development of children. Through computer games children can learn new languages by using games that understand and produce voice and text. And most importantly, they can interact with the computer game at their convinience at home. Therefore they can spend a lot more time using and developing language skills through computer games than just learning them during school time.

Computer and tablet games can also be very helpfull for learning math and algebra. There are many math games for preschoolers that capture kids' attentions because they are very attractive using sound and graphics and never get tired of teaching. And then there're higher level stand alone games and websites that have games that help students to absorb much more complex ideas like algebra and geometry, in a fun way.

Another good thing about some games is they can be used to develop manual and physical skills for children. By using different computer equipment and game programs, children can learn to, for example, drive a vehicle or even fly a plane. Other games and advance equipment let children practice sport moves just like they were playing sport for real. So these games can help develop movement, coordination, and ability to see and react to things in motion.

And finally, children can play games online in real time with chat. They can do this with other children located at a distance in their country or even anywhere in the world. As they play these online games with chat, they can talk to each other about almost anything. This can lead them to develop new kinds of friendships and international understanding and make their existing relations stronger.

Of course as in everthing, games should have their limits. But from all I have argued above, computer games are and should be part of children's daily life.

Rater Comments

This 5-level response disagrees with the statement. The writer talks about ways in which computer games are valuable, providing two nicely developed examples of games that enhance learning. The response also shows how games can promote development of motor skills and how some games, via chat and online connection, can promote friendship and international understanding. In the last paragraph, the writer mentions that games should have their limits, but then does not elaborate on this remark. This is an acceptable strategy for ending this response, which overall is a well-developed explanation of the value of computer games.

TOEFL iBT Test 3

READING

This section measures your ability to understand academic passages in English.

There are three passages in the section. Give yourself 20 minutes to read each passage and answer the questions about it. The entire section will take 60 minutes to complete.

You may look back at a passage when answering the questions. You can skip questions and go back to them later as long as there is time remaining.

Directions: Read the passage. Then answer the questions. Give yourself 20 minutes to complete this practice set.

ANCIENT EGYPTIAN SCULPTURE

In order to understand ancient Egyptian art, it is vital to know as much as possible of the elite Egyptians' view of the world and the functions and contexts of the formal art produced for them. Without this knowledge we can appreciate only the formal content of Egyptian art, and we will fail to understand why it was produced or the concepts that shaped it and caused it to adopt its distinctive forms. In fact, a lack of understanding concerning the purposes of Egyptian art has often led it to be compared unfavorably with the art of other cultures: Why did the Egyptians not develop sculpture in which the body turned and twisted through space like classical Greek statuary? Why do the artists seem to get left and right confused? And why did they not discover the geometric perspective as European artists did in the Renaissance? The answer to such questions has nothing to do with a lack of skill or imagination on the part of Egyptian artists and everything to do with the purposes for which they were producing their art.

The majority of three-dimensional representations, whether standing, seated, or kneeling, exhibit what is called frontality: they face straight ahead, neither twisting nor turning. When such statues are viewed in isolation, out of their original context and without knowledge of their function, it is easy to criticize them for their rigid attitudes that remained unchanged for three thousand years. Frontality is, however, directly related to the functions of Egyptian statuary and the contexts in which the statues were set up. Statues were created not for their decorative effect but to play a primary role in the cults of the gods, the king, and the dead. They were designed to be put in places where these beings could manifest themselves in order to be the recipients of ritual actions. Thus it made sense to show the statue looking ahead at what was happening in front of it, so that the living performer of the ritual could interact with the divine or deceased recipient. Very often such statues were enclosed in rectangular shrines or wall niches whose only opening was at the front, making it natural for the statue to display frontality. Other statues were designed to be placed within an architectural setting, for instance, in front of the monumental entrance gateways to temples known as pylons, or in pillared courts, where they would be placed against or between pillars: their frontality worked perfectly within the architectural context.

Statues were normally made of stone, wood, or metal. Stone statues were worked from single rectangular blocks of material and retained the compactness of the original shape. The stone between the arms and the body and between the legs in standing figures or the legs and the seat in seated ones was not normally cut away. From a practical aspect this protected the figures against breakage and psychologically gives the images a sense of strength and power, usually enhanced by a supporting back pillar. By contrast, wooden statues were carved from several pieces of wood that were pegged together to form the finished work, and metal statues were either made by wrapping sheet metal around a wooden core or cast by the lost wax process[1]. The arms could be held away from the body and carry separate items in their hands; there is no back pillar. The effect is altogether lighter and freer than that achieved in stone, but because both perform the same function, formal wooden and metal statues still display frontality.

Apart from statues representing deities, kings, and named members of the elite that can be called formal, there is another group of three-dimensional representations that depicts generic figures, frequently servants, from the nonelite population. The function of these is quite different. Many are made to be put in the tombs of the elite in order to serve the tomb owners in the afterlife. Unlike formal statues that are limited to static poses of standing, sitting, and kneeling, these figures depict a wide range of actions, such as grinding grain, baking bread, producing pots, and making music, and they are shown in appropriate poses, bending and squatting as they carry out their tasks.

lost wax process[1]: an ancient method of casting using a wax model and clay mold

Directions: Now answer the questions.

PARAGRAPH 1

In order to understand ancient Egyptian art, it is vital to know as much as possible of the elite Egyptians' view of the world and the functions and contexts of the formal art produced for them. Without this knowledge we can appreciate only the formal content of Egyptian art, and we will fail to understand why it was produced or the concepts that shaped it and caused it to adopt its distinctive forms. In fact, a lack of understanding concerning the purposes of Egyptian art has often led it to be compared unfavorably with the art of other cultures: Why did the Egyptians not develop sculpture in which the body turned and twisted through space like classical Greek statuary? Why do the artists seem to get left and right confused? And why did they not discover the geometric perspective as European artists did in the Renaissance? The answer to such questions has nothing to do with a lack of skill or imagination on the part of Egyptian artists and everything to do with the purposes for which they were producing their art.

1. The word "vital" in the passage is closest in meaning to

   Ⓐ attractive
   Ⓑ essential
   Ⓒ usual
   Ⓓ practical

2. Paragraph 1 suggests that one reason ancient Egyptian art has been viewed less favorably than other art is that ancient Egyptian art lacks

   Ⓐ a realistic sense of human body proportion
   Ⓑ a focus on distinctive forms of varying sizes
   Ⓒ the originality of European art
   Ⓓ examples of formal art that show the human body in motion

3. In paragraph 1, the author mentions all of the following as necessary in appreciating Egyptian art EXCEPT an understanding of

   Ⓐ the reasons why the art was made
   Ⓑ the nature of aristocratic Egyptian beliefs
   Ⓒ the influences of Egyptian art on later art such as classical Greek art
   Ⓓ how the art was used

PARAGRAPH 2

The majority of three-dimensional representations, whether standing, seated, or kneeling, exhibit what is called frontality: they face straight ahead, neither twisting nor turning. When such statues are viewed in isolation, out of their original context and without knowledge of their function, it is easy to criticize them for their rigid attitudes that remained unchanged for three thousand years. Frontality is, however, directly related to the functions of Egyptian statuary and the contexts in which the statues were set up. Statues were created not for their decorative effect but to play a primary role in the cults of the gods, the king, and the dead. They were designed to be put in places where these beings could manifest themselves in order to be the recipients of ritual actions. Thus it made sense to show the statue looking ahead at what was happening in front of it, so that the living performer of the ritual could interact with the divine or deceased recipient. Very often such statues were enclosed in rectangular shrines or wall niches whose only opening was at the front, making it natural for the statue to display frontality. Other statues were designed to be placed within an architectural setting, for instance, in front of the monumental entrance gateways to temples known as pylons, or in pillared courts, where they would be placed against or between pillars: their frontality worked perfectly within the architectural context.

4. According to paragraph 2, why are Egyptian statues portrayed frontally?

Ⓐ To create a psychological effect of distance and isolation
Ⓑ To allow them to fulfill their important role in ceremonies of Egyptian life
Ⓒ To provide a contrast to statues with a decorative function
Ⓓ To suggest the rigid, unchanging Egyptian philosophical attitudes

5. The word "context" in the passage is closest in meaning to

Ⓐ connection
Ⓑ influence
Ⓒ environment
Ⓓ requirement

6. The author mentions "an architectural setting" in the passage in order to

Ⓐ suggest that architecture was as important as sculpture to Egyptian artists
Ⓑ offer a further explanation for the frontal pose of Egyptian statues
Ⓒ explain how the display of statues replaced other forms of architectural decoration
Ⓓ illustrate the religious function of Egyptian statues

7. The word "they" in the passage refers to

Ⓐ statues
Ⓑ gateways
Ⓒ temples
Ⓓ pillared courts

PARAGRAPH 3

Statues were normally made of stone, wood, or metal. Stone statues were worked from single rectangular blocks of material and retained the compactness of the original shape. The stone between the arms and the body and between the legs in standing figures or the legs and the seat in seated ones was not normally cut away. From a practical aspect this protected the figures against breakage and psychologically gives the images a sense of strength and power, usually enhanced by a supporting back pillar. By contrast, wooden statues were carved from several pieces of wood that were pegged together to form the finished work, and metal statues were either made by wrapping sheet metal around a wooden core or cast by the lost wax process. The arms could be held away from the body and carry separate items in their hands; there is no back pillar. The effect is altogether lighter and freer than that achieved in stone, but because both perform the same function, formal wooden and metal statues still display frontality.

8. According to paragraph 3, why were certain areas of a stone statue left uncarved?

Ⓐ To prevent damage by providing physical stability
Ⓑ To emphasize that the material was as important as the figure itself
Ⓒ To emphasize that the figure was not meant to be a real human being
Ⓓ To provide another artist with the chance to finish the carving

9. The word "core" in the passage is closest in meaning to

Ⓐ material
Ⓑ layer
Ⓒ center
Ⓓ frame

10. According to paragraph 3, which of the following statements about wooden statues is true?

Ⓐ Wooden statues were usually larger than stone statues.
Ⓑ Wooden statues were made from a single piece of wood.
Ⓒ Wooden statues contained pieces of metal or stone attached to the front.
Ⓓ Wooden statues had a different effect on the viewer than stone statues.

PARAGRAPH 4

Apart from statues representing deities, kings, and named members of the elite that can be called formal, there is another group of three-dimensional representations that depicts generic figures, frequently servants, from the nonelite population. The function of these is quite different. Many are made to be put in the tombs of the elite in order to serve the tomb owners in the afterlife. Unlike formal statues that are limited to static poses of standing, sitting, and kneeling, these figures depict a wide range of actions, such as grinding grain, baking bread, producing pots, and making music, and they are shown in appropriate poses, bending and squatting as they carry out their tasks.

11. The word "depicts" in the passage is closest in meaning to

Ⓐ imagines
Ⓑ classifies
Ⓒ elevates
Ⓓ portrays

12. According to paragraph 4, what is the difference between statues that represent the Egyptian elite and statues that represent the nonelite classes?

    Ⓐ Statues of the elite are included in tombs, but statues of the nonelite are not.
    Ⓑ Statues of the elite are in motionless poses, while statues of the nonelite are in active poses.
    Ⓒ Statues of the elite are shown standing, while statues of the nonelite are shown sitting or kneeling.
    Ⓓ Statues of the elite serve an important function, while statues of the nonelite are decorative.

PARAGRAPH 4

Apart from statues representing deities, kings, and named members of the elite that can be called formal, there is another group of three-dimensional representations that depicts generic figures, frequently servants, from the nonelite population. **(A)** The function of these is quite different. **(B)** Many are made to be put in the tombs of the elite in order to serve the tomb owners in the afterlife. **(C)** Unlike formal statues that are limited to static poses of standing, sitting, and kneeling, these figures depict a wide range of actions, such as grinding grain, baking bread, producing pots, and making music, and they are shown in appropriate poses, bending and squatting as they carry out their tasks. **(D)**

13. **Directions:** Look at the part of the passage that is displayed above. The letters **(A)**, **(B)**, **(C)**, and **(D)** indicate where the following sentence could be added.

    In fact, it is the action and not the figure itself that is important.

    Where would the sentence best fit?

    Ⓐ Choice A
    Ⓑ Choice B
    Ⓒ Choice C
    Ⓓ Choice D

14. **Directions:** An introductory sentence for a brief summary of the passage is provided below. Complete the summary by selecting the THREE answer choices that express the most important ideas in the passage. Some sentences do not belong in the summary because they express ideas that are not presented in the passage or are minor ideas in the passage.

    Write your answer choices in the spaces where they belong. You can either write the letter of your answer choice or you can copy the sentence.

    The distinctive look of ancient Egyptian sculpture was determined largely by its function.

    •

    •

    •

Answer Choices

[A] The twisted forms of Egyptian statues indicate their importance in ritual actions.
[B] The reason Egyptian statues are motionless is linked to their central role in cultural rituals.
[C] Stone, wood, and metal statues all display the feature of frontality.
[D] Statues were more often designed to be viewed in isolation rather than placed within buildings.
[E] The contrasting poses used in statues of elite and nonelite Egyptians reveal their difference in social status.
[F] Although the appearances of formal and generic statues differ, they share the same function.

Directions: Read the passage. Then answer the questions. Give yourself 20 minutes to complete this practice set.

ORIENTATION AND NAVIGATION

To South Americans, robins are birds that fly north every spring. To North Americans, the robins simply vacation in the south each winter. Furthermore, they fly to very specific places in South America and will often come back to the same trees in North American yards the following spring. The question is not why they would leave the cold of winter so much as how they find their way around. The question perplexed people for years, until, in the 1950's, a German scientist named Gustave Kramer provided some answers and, in the process, raised new questions.

Kramer initiated important new kinds of research regarding how animals orient and navigate. Orientation is simply facing in the right direction; navigation involves finding one's way from point A to point B.

Early in his research, Kramer found that caged migratory birds became very restless at about the time they would normally have begun migration in the wild. Furthermore, he noticed that as they fluttered around in the cage, they often launched themselves in the direction of their normal migratory route. He then set up experiments with caged starlings and found that their orientation was, in fact, in the proper migratory direction except when the sky was overcast, at which times there was no clear direction to their restless movements. Kramer surmised, therefore, that they were orienting according to the position of the Sun. To test this idea, he blocked their view of the Sun and used mirrors to change its apparent position. He found that under these circumstances, the birds oriented with respect to the new "Sun." They seemed to be using the Sun as a compass to determine direction. At the time, this idea seemed preposterous. How could a bird navigate by the Sun when some of us lose our way with road maps? Obviously, more testing was in order.

So, in another set of experiments, Kramer put identical food boxes around the cage, with food in only one of the boxes. The boxes were stationary, and the one containing food was always at the same point of the compass. However, its position with respect to the surroundings could be changed by revolving either the inner cage containing the birds or the outer walls, which served as the background. As long as the birds could see the Sun, no matter how their surroundings were altered, they went directly to the correct food box. Whether the box appeared in front of the right wall or the left wall, they showed no signs of confusion. On overcast days, however, the birds were disoriented and had trouble locating their food box.

In experimenting with artificial suns, Kramer made another interesting discovery. If the artificial Sun remained stationary, the birds would shift their direction with respect to it at a rate of about 15 degrees per hour, the Sun's rate of movement across the sky. Apparently, the birds were assuming that the "Sun" they saw was moving at that rate. When the real Sun was visible, however, the birds maintained a constant direction as it moved across the sky. In other words, they were able to compensate for the Sun's movement. This meant that some sort of biological clock was operating–and a very precise clock at that.

What about birds that migrate at night? Perhaps they navigate by the night sky. To test the idea, caged night-migrating birds were placed on the floor of a planetarium during their migratory period. A planetarium is essentially a theater with a domelike ceiling onto which a night sky can be projected for any night of the year. When the planetarium sky matched the sky outside, the birds fluttered in the direction of their normal migration. But when the dome was rotated, the birds changed their direction to match the artificial sky. The results clearly indicated that the birds were orienting according to the stars.

There is accumulating evidence indicating that birds navigate by using a wide variety of environmental cues. Other areas under investigation include magnetism, landmarks, coastlines, sonar, and even smells. The studies are complicated by the fact that the data are sometimes contradictory and the mechanisms apparently change from time to time. Furthermore, one sensory ability may back up another.

Directions: Now answer the questions.

PARAGRAPH 1

To South Americans, robins are birds that fly north every spring. To North Americans, the robins simply vacation in the south each winter. Furthermore, they fly to very specific places in South America and will often come back to the same trees in North American yards the following spring. The question is not why they would leave the cold of winter so much as how they find their way around. The question perplexed people for years, until, in the 1950's, a German scientist named Gustave Kramer provided some answers and, in the process, raised new questions.

15. The word "perplexed" in the passage is closest in meaning to

Ⓐ defeated
Ⓑ interested
Ⓒ puzzled
Ⓓ occupied

16. Which of the following can be inferred about bird migration from paragraph 1?

Ⓐ Birds will take the most direct migratory route to their new habitat.
Ⓑ The purpose of migration is to join with larger groups of birds.
Ⓒ Bird migration generally involves moving back and forth between north and south.
Ⓓ The destination of birds' migration can change from year to year.

PARAGRAPH 3

Early in his research, Kramer found that caged migratory birds became very restless at about the time they would normally have begun migration in the wild. Furthermore, he noticed that as they fluttered around in the cage, they often launched themselves in the direction of their normal migratory route. He then set up experiments with caged starlings and found that their orientation was, in fact, in the proper migratory direction except when the sky was overcast, at which times there was no clear direction to their restless movements. Kramer surmised, therefore, that they were orienting according to the position of the Sun. To test this idea, he blocked their view of the Sun and used mirrors to change its apparent position. He found that under these circumstances, the birds oriented with respect to the new "Sun." They seemed to be using the Sun as a compass to determine direction. At the time, this idea seemed preposterous. How could a bird navigate by the Sun when some of us lose our way with road maps? Obviously, more testing was in order.

17. Which of the sentences below best expresses the essential information in the highlighted sentence in the passage? Incorrect choices change the meaning in important ways or leave out essential information.

Ⓐ Experiments revealed that caged starlings displayed a lack of directional sense and restless movements.
Ⓑ Experiments revealed that caged starlings were unable to orient themselves in the direction of their normal migratory route.
Ⓒ Experiments revealed that the restless movement of caged starlings had no clear direction.
Ⓓ Experiments revealed that caged starlings' orientation was accurate unless the weather was overcast.

18. The word "preposterous" in the passage is closest in meaning to

Ⓐ unbelievable
Ⓑ inadequate
Ⓒ limited
Ⓓ creative

19. According to paragraph 3, why did Kramer use mirrors to change the apparent position of the Sun?

Ⓐ To test the effect of light on the birds' restlessness
Ⓑ To test whether birds were using the Sun to navigate
Ⓒ To simulate the shifting of light the birds would encounter along their regular migratory route
Ⓓ To cause the birds to migrate at a different time than they would in the wild

20. According to paragraph 3, when do caged starlings become restless?

Ⓐ When the weather is overcast
Ⓑ When they are unable to identify their normal migratory route
Ⓒ When their normal time for migration arrives
Ⓓ When mirrors are used to change the apparent position of the Sun

PARAGRAPH 4

So, in another set of experiments, Kramer put identical food boxes around the cage, with food in only one of the boxes. The boxes were stationary, and the one containing food was always at the same point of the compass. However, its position with respect to the surroundings could be changed by revolving either the inner cage containing the birds or the outer walls, which served as the background. As long as the birds could see the Sun, no matter how their surroundings were altered, they went directly to the correct food box. Whether the box appeared in front of the right wall or the left wall, they showed no signs of confusion. On overcast days, however, the birds were disoriented and had trouble locating their food box.

21. Which of the following can be inferred from paragraph 4 about Kramer's reason for filling one food box and leaving the rest empty?

    Ⓐ He believed the birds would eat food from only one box.
    Ⓑ He wanted to see whether the Sun alone controlled the birds' ability to navigate toward the box with food.
    Ⓒ He thought that if all the boxes contained food, this would distract the birds from following their migratory route.
    Ⓓ He needed to test whether the birds preferred having the food at any particular point of the compass.

PARAGRAPH 5

In experimenting with artificial suns, Kramer made another interesting discovery. If the artificial Sun remained stationary, the birds would shift their direction with respect to it at a rate of about 15 degrees per hour, the Sun's rate of movement across the sky. Apparently, the birds were assuming that the "Sun" they saw was moving at that rate. When the real Sun was visible, however, the birds maintained a constant direction as it moved across the sky. In other words, they were able to compensate for the Sun's movement. This meant that some sort of biological clock was operating–and a very precise clock at that.

22. According to paragraph 5, how did the birds fly when the real Sun was visible?

    Ⓐ They kept the direction of their flight constant.
    Ⓑ They changed the direction of their flight at a rate of 15 degrees per hour.
    Ⓒ They kept flying toward the Sun.
    Ⓓ They flew in the same direction as the birds that were seeing the artificial Sun.

23. The experiment described in paragraph 5 caused Kramer to conclude that birds possess a biological clock because

    Ⓐ when birds navigate they are able to compensate for the changing position of the Sun in the sky
    Ⓑ birds' innate bearings keep them oriented in a direction that is within 15 degrees of the Sun's direction
    Ⓒ birds' migration is triggered by natural environmental cues, such as the position of the Sun
    Ⓓ birds shift their direction at a rate of 15 degrees per hour whether the Sun is visible or not

PARAGRAPH 6

What about birds that migrate at night? Perhaps they navigate by the night sky. To test the idea, caged night-migrating birds were placed on the floor of a planetarium during their migratory period. A planetarium is essentially a theater with a domelike ceiling onto which a night sky can be projected for any night of the year. When the planetarium sky matched the sky outside, the birds fluttered in the direction of their normal migration. But when the dome was rotated, the birds changed their direction to match the artificial sky. The results clearly indicated that the birds were orienting according to the stars.

24. According to paragraph 6, how did the birds navigate in the planetarium's nighttime environment?

Ⓐ By waiting for the dome to stop rotating
Ⓑ By their position on the planetarium floor
Ⓒ By orienting themselves to the stars in the artificial night sky
Ⓓ By navigating randomly until they found the correct orientation

PARAGRAPHS 1 2 3 4 5 6 & 7

To South Americans, robins are birds that fly north every spring. To North Americans, the robins simply vacation in the south each winter. Furthermore, they fly to very specific places in South America and will often come back to the same trees in North American yards the following spring. The question is not why they would leave the cold of winter so much as how they find their way around. The question perplexed people for years, until, in the 1950's, a German scientist named Gustave Kramer provided some answers and, in the process, raised new questions.

Kramer initiated important new kinds of research regarding how animals orient and navigate. Orientation is simply facing in the right direction; navigation involves finding one's way from point A to point B.

Early in his research, Kramer found that caged migratory birds became very restless at about the time they would normally have begun migration in the wild. Furthermore, he noticed that as they fluttered around in the cage, they often launched themselves in the direction of their normal migratory route. He then set up experiments with caged starlings and found that their orientation was, in fact, in the proper migratory direction except when the sky was overcast, at which times there was no clear direction to their restless movements. Kramer surmised, therefore, that they were orienting according to the position of the Sun. To test this idea, he blocked their view of the Sun and used mirrors to change its apparent position. He found that under these circumstances, the birds oriented with respect to the new "Sun." They seemed to be using the Sun as a compass to determine direction. At the time, this idea seemed preposterous. How could a bird navigate by the Sun when some of us lose our way with road maps? Obviously, more testing was in order.

So, in another set of experiments, Kramer put identical food boxes around the cage, with food in only one of the boxes. The boxes were stationary, and the one containing food was always at the same point of the compass. However, its position with respect to the surroundings could be changed by revolving either the inner cage containing the birds or the outer walls, which served as the background. As long as the birds could see the Sun, no matter how their surroundings were altered, they went directly to the correct food box. Whether the box appeared in front of the right wall or the left wall, they showed no signs of confusion. On overcast days, however, the birds were disoriented and had trouble locating their food box.

In experimenting with artificial suns, Kramer made another interesting discovery. If the artificial Sun remained stationary, the birds would shift their direction with respect to it at a rate of about 15 degrees per hour, the Sun's rate of movement across the sky. Apparently, the birds were assuming that the "Sun" they saw was moving at that rate. When the real Sun was visible, however, the birds maintained a constant direction as it moved across the sky. In other words, they were able to compensate for the Sun's movement. This meant that some sort of biological clock was operating—and a very precise clock at that.

What about birds that migrate at night? Perhaps they navigate by the night sky. To test the idea, caged night-migrating birds were placed on the floor of a planetarium during their migratory period. A planetarium is essentially a theater with a domelike ceiling onto which a night sky can be projected for any night of the year. When the planetarium sky matched the sky outside, the birds fluttered in the direction of their normal migration. But when the dome was rotated, the birds changed their direction to match the artificial sky. The results clearly indicated that the birds were orienting according to the stars.

There is accumulating evidence indicating that birds navigate by using a wide variety of environmental cues. Other areas under investigation include magnetism, landmarks, coastlines, sonar, and even smells. The studies are complicated by the fact that the data are sometimes contradictory and the mechanisms apparently change from time to time. Furthermore, one sensory ability may back up another.

25. Which of the following best describes the author's presentation of information in the passage?

Ⓐ A number of experiments are described to support the idea that birds use the Sun and the night sky to navigate.
Ⓑ The author uses logic to show that the biological clock in birds is inaccurate.
Ⓒ A structured argument about the importance of internal versus external cues for navigation is presented.
Ⓓ The opposing points of view about bird migration are clarified through the study of contrasting experiments.

PARAGRAPH 7

There is accumulating evidence indicating that birds navigate by using a wide variety of environmental cues. Other areas under investigation include magnetism, landmarks, coastlines, sonar, and even smells. The studies are complicated by the fact that the data are sometimes contradictory and the mechanisms apparently change from time to time. Furthermore, one sensory ability may back up another.

26. The word "accumulating" in the passage is closest in meaning to

Ⓐ new
Ⓑ increasing
Ⓒ convincing
Ⓓ extensive

PARAGRAPH 4

So, in another set of experiments, Kramer put identical food boxes around the cage, with food in only one of the boxes. **(A)** The boxes were stationary, and the one containing food was always at the same point of the compass. **(B)** However, its position with respect to the surroundings could be changed by revolving either the inner cage containing the birds or the outer walls, which served as the background. **(C)** As long as the birds could see the Sun, no matter how their surroundings were altered, they went directly to the correct food box. **(D)** Whether the box appeared in front of the right wall or the left wall, they showed no signs of confusion. On overcast days, however, the birds were disoriented and had trouble locating their food box.

27. **Directions:** Look at the part of the passage that is displayed above. The letters **(A)**, **(B)**, **(C)**, and **(D)** indicate where the following sentence could be added.

    He arranged the feed boxes at various positions on a compass.

    Where would the sentence best fit?

    Ⓐ Choice A
    Ⓑ Choice B
    Ⓒ Choice C
    Ⓓ Choice D

28. **Directions:** An introductory sentence for a brief summary of the passage is provided below. Complete the summary by selecting the THREE answer choices that express the most important ideas in the passage. Some sentences do not belong in the summary because they express ideas that are not presented in the passage or are minor ideas in the passage.

    Write your answer choices in the spaces where they belong. You can either write the letter of your answer choice or you can copy the sentence.

    Gustave Kramer conducted important research related to the ability of birds to orient and navigate.

    •
    •
    •

Answer Choices

[A] Because caged birds become disoriented when the sky is overcast, Kramer hypothesized that birds orient themselves according to the Sun's position.

[B] In one set of experiments, Kramer placed the box containing food at the same point of the compass each time he put food boxes in the birds' environment.

[C] Kramer demonstrated that an internal biological clock allows birds to compensate for the Sun's movement.

[D] After several studies, Kramer surmised that an internal biological clock allows some species of birds to navigate at night.

[E] The role of environmental cues in birds' navigation is clear, for on overcast days, birds use objects besides the Sun to orient themselves.

[F] Kramer showed that night-migrating birds use the sky to navigate by the stars.

Directions: Read the passage. Then answer the questions. Give yourself 20 minutes to complete this practice set.

BEGGING BY NESTLINGS

Many signals that animals make seem to impose on the signalers costs that are overly damaging. A classic example is noisy begging by nestling songbirds when a parent returns to the nest with food. These loud cheeps and peeps might give the location of the nest away to a listening hawk or raccoon, resulting in the death of the defenseless nestlings. In fact, when tapes of begging tree swallows were played at an artificial swallow nest containing an egg, the egg in that "noisy" nest was taken or destroyed by predators before the egg in a nearby quiet nest in 29 of 37 trials.

Further evidence for the costs of begging comes from a study of differences in the begging calls of warbler species that nest on the ground versus those that nest in the relative safety of trees. The young of ground-nesting warblers produce begging cheeps of higher frequencies than do their tree-nesting relatives. These higher-frequency sounds do not travel as far, and so may better conceal the individuals producing them, who are especially vulnerable to predators in their ground nests. David Haskell created artificial nests with clay eggs and placed them on the ground beside a tape recorder that played the begging calls of either tree-nesting or of ground-nesting warblers. The eggs "advertised" by the tree-nesters' begging calls were found bitten significantly more often than the eggs associated with the ground-nesters' calls.

The hypothesis that begging calls have evolved properties that reduce their potential for attracting predators yields a prediction: baby birds of species that experience high rates of nest predation should produce softer begging signals of higher frequency than nestlings of other species less often victimized by nest predators. This prediction was supported by data collected in one survey of 24 species from an Arizona forest, more evidence that predator pressure favors the evolution of begging calls that are hard to detect and pinpoint.

Given that predators can make it costly to beg for food, what benefit do begging nestlings derive from their communications? One possibility is that a noisy baby bird provides accurate signals of its real hunger and good health, making it worthwhile for the listening parent to give it food in a nest where several other offspring are usually available to be fed. If this hypothesis is true, then it follows that nestlings should adjust the intensity of their signals in relation to the signals produced by their nestmates, who are competing for parental attention. When experimentally deprived baby robins are placed in a nest with normally fed siblings, the hungry nestlings beg more loudly than usual—but so do their better-fed siblings, though not as loudly as the hungrier birds.

If parent birds use begging intensity to direct food to healthy offspring capable of vigorous begging, then parents should make food delivery decisions on the basis of their offspring's calls. Indeed, if you take baby tree swallows out of a nest for an hour, feeding half the set and starving the other half, when the birds are replaced in the nest, the starved youngsters beg more loudly than the fed birds, and the parent birds feed the active beggars more than those who beg less vigorously.

As these experiments show, begging apparently provides a signal of need that parents use to make judgments about which offspring can benefit most from a feeding. But the question arises, why don't nestlings beg loudly when they aren't all that hungry? By doing so, they could possibly secure more food, which should result in more rapid growth or larger size, either of which is advantageous. The answer lies apparently not in the increased energy costs of exaggerated begging—such energy costs are small relative to the potential gain in calories—but rather in the damage that any successful cheater would do to its siblings, which share genes with one another. An individual's success in propagating his or her genes can be affected by more than just his or her own personal reproductive success. Because close relatives have many of the same genes, animals that harm their close relatives may in effect be destroying some of their own genes. Therefore, a begging nestling that secures food at the expense of its siblings might actually leave behind fewer copies of its genes overall than it might otherwise.

Directions: Now answer the questions.

PARAGRAPH 1

Many signals that animals make seem to impose on the signalers costs that are overly damaging. A classic example is noisy begging by nestling songbirds when a parent returns to the nest with food. These loud cheeps and peeps might give the location of the nest away to a listening hawk or raccoon, resulting in the death of the defenseless nestlings. In fact, when tapes of begging tree swallows were played at an artificial swallow nest containing an egg, the egg in that "noisy" nest was taken or destroyed by predators before the egg in a nearby quiet nest in 29 of 37 trials.

29. The phrase "impose on" in the passage is closest in meaning to

Ⓐ increase for
Ⓑ remove from
Ⓒ place on
Ⓓ distribute to

30. According to paragraph 1, the experiment with tapes of begging tree swallows establishes which of the following?

Ⓐ Begging by nestling birds can attract the attention of predators to the nest.
Ⓑ Nest predators attack nests that contain nestlings more frequently than they attack nests that contain only eggs.
Ⓒ Tapes of begging nestlings attract predators to the nest less frequently than real begging calls do.
Ⓓ Nest predators have no other means of locating bird nests except the begging calls of nestling birds.

PARAGRAPH 2

Further evidence for the costs of begging comes from a study of differences in the begging calls of warbler species that nest on the ground versus those that nest in the relative safety of trees. The young of ground-nesting warblers produce begging cheeps of higher frequencies than do their tree-nesting relatives. These higher-frequency sounds do not travel as far, and so may better conceal the individuals producing them, who are especially vulnerable to predators in their ground nests. David Haskell created artificial nests with clay eggs and placed them on the ground beside a tape recorder that played the begging calls of either tree-nesting or of ground-nesting warblers. The eggs "advertised" by the tree-nesters' begging calls were found bitten significantly more often than the eggs associated with the ground-nesters' calls.

31. The word "artificial" in the passage is closest in meaning to

Ⓐ attractive
Ⓑ not real
Ⓒ short-term
Ⓓ well designed

32. Paragraph 2 indicates that the begging calls of tree-nesting warblers

Ⓐ put them at more risk than ground-nesting warblers experience
Ⓑ can be heard from a greater distance than those of ground-nesting warblers
Ⓒ are more likely to conceal the signaler than those of ground-nesting warblers
Ⓓ have higher frequencies than those of ground-nesting warblers

33. The experiment described in paragraph 2 supports which of the following conclusions?

Ⓐ Predators are unable to distinguish between the begging cheeps of ground-nesting and those of tree-nesting warblers except by the differing frequencies of the calls.
Ⓑ When they can find them, predators prefer the eggs of tree-nesting warblers to those of ground-nesting warblers.
Ⓒ The higher frequencies of the begging cheeps of ground-nesting warblers are an adaptation to the threat that ground-nesting birds face from predators.
Ⓓ The danger of begging depends more on the frequency of the begging cheep than on how loud it is.

PARAGRAPH 3

The hypothesis that begging calls have evolved properties that reduce their potential for attracting predators yields a prediction: baby birds of species that experience high rates of nest predation should produce softer begging signals of higher frequency than nestlings of other species less often victimized by nest predators. This prediction was supported by data collected in one survey of 24 species from an Arizona forest, more evidence that predator pressure favors the evolution of begging calls that are hard to detect and pinpoint.

34. The word "prediction" in the passage is closest in meaning to

Ⓐ surprise
Ⓑ discovery
Ⓒ explanation
Ⓓ expectation

35. The word "pinpoint" in the passage is closest in meaning to

Ⓐ observe
Ⓑ locate exactly
Ⓒ copy accurately
Ⓓ recognize

PARAGRAPH 4

Given that predators can make it costly to beg for food, what benefit do begging nestlings derive from their communications? One possibility is that a noisy baby bird provides accurate signals of its real hunger and good health, making it worthwhile for the listening parent to give it food in a nest where several other offspring are usually available to be fed. If this hypothesis is true, then it follows that nestlings should adjust the intensity of their signals in relation to the signals produced by their nestmates, who are competing for parental attention. When experimentally deprived baby robins are placed in a nest with normally fed siblings, the hungry nestlings beg more loudly than usual—but so do their better-fed siblings, though not as loudly as the hungrier birds.

36. The word "derive" in the passage is closest in meaning to

Ⓐ require
Ⓑ gain
Ⓒ use
Ⓓ produce

PARAGRAPHS 4 & 5

Given that predators can make it costly to beg for food, what benefit do begging nestlings derive from their communications? One possibility is that a noisy baby bird provides accurate signals of its real hunger and good health, making it worthwhile for the listening parent to give it food in a nest where several other offspring are usually available to be fed. If this hypothesis is true, then it follows that nestlings should adjust the intensity of their signals in relation to the signals produced by their nestmates, who are competing for parental attention. When experimentally deprived baby robins are placed in a nest with normally fed siblings, the hungry nestlings beg more loudly than usual—but so do their better-fed siblings, though not as loudly as the hungrier birds.

If parent birds use begging intensity to direct food to healthy offspring capable of vigorous begging, then parents should make food delivery decisions on the basis of their offspring's calls. Indeed, if you take baby tree swallows out of a nest for an hour, feeding half the set and starving the other half, when the birds are replaced in the nest, the starved youngsters beg more loudly than the fed birds, and the parent birds feed the active beggars more than those who beg less vigorously.

37. In paragraphs 4 and 5, what evidence supports the claim that the intensity of nestling begging calls is a good indicator of which offspring in a nest would most benefit from a feeding?

Ⓐ When placed in a nest with hungry robins, well-fed robins did not beg for food.
Ⓑ Among robin nestlings, the intensity of begging decreased the more the nestlings were fed.
Ⓒ Hungry tree swallow nestlings begged louder than well-fed nestlings in the same nest.
Ⓓ Hungry tree swallow nestlings continued to beg loudly until they were fed whereas well-fed nestlings soon stopped begging.

38. It can be inferred from paragraphs 4 and 5 that parent songbirds normally do not feed

Ⓐ nestlings that are too weak to beg for food as vigorously as their nestmates
Ⓑ more than one hungry nestling during a single visit to the nest
Ⓒ offspring that were fed by the parents on the previous visit to the nest
Ⓓ nestlings that have been removed and then later put back into their nest

PARAGRAPH 6

As these experiments show, begging apparently provides a signal of need that parents use to make judgments about which offspring can benefit most from a feeding. But the question arises, why don't nestlings beg loudly when they aren't all that hungry? By doing so, they could possibly secure more food, which should result in more rapid growth or larger size, either of which is advantageous. The answer lies apparently not in the increased energy costs of exaggerated begging—such energy costs are small relative to the potential gain in calories—but rather in the damage that any successful cheater would do to its siblings, which share genes with one another. An individual's success in propagating his or her genes can be affected by more than just his or her own personal reproductive success. Because close relatives have many of the same genes, animals that harm their close relatives may in effect be destroying some of their own genes. Therefore, a begging nestling that secures food at the expense of its siblings might actually leave behind fewer copies of its genes overall than it might otherwise.

39. In paragraph 6, the author compares the energy costs of vigorous begging with the potential gain in calories from such begging in order to

Ⓐ explain why begging for food vigorously can lead to faster growth and increased size
Ⓑ explain how begging vigorously can increase an individual's chances of propagating its own genes
Ⓒ point out a weakness in a possible explanation for why nestlings do not always beg vigorously
Ⓓ argue that the benefits of vigorous begging outweigh any possible disadvantages

40. According to paragraph 6, which of the following explains the fact that a well-fed nestling does not beg loudly for more food?

Ⓐ There is no benefit for a nestling to get more food than it needs to survive.
Ⓑ By begging loudly for food it does not need, a nestling would unnecessarily expose itself to danger from predators.
Ⓒ If a nestling begs loudly when it is not truly hungry, then when it is truly hungry its own begging may be drowned out by that of its well-fed siblings.
Ⓓ More of a nestling's genes will be passed to the next generation if its hungry siblings get enough food to survive.

PARAGRAPH 1

Many signals that animals make seem to impose on the signalers costs that are overly damaging. **(A)** A classic example is noisy begging by nestling songbirds when a parent returns to the nest with food. **(B)** These loud cheeps and peeps might give the location of the nest away to a listening hawk or raccoon, resulting in the death of the defenseless nestlings. **(C)** In fact, when tapes of begging tree swallows were played at an artificial swallow nest containing an egg, the egg in that "noisy" nest was taken or destroyed by predators before the egg in a nearby quiet nest in 29 of 37 trials. **(D)**

41. **Directions:** Look at the part of the passage that is displayed above. The letters **(A)**, **(B)**, **(C)**, and **(D)** indicate where the following sentence could be added.

The cheeping provides important information to the parent, but it could also attract the attention of others.

Where would the sentence best fit?

Ⓐ Choice A
Ⓑ Choice B
Ⓒ Choice C
Ⓓ Choice D

42. **Directions:** An introductory sentence for a brief summary of the passage is provided below. Complete the summary by selecting the THREE answer choices that express the most important ideas in the passage. Some sentences do not belong in the summary because they express ideas that are not presented in the passage or are minor ideas in the passage.

Write your answer choices in the spaces where they belong. You can either write the letter of your answer choice or you can copy the sentence.

Experiments have shed much light on the begging behaviors of baby songbirds.

-
-
-

Answer Choices

A Songbird species that are especially vulnerable to predators have evolved ways of reducing the dangers associated with begging calls.

B Songbird parents focus their feeding effort on the nestlings that beg loudest for food.

C It is genetically disadvantageous for nestlings to behave as if they are really hungry when they are not really hungry.

D The begging calls of songbird nestlings provide a good example of overly damaging cost to signalers of signaling.

E The success with which songbird nestlings communicate their hunger to their parents is dependent on the frequencies of the nestlings' begging calls.

F Songbird nestlings have evolved several different ways to communicate the intensity of their hunger to their parents.

LISTENING

This section measures your ability to understand conversations and lectures in English.

Listen to each conversation and lecture only one time. After each conversation and lecture, you will answer some questions about it. Answer each question based on what is stated or implied by the speakers.

You may take notes while you listen and use your notes to help you answer the questions. Your notes will not be scored.

Answer each question before moving on. Do not return to previous questions.

It will take about 60 minutes to listen to the conversations and lectures and answer the questions about them.

Directions: Listen to Track 65.

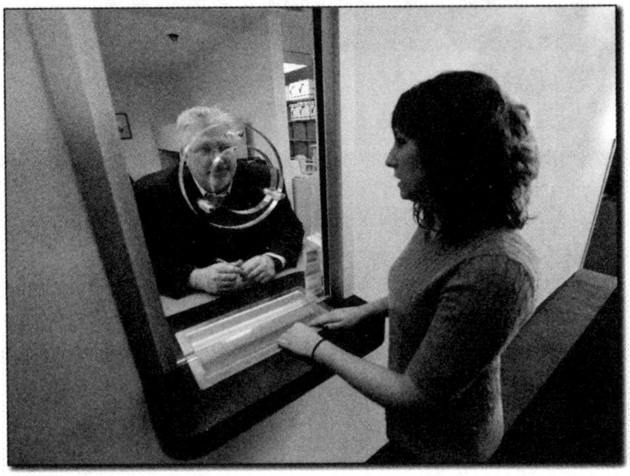

Directions: Now answer the questions.

1. What are the speakers mainly discussing?

   Ⓐ What the gym pass is used for
   Ⓑ How to try out for the swimming team
   Ⓒ The popularity of the new exercise classes at the gym
   Ⓓ The schedule of exercise classes at the gym

2. Why does the woman's initial excitement turn to disappointment?

   Ⓐ She is told that all swimming classes are full.
   Ⓑ She learns that she will have to pay extra for classes.
   Ⓒ She finds out that there are no swimming classes at her level.
   Ⓓ She thought all sports activities were supervised by coaches.

3. What does the man imply about people who play sports in the gym?

   Ⓐ They do not need an instructor to coach them.
   Ⓑ They do not usually take swimming classes.
   Ⓒ They must pay an extra fee to use the equipment.
   Ⓓ They do not need a gym pass.

4. Why does the woman make an appointment with the swimming instructor?

   Ⓐ To find out when the pool is available
   Ⓑ To apply for a job as assistant swim instructor
   Ⓒ To complain about the gym's policy
   Ⓓ To find out which swimming class she should take

5. Listen to Track 66.

Ⓐ He wants to change the subject.
Ⓑ He wants to tell a story.
Ⓒ He disagrees with the woman.
Ⓓ He understands the woman's point.

Directions: Listen to Track 67.

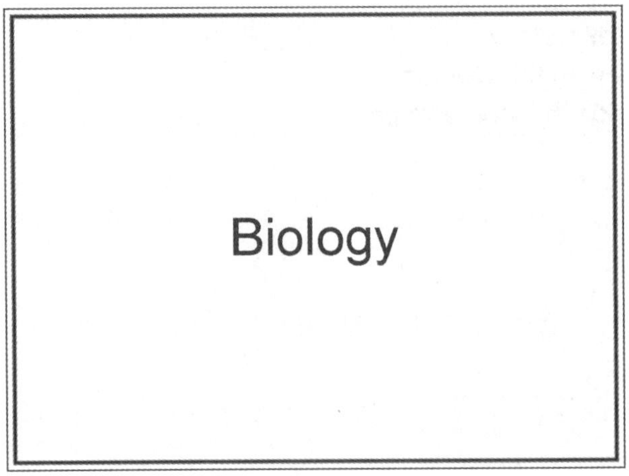

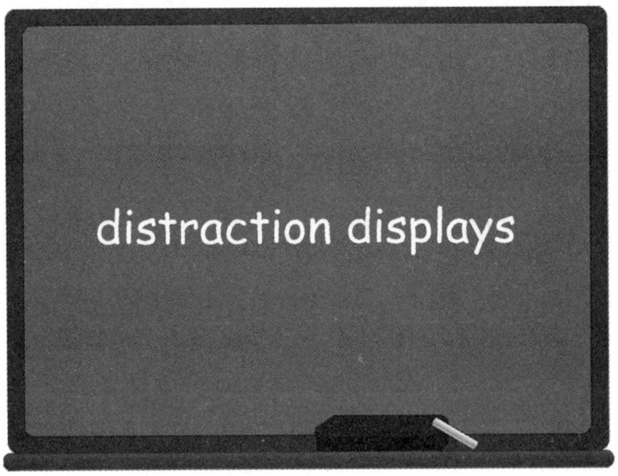

Directions: Now answer the questions.

6. What is the talk mainly about?

Ⓐ Various predators that threaten young birds
Ⓑ Various patterns of growth in young birds
Ⓒ One way that birds protect their young
Ⓓ One way that birds provide food for their young

7. According to the lecture, what do birds usually do when putting on a distraction display? *Choose 2 answers.*

[A] They imitate another kind of animal.
[B] They fly in circles around their nest.
[C] They cover their nest with their wings.
[D] They pretend they are sick or injured.

8. According to the lecture, when do birds put on their most conspicuous distraction displays?

Ⓐ Just before they lay their eggs
Ⓑ Immediately after they have laid their eggs
Ⓒ Just before their young become independent
Ⓓ Immediately after their young have left the nest

9. Listen to Track 68.

Ⓐ To introduce an explanation
Ⓑ To express uncertainty
Ⓒ To point out an error
Ⓓ To emphasize a point that should be obvious

10. Listen to Track 69.

Ⓐ To explain the behavior of the predator
Ⓑ To emphasize that predators have excellent hunting skills
Ⓒ To state the purpose of the birds' behavior
Ⓓ To emphasize the risks involved in a distraction display

11. Listen to Track 70.

Ⓐ To describe the behavior of an injured sandpiper
Ⓑ To give an example of a well-performed broken-wing display
Ⓒ To show why some sandpipers fail to distract predators
Ⓓ To distinguish the sandpiper's display from another kind of display

Directions: Listen to Track 71.

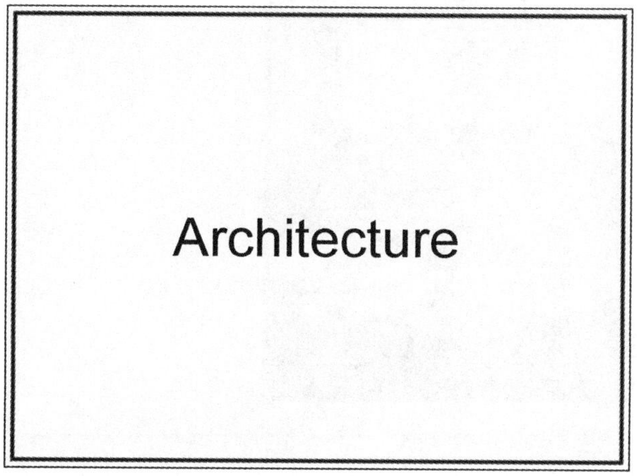

Cape Cod house

Directions: Now answer the questions.

12. What aspect of architecture in the United States is the lecture mainly about?

    Ⓐ The differences between rural and urban styles of housing
    Ⓑ The reasons for the popularity of a particular type of house
    Ⓒ The various styles of houses that are popular in New England
    Ⓓ The decorative details that are typical of houses built in New England

13. What is mentioned in the lecture as an application of the principle that "form follows function"?

    Ⓐ Smaller houses should have fewer rooms.
    Ⓑ A house's design should reflect the inhabitants' needs.
    Ⓒ The materials for a house should be selected before the house is designed.
    Ⓓ Houses in cold, harsh climates should be built with inexpensive materials.

14. Why does the woman refer to visiting her grandparents?

    Ⓐ To explain why she is interested in residential architecture
    Ⓑ To explain why she knows a lot about the history of Cape Cod
    Ⓒ To explain why she is familiar with Cape Cod houses
    Ⓓ To explain why she enjoys visiting rural New England

15. According to the lecture, what are two features of Cape Cod houses that were influenced by climate? *Choose 2 answers.*

    [A] The thickness of the walls
    [B] The slope of the roofs
    [C] The number of windows
    [D] The simplicity of the exterior
    [E] The size of the chimney

16. According to the professor, what contributed to the attitude of conformity in rural New England communities during the 1600s and 1700s?

    Ⓐ People depended on their neighbors for their own survival.
    Ⓑ People living in rural areas often had moved there from cities.
    Ⓒ People had to live very close to their neighbors.
    Ⓓ People had limited access to information from outside their community.

17. Listen to Track 72.

    Ⓐ To indicate that the student's answer is wrong
    Ⓑ To determine whether the student has prepared for the class
    Ⓒ To point out that housing styles across the United States are very similar
    Ⓓ To ask about students' preferences in architectural styles

Directions: Listen to Track 73.

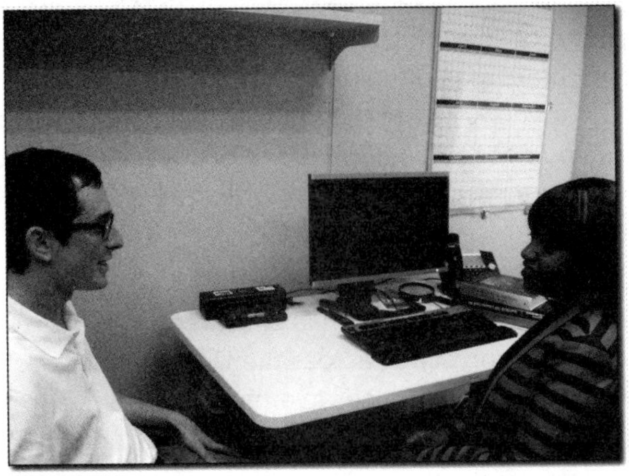

Directions: Now answer the questions.

18. Why does the professor want to see the student?

    Ⓐ To discuss the student's grade on a paper
    Ⓑ To invite the student to work on a committee
    Ⓒ To inform the student about a change in the class schedule
    Ⓓ To ask the student to become her research assistant

19. Why does the student say he is interested in doing what the professor asks?

    Ⓐ He thinks it may help him improve his research skills.
    Ⓑ He thinks it will enable him to get a better grade in the professor's class.
    Ⓒ He thinks it may help him get into graduate school.
    Ⓓ He thinks it will be good teaching practice for him.

20. What will the applicants talk about?

    Ⓐ An academic interest they have
    Ⓑ Reasons why they deserve to be hired
    Ⓒ Their educational background
    Ⓓ The classes they hope to teach

21. Why does the professor mention that one of the applicants will give a talk on a topic the student is particularly interested in?

    Ⓐ To see if the student would enjoy joining the applicant's research team
    Ⓑ To suggest that the student may not totally agree with what the applicant has to say
    Ⓒ To persuade the student to come to a talk on Friday
    Ⓓ To warn the student to focus on the applicant's teaching ability

22. Listen to Track 74.

Ⓐ He does not know of any job applicants.
Ⓑ He is not interested in learning about the hiring process.
Ⓒ He does not want to be responsible for any decisions that are made.
Ⓓ He does not understand why the professor has asked him the question.

Directions: Listen to Track 75.

Directions: Now answer the questions.

23. What is the lecture mainly about?

Ⓐ The effect of the decrease in temperatures on wetlands
Ⓑ The use of computer models to analyze temperature patterns
Ⓒ The theory that land development affected the climate of south Florida
Ⓓ The importance of the citrus industry to the south Florida economy

24. Why does the professor mention the building of canals in the wetlands?

Ⓐ To describe what the wetlands used to look like
Ⓑ To emphasize that farmers need to transport their crops to other areas
Ⓒ To explain how the wetlands were transformed into farmland
Ⓓ To explain why people want to build farms there

25. What does the professor imply about major weather patterns such as El Niño?

Ⓐ She does not believe they are the main cause of the changes in Florida's climate.
Ⓑ She is certain that they have caused a worldwide decrease in the number of frosts.
Ⓒ She believes they contributed to the increase of citrus production in Florida.
Ⓓ She does not fully understand what causes them.

26. What point about bodies of water does the professor emphasize to the students?

Ⓐ Bodies of water in Florida are slightly warmer now than they were 100 years ago.
Ⓑ Bodies of water in south Florida are increasing in size.
Ⓒ Bodies of water release heat back into the environment.
Ⓓ Bodies of water are a source of moisture for crops.

27. What data from 100 years ago and today were entered into the computer model that the professor discusses?

    Ⓐ The average temperatures in south Florida
    Ⓑ The market prices of citrus fruit grown in south Florida
    Ⓒ The numbers of animal species in south Florida wetlands
    Ⓓ The landscape characteristics of south Florida

28. Listen to Track 76.

    Ⓐ To remind the professor of her previous point
    Ⓑ To check if he understood the professor's point
    Ⓒ To express surprise at what the professor said
    Ⓓ To answer the professor's question about the farmers

Directions: Listen to Track 77.

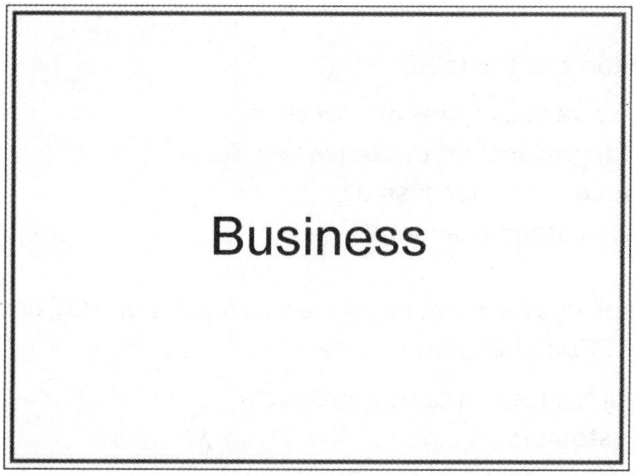

Directions: Now answer the questions.

29. What is the main topic of the talk?

Ⓐ How to analyze various types of advertising
Ⓑ How to develop products that people will like
Ⓒ How to use advertising successfully
Ⓓ How to satisfy customer demands

30. According to the professor, what might be two results of NOT having a good advertising plan? *Choose 2 answers.*

[A] Delays in the introduction of new products
[B] The loss of customers
[C] Too much attention focused on one product
[D] The unnecessary spending of money

31. Why does the professor talk about teachers?

Ⓐ To emphasize the advantages of marketing products to specific groups of people
Ⓑ To illustrate how to select the most appropriate media for advertising a product
Ⓒ To prove that it is not necessary to spend money on advertisements
Ⓓ To show how a poorly communicated message can ruin a business

32. In the example about sports equipment, what does the professor imply about spending money on advertising?

Ⓐ It is most effective just before holidays when people give gifts.
Ⓑ It may require quick decision making.
Ⓒ It is a waste, since many consumers select products based on their previous experiences.
Ⓓ It is better guided by good research than by good theories.

33. What is the professor's point when she talks about a soup shop?

Ⓐ It is difficult to understand how some customers react to advertising.
Ⓑ It is important to ensure the quality of a product before advertising it.
Ⓒ A poorly chosen advertising message can have negative consequences.
Ⓓ Some businesses remain unsuccessful even when they focus on the four M's.

34. Listen to Track 78.

Ⓐ She is eager to share an amusing story.
Ⓑ She made up the story she is about to tell.
Ⓒ She believes humor in advertising is important.
Ⓓ She will tell a story about a popular celebrity.

SPEAKING

This section measures your ability to speak in English about a variety of topics.

There are six questions in this section. For each question, you will be given a short time to prepare your response. When the preparation time is up, answer the question as completely as possible in the time indicated for that question. You should record your responses so that you can review them later and compare them with the answer key and scoring rubrics.

Directions: You will now be asked to speak about a familiar topic. Give yourself 15 seconds to prepare your response. Then record yourself speaking for 45 seconds.

1. Listen to Track 79.

> Talk about an interesting book you have read. Explain why you thought the book was interesting. Give specific details and examples to explain your answer.
>
> **Preparation Time: 15 seconds**
> **Response Time: 45 seconds**

Directions: You will now be asked to give your opinion about a familiar topic. Give yourself 15 seconds to prepare your response. Then record yourself speaking for 45 seconds.

2. Listen to Track 80.

> Some people think that children should be allowed to watch whatever television programs they choose to. Others think that parents should exercise control over the television programs their children watch. Which do you agree with? Explain why.
>
> **Preparation Time: 15 seconds**
> **Response Time: 45 seconds**

Directions: You will now read a short passage and listen to a conversation on the same topic. You will then be asked a question about them. After you hear the question, give yourself 30 seconds to prepare your response. Then record yourself speaking for 60 seconds.

Listen to Track 81.

Reading Time: 45 seconds

Housing Renovations Planned

Over the last ten years, the number of Central College students living on campus in dormitories has decreased by twenty percent. In an effort to counteract the trend, the college has announced a plan to renovate its on-campus housing. The renovations will take two years, and they will include improvements to the bathrooms, lighting, and heating in the dormitories. "A lot of people are moving off campus because the dorms aren't in great shape," explained the college president. "By renovating the dorms, we can make them more appealing than off-campus housing, and more students will choose to remain on campus."

Listen to Track 82.

3. The woman expresses her opinion about the college's plan. State her opinion and explain the reasons she gives for holding that opinion.

Preparation Time: 30 seconds

Response Time: 60 seconds

Directions: You will now read a short passage and listen to a lecture on the same topic. You will then be asked a question about them. After you hear the question, give yourself 30 seconds to prepare your response. Then record yourself speaking for 60 seconds.

Listen to Track 83.

Reading Time: 45 seconds

Outsider Art

Outsider Art is a term used to describe art that is made by people who choose to live and work outside society. The artists who produce this kind of art—Outsider Artists—work in isolation from other artists and have little or no formal artistic training. Because they do not learn conventional artistic techniques from teachers or other artists, Outsider Artists must invent their own ways of doing things. As a result of the unconventional methods that Outsider Artists often use, their work can look strange and not at all like traditional art to the observer.

Listen to Track 84.

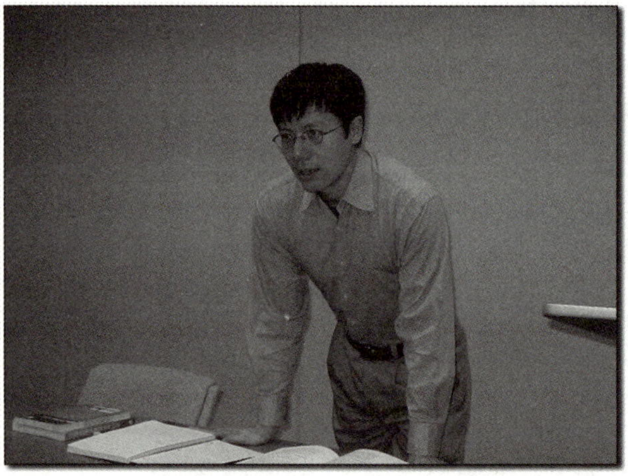

4. Explain why Henry Darger is considered an Outsider Artist.

Preparation Time: 30 seconds

Response Time: 60 seconds

Directions: You will now listen to part of a conversation. You will then be asked a question about it. After you hear the question, give yourself 20 seconds to prepare your response. Then record yourself speaking for 60 seconds.

Listen to Track 85.

5. The students discuss a problem and two possible solutions. Briefly summarize the problem. Then state which of the two solutions you prefer and explain why.

Preparation Time: 20 seconds
Response Time: 60 seconds

Directions: You will now listen to part of a lecture. You will then be asked a question about it. After you hear the question, give yourself 20 seconds to prepare your response. Then record yourself speaking for 60 seconds.

Listen to Track 86.

6. Using the points and examples from the lecture, explain what unity and contrast are, and how they make interior design more effective.

Preparation Time: 20 seconds

Response Time: 60 seconds

WRITING

This section measures your ability to write in English to communicate in an academic environment.

There are two writing questions in this section.

For question 1, you will read a passage and listen to a lecture about the same topic. You may take notes while you read and listen. Then you will write a response to a question based on what you have read and heard. You may look back at the passage when answering the question. You may use your notes to help you answer the question. You have 20 minutes to plan and write your response.

For question 2, you will write an essay based on your own knowledge and experience. You have 30 minutes to plan and complete your essay.

Directions: Give yourself 3 minutes to read the passage.

Reading Time: 3 minutes

A recent study reveals that people, especially young people, are reading far less literature—novels, plays, and poems—than they used to. This is troubling because the trend has unfortunate effects for the reading public, for culture in general, and for the future of literature itself.

While there has been a decline in book reading generally, the decline has been especially sharp for literature. This is unfortunate because nothing else provides the intellectual stimulation that literature does. Literature encourages us to exercise our imaginations, empathize with others, and expand our understanding of language. So by reading less literature, the reading public is missing out on important benefits.

Unfortunately, missing out on the benefits of literature is not the only problem. What are people reading instead? Consider the prevalence of self-help books on lists of best sellers. These are usually superficial, poorly written, and intellectually undemanding. Additionally, instead of sitting down with a challenging novel, many persons are now more likely to turn on the television, watch a music video, or read a Web page. Clearly, diverting time previously spent in reading literature to trivial forms of entertainment has lowered the level of culture in general.

The trend of reading less literature is all the more regrettable because it is taking place during a period when good literature is being written. There are many talented writers today, but they lack an audience. This fact is bound to lead publishers to invest less in literature and so support fewer serious writers. Thus, the writing as well as the reading of literature is likely to decline because of the poor standards of today's readers.

Listen to Track 87.

Directions: You have 20 minutes to plan and write your response. Your response will be judged on the basis of the quality of your writing and on how well your response presents the points in the lecture and their relationship to the reading passage. Typically, an effective response will be 150 to 225 words.

Listen to Track 88.

Response Time: 20 minutes

1. Summarize the points made in the lecture, being sure to explain how they cast doubt on specific points made in the reading passage.

Directions: Read the question below. You have 30 minutes to plan, write, and revise your essay. Typically, an effective response will contain a minimum of 300 words.

Response Time: 30 minutes

2. **Some people say that the Internet provides people with a lot of valuable information. Others think access to so much information creates problems. Which view do you agree with?**

   Use specific reasons and examples to support your answer.

ANSWERS

Reading Section

1. B
2. D
3. C
4. B
5. C
6. B
7. A
8. A
9. C
10. D
11. D
12. B
13. D
14. B, C, E
15. C
16. C
17. D
18. A
19. B
20. C
21. B
22. A
23. A
24. C
25. A
26. B
27. A
28. A, C, F
29. C
30. A
31. B
32. B
33. C
34. D
35. B
36. B
37. C
38. A
39. C
40. D
41. B
42. A, B, C

Listening Section

1. A
2. B
3. A
4. D
5. C
6. C
7. A, D
8. C
9. A
10. C
11. D
12. B
13. B
14. C
15. B, D
16. A
17. A
18. B
19. C
20. A
21. D
22. D
23. C
24. C
25. A
26. C
27. D
28. A
29. C
30. B, D
31. B
32. D
33. C
34. A

Speaking Section

Prompts, Important Points, and Sample Responses with Rater Comments

Use the sample Independent and Integrated Speaking Rubrics in Appendix A to see how responses are scored. The raters who listen to your responses will analyze them in three general categories. These categories are Delivery, Language Use, and Topic Development. All three categories have equal importance.

This section includes important points that should be covered when answering each question. All of these points must be present in a response in order for it to receive the highest score in the Topic Development category. These important points are guides to the kind of information raters expect to hear in a high-level response.

This section also refers to sample responses, which can be found on the accompanying DVD. Some responses were scored at the highest level, which others were not. The responses are followed by comments from certified ETS raters.

Question 1

Prompt

Talk about an interesting book you have read. Explain why you thought the book was interesting. Give specific details and examples to explain your answer.

Important Points

When answering this question, you should choose one book you have read and explain why you found it interesting. You are not required to spend time giving a summary of the book, but you should be sure to provide examples from the book while you are explaining why it was interesting.

High-level Response: Listen to Track 89.

Rater Comments

This speaker states the book that she has chosen to talk about and provides two reasons why she likes the book and thinks it is interesting. She does not spend time specifically talking about the story that takes place in the book, but rather focuses on what she likes about the book, and in her description of what she likes, she reveals parts of the story. For example, she provides some description of the book while focusing on answering the question when she says, *"I like this because . . . it shows how a boy grows up . . . he's different from others . . . the book describes that he's special situation in this world."* She also describes characteristics of the book that don't have to do with the story: *"The way the writer uh communicate with the readers . . . their beautiful language is um very enjoyable . . ."* Although the speaker pauses and hesitates at times during her response and makes minor grammatical errors, it is easy to understand her and follow what she is saying.

Low-level Response: Listen to Track 90.

Rater Comments

This speaker does not make it clear that she is talking about a specific book, and it seems that she is talking about a type of book that she enjoys instead. She does not connect her reason for finding this type of book interesting/enjoyable to an actual book, and instead just talks about her own interests. When she does start to try and connect her ideas to a book, she runs out of time, partly due to her slow and choppy pace of speaking: *"It's—in the book, it's, it's really interesting is because it's—."* Her use of vocabulary is at times imprecise and leads to confusion for the listener, such as when she says, *". . . the different character and behavior will impact on the decision that they make . . ."* She should more precisely have said, ". . . the different *characteristics* and how they *affect buying behavior*." Overall, her response is incomplete and somewhat difficult to follow.

Question 2

Prompt

Some people think that children should be allowed to watch whatever television programs they choose to. Others think that parents should exercise control over the television programs their children watch. Which do you agree with? Explain why.

Important Points

In this question you need to choose the statement that you agree with and explain why you agree with it. In order to give an effective response, you should provide clear, specific reasons that support your opinion. You will not be scored on which statement you agree with, but rather on how effectively you are able to present and support your opinion.
A reason to support the first statement could be that learning to make good decisions is an important part of growing up and rather than restricting a child's viewing, a parent should focus on teaching the child to make good decisions. A reason to support the second statement might include an example of an inappropriate program that parents should not let their children watch and explain why watching that program might have a negative effect on a child.

High-level Response: Listen to Track 91.

Rater Comments

This speaker demonstrates good control in language use and accurately uses a variety of grammatical structures and effective vocabulary. Her pronunciation is clear throughout and her use of intonation is appropriate.
She chooses to develop the idea of parental responsibility towards children and explains why she thinks this is important. The response would have been even fuller if she had given an example of a program that is not suitable for young children and why.

Mid-level Response: Listen to Track 92.

Rater Comments

This speaker states his opinion clearly but does not develop his ideas fully with clear support. He does provide a reason for his opinion that children should be able to watch whatever they want: that they can tell real things apart from *"not real things."* He then repeats the same basic idea in other words with imprecise language: *"I sure that a child view television with an enjoy and not with a real situation."* The speaker does not demonstrate that he can use a variety of grammatical structures or that he has a wide range of vocabulary. Though an accent is evident, pronunciation is generally clear overall.

Question 3

Prompt

The woman expresses her opinion about the college's plan. State her opinion and explain the reasons she gives for holding that opinion.

Important Points

To respond to this item, you should explain that the woman does not believe that the university's plan to renovate the dormitories in order to get more students to live on campus will work. To explain the points she makes, you could say that she argues that the renovations will create noise or disturbances, and that people will actually move off campus because of that in the short term. You should also point out her argument that in the long term students will likely remain in off-campus housing after the construction ends, since the university will have to raise the cost of housing to pay for the renovations.

High-level Response: Listen to Track 93.

Rater Comments

This speaker demonstrates a clear understanding of the information from both the reading and the conversation. He doesn't say until the end of his response that the woman disagrees with the plan, and that she doesn't think it will work. However, this doesn't prevent the listener from following the logic of the response. Consider this sentence from his response: *"She saying the price of the dorm fee will be raised . . . and it will go back to the student, and therefore student will look for the off campus apartment, which seems cheaper."* We see some minor grammatical errors here, and the speaker mispronounces a few select words (*price, cheaper*), but he uses intonation well and is able to communicate the point effectively. Overall, this is a well-developed and easy to understand response.

Mid-level Response: Listen to Track 94.

Rater Comments

In this response, the speaker touches on most of the important points; however, she does not do so with the fluidity and clarity characteristic of a high-level response. Her vocabulary is limited, and she hesitates and repeats words and phrases frequently, which requires listener effort. For example, it is hard to follow when she says, *"and and after the construction, the man was saying that maybe it's good after the construction."* She also does not explicitly explain that the noise from the renovations will cause students to move off-campus, and that later on, they will not move back because the renovations will be paid for by raising the price of housing.

Question 4

Prompt

Explain why Henry Darger is considered an Outsider Artist.

Important Points

In this item, you need to explain how Henry Darger fits the description of an Outsider Artist as described in the reading passage. Since Outsider Artists live and work outside of society, they produce art that is unusual and is made in ways that are different from other artists. Henry Darger fits this description because he lived and worked alone and taught himself to paint. Therefore his art looked different from other artists' work; for example, in one painting he cut out pictures of children from magazines and put them in his painting (and they also had more detail and were longer than paintings by most other artists).

High-level Response: Listen to Track 95.

Rater Comments

The speaker does a very good job of choosing details from the lecture that illustrate why Henry Darger is considered an Outsider Artist. He first describes characteristics of Outsider Artists, then describes how Darger matches these characteristics: "*He lived alone; he had no friends . . . he never showed those paintings to anybody; he never studied art. And his work is a unique work, and he has his own style.*" Occasionally he uses the wrong vocabulary word, such as using "conversation" instead of "lecture," but these errors do not ever make his ideas hard to follow. His response is also fluent, and his pronunciation is almost always easy to understand.

Mid-level Response: Listen to Track 96.

Rater Comments

The speaker organizes her response well, giving two main reasons that Darger was considered an Outsider Artist. However, she does not quite show how living and working alone or lacking a formal art education made him an Outsider Artist—she just seems to be explaining why he is a modern artist. Most of her pronunciation is clear, but sometimes it is difficult to understand certain phrases. She also makes a number of grammar mistakes "*that's why he has make a big difference,*" "*his production was totally innovate,*" "*he was a man who were different.*" Because of how often she makes these mistakes, the listener sometimes has to work harder to follow her ideas.

Question 5

Prompt

The students discuss a problem and two possible solutions. Briefly summarize the problem. Then state which of the two solutions you prefer and explain why.

Important Points

For this task, the prompt asks you to summarize the man's problem and recommend *one* of the solutions. Summarizing both solutions is not required and may take up too much of your response time. It is important to offer reasons to support the solution you choose. In this conversation, the man has been offered a summer research position, but he found out about the position too late to apply for campus housing for the summer. He has two possibilities: he can live with his parents (who are far from campus), or he can rent an apartment off-campus. If you recommend the first solution—that he live with his parents and drive to campus everyday—you could provide the reasons for your choice by explaining why the alternate solution is not good. For example, it may be difficult to find an apartment to rent for just a few months. Paying rent for an apartment will probably cost him more than he would pay for gas.

High-level Response: Listen to Track 97.

Rater Comments

In this response, the speaker begins with a brief summary of the problem and the two possible solutions. Even though she mentions both solutions, which is not necessary, she is able to summarize both quickly and allow time for her opinion. She runs out of time at the end, but it does not hurt her response because her opinion is clear and she justifies it well ("*. . . even if the cost is higher because he has to concentrate on this important research project and it will benefit on the long run . . .*"). She has a good command of vocabulary; however, she does make some minor grammar mistakes, especially at the end, when she is trying to finish her response. However, for the most part, her response is clear and easy to follow. Overall, she is a fairly fluent speaker, although there is sometimes an unevenness caused by rephrasing or searching for words.

Mid-level Response: Listen to Track 98.

Rater Comments

The speaker does summarize the problem from the conversation, but his explanation is a little unclear (*"he didn't hear from his professor or his instructor any-anything, so he didn't apply to the dormitory or in campus . . ."*). He also spends too much time summarizing the two possible solutions, which does not leave him enough time to explain his opinion fully. He does manage to insert his opinion briefly into the summaries of the solutions (*"I think it's a headache to drive . . ."*), but if he had focused on only including important details from the problem, he would have had more time to develop his opinion. Overall, he has good pronunciation and only minor grammar mistakes, but he also has several very noticeable pauses in his response, which suggest that he is searching for words and not able to give a full response without hesitation.

Question 6

Prompt

Using the points and examples from the lecture, explain what unity and contrast are, and how they make interior design more effective.

Important Points

In this item, your summary of the key ideas from the lecture should include the definitions of unity and contrast described by the professor. You should also describe how interior designers use unity and contrast, connecting the concepts to the specific examples mentioned. *Unity* is the repetition of similar elements, which creates a sense of order and comfort. For example, a designer might use similar colors throughout a room. *Contrast* is an occasional break in unity, which makes the design more interesting. For example, a designer might introduce a strikingly different color in one or two places. Contrast makes the design more interesting; however, too much contrast will make the room feel busy. Effective design creates a balance between unity and contrast. The order in which you present these ideas does not matter, as long as the response is logical and coherent.

High-level Response: Listen to Track 99.

Rater Comments

This is a complete and coherent response that presents the principles of unity and contrast, connects them clearly to the examples given, and explains why both are necessary for effective interior design. The speaker's logical organization of information and effective use of transitions make the response easy to follow (for example "*however, too much of unity is also boring . . . and therefore, comes into picture the second important aspect, which is contrast*"). Note that although the speaker makes occasional minor errors in grammar and usage, the meaning remains clear. The influence of the speaker's native language may be heard in the pronunciation and intonation, but he is still easy to understand. The speaker generally uses pauses and stress to communicate emphasis appropriately and make the response easier to follow, for example "what *it will* bring *is* [pause] disruption."

Mid-level Response: Listen to Track 100.

Rater Comments

This response describes unity and contrast and provides examples, but the explanation is not as full and clear as it could be. For example, the speaker describes unity as just using the same colors in a design, rather than similar elements in general, and does not mention the purpose of unity (order and comfort). At times, inaccurate words or phrases make it difficult to guess what the speaker means (*"You need contrasting thing to blend [plant?] the application"*). The speaker would also benefit from more careful pronunciation in general as some sections are very difficult to understand, thus obscuring her ideas. Overall, the speaker does not communicate her ideas as clearly as the high-level speaker does.

Writing Section

Prompts, Topic Notes, and Sample Responses with Rater Comments

Use the sample Integrated and Independent Writing Rubrics in Appendix A to see how responses are scored.

This section includes topic notes that are guides to the kind of information raters expect to read in a high-level response.

This section also refers to sample responses, which can be found on the accompanying DVD. These responses were scored at the highest level. The responses are followed by comments from certified ETS raters.

Question 1

Prompt

Summarize the points made in the lecture, being sure to explain how they cast doubt on the specific points made in the reading passage.

Topic Notes

The reading discusses three bad effects of people reading less literature than they used to. The lecture shows why these effects are not so bad or are caused by something other than people choosing not to read so much literature.

Point made in the reading	Corresponding point from the lecture
The passage argues that reading less literature means that readers are missing out on ways to stimulate their imagination and help with their mental development.	The lecturer points out that there are other forms of writing that are of high quality and just as intellectually stimulating as literature.
The passage argues that many of the kinds of reading that people currently spend time on instead of literature are just trivial entertainment and lead to lower cultural standards.	The lecturer argues that people spend time on culturally valuable activities such as listening to good music or watching good movies. The definition of culture is changing.
The passage says that another bad effect of the decline in reading literature is that talented writers of literature are not being supported.	The lecturer argues that maybe there is less readership of literature because the writers of literature nowadays are making their books/works too hard to understand.

Responses with scores of 4 and 5 typically discuss all three points in the table with good accuracy. There can be some blending of the ideas in the first two points.

Sample Response

The lecturer discusses the points made in the text but reaches a different conclusion in each case. For one thing, she states that yes, people are reading less literature then they were in earlier times but this does not equal an imediate decline of culture. On the contrary, in her opinion our culture is simply evolving and changing. Although literature is one of the most obvious elements of culture, there are also lots of other forms of artistic expression in our everchanging culture, e.g. music. And those elements are not less valuable and less creative then literature and they appeal to more modern concerns than literature.

Also the lecturer disputes the text that says we are going to lose interesting writers of literature. She says that today literature is not interesting enough for the reader! In the lecturers opinion this is mainly due to the fact that modern literature is often written with the intention of beeing difficult to understand, which does not make it very attractive for the modern reader.

And finally just because people are not reading literature anymore this does not mean they are not reading at all and losing their imagination and empathy; instead there are many other valuable types of books which people are reading, e.g. science textbooks and political analyzis. These books can stimulate readers and provide satisfaction and learning.

Rater Comments

This response earns a score of 5. The response clearly conveys the key ideas contained in the three points from the lecture. Notice that the points are not presented in the order they are discussed in the reading and lecture, but the way that this writer has presented them is coherent and accurate. Grammatical errors such as "then" instead of "than" in the first paragraph and a missing possessive apostrophe with "lecturers" in the second paragraph are few and minor. Grammatical variety and complexity are clearly present.

Question 2

Prompt

Some people say that the Internet provides people with a lot of valuable information. Others think access to so much information creates problems. Which view do you agree with?

Topic Notes

This topic asks you to assess the value of the access to a large quantity of information that the Internet provides us with these days. Successful responses can agree with the statement, disagree with the statement, or show the merits of both positions. No matter which position you take, it is important to support your opinion with details and examples.

If you agree with the statement, you should present and develop reasons that the quantity of information available is a good thing and has value. A reason may include the idea that the Internet has allowed people to learn about topics that they would not have had exposure to before the Internet became widely available. As part of supporting that approach, you could explain that some topic you have researched on the Internet would have either been impossible or have taken a very long time to get information about if you were limited to looking up the topic in books at your local library.

If you disagree with the statement, you should present and develop reasons that the quantity of information now available can be overwhelming and detrimental to learners, consumers, or some other audience. A reason may include the idea that many people can't distinguish between good and poor quality information on the Internet, for example, when choosing a particular product to buy, and so they are no better off in terms of getting valuable information about the product than if they had just gone to a shop to ask the salesperson about it.

If you believe that both of these positions have merit, you can present a balanced argument that presents both sides of the issues.

Sample Response

It is a fact that in the past few years, the Internet has exploded in terms of size, amount of information and accessibility.

The usage of the Internet encompasses every aspect of day-to-day life with a few examples being Shopping, News, Weather, Live Webcasts and much more. People who used to rely on traditional sources of information like the radio, TV, Newspapers are now increasingly flocking to the Internet or the "Web" as it's popularly called.

As more and more people get on the Web, it becomes increasingly effective for companies to use the web to reach out for the consumers. This also applies for Advertisers, Marketers, Content Providers, Newsmakers etc to adopt the same strategies. All the information is now available online and when it all adds up, there is a wealth of information that is now available to whoever seeks to find them. So, I strongly agree with view that the Internet provides people with a lot of valuable information, much more than what is actually necessary.

Now, providing too much information can also prove to be counter-productive. How does a consumer pick the right information, when there is so much available online? How does he filter to get the data that he needs? Is there a chance that the data he needs is buried somewhere in the middle? It is highly probable, or let me say, this was the case a few years back. So, technically, people were correct when they said too much information also created problems.

Fortunately, Technology finds ways to make it easier to use an innovation over a period of time. In the last few years, Internet search engines have been getting smarter everyday. They enable a user to enter a search string and then it searches the Internet for the most relevant and appropriate data and presents them to the user, with the results listed in the order of importance. They also offer the user several options to further filter the provided results, making it easier to zone on the correct data.

In summary, while it is true that there is a lot of not very valuable information on the web, which may be counter-productive for users, there are also means to effectively seek and find the appropriate information, thus providing a great deal of value to people who are looking to learn about a subject, buy the best product for their needs, or any one of many other activities that people need to do nowadays.

Rater Comments

This 5-level response acknowledges the merits of both positions, while ultimately coming out in favor of the idea that the Internet provides a lot of valuable information. The writer describes some reasons why people use the Internet, explains how helpful it can be for both individuals and companies, and concedes in the fourth paragraph that access to too much information online can be a bad thing. In the fifth paragraph, the writer explains how technology is advancing so that the negative aspects mentioned in the preceding paragraph are becoming less and less problematic. The writer goes on to conclude that in spite of some drawbacks, overall the Internet is quite valuable in what it provides to us. This is a good progression of ideas, and the writer has expressed those ideas by using, mostly accurately, a good range of vocabulary and sentence structure. Errors such as "reach out for the consumers" instead of "reach out *to* consumers" are minor and do not interfere with meaning.

TOEFL iBT Test 4

READING

This section measures your ability to understand academic passages in English.

There are three passages in the section. Give yourself 20 minutes to read each passage and answer the questions about it. The entire section will take 60 minutes to complete.

You may look back at a passage when answering the questions. You can skip questions and go back to them later as long as there is time remaining.

Directions: Read the passage. Then answer the questions. Give yourself 20 minutes to complete this practice set.

WHICH HAND DID THEY USE?

We all know that many more people today are right-handed than left-handed. Can one trace this same pattern far back in prehistory? Much of the evidence about right-hand versus left-hand dominance comes from stencils and prints found in rock shelters in Australia and elsewhere, and in many Ice Age caves in France, Spain, and Tasmania. When a left hand has been stenciled, this implies that the artist was right-handed, and vice versa. Even though the paint was often sprayed on by mouth, one can assume that the dominant hand assisted in the operation. One also has to make the assumption that hands were stenciled palm downward—a left hand stenciled palm upward might of course look as if it were a right hand. Of 158 stencils in the French cave of Gargas, 136 have been identified as left, and only 22 as right; right-handedness was therefore heavily predominant.

Cave art furnishes other types of evidence of this phenomenon. Most engravings, for example, are best lit from the left, as befits the work of right-handed artists, who generally prefer to have the light source on the left so that the shadow of their hand does not fall on the tip of the engraving tool or brush. In the few cases where an Ice Age figure is depicted holding something, it is mostly, though not always, in the right hand.

Clues to right-handedness can also be found by other methods. Right-handers tend to have longer, stronger, and more muscular bones on the right side, and Marcellin Boule as long ago as 1911 noted the La Chapelle-aux-Saints Neanderthal skeleton had a right upper arm bone that was noticeably stronger than the left. Similar observations have been made on other Neanderthal skeletons such as La Ferrassie I and Neanderthal itself.

Fractures and other cut marks are another source of evidence. Right-handed soldiers tend to be wounded on the left. The skeleton of a 40- or 50-year-old Nabatean warrior, buried 2,000 years ago in the Negev Desert, Israel, had multiple healed fractures to the skull, the left arm, and the ribs.

Tools themselves can be revealing. Long-handed Neolithic spoons of yew wood preserved in Alpine villages dating to 3000 B.C. have survived; the signs of rubbing on their left side indicate that their users were right-handed. The late Ice Age rope found in the French cave of Lascaux consists of fibers spiraling to the right, and was therefore tressed by a right-hander.

Occasionally one can determine whether stone tools were used in the right hand or the left, and it is even possible to assess how far back this feature can be traced. In stone toolmaking experiments, Nick Toth, a right-hander, held the core (the stone that would become the tool) in his left hand and the hammer stone in his right. As the tool was made, the core was rotated clockwise, and the flakes, removed in sequence, had a little crescent of cortex (the core's outer surface) on the side. Toth's knapping produced 56 percent flakes with the cortex on the right, and 44 percent left-oriented flakes. A left-handed toolmaker would produce the opposite pattern. Toth has applied these criteria to the similarly made pebble tools from a number of early sites (before 1.5 million years) at Koobi Fora, Kenya, probably made by *Homo habilis*. At seven sites he found that 57 percent of the flakes were right-oriented, and 43 percent left, a pattern almost identical to that produced today.

About 90 percent of modern humans are right-handed: we are the only mammal with a preferential use of one hand. The part of the brain responsible for fine control and movement is located in the left cerebral hemisphere, and the findings above suggest that the human brain was already asymmetrical in its structure and function not long after 2 million years ago. Among Neanderthalers of 70,000–35,000 years ago, Marcellin Boule noted that the La Chapelle-aux-Saints individual had a left hemisphere slightly bigger than the right, and the same was found for brains of specimens from Neanderthal, Gibraltar, and La Quina.

Directions: Now answer the questions.

PARAGRAPH 1

We all know that many more people today are right-handed than left-handed. Can one trace this same pattern far back in prehistory? Much of the evidence about right-hand versus left-hand dominance comes from stencils and prints found in rock shelters in Australia and elsewhere, and in many Ice Age caves in France, Spain, and Tasmania. When a left hand has been stenciled, this implies that the artist was right-handed, and vice versa. Even though the paint was often sprayed on by mouth, one can assume that the dominant hand assisted in the operation. One also has to make the assumption that hands were stenciled palm downward—a left hand stenciled palm upward might of course look as if it were a right hand. Of 158 stencils in the French cave of Gargas, 136 have been identified as left, and only 22 as right; right-handedness was therefore heavily predominant.

1. The phrase "assisted in" in the passage is closest in meaning to

Ⓐ initiated
Ⓑ dominated
Ⓒ helped with
Ⓓ set up

2. It can be inferred from paragraph 1 that even when paint was sprayed by mouth to make a hand stencil

Ⓐ there was no way to tell which hand was stenciled
Ⓑ the stenciled hand was the weaker hand
Ⓒ the stenciled hand was the dominant hand
Ⓓ artists stenciled more images of the dominant hand than they did of the weak

PARAGRAPH 2

Cave art furnishes other types of evidence of this phenomenon. Most engravings, for example, are best lit from the left, as befits the work of right-handed artists, who generally prefer to have the light source on the left so that the shadow of their hand does not fall on the tip of the engraving tool or brush. In the few cases where an Ice Age figure is depicted holding something, it is mostly, though not always, in the right hand.

3. The word "depicted" in the passage is closest in meaning to

Ⓐ identified
Ⓑ revealed
Ⓒ pictured
Ⓓ imagined

4. Which of the sentences below best expresses the essential information in the highlighted sentence in the passage? Incorrect choices change the meaning in important ways or leave out essential information.

   Ⓐ Right-handed artists could more easily have avoided casting shadows on their work, because engravings in prehistoric caves were lit from the left.
   Ⓑ The tips of engraving tools and brushes indicate that these instruments were used by right-handed artists whose work was lit from the left.
   Ⓒ The best lighting for most engravings suggests that they were made by right-handed people trying to avoid the shadow of their hands interfering with their work.
   Ⓓ Right-handed artists try to avoid having the brush they are using interfere with the light source.

PARAGRAPHS 1 & 2

We all know that many more people today are right-handed than left-handed. Can one trace this same pattern far back in prehistory? Much of the evidence about right-hand versus left-hand dominance comes from stencils and prints found in rock shelters in Australia and elsewhere, and in many Ice Age caves in France, Spain, and Tasmania. When a left hand has been stenciled, this implies that the artist was right-handed, and vice versa. Even though the paint was often sprayed on by mouth, one can assume that the dominant hand assisted in the operation. One also has to make the assumption that hands were stenciled palm downward—a left hand stenciled palm upward might of course look as if it were a right hand. Of 158 stencils in the French cave of Gargas, 136 have been identified as left, and only 22 as right; right-handedness was therefore heavily predominant.

Cave art furnishes other types of evidence of this phenomenon. Most engravings, for example, are best lit from the left, as befits the work of right-handed artists, who generally prefer to have the light source on the left so that the shadow of their hand does not fall on the tip of the engraving tool or brush. In the few cases where an Ice Age figure is depicted holding something, it is mostly, though not always, in the right hand.

5. All of the following are mentioned in paragraphs 1 and 2 as evidence of right-handedness in art and artists EXCEPT

   Ⓐ the ideal source of lighting for most engravings
   Ⓑ the fact that a left hand stenciled palm upward might look like a right hand
   Ⓒ the prevalence of outlines of left hands
   Ⓓ figures in prehistoric art holding objects with the right hand

PARAGRAPH 3

Clues to right-handedness can also be found by other methods. Right-handers tend to have longer, stronger, and more muscular bones on the right side, and Marcellin Boule as long ago as 1911 noted the La Chapelle-aux-Saints Neanderthal skeleton had a right upper arm bone that was noticeably stronger than the left. Similar observations have been made on other Neanderthal skeletons such as La Ferrassie I and Neanderthal itself.

6. According to paragraph 3, the La Chapelle-aux-Saints Neanderthal skeleton can be identified as right-handed because

   Ⓐ other Neanderthal skeletons found nearby are also right-handed
   Ⓑ the right arm bone is stronger than the left
   Ⓒ it is similar to skeletons of La Ferrassie I and Neanderthal
   Ⓓ the right side of the skeleton shows less evidence of fractures

PARAGRAPH 4

Fractures and other cut marks are another source of evidence. Right-handed soldiers tend to be wounded on the left. The skeleton of a 40- or 50-year-old Nabatean warrior, buried 2,000 years ago in the Negev Desert, Israel, had multiple healed fractures to the skull, the left arm, and the ribs.

7. Which of the following statements about fractures and cut marks can be inferred from paragraph 4?

   Ⓐ Fractures and cut marks caused by right-handed soldiers tend to occur on the right side of the injured party's body.
   Ⓑ The right arm sustains more injuries because, as the dominant arm, it is used more actively.
   Ⓒ In most people, the left side of the body is more vulnerable to injury since it is not defended effectively by the dominant arm.
   Ⓓ Fractures and cut marks on fossil humans probably occurred after death.

PARAGRAPH 5

Tools themselves can be revealing. Long-handed Neolithic spoons of yew wood preserved in Alpine villages dating to 3000 B.C. have survived; the signs of rubbing on their left side indicate that their users were right-handed. The late Ice Age rope found in the French cave of Lascaux consists of fibers spiraling to the right, and was therefore tressed by a right-hander.

8. According to paragraph 5, what characteristic of a Neolithic spoon would imply that the spoon's owner was right-handed?

   Ⓐ The direction of the fibers
   Ⓑ Its long handle
   Ⓒ The yew wood it is carved from
   Ⓓ Wear on its left side

9. In paragraph 5, why does the author mention the Ice Age rope found in the French cave of Lascaux?

Ⓐ As an example of an item on which the marks of wear imply that it was used by a right-handed person
Ⓑ Because tressing is an activity that is easier for a right-handed person than for a left-handed person
Ⓒ Because the cave of Lascaux is the site where researchers have found several prehistoric tools made for right-handed people
Ⓓ As an example of an item whose construction shows that it was made by a right-handed person

PARAGRAPH 6

Occasionally one can determine whether stone tools were used in the right hand or the left, and it is even possible to assess how far back this feature can be traced. In stone toolmaking experiments, Nick Toth, a right-hander, held the core (the stone that would become the tool) in his left hand and the hammer stone in his right. As the tool was made, the core was rotated clockwise, and the flakes, removed in sequence, had a little crescent of cortex (the core's outer surface) on the side. Toth's knapping produced 56 percent flakes with the cortex on the right, and 44 percent left-oriented flakes. A left-handed toolmaker would produce the opposite pattern. Toth has applied these criteria to the similarly made pebble tools from a number of early sites (before 1.5 million years) at Koobi Fora, Kenya, probably made by *Homo habilis*. At seven sites he found that 57 percent of the flakes were right-oriented, and 43 percent left, a pattern almost identical to that produced today.

10. The word "criteria" in the passage is closest in meaning to

Ⓐ standards
Ⓑ findings
Ⓒ ideas
Ⓓ techniques

11. What was the purpose of Toth's toolmaking experiment described in paragraph 6?

Ⓐ To shape tools that could be used by either hand
Ⓑ To produce replicas of early tools for display in museums
Ⓒ To imitate the production of pebble tools from early sites
Ⓓ To determine which hand made the early tools

PARAGRAPH 7

About 90 percent of modern humans are right-handed: we are the only mammal with a preferential use of one hand. The part of the brain responsible for fine control and movement is located in the left cerebral hemisphere, and the findings above suggest that the human brain was already asymmetrical in its structure and function not long after 2 million years ago. Among Neanderthalers of 70,000–35,000 years ago, Marcellin Boule noted that the La Chapelle-aux-Saints individual had a left hemisphere slightly bigger than the right, and the same was found for brains of specimens from Neanderthal, Gibraltar, and La Quina.

12. What is the author's primary purpose in paragraph 7?

    Ⓐ To illustrate the importance of studying the brain
    Ⓑ To demonstrate that human beings are the only mammal to desire fine control of movement
    Ⓒ To contrast the functions of the two hemispheres of the brain
    Ⓓ To demonstrate that right-hand preference has existed for a long time

PARAGRAPH 1

We all know that many more people today are right-handed than left-handed. Can one trace this same pattern far back in prehistory? **(A)** Much of the evidence about right-hand versus left-hand dominance comes from stencils and prints found in rock shelters in Australia and elsewhere, and in many Ice Age caves in France, Spain, and Tasmania. **(B)** When a left hand has been stenciled, this implies that the artist was right-handed, and vice versa. **(C)** Even though the paint was often sprayed on by mouth, one can assume that the dominant hand assisted in the operation. One also has to make the assumption that hands were stenciled palm downward—a left hand stenciled palm upward might of course look as if it were a right hand. **(D)** Of 158 stencils in the French cave of Gargas, 136 have been identified as left, and only 22 as right; right-handedness was therefore heavily predominant.

13. **Directions:** Look at the part of the passage that is displayed above. The letters **(A)**, **(B)**, **(C)**, and **(D)** indicate where the following sentence could be added.

    The stencils of hands found in these shelters and caves allow us to draw conclusions about which hand was dominant.

    Where would the sentence best fit?

    Ⓐ Choice A
    Ⓑ Choice B
    Ⓒ Choice C
    Ⓓ Choice D

14. **Directions:** An introductory sentence for a brief summary of the passage is provided below. Complete the summary by selecting the THREE answer choices that express the most important ideas in the passage. Some sentences do not belong in the summary because they express ideas that are not presented in the passage or are minor ideas in the passage.

    Write your answer choices in the spaces where they belong. You can either write the letter of your answer choice or you can copy the sentence.

Several categories of evidence indicate that people have always been predominantly right-handed.

-
-
-

Answer Choices

[A] Stencils of right-handed figures are characteristic of cave art in France, Spain, and Tasmania.

[B] The amount of prehistoric art created by right-handed artists indicates that left-handed people were in the minority.

[C] Signs on the skeletal remains of prehistoric figures, including arm-bone size and injury marks, imply that these are the remains of right-handed people.

[D] Neanderthal skeletons often have longer finger bones in the right hand, which is evidence that the right hand was stronger.

[E] Instruments such as spoons, ropes, and pebble tools show signs that indicate they were used or constructed by right-handed people.

[F] Nick Toth, a modern right-handed toolmaker, has shown that prehistoric tools were knapped to fit the right hand.

Directions: Read the passage. Then answer the questions. Give yourself 20 minutes to complete this practice set.

TRANSITION TO SOUND IN FILM

The shift from silent to sound film at the end of the 1920's marks, so far, the most important transformation in motion picture history. Despite all the highly visible technological developments in theatrical and home delivery of the moving image that have occurred over the decades since then, no single innovation has come close to being regarded as a similar kind of watershed. In nearly every language, however the words are phrased, the most basic division in cinema history lies between films that are mute and films that speak.

Yet this most fundamental standard of historical periodization conceals a host of paradoxes. Nearly every movie theater, however modest, had a piano or organ to provide musical accompaniment to silent pictures. In many instances, spectators in the era before recorded sound experienced elaborate aural presentations alongside movies' visual images, from the Japanese *benshi* (narrators) crafting multivoiced dialogue narratives to original musical compositions performed by symphony-size orchestras in Europe and the United States. In Berlin, for the premiere performance outside the Soviet Union of *The Battleship Potemkin*, film director Sergei Eisenstein worked with Austrian composer Edmund Meisel (1874–1930) on a musical score matching sound to image; the Berlin screenings with live music helped to bring the film its wide international fame.

Beyond that, the triumph of recorded sound has overshadowed the rich diversity of technological and aesthetic experiments with the visual image that were going forward simultaneously in the 1920's. New color processes, larger or differently shaped screen sizes, multiple-screen projections, even television, were among the developments invented or tried out during the period, sometimes with startling success. The high costs of converting to sound and the early limitations of sound technology were among the factors that suppressed innovations or retarded advancement in these other areas. The introduction of new screen formats was put off for a quarter century, and color, though utilized over the next two decades for special productions, also did not become a norm until the 1950's.

Though it may be difficult to imagine from a later perspective, a strain of critical opinion in the 1920's predicted that sound film would be a technical novelty that would soon fade from sight, just as had many previous attempts, dating well back before the First World War, to link images with recorded sound. These critics were making a common assumption—that the technological inadequacies of earlier efforts (poor synchronization, weak sound amplification, fragile sound recordings) would invariably occur again. To be sure, their evaluation of the technical flaws in 1920's sound experiments was not so far off the mark, yet they neglected to take into account important new forces in the motion picture field that, in a sense, would not take no for an answer.

These forces were the rapidly expanding electronics and telecommunications companies that were developing and linking telephone and wireless technologies in the 1920's. In the United States, they included such firms as American Telephone and Telegraph, General Electric, and Westinghouse. They were interested in all forms of sound technology and all potential avenues for commercial exploitation. Their competition and collaboration were creating the broadcasting industry in the United States, beginning with the introduction of commercial radio programming in the early 1920's. With financial assets considerably greater than those in the motion picture industry, and perhaps a wider vision of the relationships among entertainment and communications media, they revitalized research into recording sound for motion pictures.

In 1929 the United States motion picture industry released more than 300 sound films—a rough figure, since a number were silent films with music tracks, or films prepared in dual versions, to take account of the many cinemas not yet wired for sound. At the production level, in the United States the conversion was virtually complete by 1930. In Europe it took a little longer, mainly because there were more small producers for whom the costs of sound were prohibitive, and in other parts of the world problems with rights or access to equipment delayed the shift to sound production for a few more years (though cinemas in major cities may have been wired in order to play foreign sound films). The triumph of sound cinema was swift, complete, and enormously popular.

Directions: Now answer the questions.

PARAGRAPH 1

The shift from silent to sound film at the end of the 1920's marks, so far, the most important transformation in motion picture history. Despite all the highly visible technological developments in theatrical and home delivery of the moving image that have occurred over the decades since then, no single innovation has come close to being regarded as a similar kind of watershed. In nearly every language, however the words are phrased, the most basic division in cinema history lies between films that are mute and films that speak.

15. The word "regarded" in the passage is closest in meaning to

Ⓐ analyzed
Ⓑ considered
Ⓒ altered
Ⓓ criticized

16. According to paragraph 1, which of the following is the most significant development in the history of film?

Ⓐ The technological innovation of sound film during the 1920's
Ⓑ The invention of a method for delivering movies to people's homes
Ⓒ The development of a technology for translating films into other languages
Ⓓ The technological improvements allowing clearer images in films

PARAGRAPH 2

Yet this most fundamental standard of historical periodization conceals a host of paradoxes. Nearly every movie theater, however modest, had a piano or organ to provide musical accompaniment to silent pictures. In many instances, spectators in the era before recorded sound experienced elaborate aural presentations alongside movies' visual images, from the Japanese *benshi* (narrators) crafting multivoiced dialogue narratives to original musical compositions performed by symphony-size orchestras in Europe and the United States. In Berlin, for the premiere performance outside the Soviet Union of *The Battleship Potemkin*, film director Sergei Eisenstein worked with Austrian composer Edmund Meisel (1874–1930) on a musical score matching sound to image; the Berlin screenings with live music helped to bring the film its wide international fame.

17. The word "paradoxes" in the passage is closest in meaning to

Ⓐ difficulties
Ⓑ accomplishments
Ⓒ parallels
Ⓓ contradictions

18. Why does the author mention "Japanese *benshi* " and "original musical compositions"?

Ⓐ To suggest that audiences preferred other forms of entertainment to film before the transition to sound in the 1920's
Ⓑ To provide examples of some of the first sounds that were recorded for film
Ⓒ To indicate some ways in which sound accompanied film before the innovation of sound films in the late 1920's
Ⓓ To show how the use of sound in films changed during different historical periods

19. Paragraph 2 suggests which of the following about Eisenstein's film *The Battleship Potemkin*?

Ⓐ The film was not accompanied by sound before its Berlin screening.
Ⓑ The film was unpopular in the Soviet Union before it was screened in Berlin.
Ⓒ Eisenstein's film was the first instance of collaboration between a director and a composer.
Ⓓ Eisenstein believed that the musical score in a film was as important as dialogue.

PARAGRAPH 3

Beyond that, the triumph of recorded sound has overshadowed the rich diversity of technological and aesthetic experiments with the visual image that were going forward simultaneously in the 1920's. New color processes, larger or differently shaped screen sizes, multiple-screen projections, even television, were among the developments invented or tried out during the period, sometimes with startling success. The high costs of converting to sound and the early limitations of sound technology were among the factors that suppressed innovations or retarded advancement in these other areas. The introduction of new screen formats was put off for a quarter century, and color, though utilized over the next two decades for special productions, also did not become a norm until the 1950's.

20. The word "overshadowed" in the passage is closest in meaning to

Ⓐ distracted from
Ⓑ explained
Ⓒ conducted
Ⓓ coordinated with

21. According to paragraph 3, which of the following is NOT true of the technological and aesthetic experiments of the 1920's?

Ⓐ Because the costs of introducing recorded sound were low, it was the only innovation that was put to use in the 1920's.
Ⓑ The introduction of recorded sound prevented the development of other technological innovations in the 1920's.
Ⓒ The new technological and aesthetic developments of the 1920's included the use of color, new screen formats, and television.
Ⓓ Many of the innovations developed in the 1920's were not widely introduced until as late as the 1950's.

PARAGRAPH 4

Though it may be difficult to imagine from a later perspective, a strain of critical opinion in the 1920's predicted that sound film would be a technical novelty that would soon fade from sight, just as had many previous attempts, dating well back before the First World War, to link images with recorded sound. These critics were making a common assumption—that the technological inadequacies of earlier efforts (poor synchronization, weak sound amplification, fragile sound recordings) would invariably occur again. To be sure, their evaluation of the technical flaws in 1920's sound experiments was not so far off the mark, yet they neglected to take into account important new forces in the motion picture field that, in a sense, would not take no for an answer.

22. Which of the sentences below best expresses the essential information in the highlighted sentence in the passage? Incorrect choices change the meaning in important ways or leave out essential information.

Ⓐ It was difficult for some critics in the 1920's to imagine why the idea of sound film had faded from sight well before the First World War.
Ⓑ As surprising as it seems today, some critics in the 1920's believed that the new attempts at sound films would fade just as quickly as the attempts made before the First World War.
Ⓒ Though some early critics thought that sound film would fade, its popularity during the First World War proved that it was not simply a technical novelty.
Ⓓ Although some critics predicted well before the First World War that sound film would be an important technical innovation, it was not attempted until the 1920's.

23. The word "neglected" in the passage is closest in meaning to

Ⓐ failed
Ⓑ needed
Ⓒ started
Ⓓ expected

24. According to paragraph 4, which of the following is true about the technical problems of early sound films?

Ⓐ Linking images with recorded sound was a larger obstacle than weak sound amplification or fragile sound recordings.

Ⓑ Sound films in the 1920's were unable to solve the technical flaws found in sound films before the First World War.

Ⓒ Technical inadequacies occurred less frequently in early sound films than critics suggested.

Ⓓ Critics assumed that it would be impossible to overcome the technical difficulties experienced with earlier sound films.

PARAGRAPH 5

These forces were the rapidly expanding electronics and telecommunications companies that were developing and linking telephone and wireless technologies in the 1920's. In the United States, they included such firms as American Telephone and Telegraph, General Electric, and Westinghouse. They were interested in all forms of sound technology and all potential avenues for commercial exploitation. Their competition and collaboration were creating the broadcasting industry in the United States, beginning with the introduction of commercial radio programming in the early 1920's. With financial assets considerably greater than those in the motion picture industry, and perhaps a wider vision of the relationships among entertainment and communications media, they revitalized research into recording sound for motion pictures.

25. In paragraph 5, commercial radio programming is best described as the result of

Ⓐ a financially successful development that enabled large telecommunications firms to weaken their competition

Ⓑ the desire of electronics and telecommunications companies to make sound technology profitable

Ⓒ a major development in the broadcasting industry that occurred before the 1920's

Ⓓ the cooperation between telecommunications companies and the motion picture industry

PARAGRAPH 6

In 1929 the United States motion picture industry released more than 300 sound films—a rough figure, since a number were silent films with music tracks, or films prepared in dual versions, to take account of the many cinemas not yet wired for sound. At the production level, in the United States the conversion was virtually complete by 1930. In Europe it took a little longer, mainly because there were more small producers for whom the costs of sound were prohibitive, and in other parts of the world problems with rights or access to equipment delayed the shift to sound production for a few more years (though cinemas in major cities may have been wired in order to play foreign sound films). The triumph of sound cinema was swift, complete, and enormously popular.

26. According to paragraph 6, which of the following accounts for the delay in the conversion to sound films in Europe?

    Ⓐ European producers often lacked knowledge about the necessary equipment for the transition to sound films.
    Ⓑ Smaller European producers were often unable to afford to add sound to their films.
    Ⓒ It was often difficult to wire older cinemas in the major cities to play sound films.
    Ⓓ Smaller European producers believed that silent films with music accompaniment were aesthetically superior to sound films.

PARAGRAPHS 5 & 6

These forces were the rapidly expanding electronics and telecommunications companies that were developing and linking telephone and wireless technologies in the 1920's. In the United States, they included such firms as American Telephone and Telegraph, General Electric, and Westinghouse. They were interested in all forms of sound technology and all potential avenues for commercial exploitation. Their competition and collaboration were creating the broadcasting industry in the United States, beginning with the introduction of commercial radio programming in the early 1920's. **(A)** With financial assets considerably greater than those in the motion picture industry, and perhaps a wider vision of the relationships among entertainment and communications media, they revitalized research into recording sound for motion pictures.

(B) In 1929 the United States motion picture industry released more than 300 sound films—a rough figure, since a number were silent films with music tracks, or films prepared in dual versions, to take account of the many cinemas not yet wired for sound. **(C)** At the production level, in the United States the conversion was virtually complete by 1930. **(D)** In Europe it took a little longer, mainly because there were more small producers for whom the costs of sound were prohibitive, and in other parts of the world problems with rights or access to equipment delayed the shift to sound production for a few more years (though cinemas in major cities may have been wired in order to play foreign sound films). The triumph of sound cinema was swift, complete, and enormously popular.

27. **Directions:** Look at the part of the passage that is displayed above. The letters **(A)**, **(B)**, **(C)**, and **(D)** indicate where the following sentence could be added.

    When this research resulted in the development of vastly improved sound techniques, film studios became convinced of the importance of converting to sound.

    Where would the sentence best fit?

    Ⓐ Choice A
    Ⓑ Choice B
    Ⓒ Choice C
    Ⓓ Choice D

28. **Directions:** An introductory sentence for a brief summary of the passage is provided below. Complete the summary by selecting the THREE answer choices that express the most important ideas in the passage. Some sentences do not belong in the summary because they express ideas that are not presented in the passage or are minor ideas in the passage.

Write your answer choices in the spaces where they belong. You can either write the letter of your answer choice or you can copy the sentence.

The transition from silent to sound films was the most important development in film history.

-
-
-

Answer Choices

[A] Although music and speech had frequently accompanied film presentations before the 1920's, there was a strong desire to add sound to the films themselves.

[B] Japanese filmmakers had developed the technology for creating sound films before directors in Europe and the United States began experimenting with sound.

[C] Because of intense interest in developing and introducing sound in film, the general use of other technological innovations being developed in the 1920's was delayed.

[D] Before the First World War, film directors showed little interest in linking images with recorded sound.

[E] The rapid progress in sound technology made possible by the involvement of telecommunications companies transformed the motion picture industry.

[F] The arrival of sound film technology in the United States forced smaller producers in the motion picture industry out of business.

Directions: Read the passage. Then answer the questions. Give yourself 20 minutes to complete this practice set.

WATER IN THE DESERT

Rainfall is not completely absent in desert areas, but it is highly variable. An annual rainfall of four inches is often used to define the limits of a desert. The impact of rainfall upon the surface water and groundwater resources of the desert is greatly influenced by landforms. Flats and depressions where water can collect are common features, but they make up only a small part of the landscape.

Arid lands, surprisingly, contain some of the world's largest river systems, such as the Murray-Darling in Australia, the Rio Grande in North America, the Indus in Asia, and the Nile in Africa. These rivers and river systems are known as "exogenous" because their sources lie outside the arid zone. They are vital for sustaining life in some of the driest parts of the world. For centuries, the annual floods of the Nile, Tigris, and Euphrates, for example, have brought fertile silts and water to the inhabitants of their lower valleys. Today, river discharges are increasingly controlled by human intervention, creating a need for international river-basin agreements. The filling of the Ataturk and other dams in Turkey has drastically reduced flows in the Euphrates, with potentially serious consequences for Syria and Iraq.

The flow of exogenous rivers varies with the season. The desert sections of long rivers respond several months after rain has fallen outside the desert, so that peak flows may be in the dry season. This is useful for irrigation, but the high temperatures, low humidities, and different day lengths of the dry season, compared to the normal growing season, can present difficulties with some crops.

Regularly flowing rivers and streams that originate within arid lands are known as "endogenous." These are generally fed by groundwater springs, and many issue from limestone massifs, such as the Atlas Mountains in Morocco. Basaltic rocks also support springs, notably at the Jabal Al-Arab on the Jordan-Syria border. Endogenous rivers often do not reach the sea but drain into inland basins, where the water evaporates or is lost in the ground. Most desert streambeds are normally dry, but they occasionally receive large flows of water and sediment.

Deserts contain large amounts of groundwater when compared to the amounts they hold in surface stores such as lakes and rivers. But only a small fraction of groundwater enters the hydrological cycle—feeding the flows of streams, maintaining lake levels, and being recharged (or refilled) through surface flows and rainwater. In recent years, groundwater has become an increasingly important source of freshwater for desert dwellers. The United Nations Environment Programme and the World Bank have funded attempts to survey the groundwater resources of arid lands and to develop appropriate extraction techniques. Such programs are much needed because in many arid lands there is only a vague idea of the extent of groundwater resources. It is known, however, that the distribution of groundwater is uneven, and that much of it lies at great depths.

Groundwater is stored in the pore spaces and joints of rocks and unconsolidated (unsolidified) sediments or in the openings widened through fractures and weathering. The water-saturated rock or sediment is known as an "aquifer." Because they are porous, sedimentary rocks, such as sandstones and conglomerates, are important potential sources of groundwater. Large quantities of water may also be stored in limestones when joints and cracks have been enlarged to form cavities. Most limestone and sandstone aquifers are deep and extensive but may contain groundwaters that are not being recharged. Most shallow aquifers in sand and gravel deposits produce lower yields, but they can be rapidly recharged. Some deep aquifers are known as "fossil" waters. The term "fossil" describes water that has been present for several thousand years. These aquifers became saturated more than 10,000 years ago and are no longer being recharged.

Water does not remain immobile in an aquifer but can seep out at springs or leak into other aquifers. The rate of movement may be very slow: in the Indus plain, the movement of saline (salty) groundwaters has still not reached equilibrium after 70 years of being tapped. The mineral content of groundwater normally increases with the depth, but even quite shallow aquifers can be highly saline.

Directions: Now answer the questions.

PARAGRAPH 1

Rainfall is not completely absent in desert areas, but it is highly variable. An annual rainfall of four inches is often used to define the limits of a desert. The impact of rainfall upon the surface water and groundwater resources of the desert is greatly influenced by landforms. Flats and depressions where water can collect are common features, but they make up only a small part of the landscape.

29. Which of the following statements about annual rainfall can be inferred from paragraph 1?

    (A) Flat desert areas receive more annual rainfall than desert areas with mountains.
    (B) Areas that receive more than four inches of rain per year are not considered deserts.
    (C) Many areas receive less than four inches of annual rainfall, but only a few are deserts.
    (D) Annual rainfall has no impact on the groundwater resources of desert areas.

PARAGRAPH 2

Arid lands, surprisingly, contain some of the world's largest river systems, such as the Murray-Darling in Australia, the Rio Grande in North America, the Indus in Asia, and the Nile in Africa. These rivers and river systems are known as "exogenous" because their sources lie outside the arid zone. They are vital for sustaining life in some of the driest parts of the world. For centuries, the annual floods of the Nile, Tigris, and Euphrates, for example, have brought fertile silts and water to the inhabitants of their lower valleys. Today, river discharges are increasingly controlled by human intervention, creating a need for international river-basin agreements. The filling of the Ataturk and other dams in Turkey has drastically reduced flows in the Euphrates, with potentially serious consequences for Syria and Iraq.

30. The word "drastically" in the passage is closest in meaning to

Ⓐ obviously
Ⓑ unfortunately
Ⓒ rapidly
Ⓓ severely

31. In paragraph 2, why does the author mention the Ataturk and other dams in Turkey?

Ⓐ To contrast the Euphrates River with other exogenous rivers
Ⓑ To illustrate the technological advances in dam building
Ⓒ To argue that dams should not be built on the Euphrates River
Ⓓ To support the idea that international river-basin agreements are needed

32. According to paragraph 2, which of the following is true of the Nile River?

Ⓐ The Nile's flow in its desert sections is at its lowest during the dry season.
Ⓑ The Nile's sources are located in one of the most arid zones of the world.
Ⓒ The Nile's annual floods bring fertile silts and water to its lower valley.
Ⓓ The Nile's periodic flooding hinders the growth of some crops.

PARAGRAPH 5

Deserts contain large amounts of groundwater when compared to the amounts they hold in surface stores such as lakes and rivers. But only a small fraction of groundwater enters the hydrological cycle—feeding the flows of streams, maintaining lake levels, and being recharged (or refilled) through surface flows and rainwater. In recent years, groundwater has become an increasingly important source of freshwater for desert dwellers. The United Nations Environment Programme and the World Bank have funded attempts to survey the groundwater resources of arid lands and to develop appropriate extraction techniques. Such programs are much needed because in many arid lands there is only a vague idea of the extent of groundwater resources. It is known, however, that the distribution of groundwater is uneven, and that much of it lies at great depths.

33. The word "dwellers" in the passage is closest in meaning to

Ⓐ settlements
Ⓑ farmers
Ⓒ tribes
Ⓓ inhabitants

34. Paragraph 5 supports all of the following statements about the groundwater in deserts EXCEPT:

Ⓐ The groundwater is consistently found just below the surface.
Ⓑ A small part of the groundwater helps maintain lake levels.
Ⓒ Most of the groundwater is not recharged through surface water.
Ⓓ The groundwater is increasingly used as a source of freshwater.

PARAGRAPH 6

Groundwater is stored in the pore spaces and joints of rocks and unconsolidated (unsolidified) sediments or in the openings widened through fractures and weathering. The water-saturated rock or sediment is known as an "aquifer." Because they are porous, sedimentary rocks, such as sandstones and conglomerates, are important potential sources of groundwater. Large quantities of water may also be stored in limestones when joints and cracks have been enlarged to form cavities. Most limestone and sandstone aquifers are deep and extensive but may contain groundwaters that are not being recharged. Most shallow aquifers in sand and gravel deposits produce lower yields, but they can be rapidly recharged. Some deep aquifers are known as "fossil" waters. The term "fossil" describes water that has been present for several thousand years. These aquifers became saturated more than 10,000 years ago and are no longer being recharged.

35. The word "fractures" in the passage is closest in meaning to

Ⓐ streams
Ⓑ cracks
Ⓒ storms
Ⓓ earthquakes

36. According to paragraph 6, which of the following statements about aquifers in deserts is true?

Ⓐ Water from limestone and sandstone aquifers is generally better to drink than water from sand and gravel aquifers.
Ⓑ Sand and gravel aquifers tend to contain less groundwater than limestone or sandstone aquifers.
Ⓒ Groundwater in deep aquifers is more likely to be recharged than groundwater in shallow aquifers.
Ⓓ Sedimentary rocks, because they are porous, are not capable of storing large amounts of groundwater.

37. According to paragraph 6, the aquifers called "fossil" waters

Ⓐ contain fossils that are thousands of years old
Ⓑ took more than 10,000 years to become saturated with water
Ⓒ have not gained or lost any water for thousands of years
Ⓓ have been collecting water for the past 10,000 years

PARAGRAPH 7

Water does not remain immobile in an aquifer but can seep out at springs or leak into other aquifers. The rate of movement may be very slow: in the Indus plain, the movement of saline (salty) groundwaters has still not reached equilibrium after 70 years of being tapped. The mineral content of groundwater normally increases with the depth, but even quite shallow aquifers can be highly saline.

38. The word "immobile" in the passage is closest in meaning to

Ⓐ enclosed
Ⓑ permanent
Ⓒ motionless
Ⓓ intact

PARAGRAPHS 1 2 3 4 5 6 & 7

Rainfall is not completely absent in desert areas, but it is highly variable. An annual rainfall of four inches is often used to define the limits of a desert. The impact of rainfall upon the surface water and groundwater resources of the desert is greatly influenced by landforms. Flats and depressions where water can collect are common features, but they make up only a small part of the landscape.

Arid lands, surprisingly, contain some of the world's largest river systems, such as the Murray-Darling in Australia, the Rio Grande in North America, the Indus in Asia, and the Nile in Africa. These rivers and river systems are known as "exogenous" because their sources lie outside the arid zone. They are vital for sustaining life in some of the driest parts of the world. For centuries, the annual floods of the Nile, Tigris, and Euphrates, for example, have brought fertile silts and water to the inhabitants of their lower valleys. Today, river discharges are increasingly controlled by human intervention, creating a need for international river-basin agreements. The filling of the Ataturk and other dams in Turkey has drastically reduced flows in the Euphrates, with potentially serious consequences for Syria and Iraq.

The flow of exogenous rivers varies with the season. The desert sections of long rivers respond several months after rain has fallen outside the desert, so that peak flows may be in the dry season. This is useful for irrigation, but the high temperatures, low humidities, and different day lengths of the dry season, compared to the normal growing season, can present difficulties with some crops.

Regularly flowing rivers and streams that originate within arid lands are known as "endogenous." These are generally fed by groundwater springs, and many issue from limestone massifs, such as the Atlas Mountains in Morocco. Basaltic rocks also support springs, notably at the Jabal Al-Arab on the Jordan-Syria border. Endogenous rivers often do not reach the sea but drain into inland basins, where the water evaporates or is lost in the ground. Most desert streambeds are normally dry, but they occasionally receive large flows of water and sediment.

Deserts contain large amounts of groundwater when compared to the amounts they hold in surface stores such as lakes and rivers. But only a small fraction of groundwater enters the hydrological cycle—feeding the flows of streams, maintaining lake levels, and being recharged (or refilled) through surface flows and rainwater. In recent years, groundwater has become an increasingly important source of freshwater for desert dwellers. The United Nations Environment Programme and the World Bank have funded attempts to survey the groundwater resources of arid lands and to develop appropriate extraction techniques. Such programs are much needed because in many arid lands there is only a vague idea of the extent of groundwater resources. It is known, however, that the distribution of groundwater is uneven, and that much of it lies at great depths.

Groundwater is stored in the pore spaces and joints of rocks and unconsolidated (unsolidified) sediments or in the openings widened through fractures and weathering. The water-saturated rock or sediment is known as an "aquifer." Because they are porous, sedimentary rocks, such as sandstones and conglomerates, are important potential sources of groundwater. Large quantities of water may also be stored in limestones when joints and cracks have been enlarged to form cavities. Most limestone and sandstone aquifers are deep and extensive but may contain groundwaters that are not being recharged. Most shallow aquifers in sand and gravel deposits produce lower yields, but they can be rapidly recharged. Some deep aquifers are known as "fossil" waters. The term "fossil" describes water that has been present for several thousand years. These aquifers became saturated more than 10,000 years ago and are no longer being recharged.

Water does not remain immobile in an aquifer but can seep out at springs or leak into other aquifers. The rate of movement may be very slow: in the Indus plain, the movement of saline (salty) groundwaters has still not reached equilibrium after 70 years of being tapped. The mineral content of groundwater normally increases with the depth, but even quite shallow aquifers can be highly saline.

39. The passage supports which of the following statements about water in the desert?

Ⓐ The most visible forms of water are not the most widespread forms of water in the desert.

Ⓑ Groundwater in the desert cannot become a source of drinking water but can be used for irrigation.

Ⓒ Most of the water in the desert is contained in shallow aquifers that are being rapidly recharged.

Ⓓ Desert areas that lack endogenous or exogenous rivers and streams cannot support life.

PARAGRAPHS 4 & 5

Regularly flowing rivers and streams that originate within arid lands are known as "endogenous." These are generally fed by groundwater springs, and many issue from limestone massifs, such as the Atlas Mountains in Morocco. Basaltic rocks also support springs, notably at the Jabal Al-Arab on the Jordan-Syria border. **(A)** Endogenous rivers often do not reach the sea but drain into inland basins, where the water evaporates or is lost in the ground. **(B)** Most desert streambeds are normally dry, but they occasionally receive large flows of water and sediment. **(C)**

Deserts contain large amounts of groundwater when compared to the amounts they hold in surface stores such as lakes and rivers. **(D)** But only a small fraction of groundwater enters the hydrological cycle—feeding the flows of streams, maintaining lake levels, and being recharged (or refilled) through surface flows and rainwater. In recent years, groundwater has become an increasingly important source of freshwater for desert dwellers. The United Nations Environment Programme and the World Bank have funded attempts to survey the groundwater resources of arid lands and to develop appropriate extraction techniques. Such programs are much needed because in many arid lands there is only a vague idea of the extent of groundwater resources. It is known, however, that the distribution of groundwater is uneven, and that much of it lies at great depths.

40. **Directions:** Look at the part of the passage that is displayed above. The letters **(A)**, **(B)**, **(C)**, and **(D)** indicate where the following sentence could be added.

These sudden floods provide important water supplies but can also be highly destructive.

Where would the sentence best fit?

Ⓐ Choice A
Ⓑ Choice B
Ⓒ Choice C
Ⓓ Choice D

41. **Directions:** Select from the seven sentences below, the two sentences that correctly characterize endogenous rivers and the three sentences that correctly characterize exogenous rivers. Write your answer choices in the appropriate column of the table. You can either write the letter of your answer choice or you can copy the sentence. Two of the sentences will NOT be used.

Endogenous Rivers	**Exogenous Rivers**
•	•
•	•
	•

Answer Choices

- [A] Their water generally comes from groundwater springs.
- [B] Their water is saltier than the water of most other rivers.
- [C] They include some of the world's largest rivers.
- [D] They originate outside the desert.
- [E] They often drain into inland basins and do not reach the sea.
- [F] They contain too much silt to be useful for irrigation.
- [G] Their water flow generally varies with the season of the year.

LISTENING

This section measures your ability to understand conversations and lectures in English.

Listen to each conversation and lecture only one time. After each conversation and lecture, you will answer some questions about it. Answer each question based on what is stated or implied by the speakers.

You may take notes while you listen and use your notes to help you answer the questions. Your notes will not be scored.

Answer each question before moving on. Do not return to previous questions.

It will take about 60 minutes to listen to the conversations and lectures and answer the questions about them.

Directions: Listen to Track 101.

Directions: Now answer the questions.

1. Why does the professor ask the man to come to her office?
   Ⓐ To check on the man's progress on a paper he is writing
   Ⓑ To show the man techniques for organizing his time
   Ⓒ To encourage the man to revise a paper he wrote
   Ⓓ To clarify her comments on a paper the man wrote

2. Why does the man hesitate before agreeing to the professor's request?
   Ⓐ He is not sure his effort would be successful.
   Ⓑ He feels overwhelmed by all his schoolwork.
   Ⓒ He is unclear about what the professor wants him to do.
   Ⓓ He does not like to work on more than one assignment at a time.

3. What is the professor's main criticism of the man's paper?
   Ⓐ It included unnecessary information.
   Ⓑ It did not include enough examples to illustrate the main point.
   Ⓒ The main point was expressed too abstractly.
   Ⓓ The paper ignored a key historical fact.

4. Why does the professor suggest that the student change the introduction of his paper?

   Ⓐ To make it less repetitive
   Ⓑ To more clearly state the man's point of view
   Ⓒ To correct spelling and grammar mistakes
   Ⓓ To reflect changes made elsewhere in the paper

5. Listen to Track 102.

   Ⓐ She understands the student's problem.
   Ⓑ She wants the student to explain his comment.
   Ⓒ She did not hear what the student said.
   Ⓓ She does not accept the student's excuse.

Directions: Listen to Track 103.

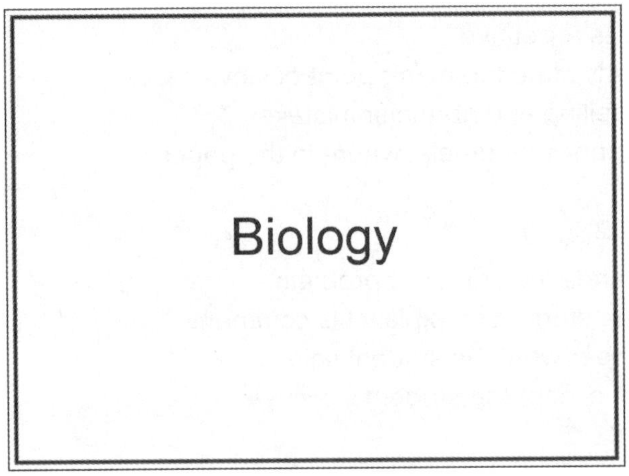

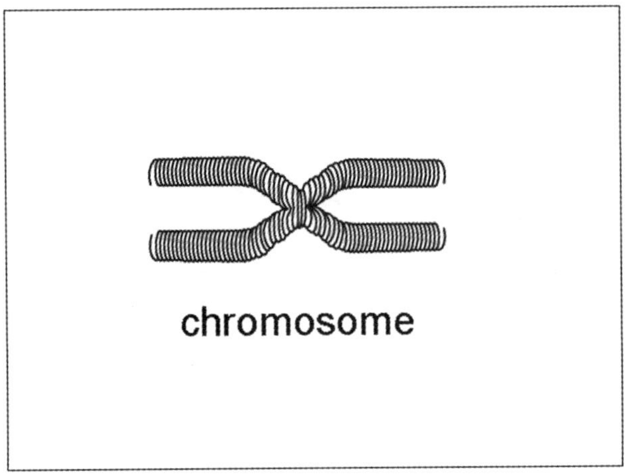

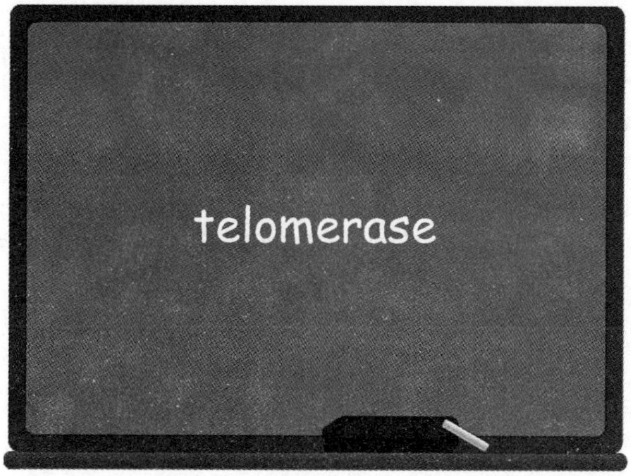

Directions: Now answer the questions.

6. What does the professor mainly discuss?

   Ⓐ How genes control human development
   Ⓑ Why various types of human cells divide at different rates
   Ⓒ How human chromosomes differ from one another
   Ⓓ Why most human cells cannot keep dividing successfully

7. The professor discusses research about the percentage of a chromosome's DNA that contains genetic information. How did she feel about this research?

   Ⓐ She doubted its accuracy.
   Ⓑ She was surprised by its conclusion.
   Ⓒ She was concerned about its implications.
   Ⓓ She thought it was unnecessary.

8. What does the professor say about the DNA in a telomere?

   Ⓐ It causes a cell to begin dividing.
   Ⓑ It separates one gene from another.
   Ⓒ It is genetically meaningless.
   Ⓓ It has no function.

9. Why does the professor mention shoelaces?

   Ⓐ To point out that chromosomes are arranged in pairs
   Ⓑ To describe the coiled shape of a chromosome
   Ⓒ To illustrate how chromosomes are protected from damage
   Ⓓ To explain how chromosomes are joined before dividing

10. What does the professor imply about the length of the telomeres on a cell's chromosomes?

    Ⓐ Longer telomeres allow the cell to divide more times.
    Ⓑ Longer telomeres contain more genetic information.
    Ⓒ Shorter telomeres are wound into tighter coils.
    Ⓓ Shorter telomeres are less likely to break.

11. According to the professor, how is the chemical telomerase related to the telomere?

    Ⓐ It resembles the telomere in structure.
    Ⓑ It helps repair broken telomeres.
    Ⓒ It is produced at the end of the telomere.
    Ⓓ It prevents telomeres from becoming too long.

Directions: Listen to Track 104.

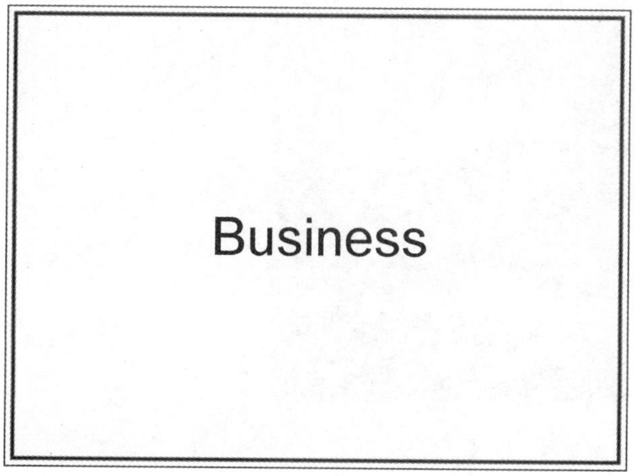

Directions: Now answer the questions.

12. What is the lecture mainly about?

    Ⓐ Two competing theories of business management
    Ⓑ Tools that business managers can use to improve the efficiency of their employees
    Ⓒ A method for businesses to learn about the needs of their customers
    Ⓓ A way that business managers can better relate to their employees

13. According to the discussion, what is a potential drawback of MBWA?

    Ⓐ MBWA provides information about the opinions of a small number of people.
    Ⓑ MBWA can provide conflicting information.
    Ⓒ Customers often are reluctant to share their opinions.
    Ⓓ Customers may be annoyed about being observed while they shop.

14. What does the professor say about the relationship between MBWA and market research?

    Ⓐ MBWA is a refined version of a market research technique.
    Ⓑ Market research information is more valuable than information from MBWA.
    Ⓒ Information provided by MBWA complements information collected from market research.
    Ⓓ Business managers should replace market research with MBWA.

15. Why does the professor mention Dalton's soup and Elkin jeans?

    Ⓐ To illustrate that the success of MBWA often depends on the product involved
    Ⓑ To give examples of two companies that were resistant to trying MBWA
    Ⓒ To contrast a successful use of MBWA with an unsuccessful use
    Ⓓ To give examples of how the technique of MBWA is used in practice

16. Why does the professor discuss the mayor of Baltimore?

Ⓐ To explain the origins of the method of MBWA
Ⓑ To demonstrate that MBWA can be useful outside the business world
Ⓒ To provide an example of how MBWA can sometimes fail
Ⓓ To give an example where market research and MBWA provide similar types of information

17. Listen to Track 105.

Ⓐ It is surprising that Dalton's tried to use MBWA.
Ⓑ It is surprising that MBWA was successful for Dalton's.
Ⓒ She does not have a high opinion of the quality of Dalton's soups.
Ⓓ Dalton's positive experience with MBWA led many other companies to try MBWA.

Directions: Listen to Track 106.

Directions: Now answer the questions.

18. What is the student's problem?
    (A) He missed the tuition due date.
    (B) He has not been paid.
    (C) His bank lost his paycheck.
    (D) His tuition payment got lost.

19. What happened at the payroll department?
    (A) A new computer system was installed.
    (B) Information was entered into the computer system incorrectly.
    (C) Some employee information got lost.
    (D) Paychecks were distributed for the wrong amount.

20. What does the woman imply about the people who work in the payroll office?
    (A) They did not realize they had a problem.
    (B) They are rather disorganized.
    (C) They had tried to contact the man several times.
    (D) They prefer to process checks manually.

21. What will the student probably need to do to get paid?

Ⓐ Talk to the person who hired him
Ⓑ Go to the payroll department
Ⓒ Call the director of the payroll department
Ⓓ Resubmit the payroll paperwork

22. How does the student's attitude change during the conversation?

Ⓐ From annoyed to appreciative
Ⓑ From frustrated to excited
Ⓒ From surprised to frustrated
Ⓓ From appreciative to surprised

Directions: Listen to Track 107.

Directions: Now answer the questions.

23. What is the lecture mainly about? *Choose 2 answers.*

    [A] Some changes that took place in the early years of opera
    [B] Differences between opera and other forms of music
    [C] Italy's musical influence throughout Europe
    [D] Reasons that early French and Italian opera did not survive

24. According to the professor, what happened after the Italian language replaced Latin in Italian opera?

    (A) Operas became much longer.
    (B) Operas began to express secular ideas.
    (C) Music in opera became more complex.
    (D) Opera was used to teach theology to the general public.

25. Why does the professor mention ancient Greek theater?

Ⓐ To give an example of a culture that adopted opera from the Italians
Ⓑ To describe the type of setting in which opera was typically performed
Ⓒ To point out a precursor of opera
Ⓓ To explain how opera was introduced into French society

26. What does the professor say about music in French opera?

Ⓐ It resembled sacred church music.
Ⓑ It often inspired French novelists to write great pieces of literature.
Ⓒ It revolved mainly around solo pieces.
Ⓓ It was secondary to the rhythmic flow of language.

27. Listen to Track 108.

Ⓐ To show differences between English and Italian opera
Ⓑ To give one instance in the evolution of opera
Ⓒ To discuss the popularity of opera in England at the time
Ⓓ To point out that English and Italian opera companies often worked together

28. Listen to Track 109.

Ⓐ He agrees with Chapman about opera and society.
Ⓑ He thinks Chapman's approach to opera is confusing.
Ⓒ He is concerned that Chapman's ideas are often misunderstood.
Ⓓ He thinks Chapman's questions are difficult to answer.

Directions: Listen to Track 110.

Environmental Science

Directions: Now answer the questions.

29. What is this lecture mainly about?

   Ⓐ An efficient solution to the problem of storing solar energy
   Ⓑ Energy policies in the twentieth century
   Ⓒ Reasons that solar energy is not more widely used
   Ⓓ The superiority of solar energy to oil and natural gas

30. What are the two main problems solar power presents as an energy source?
   Choose 2 answers.

   [A] It is a potentially dangerous source.
   [B] It is difficult to concentrate.
   [C] It is scientifically unsound.
   [D] It needs to be stored.

31. According to the professor, what led to the popularity of solar energy in the 1970s?

Ⓐ New solar energy technologies
Ⓑ Advertising campaigns by solar energy companies
Ⓒ An increase in the price of oil and natural gas
Ⓓ The depletion of Earth's reserves of oil and natural gas

32. What is the difference between passive and active heating systems?

Ⓐ Passive systems are less reliable.
Ⓑ Passive systems are difficult to install.
Ⓒ Passive systems can be used at any location.
Ⓓ Passive systems work without mechanical support.

33. What is the professor's opinion about the future of the Kramer Junction power plant?

Ⓐ He is uncertain about the future of the Kramer Junction plant.
Ⓑ He believes the Kramer Junction plant will become a major source of power.
Ⓒ He is certain the Kramer Junction plant will not be able to increase its capacity.
Ⓓ He thinks the Kramer Junction plant will have many competitors.

34. Listen to Track 111.

Ⓐ He thinks the student should know the answer.
Ⓑ He thinks the student has raised an important issue.
Ⓒ He wants the student to repeat his question.
Ⓓ He will answer the question later in the lecture.

SPEAKING

This section measures your ability to speak in English about a variety of topics.

There are six questions in this section. For each question, you will be given a short time to prepare your response. When the preparation time is up, answer the question as completely as possible in the time indicated for that question. You should record your responses so that you can review them later and compare them with the answer key and scoring rubrics.

Directions: You will now be asked to speak about a familiar topic. Give yourself 15 seconds to prepare your response. Then record yourself speaking for 45 seconds.

1. Listen to Track 112.

What is the most efficient type of transportation in your country? Explain why you think it is efficient. Include specific reasons or examples.

Preparation Time: 15 seconds
Response Time: 45 seconds

Directions: You will now be asked to give your opinion about a familiar topic. Give yourself 15 seconds to prepare your response. Then record yourself speaking for 45 seconds.

2. Listen to Track 113.

Some people believe it's essential for a person's education to learn to play a musical instrument. Others don't believe music education is important. Which view do you agree with? Explain why.

Preparation Time: 15 seconds
Response Time: 45 seconds

Directions: You will now read a short passage and listen to a conversation on the same topic. You will then be asked a question about them. After you hear the question, give yourself 30 seconds to prepare your response. Then record yourself speaking for 60 seconds.

Listen to Track 114.

Reading Time: 45 seconds

College Radio Station to Undergo Major Changes?

The university is considering making major changes to the college radio station. Changes would include an expansion of the station's broadcasting range, which would allow the radio's programming to reach nearby towns. One goal of the plan is to attract more students to apply to its communications program. Another goal is to provide the university with an extra source of revenue. University officials expect the enhanced radio station to significantly increase the number of listeners, which will in turn encourage businesses to place commercials on the radio.

Listen to Track 115.

3. The woman supports the proposal described in the article. Explain why she thinks it will achieve the university's goals.

Preparation Time: 30 seconds

Response Time: 60 seconds

Directions: You will now read a short passage and listen to a lecture on the same topic. You will then be asked a question about them. After you hear the question, give yourself 30 seconds to prepare your response. Then record yourself speaking for 60 seconds.

Listen to Track 116.

Reading Time: 50 seconds

Subliminal Perception

Humans are constantly perceiving visual and auditory stimuli. Sometimes our perception of these stimuli occurs consciously; we are aware of a stimulus and know that we are perceiving it. But our perception of a stimulus can also occur without our awareness: an image might appear and disappear before our eyes too quickly for us to notice that we saw it, or a sound might be too faint for us to realize that we heard it. This phenomenon—the perception of a stimulus just below the threshold of conscious awareness—is called subliminal perception. Experiments have shown that subliminally perceived stimuli can influence people's thoughts and attitudes.

Listen to Track 117.

4. Describe what subliminal perception is and explain how the experiment discussed by the professor illustrates this phenomenon.

Preparation Time: 30 seconds

Response Time: 60 seconds

Directions: You will now listen to part of a conversation. You will then be asked a question about it. After you hear the question, give yourself 20 seconds to prepare your response. Then record yourself speaking for 60 seconds.

Listen to Track 118.

5. The speakers discuss two possible solutions to the woman's problem. Briefly summarize the problem. Then state which of the solutions you recommend and explain why.

Preparation Time: 20 seconds

Response Time: 60 seconds

Directions: You will now listen to part of a lecture. You will then be asked a question about it. After you hear the question, give yourself 20 seconds to prepare your response. Then record yourself speaking for 60 seconds.

Listen to Track 119.

6. Using the points and examples from the talk, explain how substitute goods and complement goods influence demand for a particular product.

Preparation Time: 20 seconds
Response Time: 60 seconds

WRITING

This section measures your ability to write in English to communicate in an academic environment.

There are two writing questions in this section.

For question 1, you will read a passage and listen to a lecture about the same topic. You may take notes while you read and listen. Then you will write a response to a question based on what you have read and heard. You may look back at the passage when answering the question. You may use your notes to help you answer the question. You have 20 minutes to plan and write your response.

For question 2, you will write an essay based on your own knowledge and experience. You have 30 minutes to plan and complete your essay.

Directions: Give yourself 3 minutes to read the passage.

Reading Time: 3 minutes

Jane Austen (1775–1817) is one of the most famous of all English novelists, and today her novels are more popular than ever, with several recently adapted as Hollywood movies. But we do not have many records of what she looked like. For a long time, the only accepted image of Austen was an amateur sketch of an adult Austen made by her sister Cassandra. However, recently a professionally painted, full-length portrait of a teenage girl owned by a member of the Austen family has come up for sale. Although the professional painting is not titled *Jane Austen*, there are good reasons to believe she is the subject.

First, in 1882, several decades after Austen's death, Austen's family gave permission to use the portrait as an illustration in an edition of her letters. Austen's family clearly recognized it as a portrait of the author. So, for over a century now, the Austen family itself has endorsed the claim that the girl in the portrait is Jane Austen.

Second, the face in the portrait clearly resembles the one in Cassandra's sketch, which we know depicts Austen. Though somewhat amateurish, the sketch communicates definite details about Austen's face. Even though the Cassandra sketch is of an adult Jane Austen, the features are still similar to those of the teenage girl in the painting. The eyebrows, nose, mouth, and overall shape of the face are very much like those in the full-length portrait.

Third, although the painting is unsigned and undated, there is evidence that it was painted when Austen was a teenager. The style links it to Ozias Humphrey, a society portrait painter who was the kind of professional the wealthy Austen family would hire. Humphrey was active in the late 1780s and early 1790s, exactly the period when Jane Austen was the age of the girl in the painting.

Listen to Track 120.

Directions: You have 20 minutes to plan and write your response. Your response will be judged on the basis of the quality of your writing and on how well your response presents the points in the lecture and their relationship to the reading passage. Typically, an effective response will be 150 to 225 words.

Listen to Track 121.

Response Time: 20 minutes

1. Summarize the points made in the lecture, being sure to explain how they respond to the specific arguments made in the reading passage.

Directions: Read the question below. You have 30 minutes to plan, write, and revise your essay. Typically, an effective response will contain a minimum of 300 words.

Response Time: 30 minutes

2. Do you agree or disagree with the following statement?

   It is better to have broad knowledge of many academic subjects than to specialize in one specific subject.

   Use specific reasons and examples to support your answer.

ANSWERS

Reading Section

1. C
2. B
3. C
4. C
5. B
6. B
7. C
8. D
9. D
10. A
11. D
12. D
13. B
14. B, C, E
15. B
16. A
17. D
18. C
19. A
20. A
21. A
22. B
23. A
24. D
25. B
26. B
27. B
28. A, C, E
29. B
30. D
31. D
32. C
33. D
34. A
35. B
36. B
37. C
38. C
39. A
40. C
41.

Endogenous Rivers	Exogenous Rivers
• Their water generally comes from groundwater springs. • They often drain into inland basins and do not reach the sea.	• They include some of the world's largest rivers. • They originate outside the desert. • Their water flow generally varies with the season of the year.

Listening Section

1. C
2. B
3. A
4. D
5. A
6. D
7. B
8. C
9. C
10. A
11. B
12. C
13. A
14. C
15. D
16. B
17. A
18. B
19. C
20. B
21. D
22. A
23. A, C
24. B
25. C
26. D
27. B
28. A
29. C
30. B, D
31. C
32. D
33. A
34. B

Speaking Section

Prompts, Important Points, and Sample Responses with Rater Comments

Use the sample Independent and Integrated Speaking Rubrics in Appendix A to see how responses are scored. The raters who listen to your responses will analyze them in three general categories. These categories are Delivery, Language Use, and Topic Development. All three categories have equal importance.

This section includes important points that should be covered when answering each question. All of these points must be present in a response in order for it to receive the highest score in the Topic Development category. These important points are guides to the kind of information raters expect to hear in a high-level response.

This section also refers to sample responses, which can be found on the accompanying DVD. Some responses were scored at the highest level, which others were not. The responses are followed by comments from certified ETS raters.

Question 1

Prompt

What is the most efficient type of transportation in your country? Explain why you think it is efficient. Include specific reasons or examples.

Important Points

In this item, you should talk about the type of transportation in your country that you think is the most efficient and explain why.

You could discuss factors such as speed, cost, or convenience, giving examples for how the type of transportation you chose is preferable in those categories. It is OK to talk about other advantages of that kind of transportation, such as comfort, but you should focus mainly on what makes it most efficient.

High-level Response: Listen to Track 122.

Rater Comments

This speaker speaks quite naturally and uses stress and intonation well, which helps the listener to follow and understand his response easily. For example, the way he says, "*it's* so *much easier*," helps to make his point about the ease of using a car instead of the bus. He is also able to use rather advanced structures to effectively make this comparison: "*compared with the other transportation devices, it's so much faster.*" (Note that "device" is an incorrect word choice here.) The speaker does hesitate and repeat words at times, but this is not overly distracting. He develops his response well, using the personal example of how long it takes him to get to the movie theater using both modes of transportation.

Mid-level Response: Listen to Track 123.

Rater Comments

This speaker provides several good reasons and details to justify his choice of the subway as the most efficient. In terms of content, this is a strong response. However, the speaker is hard to follow at times. In contrast to the high-level response, which used stress patterns effectively to convey meaning, this speaker speaks in a flat tone, pausing infrequently and at odd places. This means that the listener has to make an effort to separate his ideas and understand what he is saying. Some mistakes in pronunciation ("*scheduled*"), misused words ("electronic" instead of "electricity"), and some long hesitations also prevent this response from reaching the high level.

Question 2

Prompt

Some people believe it's essential for a person's education to learn to play a musical instrument. Others don't believe music education is important. Which view do you agree with? Explain why.

Important Points

When answering this question, you should take a clear stance and explain whether you think that music education or playing a musical instrument is important. You should provide at least one reason to support your point of view and you should explain that reason in detail. It is acceptable to list several reasons for agreeing or disagreeing with the importance of music education, but you should not simply make a list of reasons without providing any support or explanation for them.

High-level Response: Listen to Track 124.

Rater Comments

In this response, the speaker takes an interesting stance by disagreeing with both statements, though he expresses a clear opinion and gives support for that opinion. He believes that music education is important but not essential. He is able to give reasons for his point of view and support for these reasons. He speaks about people who "*have gone through life successfully without having to learn a musical instrument.*" But he also mentions that learning a musical instrument can help with other skills, such as "*logical thinking and math skills,*" and he references studies which have proven this point. He has some minor hesitations in his speech, but he is able to correct himself easily, and he is very easy to understand.

Mid-level Response: Listen to Track 125.

Rater Comments

In this response, the speaker agrees that learning to play a musical instrument is essential. The general content of this response is very close to the high-level response, but this speaker does not express her ideas as clearly. She is able to list several reasons for her opinion, but her explanations are sometimes not well developed and therefore not clear (*"It's very helpful to develop their brain also because they use in the tip of the fingers, for example, keyboard instrument"*). Her pronunciation is mostly clear and easy to understand, but her speech is not always smooth (she pauses frequently and uses words like *"um"*). Her word choice is sometimes inaccurate (*"develop their emotional feeling"*), and she makes small grammatical errors, but she mostly communicates her point of view successfully.

Question 3

Prompt

The woman supports the proposal described in the article. Explain why she thinks it will achieve the university's goals.

Important Points

In your answer to this prompt, you should explain that the woman thinks the proposal to expand the student radio station will attract more students to the communications program and allow the university to make money. She thinks that more students will be attracted to the communications program because the proposed changes would allow the radio station to reach a larger audience, which will enable students to get real-life work experience and get better jobs when they graduate. She also thinks that the changes to the radio station will allow the university to make extra money by adding commercials. The extra money made from commercials can be used to offer more scholarships or to help fund other projects in the program. Note that it is not necessary to explain the technical aspects of expanding the broadcasting range of the radio station, as long as it's clear that the changes will allow the station to reach a larger audience.

High-level Response: Listen to Track 126.

Rater Comments

The speaker clearly explains why the woman thinks the plan will benefit the school. Both goals (improving job prospects for students and generating money through commercials) are addressed with an appropriate level of detail. The response is well organized, and makes logical connections between the plan and its effects (*"the staff will have . . . a better chance of getting a job, because it'll promote interacting with people that are not only students, but people who live in nearby towns."*) The idea of expanding the radio station is implied rather than directly stated (*"right now it is only limited to campus and campus students"*), but this is acceptable for this particular item since the prompt does not ask the speaker to describe the plan. Although the speaker occasionally pauses to think, he speaks for long, fluid stretches between pauses, using appropriate intonation to express meaning. He uses precise vocabulary and complex structures accurately throughout.

Mid-level Response: Listen to Track 127.

Rater Comments

Although the speaker addresses all of the points and is understandable, vagueness and simple language keep this response in the middle range. For example, when the speaker says *"more program would provide for opportunity for more students to have a real experience of what that is"* the listener has to guess what *"that"* refers to. The speaker also tends to repeat things instead of elaborating on them. For example, after the sentence quoted above, he adds *"and then they would have – get more jobs after they finish it because they get experience of doing it"* instead of adding details like the fact that the station's wider range would allow students to work with a different type of audience. Sometimes the speaker's sentence structure limits his ability to express himself and make connections between pieces of information. For example, in "*they also get more money out of it because of the commercials*", it would be better to say something like, "the radio station would also be able to earn more money because their wider audience would allow them to attract more commercials."

Question 4

Prompt

Describe what subliminal perception is and explain how the experiment discussed by the professor illustrates this phenomenon.

Important Points

In this question, you should describe what subliminal perception is, then discuss the specific information from the experiment and explain how it is related to the general idea of subliminal perception. Subliminal perception is the idea that people perceive an image or other stimulus even if they are not aware that they have experienced it. These subliminal perceptions can influence people's thoughts and actions. The professor describes an experiment in which people were subliminally exposed to different photos (an angry or a happy boy) and then shown a second photo of a boy with a neutral expression. Those who had seen the angry boy described the neutral boy negatively, whereas those who had seen the happy boy described the neutral boy positively. This experiment shows that because of subliminal perception, people were influenced by a photo they were not aware of seeing.

High-level Response: Listen to Track 128.

Rater Comments

The speaker gives a full response. She gives a brief definition of subliminal perception, then describes the experiment in more detail, with good accuracy. She also briefly connects the specific experiment to the general idea of subliminal perception. Although she has a prominent accent, her pronunciation is clear and easy to understand. The response also progresses naturally from idea to idea, making it easier for the listener to follow. Occasional imprecise use of vocabulary or structure (for example, "*people* who were flashed with *a stimulus*") does not affect meaning. The speaker also uses self-correction effectively ("*one group looked* . . . saw *the picture* . . . *the other group looked in* . . . looked at *a picture*").

Mid-level Response: Listen to Track 129.

Rater Comments

Overall, the speaker's pronunciation is good. There is some hesitation at times in the response, but not to the extent that it creates unnecessary effort for the listener. The content at the beginning and middle of the response is good in general, but she is unable to control more difficult structures, resulting in unclear language and confusion ("*One teacher was shown with in order to the people during the experiment to watch it just a little amount of time*"). Also, although she attempts to summarize the results and connect the experiment to the general idea, she does not describe how the people in the different groups reacted differently (i.e., that one group described the boy negatively and the other group described the boy positively), which is a major omission of the content.

Question 5

Prompt

The speakers discuss two possible solutions to the woman's problem. Briefly summarize the problem. Then state which of the solutions you recommend and explain why.

Important Points

When answering this question, you should start by describing the woman's problem—she has a scheduling conflict. She won an award, but the ceremony to accept the award conflicts with/overlaps with an exam she must take. You are not required to describe the two different solutions, but you should recommend one of the solutions from the conversation (go to the award ceremony right after her exam or reschedule the exam) and provide specific support for your recommendation. For example, you could recommend that she reschedule the exam and take it early, so that she will not have to worry about being late to the ceremony and will not have to rush to finish her exam, which could affect her performance on the exam. There is no "right" solution; that is, you will not be scored based on which solution you choose, but rather on how well you are able to explain the problem and make a clear recommendation for solving it.

High-level Response: Listen to Track 130.

Rater Comments

This speaker accurately describes the problem and provides a clear recommendation (that the woman should go to the award ceremony right after her exam). She does spend some time providing a brief description of the two different solutions (which is not required), but because she is able to express herself efficiently, she still has plenty of time to provide and justify her recommendation. Her delivery is quite clear; although the listener can hear that her speech is accented, this does not make her difficult to understand. She makes use of complex grammatical structures to support her recommendation ("*I would go with the option that she should . . .*" and "*The reason I say so is that, as her friend mentions, that award ceremonies never start on time*"). Although she does make some minor errors ("*an philosophy exam*," "*secondly being*"), these do not prevent the listener from easily following her response.

Mid-level Response: Listen to Track 131.

Rater Comments

This speaker describes the problem and chooses a solution (that the girl talk with her professor in order to take the exam early or later). His solution is mostly clear, though at times issues with vocabulary and grammar make his message somewhat vague and difficult to understand. For example, he says, "*. . . it will be too risky if she get both of them at the same time.*" This statement would be clearer if he had said, "it would be too risky to take the exam when she needs to be at the award ceremony at the same time." The speaker does make effective use of some complex structures ("*If she did that—if she talked with her professor—I think she would . . .*") and his pronunciation is understandable without listener effort.

Question 6

Prompt

Using the points and examples from the talk, explain how substitute goods and complement goods influence demand for a particular product.

Important Points

In this item, you need to explain the ways the two kinds of goods—substitute goods and complement goods—have an effect on the demand for particular products. You should use the examples of butter and margarine and of CDs and CD players to help explain the effect. Substitute goods are products that are similar enough to be interchangeable, so the price of one will influence the demand for the other. For example, margarine and butter are substitute goods, so if the price goes up for butter, then the demand goes up for margarine, which can be used as a butter substitute. Complement goods are those in which two products can't be used without the other, so the price of one will influence the demand for both in the same way. For instance, compact discs (CDs) and CD players are complement goods. If the price of CDs goes up, the demand will go down not only for CDs, but also for CD players.

High-level Response: Listen to Track 132.

Rater Comments

The speaker does a good job of explaining the two kinds of goods and of using the examples to explain how they each affect the demand. It is easy to follow the organization of her ideas and her pronunciation is mostly quite clear. She mispronounces the words "*butter*" and "*margarine*," but it is still possible to understand her response. While her grammar contains some minor errors, in other areas she is able to use fairly difficult grammatical constructions easily, such as "*she stated an example . . . saying that if the price of the CD goes up, then the demands for both the CD and the CD players will go down.*" There are a few hesitations during her response as she pauses to consider what to say, but they do not interfere greatly with the flow of her response.

Mid-level Response: Listen to Track 133.

Rater Comments

The speaker does a fairly good job of explaining substitute goods and their effect on demand, but she runs out of time before she can finish talking about complement goods. She also never mentions the examples the professor gave. If she had not included an unnecessary introduction at the beginning—explaining that the professor is talking about economic theory in an economics class—she would have had a bit more time to finish discussing what the prompt required. Her speech also contains many hesitations, so listeners have to make an effort to follow her ideas. In addition, her response contains numerous minor grammatical errors, such as "*one goods,*" "*substitute of another,*" and "*the two good.*"

Writing Section

Prompts, Topic Notes, and Sample Responses with Rater Comments

Use the sample Integrated and Independent Writing Rubrics in Appendix A to see how responses are scored.

This section includes topic notes that are guides to the kind of information raters expect to read in a high-level response.

This section also refers to sample responses, which can be found on the accompanying DVD. These responses were scored at the highest level. The responses are followed by comments from certified ETS raters.

Question 1

Prompt

Summarize the points made in the lecture, being sure to explain how they respond to the specific arguments made in the reading passage.

Topic Notes

The reading discusses a painting has been identified as depicting a teenaged Jane Austen, but the lecturer presents three reasons that cast doubt on the reading's support of this:

resemblance between the Austen family members; specifically he names Mary, one of Jane's distant cousins.

Third, according to the passage the portrait was attributed to Humphrey. However, the lecture presents other evidence relating

Point made in the reading	Corresponding point from the lecture
Jane Austen's family members authorized the portrait for use in the 1882 edition of her letters.	Although Jane Austen's relatives did authorize the portrait in question for use with an edition of her letters, so much time had passed since Jane died that none of them would have actually seen the teenaged Jane.
There is a strong resemblance between Cassandra's sketch of Jane and the portrait.	The portrait could actually be of one of the many female relatives (for example, Mary Ann Campion) who may have resembled Jane, and who were teenagers at the time the portrait was painted.
Although we don't know who painted the portrait, its style is like that of a painter who was active at the same time the Austen family might have hired him to paint a teenaged Jane.	A date stamped on the canvas indicates that the canvas was sold by William Legg, who didn't begin selling canvas until Jane was older than the girl in the portrait.

Responses with scores of 4 and 5 typically discuss all three points in the table.

Sample Response

The lecture casts doubt and questions the evidence presented in the reading passage regarding a painting allegedly of Jane Austen.

First, about the family's recognition of the painting as that of Jane's as a teenager. The lecturer points out that in 1882, when the Austen family authorized the use of the painting as a portrait of Jane in the publication of her letters, Jane had been dead for 70 years. Hence, the family members who claimed this portrait to be of Jane's probably have never seen her, and don't necessarily know how she looked.

While the reading passage presents the resemblance of the face features to prove that the teenager in the portrait is indeed Jane, the lecturer sees otherwise: the teenager in the portrait could have been any cousin or niece of Jane. The lecturer claims that there was much to the date of the portrait based on the stamp on the canvas itself. According to the stamp it was sold by William Legg, who didn't sell canvas in London when Jane was a teenager. He only began selling canvas in London when Jane was 27 years old.

Rater Comments

This response earns a score of 5. It is a well organized response that successfully explains the opposing relationship between the reading and the lecture. The three main points from the lecture are clearly identified, and the writer has provided relevant details for each of those main points. One detail about the second point is presented with a minor inaccuracy – MaryAnn Campion is described by the lecturer as a niece, not a cousin, of Jane Austen – but overall the writer's coverage of this point is sufficient to achieve the highest score. The very few language errors in the response do not interfere with the clear presentation of the essential content from the reading and lecture.

Question 2

Prompt

Do you agree or disagree with the following statement?

It is better to have broad knowledge of many academic subjects than to specialize in one specific subject.

Use specific reasons and examples to support your answer.

Topic Notes

This topic requires that you compare two approaches to knowledge. For either approach you choose to write about, you should present and develop reasons for preferring this approach. As you do so, it may be helpful to identify the particular aspect or aspects of your life in which you think your choice would benefit you most; for example, if you indicate that it is better to specialize, you could explain that this will help you economically (for example, if you are studying to be a doctor and choose certain areas of specialization, you will probably make more money than if you were a general practitioner). By the same token, if you indicate that it is better to take broad knowledge, you could explain that this will help you be a well-rounded person who can enjoy exploring many interests. If you believe that broad knowledge and specialization are equally important, it might be helpful to explain how having broad knowledge will be very useful in certain aspects of your life, while having specialized knowledge will be very useful in other aspects of your life.

Sample Response

To answer this question it seems to be necessary to make clear, for what aspect of life the knowledge in general should be good. On the one hand you might think that knowledge should be useful for the success in your job or at school. On the other hand you maybe understand knowledge as a part of the human existence, that allows us to think critically and to reflect about our life which includes the whole environment surrounding us.

I want to respond the question from the second point of view. Knowledge has to be understood as much more than the ability to function in a special kind of business environment. Knowledge is the sum of all the theoretical facts and experiences a human being collects during his or her whole life. And from this position a knowledge as broad as possible must be accepted as the better alternative.

I think that it will become a very big problem in our society when we continue to concentrate the whole educational system – especially the schools – only on teaching specific subjects. Of course it is actually is very important for young people to have the right preparation for the business world. But as I already said, life must focus on much more than the economic aspect.

Even if you think that the preparation for the business world should be the main aspect of acquiring knowledge, you should still agree with the statement, because when you really analyse the requirements of work that are typical in our time, you will realize that the technologies and the methods change so quickly, that it would be a very big mistake to concentrate on a specific subject. You would always have the danger that if you concentrate on a specialized part of human knowledge, that part might become completely unimportant in the nearest future. Nowadays it seems to be useful to be able to program computers. Yet in some years computers might have the ability to program themselves.

When you have a broad knowledge than you will be able to handle all the new things that you might get confronted with. And you will not only be able to handle them – but you will have the possibility to fully understand them and take part in their development. Not only as a passive part but as a creator of your own future.

Rater Comments

The writer of this 5-level response argues in favor of having broad knowledge. The response begins by examining some different purposes of acquiring knowledge and identifies different areas or aspects of life in which we use knowledge, and then goes on to acknowledge that while acquiring specialized knowledge is useful for success at work or school, it is the other type of knowledge, broad knowledge, which is best to have. In the beginning of the response, this writer has associated this type of knowledge with critical thinking skills. The writer then goes on to argue that if we decide to pursue specialized knowledge, there is the risk that it may become obsolete. The response comes back to the idea of critical thinking skills being most valuable after the writer has presented a scenario about what would happen if somebody pursues the kind of knowledge that the writer is not coming out in favor of in this response. Although the concluding remark contains an error in structure, there are many instances of good facility with language use in the response.

TOEFL iBT Test 5

READING

This section measures your ability to understand academic passages in English.

There are three passages in the section. Give yourself 20 minutes to read each passage and answer the questions about it. The entire section will take 60 minutes to complete.

You may look back at a passage when answering the questions. You can skip questions and go back to them later as long as there is time remaining.

Directions: Read the passage. Then answer the questions. Give yourself 20 minutes to complete this practice set.

TYPES OF SOCIAL GROUPS

Life places us in a complex web of relationships with other people. Our humanness arises out of these relationships in the course of social interaction. Moreover, our humanness must be sustained through social interaction—and fairly constantly so. When an association continues long enough for two people to become linked together by a relatively stable set of expectations, it is called a relationship.

People are bound within relationships by two types of bonds: expressive ties and instrumental ties. Expressive ties are social links formed when we emotionally invest ourselves in and commit ourselves to other people. Through association with people who are meaningful to us, we achieve a sense of security, love, acceptance, companionship, and personal worth. Instrumental ties are social links formed when we cooperate with other people to achieve some goal. Occasionally, this may mean working with instead of against competitors. More often, we simply cooperate with others to reach some end without endowing the relationship with any larger significance.

Sociologists have built on the distinction between expressive and instrumental ties to distinguish between two types of groups: primary and secondary. A primary group involves two or more people who enjoy a direct, intimate, cohesive relationship with one another. Expressive ties predominate in primary groups; we view the people as ends in themselves and valuable in their own right. A secondary group entails two or more people who are involved in an impersonal relationship and have come together for a specific, practical purpose. Instrumental ties predominate in secondary groups; we perceive people as means to ends rather than as ends in their own right. Sometimes primary group relationships evolve out of secondary group relationships. This happens in many work settings. People on the job often develop close relationships with coworkers as they come to share gripes, jokes, gossip, and satisfactions.

A number of conditions enhance the likelihood that primary groups will arise. First, group size is important. We find it difficult to get to know people personally when they are milling about and dispersed in large groups. In small groups we have a better chance to initiate contact and establish rapport with them. Second, face-to-face contact allows us to size up others. Seeing and talking with one another in close physical proximity makes possible a subtle exchange of ideas and feelings. And third, the probability that we will develop primary group bonds increases as we have frequent and continuous contact. Our ties with people often deepen as we interact with them across time and gradually evolve interlocking habits and interests.

Primary groups are fundamental to us and to society. First, primary groups are critical to the socialization process. Within them, infants and children are introduced to the ways of their society. Such groups are the breeding grounds in which we acquire the norms and values that equip us for social life. Sociologists view primary groups as bridges between individuals and the larger society because they transmit, mediate, and interpret a society's cultural patterns and provide the sense of oneness so critical for social solidarity.

Second, primary groups are fundamental because they provide the settings in which we meet most of our personal needs. Within them, we experience companionship, love, security, and an overall sense of well-being. Not surprisingly, sociologists find that the strength of a group's primary ties has implications for the group's functioning. For example, the stronger the primary group ties of a sports team playing together, the better their record is.

Third, primary groups are fundamental because they serve as powerful instruments for social control. Their members command and dispense many of the rewards that are so vital to us and that make our lives seem worthwhile. Should the use of rewards fail, members can frequently win by rejecting or threatening to ostracize those who deviate from the primary group's norms. For instance, some social groups employ shunning (a person can remain in the community, but others are forbidden to interact with the person) as a device to bring into line individuals whose behavior goes beyond that allowed by the particular group. Even more important, primary groups define social reality for us by structuring our experiences. By providing us with definitions of situations, they elicit from us behavior that conforms to group-devised meanings. Primary groups, then, serve both as carriers of social norms and as enforcers of them.

Directions: Now answer the questions.

PARAGRAPH 1

Life places us in a complex web of relationships with other people. Our humanness arises out of these relationships in the course of social interaction. Moreover, our humanness must be sustained through social interaction—and fairly constantly so. When an association continues long enough for two people to become linked together by a relatively stable set of expectations, it is called a relationship.

1. The word "complex" in the passage is closest in meaning to

Ⓐ delicate
Ⓑ elaborate
Ⓒ private
Ⓓ common

2. According to paragraph 1, which of the following is true of a relationship?

Ⓐ It is a structure of associations with many people.
Ⓑ It should be studied in the course of a social interaction.
Ⓒ It places great demands on people.
Ⓓ It develops gradually over time.

PARAGRAPH 2

People are bound within relationships by two types of bonds: expressive ties and instrumental ties. Expressive ties are social links formed when we emotionally invest ourselves in and commit ourselves to other people. Through association with people who are meaningful to us, we achieve a sense of security, love, acceptance, companionship, and personal worth. Instrumental ties are social links formed when we cooperate with other people to achieve some goal. Occasionally, this may mean working with instead of against competitors. More often, we simply cooperate with others to reach some end without endowing the relationship with any larger significance.

3. The word "endowing" in the passage is closest in meaning to

   Ⓐ leaving
   Ⓑ exposing
   Ⓒ providing
   Ⓓ understanding

4. Which of the following can be inferred about instrumental ties from the author's mention of working with competitors in paragraph 2?

   Ⓐ Instrumental ties can develop even in situations in which people would normally not cooperate.
   Ⓑ Instrumental ties require as much emotional investment as expressive ties.
   Ⓒ Instrumental ties involve security, love, and acceptance.
   Ⓓ Instrumental ties should be expected to be significant.

PARAGRAPH 3

Sociologists have built on the distinction between expressive and instrumental ties to distinguish between two types of groups: primary and secondary. A primary group involves two or more people who enjoy a direct, intimate, cohesive relationship with one another. Expressive ties predominate in primary groups; we view the people as ends in themselves and valuable in their own right. A secondary group entails two or more people who are involved in an impersonal relationship and have come together for a specific, practical purpose. Instrumental ties predominate in secondary groups; we perceive people as means to ends rather than as ends in their own right. Sometimes primary group relationships evolve out of secondary group relationships. This happens in many work settings. People on the job often develop close relationships with coworkers as they come to share gripes, jokes, gossip, and satisfactions.

5. According to paragraph 3, what do sociologists see as the main difference between primary and secondary groups?

   Ⓐ Primary groups consist of people working together, while secondary groups exist outside of work settings.
   Ⓑ In primary groups people are seen as means, while in secondary groups people are seen as ends.
   Ⓒ Primary groups involve personal relationships, while secondary groups are mainly practical in purpose.
   Ⓓ Primary groups are generally small, while secondary groups often contain more than two people.

6. Which of the following can be inferred from the author's claim in paragraph 3 that primary group relationships sometimes evolve out of secondary group relationships?

   Ⓐ Secondary group relationships begin by being primary group relationships.
   Ⓑ A secondary group relationship that is highly visible quickly becomes a primary group relationship.
   Ⓒ Sociologists believe that only primary group relationships are important to society.
   Ⓓ Even in secondary groups, frequent communication serves to bring people into close relationships.

PARAGRAPH 4

A number of conditions enhance the likelihood that primary groups will arise. First, group size is important. We find it difficult to get to know people personally when they are milling about and dispersed in large groups. In small groups we have a better chance to initiate contact and establish rapport with them. Second, face-to-face contact allows us to size up others. Seeing and talking with one another in close physical proximity makes possible a subtle exchange of ideas and feelings. And third, the probability that we will develop primary group bonds increases as we have frequent and continuous contact. Our ties with people often deepen as we interact with them across time and gradually evolve interlocking habits and interests.

7. The phrase "size up" in the passage is closest in meaning to

   Ⓐ enlarge
   Ⓑ evaluate
   Ⓒ impress
   Ⓓ accept

PARAGRAPH 5

Primary groups are fundamental to us and to society. First, primary groups are critical to the socialization process. Within them, infants and children are introduced to the ways of their society. Such groups are the breeding grounds in which we acquire the norms and values that equip us for social life. Sociologists view primary groups as bridges between individuals and the larger society because they transmit, mediate, and interpret a society's cultural patterns and provide the sense of oneness so critical for social solidarity.

8. Which of the sentences below best expresses the essential information in the highlighted sentence in the passage? Incorrect choices change the meaning in important ways or leave out essential information.

   Ⓐ Sociologists think that cultural patterns establish connections between the individual and the larger society.
   Ⓑ Sociologists believe that individuals with a sense of oneness bridge the gap between society and primary groups.
   Ⓒ Sociologists think primary groups contribute to social solidarity because they help maintain a society's cultural patterns.
   Ⓓ Sociologists believe that the cultural patterns that provide social solidarity arise as bridges from primary groups.

PARAGRAPHS 1 2 3 4 5 6 & 7

Life places us in a complex web of relationships with other people. Our humanness arises out of these relationships in the course of social interaction. Moreover, our humanness must be sustained through social interaction—and fairly constantly so. When an association continues long enough for two people to become linked together by a relatively stable set of expectations, it is called a relationship.

People are bound within relationships by two types of bonds: expressive ties and instrumental ties. Expressive ties are social links formed when we emotionally invest ourselves in and commit ourselves to other people. Through association with people who are meaningful to us, we achieve a sense of security, love, acceptance, companionship, and personal worth. Instrumental ties are social links formed when we cooperate with other people to achieve some goal. Occasionally, this may mean working with instead of against competitors. More often, we simply cooperate with others to reach some end without endowing the relationship with any larger significance.

Sociologists have built on the distinction between expressive and instrumental ties to distinguish between two types of groups: primary and secondary. A primary group involves two or more people who enjoy a direct, intimate, cohesive relationship with one another. Expressive ties predominate in primary groups; we view the people as ends in themselves and valuable in their own right. A secondary group entails two or more people who are involved in an impersonal relationship and have come together for a specific, practical purpose. Instrumental ties predominate in secondary groups; we perceive people as means to ends rather than as ends in their own right. Sometimes primary group relationships evolve out of secondary group relationships. This happens in many work settings. People on the job often develop close relationships with coworkers as they come to share gripes, jokes, gossip, and satisfactions.

A number of conditions enhance the likelihood that primary groups will arise. First, group size is important. We find it difficult to get to know people personally when they are milling about and dispersed in large groups. In small groups we have a better chance to initiate contact and establish rapport with them. Second, face-to-face contact allows us to size up others. Seeing and talking with one another in close physical proximity makes possible a subtle exchange of ideas and feelings. And third, the probability that we will develop primary group bonds increases as we have frequent and continuous contact. Our ties with people often deepen as we interact with them across time and gradually evolve interlocking habits and interests.

Primary groups are fundamental to us and to society. First, primary groups are critical to the socialization process. Within them, infants and children are introduced to the ways of their society. Such groups are the breeding grounds in which we acquire the norms and values that equip us for social life. Sociologists view primary groups as bridges between individuals and the larger society because they transmit, mediate, and interpret a society's cultural patterns and provide the sense of oneness so critical for social solidarity.

Second, primary groups are fundamental because they provide the settings in which we meet most of our personal needs. Within them, we experience companionship, love, security, and an overall sense of well-being. Not surprisingly, sociologists find that the strength of a group's primary ties has implications for the group's functioning. For example, the stronger the primary group ties of a sports team playing together, the better their record is.

Third, primary groups are fundamental because they serve as powerful instruments for social control. Their members command and dispense many of the rewards that are so vital to us and that make our lives seem worthwhile. Should the use of rewards fail, members can frequently win by rejecting or threatening to ostracize those who deviate from the primary group's norms. For instance, some social groups employ shunning (a person can remain in the community, but others are forbidden to interact with the person) as a device to bring into line individuals whose behavior goes beyond that allowed by the particular group. Even more important, primary groups define social reality for us by structuring our experiences. By providing us with definitions of situations, they elicit from us behavior that conforms to group-devised meanings. Primary groups, then, serve both as carriers of social norms and as enforcers of them.

9. This passage is developed primarily by

Ⓐ drawing comparisons between theory and practice
Ⓑ presenting two opposing theories
Ⓒ defining important concepts and providing examples of them
Ⓓ discussing causes and their effects

PARAGRAPH 7

Third, primary groups are fundamental because they serve as powerful instruments for social control. Their members command and dispense many of the rewards that are so vital to us and that make our lives seem worthwhile. Should the use of rewards fail, members can frequently win by rejecting or threatening to ostracize those who deviate from the primary group's norms. For instance, some social groups employ shunning (a person can remain in the community, but others are forbidden to interact with the person) as a device to bring into line individuals whose behavior goes beyond that allowed by the particular group. Even more important, primary groups define social reality for us by structuring our experiences. By providing us with definitions of situations, they elicit from us behavior that conforms to group-devised meanings. Primary groups, then, serve both as carriers of social norms and as enforcers of them.

10. The word "deviate" in the passage is closest in meaning to

Ⓐ detract
Ⓑ advance
Ⓒ select
Ⓓ depart

11. According to paragraph 7, why would a social group use shunning?

Ⓐ To enforce practice of the kinds of behavior acceptable to the group
Ⓑ To discourage offending individuals from remaining in the group
Ⓒ To commend and reward the behavior of the other members of the group
Ⓓ To decide which behavioral norms should be passed on to the next generation

PARAGRAPH 6

Second, primary groups are fundamental because they provide the settings in which we meet most of our personal needs. **(A)** Within them, we experience companionship, love, security, and an overall sense of well-being. **(B)** Not surprisingly, sociologists find that the strength of a group's primary ties has implications for the group's functioning. **(C)** For example, the stronger the primary group ties of a sports team playing together, the better their record is. **(D)**

12. **Directions:** Look at the part of the passage that is displayed above. The letters **(A)**, **(B)**, **(C)**, and **(D)** indicate where the following sentence could be added.

    People who do not live alone, for example, tend to make healthier life choices and develop fewer pathologies than people who live by themselves.

    Where would the sentence best fit?

    Ⓐ Choice A
    Ⓑ Choice B
    Ⓒ Choice C
    Ⓓ Choice D

13. **Directions:** Complete the table below by selecting THREE answer choices that are characteristics of primary groups and TWO answer choices that are characteristics of secondary groups.

    Write your answer choices in the spaces where they belong. You can either write the letter of your answer choice or you can copy the sentence.

    Primary groups

    -
    -
    -

    Secondary groups

    -
    -

Answer Choices

[A] Developing socially acceptable behavior
[B] Working together against competitors
[C] Experiencing pressure from outside forces
[D] Viewing people as a means to an end
[E] Existing for practical purposes
[F] Providing meaning for life situations
[G] Involving close relationships

Directions: Read the passage. Then answer the questions. Give yourself 20 minutes to complete this practice set.

BIOLOGICAL CLOCKS

Survival and successful reproduction usually require the activities of animals to be coordinated with predictable events around them. Consequently, the timing and rhythms of biological functions must closely match periodic events like the solar day, the tides, the lunar cycle, and the seasons. The relations between animal activity and these periods, particularly for the daily rhythms, have been of such interest and importance that a huge amount of work has been done on them and the special research field of **chronobiology** has emerged. Normally, the constantly changing levels of an animal's activity—sleeping, feeding, moving, reproducing, metabolizing, and producing enzymes and hormones, for example—are well coordinated with environmental rhythms, but the key question is whether the animal's schedule is driven by external cues, such as sunrise or sunset, or is instead dependent somehow on internal timers that themselves generate the observed biological rhythms. Almost universally, biologists accept the idea that all eukaryotes (a category that includes most organisms except bacteria and certain algae) have internal clocks. By isolating organisms completely from external periodic cues, biologists learned that organisms have internal clocks. For instance, apparently normal daily periods of biological activity were maintained for about a week by the fungus *Neurospora* when it was intentionally isolated from all geophysical timing cues while orbiting in a space shuttle. The continuation of biological rhythms in an organism without external cues attests to its having an internal clock.

When crayfish are kept continuously in the dark, even for four to five months, their compound eyes continue to adjust on a daily schedule for daytime and nighttime vision. Horseshoe crabs kept in the dark continuously for a year were found to maintain a persistent rhythm of brain activity that similarly adapts their eyes on a daily schedule for bright or for weak light. Like almost all daily cycles of animals deprived of environmental cues, those measured for the horseshoe crabs in these conditions were not exactly 24 hours. Such a rhythm whose period is approximately—but not exactly—a day is called **circadian.** For different individual horseshoe crabs, the circadian period ranged from 22.2 to 25.5 hours. A particular animal typically maintains its own characteristic cycle duration with great precision for many days. Indeed, stability of the biological clock's period is one of its major features, even when the organism's environment is subjected to considerable changes in factors, such as temperature, that would be expected to affect biological activity strongly. Further evidence for persistent internal rhythms appears when the usual external cycles are shifted—either experimentally or by rapid east-west travel over great distances. Typically, the animal's daily internally generated cycle of activity continues without change. As a result, its activities are shifted relative to the external cycle of the new environment. The disorienting effects of this mismatch between external time cues and internal schedules may persist, like our jet lag, for several days or weeks until certain cues such as the daylight/darkness cycle reset the organism's clock to synchronize with the daily rhythm of the new environment.

Animals need natural periodic signals like sunrise to maintain a cycle whose period is precisely 24 hours. Such an external cue not only coordinates an animal's daily rhythms with particular features of the local solar day but also—because it normally does so day after day—seems to keep the internal clock's period close to that of Earth's rotation. Yet despite this synchronization of the period of the internal cycle, the animal's timer itself continues to have its own genetically built-in period close to, but different from, 24 hours. Without the external cue, the difference accumulates and so the internally regulated activities of the biological day drift continuously, like the tides, in relation to the solar day. This drift has been studied extensively in many animals and in biological activities ranging from the hatching of fruit fly eggs to wheel running by squirrels. Light has a predominating influence in setting the clock. Even a fifteen-minute burst of light in otherwise sustained darkness can reset an animal's circadian rhythm. Normally, internal rhythms are kept in step by regular environmental cycles. For instance, if a homing pigeon is to navigate with its Sun compass, its clock must be properly set by cues provided by the daylight/darkness cycle.

Directions: Now answer the questions.

PARAGRAPH 1

Survival and successful reproduction usually require the activities of animals to be coordinated with predictable events around them. Consequently, the timing and rhythms of biological functions must closely match periodic events like the solar day, the tides, the lunar cycle, and the seasons. The relations between animal activity and these periods, particularly for the daily rhythms, have been of such interest and importance that a huge amount of work has been done on them and the special research field of **chronobiology** has emerged. Normally, the constantly changing levels of an animal's activity—sleeping, feeding, moving, reproducing, metabolizing, and producing enzymes and hormones, for example—are well coordinated with environmental rhythms, but the key question is whether the animal's schedule is driven by external cues, such as sunrise or sunset, or is instead dependent somehow on internal timers that themselves generate the observed biological rhythms. Almost universally, biologists accept the idea that all eukaryotes (a category that includes most organisms except bacteria and certain algae) have internal clocks. By isolating organisms completely from external periodic cues, biologists learned that organisms have internal clocks. For instance, apparently normal daily periods of biological activity were maintained for about a week by the fungus *Neurospora* when it was intentionally isolated from all geophysical timing cues while orbiting in a space shuttle. The continuation of biological rhythms in an organism without external cues attests to its having an internal clock.

14. The word "Consequently" in the passage is closest in meaning to

Ⓐ Therefore
Ⓑ Additionally
Ⓒ Nevertheless
Ⓓ Moreover

15. In paragraph 1, the experiment on the fungus *Neurospora* is mentioned to illustrate

    Ⓐ the existence of weekly periods of activity as well as daily ones
    Ⓑ the finding of evidence that organisms have internal clocks
    Ⓒ the effect of space on the internal clocks of organisms
    Ⓓ the isolation of one part of an organism's cycle for study

16. According to paragraph 1, all the following are generally assumed to be true EXCEPT:

    Ⓐ It is important for animals' daily activities to be coordinated with recurring events in their environment.
    Ⓑ Eukaryotes have internal clocks.
    Ⓒ The relationship between biological function and environmental cycles is a topic of intense research.
    Ⓓ Animals' daily rhythms are more dependent on external cues than on internal clocks.

PARAGRAPH 2

When crayfish are kept continuously in the dark, even for four to five months, their compound eyes continue to adjust on a daily schedule for daytime and nighttime vision. Horseshoe crabs kept in the dark continuously for a year were found to maintain a persistent rhythm of brain activity that similarly adapts their eyes on a daily schedule for bright or for weak light. Like almost all daily cycles of animals deprived of environmental cues, those measured for the horseshoe crabs in these conditions were not exactly 24 hours. Such a rhythm whose period is approximately—but not exactly—a day is called **circadian.** For different individual horseshoe crabs, the circadian period ranged from 22.2 to 25.5 hours. A particular animal typically maintains its own characteristic cycle duration with great precision for many days. Indeed, stability of the biological clock's period is one of its major features, even when the organism's environment is subjected to considerable changes in factors, such as temperature, that would be expected to affect biological activity strongly. Further evidence for persistent internal rhythms appears when the usual external cycles are shifted—either experimentally or by rapid east-west travel over great distances. Typically, the animal's daily internally generated cycle of activity continues without change. As a result, its activities are shifted relative to the external cycle of the new environment. The disorienting effects of this mismatch between external time cues and internal schedules may persist, like our jet lag, for several days or weeks until certain cues such as the daylight/darkness cycle reset the organism's clock to synchronize with the daily rhythm of the new environment.

17. The word "persistent" in the passage is closest in meaning to

    Ⓐ adjusted
    Ⓑ strong
    Ⓒ enduring
    Ⓓ predicted

18. The word "duration" in the passage is closest in meaning to

Ⓐ length
Ⓑ feature
Ⓒ process
Ⓓ repetition

19. Which of the sentences below best expresses the essential information in the highlighted sentence in the passage? Incorrect choices change the meaning in important ways or leave out essential information.

Ⓐ Stability, a feature of the biological clock's period, depends on changeable factors such as temperature.
Ⓑ A major feature of the biological clock is that its period does not change despite significant changes in the environment.
Ⓒ A factor such as temperature is an important feature in the establishment of the biological clock's period.
Ⓓ Biological activity is not strongly affected by changes in temperature.

20. According to paragraph 2, which of the following is true about the circadian periods of animals deprived of environmental cues?

Ⓐ They have the same length as the daily activity cycles of animals that are not deprived of such cues.
Ⓑ They can vary significantly from day to day.
Ⓒ They are not the same for all members of a single species.
Ⓓ They become longer over time.

21. According to paragraph 2, what will an animal experience when its internal rhythms no longer correspond with the daily cycle of the environment?

Ⓐ Disorientation
Ⓑ Change in period of the internal rhythms
Ⓒ Complete reversal of day and night activities
Ⓓ Increased sensitivity to environmental factors

22. In paragraph 2, the author provides evidence for the role of biological clocks by

Ⓐ listing the daily activities of an animal's cycle: sleeping, feeding, moving, reproducing, metabolizing, and producing enzymes and hormones
Ⓑ describing the process of establishing the period of a biological clock
Ⓒ presenting cases in which an animal's daily schedule remained stable despite lack of environmental cues
Ⓓ contrasting animals whose daily schedules fluctuate with those of animals whose schedules are constant

23. In paragraph 2, why does the author mention that the period for different horseshoe crabs ranges from 22.2 to 25.5 hours?

Ⓐ To illustrate that an animal's internal clock seldom has a 24-hour cycle
Ⓑ To argue that different horseshoe crabs will shift from daytime to nighttime vision at different times
Ⓒ To illustrate the approximate range of the circadian rhythm of all animals
Ⓓ To support the idea that external cues are the only factors affecting an animal's periodic behavior

PARAGRAPH 3

Animals need natural periodic signals like sunrise to maintain a cycle whose period is precisely 24 hours. Such an external cue not only coordinates an animal's daily rhythms with particular features of the local solar day but also—because it normally does so day after day—seems to keep the internal clock's period close to that of Earth's rotation. Yet despite this synchronization of the period of the internal cycle, the animal's timer itself continues to have its own genetically built-in period close to, but different from, 24 hours. Without the external cue, the difference accumulates and so the internally regulated activities of the biological day drift continuously, like the tides, in relation to the solar day. This drift has been studied extensively in many animals and in biological activities ranging from the hatching of fruit fly eggs to wheel running by squirrels. Light has a predominating influence in setting the clock. Even a fifteen-minute burst of light in otherwise sustained darkness can reset an animal's circadian rhythm. Normally, internal rhythms are kept in step by regular environmental cycles. For instance, if a homing pigeon is to navigate with its Sun compass, its clock must be properly set by cues provided by the daylight/darkness cycle.

24. The word "it" in the passage refers to

Ⓐ an external cue such as sunrise
Ⓑ the daily rhythm of an animal
Ⓒ the local solar day
Ⓓ a cycle whose period is precisely 24 hours

25. The word "sustained" in the passage is closest in meaning to

Ⓐ intense
Ⓑ uninterrupted
Ⓒ natural
Ⓓ periodic

PARAGRAPH 3

Animals need natural periodic signals like sunrise to maintain a cycle whose period is precisely 24 hours. **(A)** Such an external cue not only coordinates an animal's daily rhythms with particular features of the local solar day but also—because it normally does so day after day—seems to keep the internal clock's period close to that of Earth's rotation. **(B)** Yet despite this synchronization of the period of the internal cycle, the animal's timer itself continues to have its own genetically built-in period close to, but different from, 24 hours. **(C)** Without the external cue, the difference accumulates and so the internally regulated activities of the biological day drift continuously, like the tides, in relation to the solar day. **(D)** This drift has been studied extensively in many animals and in biological activities ranging from the hatching of fruit fly eggs to wheel running by squirrels. Light has a predominating influence in setting the clock. Even a fifteen-minute burst of light in otherwise sustained darkness can reset an animal's circadian rhythm. Normally, internal rhythms are kept in step by regular environmental cycles. For instance, if a homing pigeon is to navigate with its Sun compass, its clock must be properly set by cues provided by the daylight/darkness cycle.

26. **Directions:** Look at the part of the passage that is displayed above. The letters **(A)**, **(B)**, **(C)**, and **(D)** indicate where the following sentence could be added.

    Because the internal signals that regulate waking and going to sleep tend to align themselves with these external cues, the external clock appears to dominate the internal clock.

    Where would the sentence best fit?

    Ⓐ Choice A
    Ⓑ Choice B
    Ⓒ Choice C
    Ⓓ Choice D

27. **Directions:** An introductory sentence for a brief summary of the passage is provided below. Complete the summary by selecting the THREE answer choices that express the most important ideas in the passage. Some sentences do not belong in the summary because they express ideas that are not presented in the passage or are minor ideas in the passage.

    Write your answer choices in the spaces where they belong. You can either write the letter of your answer choice or you can copy the sentence.

    The activity of animals is usually coordinated with periodically recurring events in the environment.

    •

    •

    •

Answer Choices

[A] Most animals survive and reproduce successfully without coordinating their activities to external environmental rhythms.

[B] Animals have internal clocks that influence their activities even when environmental cues are absent.

[C] The circadian period of an animal's internal clock may vary slightly for different individuals but is generally quite stable for any one individual.

[D] Animals are less affected by large differences between their internal rhythms and the local solar day than are humans.

[E] Environmental cues such as a change in temperature are enough to reset an animal's clock.

[F] Because an animal's internal clock does not operate on a 24-hour cycle, environmental stimuli are needed to keep the biological day aligned with the solar day.

Directions: Read the passage. Then answer the questions. Give yourself 20 minutes to complete this practice set.

METHODS OF STUDYING INFANT PERCEPTION

In the study of perceptual abilities of infants, a number of techniques are used to determine infants' responses to various stimuli. Because they cannot verbalize or fill out questionnaires, indirect techniques of naturalistic observation are used as the primary means of determining what infants can see, hear, feel, and so forth. Each of these methods compares an infant's state prior to the introduction of a stimulus with its state during or immediately following the stimulus. The difference between the two measures provides the researcher with an indication of the level and duration of the response to the stimulus. For example, if a uniformly moving pattern of some sort is passed across the visual field of a neonate (newborn), repetitive following movements of the eye occur. The occurrence of these eye movements provides evidence that the moving pattern is perceived at some level by the newborn. Similarly, changes in the infant's general level of motor activity—turning the head, blinking the eyes, crying, and so forth—have been used by researchers as visual indicators of the infant's perceptual abilities.

Such techniques, however, have limitations. First, the observation may be unreliable in that two or more observers may not agree that the particular response occurred, or to what degree it occurred. Second, responses are difficult to quantify. Often the rapid and diffuse movements of the infant make it difficult to get an accurate record of the number of responses. The third, and most potent, limitation is that it is not possible to be certain that the infant's response was due to the stimulus presented or to a change from no stimulus to a stimulus. The infant may be responding to aspects of the stimulus different than those identified by the investigator. Therefore, when observational assessment is used as a technique for studying infant perceptual abilities, care must be taken not to overgeneralize from the data or to rely on one or two studies as conclusive evidence of a particular perceptual ability of the infant.

Observational assessment techniques have become much more sophisticated, reducing the limitations just presented. Film analysis of the infant's responses, heart and respiration rate monitors, and nonnutritive sucking devices are used as effective tools in understanding infant perception. Film analysis permits researchers to carefully study the infant's responses over and over and in slow motion. Precise measurements can be made of the length and frequency of the infant's attention between two stimuli. Heart and respiration monitors provide the investigator with the number of heartbeats or breaths taken when a new stimulus is presented. Numerical increases are used as quantifiable indicators of heightened interest in the new stimulus. Increases in nonnutritive sucking were first used as an assessment measure by researchers in 1969. They devised an apparatus that connected a baby's pacifier[1] to a counting device. As stimuli were presented, changes in the infant's sucking behavior were recorded. Increases in the number of sucks were used as an indicator of the infant's attention to or preference for a given visual display.

Two additional techniques of studying infant perception have come into vogue. The first is the habituation-dishabituation technique, in which a single stimulus is presented repeatedly to the infant until there is a measurable decline (habituation) in whatever attending behavior is being observed. At that point a new stimulus is presented, and any recovery (dishabituation) in responsiveness is recorded. If the infant fails to dishabituate and continues to show habituation with the new stimulus, it is assumed that the baby is unable to perceive the new stimulus as different. The habituation-dishabituation paradigm has been used most extensively with studies of auditory and olfactory perception in infants. The second technique relies on evoked potentials, which are electrical brain responses that may be related to a particular stimulus because of where they originate. Changes in the electrical pattern of the brain indicate that the stimulus is getting through to the infant's central nervous system and eliciting some form of response.

Each of the preceding techniques provides the researcher with evidence that the infant can detect or discriminate between stimuli. With these sophisticated observational assessment and electro physiological measures, we know that the neonate of only a few days is far more perceptive than previously suspected. However, these measures are only "indirect" indicators of the infant's perceptual abilities.

pacifier[1]: a small plastic device for babies to suck or bite on

Directions: Now answer the questions.

PARAGRAPH 1

In the study of perceptual abilities of infants, a number of techniques are used to determine infants' responses to various stimuli. Because they cannot verbalize or fill out questionnaires, indirect techniques of naturalistic observation are used as the primary means of determining what infants can see, hear, feel, and so forth. Each of these methods compares an infant's state prior to the introduction of a stimulus with its state during or immediately following the stimulus. The difference between the two measures provides the researcher with an indication of the level and duration of the response to the stimulus. For example, if a uniformly moving pattern of some sort is passed across the visual field of a neonate (newborn), repetitive following movements of the eye occur. The occurrence of these eye movements provides evidence that the moving pattern is perceived at some level by the newborn. Similarly, changes in the infant's general level of motor activity—turning the head, blinking the eyes, crying, and so forth—have been used by researchers as visual indicators of the infant's perceptual abilities.

28. The word "uniformly" in the passage is closest in meaning to

Ⓐ clearly
Ⓑ quickly
Ⓒ consistently
Ⓓ occasionally

29. Paragraph 1 indicates that researchers use indirect methods primarily to observe the

Ⓐ range of motor activity in neonates
Ⓑ frequency and duration of various stimuli
Ⓒ change in an infant's state following the introduction of a stimulus
Ⓓ range of an infant's visual field

30. Why does the author mention "repetitive following movements of the eye"?

Ⓐ To identify a response that indicates a neonate's perception of a stimulus
Ⓑ To explain why a neonate is capable of responding to stimuli only through repetitive movements
Ⓒ To argue that motor activity in a neonate may be random and unrelated to stimuli
Ⓓ To emphasize that responses to stimuli vary in infants according to age

PARAGRAPH 2

Such techniques, however, have limitations. First, the observation may be unreliable in that two or more observers may not agree that the particular response occurred, or to what degree it occurred. Second, responses are difficult to quantify. Often the rapid and diffuse movements of the infant make it difficult to get an accurate record of the number of responses. The third, and most potent, limitation is that it is not possible to be certain that the infant's response was due to the stimulus presented or to a change from no stimulus to a stimulus. The infant may be responding to aspects of the stimulus different than those identified by the investigator. Therefore, when observational assessment is used as a technique for studying infant perceptual abilities, care must be taken not to overgeneralize from the data or to rely on one or two studies as conclusive evidence of a particular perceptual ability of the infant.

31. Which of the following is NOT mentioned in paragraph 2 as a problem in using the technique of direct observation?

Ⓐ It is impossible to be certain of the actual cause of an infant's response.
Ⓑ Infants' responses, which occur quickly and diffusely, are often difficult to measure.
Ⓒ Infants do not respond well to stimuli presented in an unnatural laboratory setting.
Ⓓ It may be difficult for observers to agree on the presence or the degree of a response.

32. The word "potent" in the passage is closest in meaning to

Ⓐ artificial
Ⓑ powerful
Ⓒ common
Ⓓ similar

33. Which of the sentences below best expresses the essential information in the highlighted sentence in the passage? Incorrect choices change the meaning in important ways or leave out essential information.

    Ⓐ Researchers using observational assessment techniques on infants must not overgeneralize and must base their conclusions on data from many studies.
    Ⓑ On the basis of the data from one or two studies, it seems that some infants develop a particular perceptual ability not observed in others.
    Ⓒ To use data from one or two studies on infants' perceptual abilities, it is necessary to use techniques that will provide conclusive evidence.
    Ⓓ When researchers fail to make generalizations from their studies, their observed data is often inconclusive.

PARAGRAPH 3

Observational assessment techniques have become much more sophisticated, reducing the limitations just presented. Film analysis of the infant's responses, heart and respiration rate monitors, and nonnutritive sucking devices are used as effective tools in understanding infant perception. Film analysis permits researchers to carefully study the infant's responses over and over and in slow motion. Precise measurements can be made of the length and frequency of the infant's attention between two stimuli. Heart and respiration monitors provide the investigator with the number of heartbeats or breaths taken when a new stimulus is presented. Numerical increases are used as quantifiable indicators of heightened interest in the new stimulus. Increases in nonnutritive sucking were first used as an assessment measure by researchers in 1969. They devised an apparatus that connected a baby's pacifier to a counting device. As stimuli were presented, changes in the infant's sucking behavior were recorded. Increases in the number of sucks were used as an indicator of the infant's attention to or preference for a given visual display.

34. What is the author's primary purpose in paragraph 3?

    Ⓐ To explain why researchers must conduct more than one type of study when they are attempting to understand infant perception
    Ⓑ To describe new techniques for observing infant perception that overcome problems identified in the previous paragraph
    Ⓒ To present and evaluate the conclusions of various studies on infant perception
    Ⓓ To point out the strengths and weaknesses of three new methods for quantifying an infant's reaction to stimuli

35. The word "quantifiable" in the passage is closest in meaning to

    Ⓐ visual
    Ⓑ permanent
    Ⓒ meaningful
    Ⓓ measurable

36. Paragraph 3 mentions all of the following as indications of an infant's heightened interest in a new stimulus EXCEPT an increase in

Ⓐ sucking behavior
Ⓑ heart rate
Ⓒ the number of breaths taken
Ⓓ eye movements

PARAGRAPH 4

Two additional techniques of studying infant perception have come into vogue. The first is the habituation-dishabituation technique, in which a single stimulus is presented repeatedly to the infant until there is a measurable decline (habituation) in whatever attending behavior is being observed. At that point a new stimulus is presented, and any recovery (dishabituation) in responsiveness is recorded. If the infant fails to dishabituate and continues to show habituation with the new stimulus, it is assumed that the baby is unable to perceive the new stimulus as different. The habituation-dishabituation paradigm has been used most extensively with studies of auditory and olfactory perception in infants. The second technique relies on evoked potentials, which are electrical brain responses that may be related to a particular stimulus because of where they originate. Changes in the electrical pattern of the brain indicate that the stimulus is getting through to the infant's central nervous system and eliciting some form of response.

37. According to paragraph 4, which of the following leads to the conclusion that infants are able to differentiate between stimuli in a habituation-dishabituation study?

Ⓐ Dishabituation occurs with the introduction of a new stimulus.
Ⓑ Electrical responses in the infant's brain decline with each new stimulus.
Ⓒ Habituation is continued with the introduction of a new stimulus.
Ⓓ The infant displays little change in electrical brain responses.

38. In paragraph 4, what does the author suggest about the way an infant's brain perceives stimuli?

Ⓐ An infant's potential to respond to a stimulus may be related to the size of its brain.
Ⓑ Changes in the electrical patterns of an infant's brain are difficult to detect.
Ⓒ Different areas of an infant's brain respond to different types of stimuli.
Ⓓ An infant is unable to perceive more than one stimulus at a time.

PARAGRAPH 5

Each of the preceding techniques provides the researcher with evidence that the infant can detect or discriminate between stimuli. With these sophisticated observational assessment and electro physiological measures, we know that the neonate of only a few days is far more perceptive than previously suspected. However, these measures are only "indirect" indicators of the infant's perceptual abilities.

39. Paragraph 5 indicates that researchers who used the techniques described in the passage discovered that

    Ⓐ infants find it difficult to perceive some types of stimuli
    Ⓑ neonates of only a few days cannot yet discriminate between stimuli
    Ⓒ observational assessment is less useful for studying infant perception than researchers previously believed
    Ⓓ a neonate is able to perceive stimuli better than researchers once thought

PARAGRAPH 3

Observational assessment techniques have become much more sophisticated, reducing the limitations just presented. Film analysis of the infant's responses, heart and respiration rate monitors, and nonnutritive sucking devices are used as effective tools in understanding infant perception. **(A)** Film analysis permits researchers to carefully study the infant's responses over and over and in slow motion. **(B)** Precise measurements can be made of the length and frequency of the infant's attention between two stimuli. **(C)** Heart and respiration monitors provide the investigator with the number of heartbeats or breaths taken when a new stimulus is presented. **(D)** Numerical increases are used as quantifiable indicators of heightened interest in the new stimulus. Increases in nonnutritive sucking were first used as an assessment measure by researchers in 1969. They devised an apparatus that connected a baby's pacifier to a counting device. As stimuli were presented, changes in the infant's sucking behavior were recorded. Increases in the number of sucks were used as an indicator of the infant's attention to or preference for a given visual display.

40. **Directions:** Look at the part of the passage that is displayed above. The letters **(A)**, **(B)**, **(C)**, and **(D)** indicate where the following sentence could be added.

    The repetition allows researchers to observe the infant's behavior until they reach agreement about the presence and the degree of the infant's response.

    Where would the sentence best fit?

    Ⓐ Choice A
    Ⓑ Choice B
    Ⓒ Choice C
    Ⓓ Choice D

41. **Directions:** An introductory sentence for a brief summary of the passage is provided below. Complete the summary by selecting the THREE answer choices that express the most important ideas in the passage. Some sentences do not belong in the summary because they express ideas that are not presented in the passage or are minor ideas in the passage.

    Write your answer choices in the spaces where they belong. You can either write the letter of your answer choice or you can copy the sentence.

Researchers use a number of techniques to determine how infants respond to changes in their environment.

-
-
-

Answer Choices

[A] Data from observational methods must be confirmed through multiple studies.

[B] Visual indicators such as turning the head, blinking the eyes, or crying remain the best evidence of an infant's perceptual abilities.

[C] New techniques for studying infant perception have improved the accuracy with which researchers observe and quantify infant responses.

[D] Pacifiers are commonly used in studies to calm an infant who has been presented with excessive stimuli.

[E] Indirect observation is most accurate when researchers use it to test auditory and olfactory perception in neonates.

[F] Sophisticated techniques that have aided new discoveries about perception in the neonate continue to be indirect measures.

LISTENING

This section measures your ability to understand conversations and lectures in English.

Listen to each conversation and lecture only one time. After each conversation and lecture, you will answer some questions about it. Answer each question based on what is stated or implied by the speakers.

You may take notes while you listen and use your notes to help you answer the questions. Your notes will not be scored.

Answer each question before moving on. Do not return to previous questions.

It will take about 60 minutes to listen to the conversations and lectures and answer the questions about them.

Directions: Listen to Track 134.

Directions: Now answer the questions.

1. Why does the student go to see the professor?
   Ⓐ To report on the research he has done
   Ⓑ To ask for permission to observe a class
   Ⓒ To get help understanding an assignment
   Ⓓ To ask about a question on a recent test

2. According to the professor, what should the student do after completing the first observation?
   Ⓐ Look for another child to observe
   Ⓑ Research the child's developmental stage
   Ⓒ Report his progress to the class
   Ⓓ Submit the notes he took during the observation

3. Why does the student mention a child playing with a toy car?
   Ⓐ To identify a behavior that would show a child's imagination developing
   Ⓑ To identify a behavior that might illustrate egocentric thinking
   Ⓒ To give an example of a behavior he has observed
   Ⓓ To give an example of a behavior he would not need to describe

4. Why should the student contact the education department secretary?
   Ⓐ Her child attends a school run by the university.
   Ⓑ She has a list of families that might be able to help the man.
   Ⓒ She can contact students who have worked on a similar project.
   Ⓓ She will explain how to observe a class without disturbing it.

5. Listen to Track 135.

Ⓐ The man's paper has a strong introduction.
Ⓑ The man has already started his research project.
Ⓒ The assignment cannot be submitted late.
Ⓓ The man does not fully understand the assignment.

Directions: Listen to Track 136.

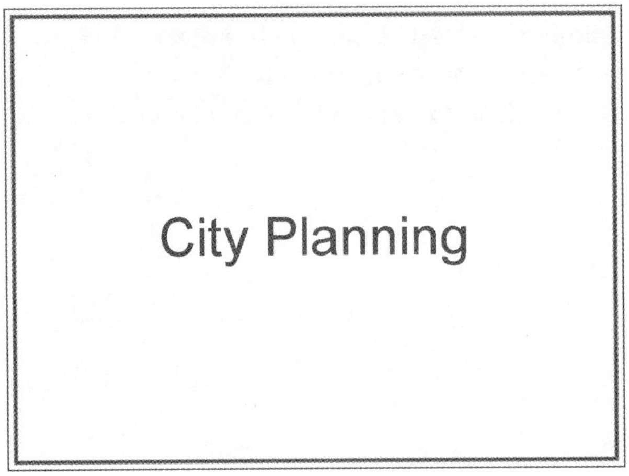

Directions: Now answer the questions.

6. What is the main topic of the lecture?

   (A) How the first pedestrian mall was developed
   (B) How pedestrian malls have affected business in America
   (C) Key considerations in creating a pedestrian mall
   (D) Ways that cities can better use pedestrian malls

7. According to the professor, what is the basic reason for building pedestrian malls in the city center?

   (A) To increase retail activity in the area
   (B) To reduce the noise made by automobile traffic
   (C) To increase shopping conveniences for city residents
   (D) To encourage people to move from the suburbs back into the city center

8. What are two aspects of location that need to be considered when planning a pedestrian mall? *Choose 2 answers.*

   [A] The proximity to the customer base
   [B] The number of nearby tourist sites
   [C] The variety of restaurants in the area
   [D] The access to public transportation

9. Why does the professor explain the design of a pedestrian mall?

   (A) To illustrate its importance to the success of a pedestrian mall
   (B) To explain why pedestrian malls are so appealing to shoppers
   (C) To point out how a pedestrian mall looks different from other malls
   (D) To show how the design is more important than the location

10. Why does the professor mention the Louisville, Kentucky, pedestrian mall?

Ⓐ To discuss her favorite pedestrian mall to visit
Ⓑ To illustrate how a pedestrian mall can overcome financial difficulties
Ⓒ To give an example of a typical American pedestrian mall
Ⓓ To show how poor planning can affect the success of a pedestrian mall

11. Listen to Track 137.

Ⓐ Art is of little importance in designing a pedestrian mall.
Ⓑ There should be a wide variety of art on display in pedestrian malls.
Ⓒ Art is a key feature in the designing of a pedestrian mall.
Ⓓ Most pedestrian mall designers do not like art as much as she does.

Directions: Listen to Track 138.

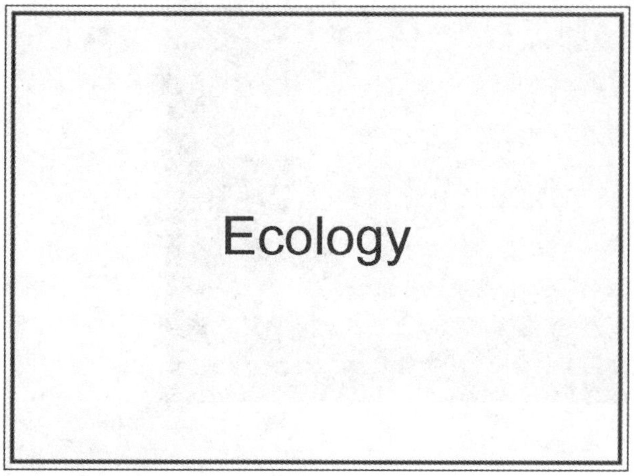

Directions: Now answer the questions.

12. What is the class mainly discussing?

Ⓐ How beavers select the ecosystems where they live
Ⓑ How ecosystems differ from one another
Ⓒ The impact of human activities on an ecosystem
Ⓓ The role of one species in an ecosystem

13. Why does the professor interrupt the student when he first mentions European settlement in North America?

Ⓐ She had already mentioned that point.
Ⓑ She thinks the information he gave is unrelated to the topic.
Ⓒ She prefers to present the information in the lecture in a specific order.
Ⓓ She questions the accuracy of his point.

14. What does the professor say about still water and swiftly flowing water?

Ⓐ Beavers cannot adapt to living near swiftly flowing water.
Ⓑ Still water and swiftly flowing water support similar ecosystems.
Ⓒ Still water supports more life than swiftly flowing water.
Ⓓ Wetland areas include large quantities of swiftly flowing water.

15. According to the professor, what was the impact of the extensive hunting of beavers in North America?

Ⓐ It led to a decrease in the number of wetlands.
Ⓑ It led to a decrease in the number of swiftly flowing streams.
Ⓒ It led to an increase in the number of other animal species in the wetlands.
Ⓓ It led to an increase in the amount of groundwater.

16. Listen to Track 139.

Ⓐ To point out that some terms have different meanings in other fields
Ⓑ To indicate that she is not going to explain the term
Ⓒ To defend a point she made earlier about ecosystems
Ⓓ To clarify a term used in biology

17. Listen to Track 140.

Ⓐ Beaver dams would cause floods in many areas where people now live.
Ⓑ Beaver dams would cause most of the water supply to be inaccessible.
Ⓒ Large areas of land would become unusable by humans.
Ⓓ More groundwater would be available for human consumption.

Directions: Listen to Track 141.

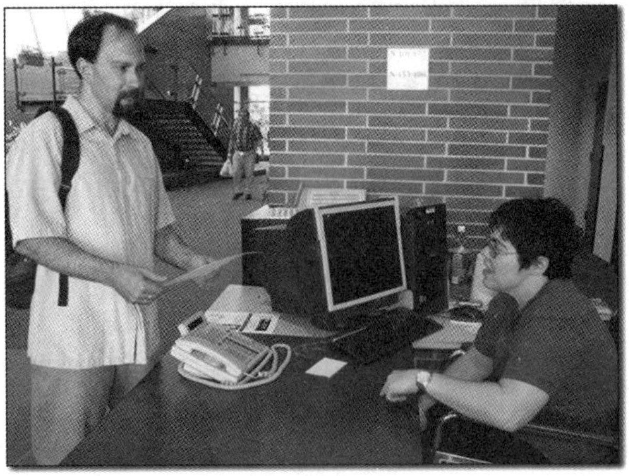

Directions: Now answer the questions.

18. What are the speakers mainly discussing?

    Ⓐ How to use the language lab
    Ⓑ How to make a video for class
    Ⓒ How to reserve a study room in the library
    Ⓓ How to improve study habits

19. How is the language lab different from the library?

    Ⓐ The language lab closes much earlier than the library does.
    Ⓑ More students go to the library after dinner than to the language lab.
    Ⓒ Students cannot remove educational materials from the language lab.
    Ⓓ There are more rooms where students can work in groups in the library.

20. When can students reserve a room in the language lab? *Choose 2 answers.*

    [A] When they arrive at the lab
    [B] After their professor signs a certain form
    [C] When all the members of a study group have signed in
    [D] The day before they want to use a room

21. What will the student probably do next?

    Ⓐ Ask a classmate to watch a video with him
    Ⓑ Sign out a Spanish video
    Ⓒ Find out when the video he needs will be available
    Ⓓ Buy a copy of the video series

22. Listen to Track 142.

Ⓐ She confused the man for another student who had visited the lab earlier in the day.
Ⓑ The man is mistaken about how many videos are in the series.
Ⓒ The language lab does not own the whole series of videos the man needs.
Ⓓ The man is not familiar with the procedures used at the language lab.

Directions: Listen to Track 143.

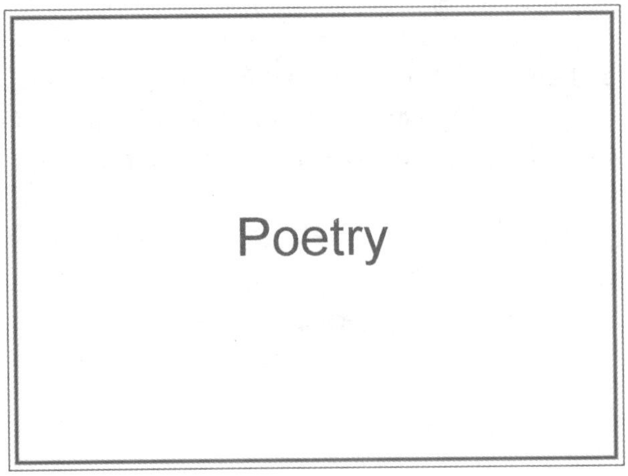

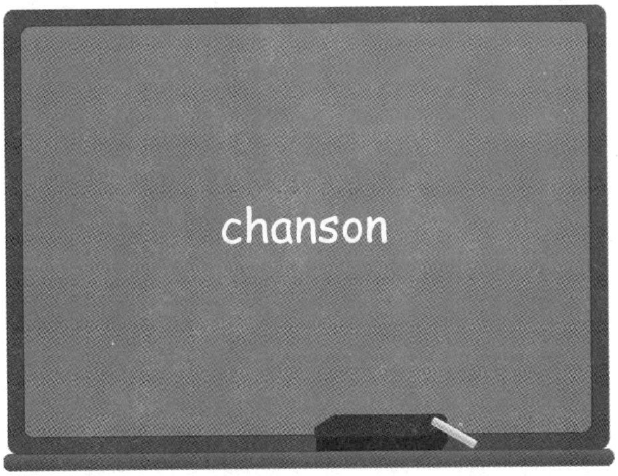

Directions: Now answer the questions.

23. What is the main purpose of the talk?

    Ⓐ To investigate the information known about the troubadours
    Ⓑ To explain the role of patriotic poetry during medieval times
    Ⓒ To explain why opinions about knights changed during the medieval period
    Ⓓ To compare two different types of medieval poems

24. According to the professor, who was the intended audience for chanson poetry? *Choose 2 answers.*

    [A] Lords
    [B] Ladies
    [C] Knights
    [D] Troubadours

25. According to the professor, what is true about the hero in chanson poetry and the hero in romance poetry? *Put a check (✓) in the correct boxes.*

	Chanson Hero	Romance Hero
Is admired for loyalty to country		
Engages in conflict for adventure		
Is willing to face extreme dangers to protect the lord		
Is concerned with individual improvement		

26. Why does the professor mention that romance poems often included biographical sketches?

Ⓐ To emphasize the similarities between chanson authors and romance authors
Ⓑ To explain why the social status of troubadours is known today
Ⓒ To point out why the biographical sketches are reliable sources of information
Ⓓ To provide evidence that many troubadours were also historians

27. What does the professor say about the political climate during the time troubadours were writing poetry?

Ⓐ It enabled chanson poetry to gain wide popularity over romance poetry.
Ⓑ It gave the troubadours time to devote themselves to writing poetry.
Ⓒ It inspired troubadours to write poetry that described their lord's deeds.
Ⓓ It made it difficult for troubadours to travel safely within their country.

28. Listen to Track 144. 

Ⓐ To indicate that he understands why the student may be confused
Ⓑ To emphasize that the student has asked a very important question
Ⓒ To remind the student that she may know the answer to her own question
Ⓓ To invite other members of the class to answer the question

Directions: Listen to Track 145.

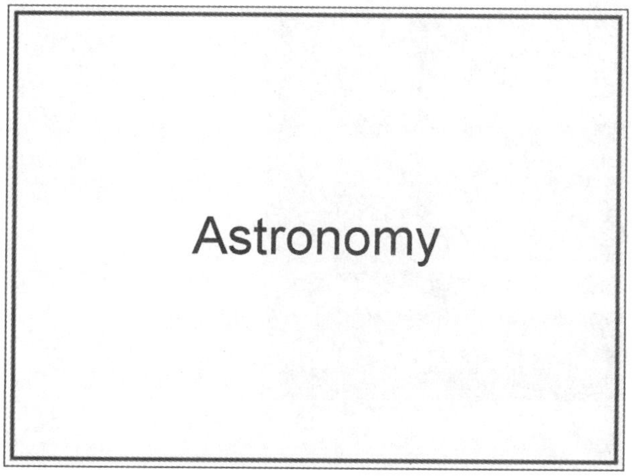

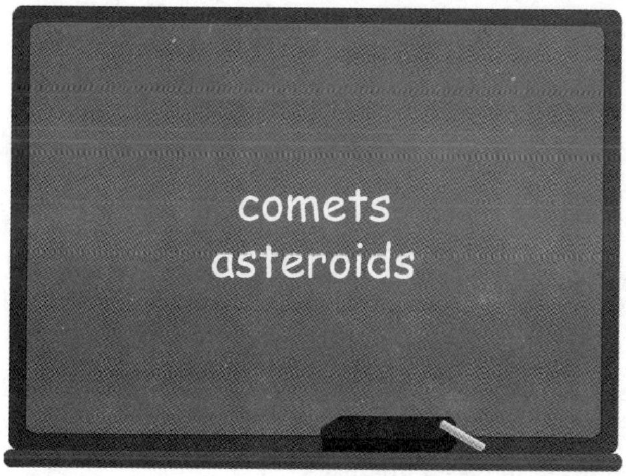

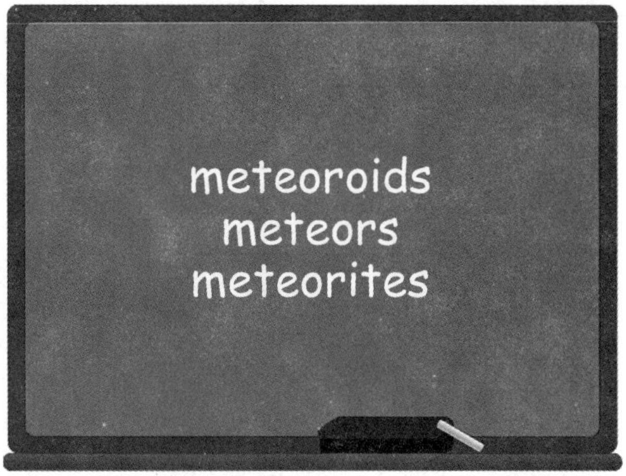

Directions: Now answer the questions.

29. What is the main topic of the lecture?

    Ⓐ The major differences between meteors and meteorites
    Ⓑ The origins of comets and asteroids
    Ⓒ The nature and origin of meteorites
    Ⓓ The similarities between objects in the inner solar system

30. What comparison does the professor make to help describe the composition of asteroids and comets?

    Ⓐ He compares them to stars.
    Ⓑ He compares them to types of planets.
    Ⓒ He compares them to rocks on Earth.
    Ⓓ He compares them to meteors and meteorites.

31. What does the professor say about the origin of meteors and meteorites?

Ⓐ They are pieces of asteroids or comets.
Ⓑ They are pieces of the planets in our solar system.
Ⓒ They are made from minerals that are otherwise uncommon in our solar system.
Ⓓ Their origin cannot be determined.

32. According to the professor, what feature of a meteoroid generally determines whether the meteoroid becomes a meteorite?

Ⓐ Whether it was originally part of a larger meteoroid
Ⓑ Whether it originated in the inner or outer solar system
Ⓒ What proportion of iron and stone it contains
Ⓓ How large it is when it enters Earth's atmosphere

33. What are two points the professor makes about stone meteorites? *Choose 2 answers.*

[A] They are the type of meteorite that most commonly falls to the ground.
[B] They are the type of meteorite most often seen in museums.
[C] They are the oldest type of meteorite found on the ground.
[D] They are the most difficult type of meteorite to find on the ground.

34. Listen to Track 146.

Ⓐ To offer a hint about the answer to a question he asked
Ⓑ To clarify a question that a student asked
Ⓒ To find out whether students understand a question he asked
Ⓓ To find out whether students understand an important comparison he made

SPEAKING

This section measures your ability to speak in English about a variety of topics.

There are six questions in this section. For each question, you will be given a short time to prepare your response. When the preparation time is up, answer the question as completely as possible in the time indicated for that question. You should record your responses so that you can review them later and compare them with the answer key and scoring rubrics.

Directions: You will now be asked to speak about a familiar topic. Give yourself 15 seconds to prepare your response. Then record yourself speaking for 45 seconds.

1. Listen to Track 147.

Talk about a game, sport or other group activity that is played in your country. Explain why you think the activity is enjoyable.

Preparation Time: 15 seconds
Response Time: 45 seconds

Directions: You will now be asked to give your opinion about a familiar topic. Give yourself 15 seconds to prepare your response. Then record yourself speaking for 45 seconds.

2. Listen to Track 148.

When looking for information for a research project, some students prefer to get their information mainly from the Internet. Others prefer to mainly use printed materials such as books and academic journals. Which do you prefer, and why?

Preparation Time: 15 seconds
Response Time: 45 seconds

Directions: You will now read a short passage and listen to a conversation on the same topic. You will then be asked a question about them. After you hear the question, give yourself 30 seconds to prepare your response. Then record yourself speaking for 60 seconds.

Listen to Track 149.

Reading Time: 45 seconds

New Stadium

A university official announced plans to spend $2 million to build a new athletic stadium, commenting that a new stadium would help the university achieve its goal of attracting more top students. The official also said that, additionally, building a new stadium would allow the university to strengthen its relationship with the town since a new and larger stadium would have the space to seat not only students, parents, and alumni, but members of the local community as well.

Listen to Track 150.

3. The woman expresses her opinion about the university's plan. State her opinion and explain the reasons she gives for holding that opinion.

Preparation Time: 30 seconds

Response Time: 60 seconds

Directions: You will now read a short passage and listen to a lecture on the same topic. You will then be asked a question about them. After you hear the question, give yourself 30 seconds to prepare your response. Then record yourself speaking for 60 seconds.

Listen to Track 151.

Reading Time: 50 seconds

Perceptual Constancy

How an object affects our senses depends in part on external conditions, and these conditions are always changing. An object viewed from one angle presents a different shape to our eye than when viewed from another angle; similarly, as the distance from which we view an object changes, the object will appear larger or smaller. In spite of this, even as conditions change and we see objects differently, we still recognize that they remain the same. This is what is known as perceptual constancy. If not for perceptual constancy, we might have difficulty recognizing familiar objects if we viewed them in a new and different context.

Listen to Track 152.

4. Explain what is meant by perceptual constancy, using the examples provided by the professor.

Preparation Time: 30 seconds
Response Time: 60 seconds

Directions: You will now listen to part of a conversation. You will then be asked a question about it. After you hear the question, give yourself 20 seconds to prepare your response. Then record yourself speaking for 60 seconds.

Listen to Track 153.

5. The speakers discuss two possible solutions to the man's problem. Briefly summarize the problem. Then state which solution you recommend and explain why.

Preparation Time: 20 seconds
Response Time: 60 seconds

Directions: You will now listen to part of a lecture. You will then be asked a question about it. After you hear the question, give yourself 20 seconds to prepare your response. Then record yourself speaking for 60 seconds.

Listen to Track 154.

6. Using the examples of the leafy sea dragon and the cuttlefish, describe two kinds of camouflage and the benefits they provide.

Preparation Time: 20 seconds
Response Time: 60 seconds

WRITING

This section measures your ability to write in English to communicate in an academic environment.

There are two writing questions in this section.

For question 1, you will read a passage and listen to a lecture about the same topic. You may take notes while you read and listen. Then you will write a response to a question based on what you have read and heard. You may look back at the passage when answering the question. You may use your notes to help you answer the question. You have 20 minutes to plan and write your response.

For question 2, you will write an essay based on your own knowledge and experience. You have 30 minutes to plan and complete your essay.

Directions: Give yourself 3 minutes to read the passage.

Reading Time: 3 minutes

Private collectors have been selling and buying fossils, the petrified remains of ancient organisms, ever since the eighteenth century. In recent years, however, the sale of fossils, particularly of dinosaurs and other large vertebrates, has grown into a big business. Rare and important fossils are now being sold to private ownership for millions of dollars. This is an unfortunate development for both scientists and the general public.

The public suffers because fossils that would otherwise be donated to museums where everyone can see them are sold to private collectors who do not allow the public to view their collections. Making it harder for the public to see fossils can lead to a decline in public interest in fossils, which would be a pity.

More importantly, scientists are likely to lose access to some of the most important fossils and thereby miss out on potentially crucial discoveries about extinct life forms. Wealthy fossil buyers with a desire to own the rarest and most important fossils can spend virtually limitless amounts of money to acquire them. Scientists and the museums and universities they work for often cannot compete successfully for fossils against millionaire fossil buyers.

Moreover, commercial fossil collectors often destroy valuable scientific evidence associated with the fossils they unearth. Most commercial fossil collectors are untrained or uninterested in carrying out the careful field work and documentation that reveal the most about animal life in the past. For example, scientists have learned about the biology of nest-building dinosaurs called oviraptors by carefully observing the exact position of oviraptor fossils in the ground and the presence of other fossils in the immediate surroundings. Commercial fossil collectors typically pay no attention to how fossils lie in the ground or to the smaller fossils that may surround bigger ones.

Listen to Track 155.

Directions: You have 20 minutes to plan and write your response. Your response will be judged on the basis of the quality of your writing and on how well your response presents the points in the lecture and their relationship to the reading passage. Typically, an effective response will be 150 to 225 words.

Listen to Track 156.

Response Time: 20 minutes

1. Summarize the points made in the lecture, being sure to explain how they oppose specific points made in the reading passage.

Directions: Read the question below. You have 30 minutes to plan, write, and revise your essay. Typically, an effective response will contain a minimum of 300 words.

Response Time: 30 minutes

2. Do you agree or disagree with the following statement?

   The extended family (grandparents, cousins, aunts, and uncles) is less important now than it was in the past.

   Use specific reasons and examples to support your answer.

ANSWERS

Reading Section

1. B
2. D
3. C
4. A
5. C
6. D
7. B
8. C
9. C
10. D
11. A
12. B
13.
    Primary groups
    - Developing socially acceptable behavior
    - Involving close relationships
    - Providing meaning for life situations

    Secondary groups
    - Viewing people as a means to an end
    - Existing for practical purposes
14. A
15. B
16. D
17. C
18. A
19. B
20. C
21. A
22. C
23. A
24. A
25. B
26. B
27. B, C, F
28. C
29. C
30. A
31. C
32. B
33. A
34. B
35. D
36. D
37. A
38. C
39. D
40. B
41. A, C, F

Listening Section

1. C
2. B
3. A
4. B
5. D
6. C
7. A
8. A, D
9. A
10. D
11. A
12. D
13. C
14. C
15. A
16. D
17. D
18. A
19. C
20. A, D
21. B
22. D
23. D
24. A, C
25.

	Chanson Hero	Romance Hero
Is admired for loyalty to country	✓	
Engages in conflict for adventure		✓
Is willing to face extreme dangers to protect the lord	✓	
Is concerned with individual improvement		✓

26. B
27. B
28. C
29. C
30. B
31. A
32. D
33. A, D
34. A

Speaking Section

Prompts, Important Points, and Sample Responses with Rater Comments

Use the sample Independent and Integrated Speaking Rubrics in Appendix A to see how responses are scored. The raters who listen to your responses will analyze them in three general categories. These categories are Delivery, Language Use, and Topic Development. All three categories have equal importance.

This section includes important points that should be covered when answering each question. All of these points must be present in a response in order for it to receive the highest score in the Topic Development category. These important points are guides to the kind of information raters expect to hear in a high-level response.

This section also refers to sample responses, which can be found on the accompanying DVD. Some responses were scored at the highest level, which others were not. The responses are followed by comments from certified ETS raters.

Question 1

Prompt

Talk about a game, sport or other group activity that is played in your country. Explain why you think the activity is enjoyable.

Important Points

In this item, you should talk about a game or sport in your country that you enjoy. You should describe the activity and explain why you enjoy it. You should be careful not to spend too much of your response time just giving a description of the activity. It is acceptable to explain why the activity is popular in your country, but you should focus mainly on why you enjoy the activity.

High-level Response: Listen to Track 157.

Rater Comments

This speaker's response is very clear and well organized. She presents several reasons to support her enjoyment of soccer: it reduces stress, it is good exercise, it encourages cooperation and teamwork. She uses good connecting phrases (*"not only can I lose weight and build self-confidence but I can also learn a sense of cooperation . . ."*), and she ends her response with a brief summary statement, which makes her point of view clear and memorable. This summary statement does contain some minor grammatical errors (*"This is the reasons why I like soccer"*), and she does have some noticeable pauses throughout her response. Overall, however, none of these errors make her response difficult to follow.

Mid-level Response: Listen to Track 158.

Rater Comments

This response is mostly intelligible, but the first sentence is very difficult to understand. The speaker's topic is clear, and she does explain why she enjoys football. (Note: this speaker uses the term football, while the previous speaker uses soccer. Either is acceptable.) Her reasons for enjoying football, however, are mostly related to teamwork, and so she actually repeats herself for most of the response (*"we have to play as a group, it's enjoyable because everyone has to support the team. You have to try to play with the people and have contact with your teammates"*). She pauses often, clearly searching for the right words. She also has some noticeable grammatical errors (*"it's a game that requires the playing in together"*), and she makes some consistent pronunciation errors (pronouncing *"very"* as *"berry"*), though she is still relatively easy to understand.

Question 2

Prompt

When looking for information for a research project, some students prefer to get their information mainly from the Internet. Others prefer to mainly use printed materials such as books and academic journals. Which do you prefer, and why?

Important Points

Speakers should both state their preference and provide support for their choice, such as preferring the internet because it allows for faster research, or preferring printed materials because they are more reliable sources. There are many ways to successfully support a choice. Speakers may provide one overarching reason and elaborate on it, or provide several different reasons. They may provide concrete examples or general logic. It is also acceptable for speakers to say they find both internet and printed materials useful in doing research, but speakers would need to clearly explain why and under what circumstances each type of source is appropriate, and this would be difficult for many speakers to do in the time given. In all cases, the listener should be able to easily follow why the speaker holds that opinion.

High-level Response: Listen to Track 159.

Rater Comments

The speaker clearly states his preference (using the internet to find information for a research project) and why he prefers it (*"because you have a wider range of information from the internet*"). He then goes on to elaborate on his reasons, explaining why printed materials are not as convenient ("*if you need a particular type of information you need to go and search for a particular journal*") and comparing them to the internet. Although he does not give specific examples, his reasons are full and clear. The lack of examples is acceptable since this particular prompt did not ask for them.

A noticeable accent and occasional mispronunciations do not prevent the listener from easily understanding the response.

Mid-level Response: Listen to Track 160.

Rater Comments

The speaker states her preference ("*I prefer to research some information from the internet*") and provides some support for her choice ("*It is easier and faster to access some informations*"). However, beyond that initial statement, only a moderate amount of relevant support is provided. The speaker has some language limitations that prevent her from providing full support: she speaks slowly and with hesitation, and does not successfully use a wide variety of vocabulary or grammatical structures. She also includes information whose relevance is not clear. For example, she says, "*I can not only save my time, but also exchange opinions with others easily.*" It is not obvious what exchanging opinions with others has to do with getting information for a research project, and the speaker does not explain the connection.

Question 3

Prompt

The woman expresses her opinion about the university's plan. State her opinion and explain the reasons she gives for holding that opinion.

Important Points

In this question, you should use the reading and listening passages to describe the university's plan (to spend money to build a new stadium), state the woman's opinion about the plan, and explain the reasons why the woman disagrees with the plan. The woman disagrees with the idea that a new stadium will attract top students because she thinks that other facilities in the university are in poor condition—including the science labs, the library, and the student center—and that money should be spent on them before a new stadium. She also disagrees that a new stadium would attract people from the local community because she thinks people don't come because the teams always lose and a larger stadium wouldn't change that.

High-level Response: Listen to Track 161.

Rater Comments

The speaker gives a full response. He organizes the response well, devoting equal time to the woman's two reasons and covering most of the material in the important points above. Note that providing every detail of the plan or the woman's reasons is not a requirement for full credit; when discussing the poor facilities, for example, the man simply says "*like the library, and other places.*" His vocabulary and language use is precise and appropriate throughout for the most part, though there are a few minor errors that do not interfere with comprehension. Pronunciation is good overall, but there is some evident hesitation throughout. The response could be more fluid, but it is not choppy to the point that it creates listener effort.

Mid-level Response: Listen to Track 162.

Rater Comments

The speaker does address all of the main points, but they are not developed fully. For one, he does not clearly state at the beginning what the plan is (to build a new stadium); this is important for the listener to understand the response fully. He also leaves out other important information, such as the condition of the other facilities he mentions, which is again important in order to understand the woman's opinion. He does include a transition ("*second, she says . . .*") before discussing her second reason, which helps organization. Though the response is understandable, the language is often imprecise and demonstrates a limited range of vocabulary and grammatical structures (for example, *"Only new stadium cannot invite top students"*). The speech is generally intelligible, but pronunciation problems, mainly with individual sounds, and hesitations when searching for language do create some listener effort.

Question 4

Prompt

Explain what is meant by perceptual constancy, using the examples provided by the professor.

Important Points

This task asks you to explain how the examples given by the professor in the lecture illustrate the concept of perceptual constancy from the reading. There are different ways you can organize your response. You might begin by explaining that *perceptual constancy* is the idea that even though objects appear different depending on external conditions, we are able to recognize that they are the same objects. Or you might choose to begin with the examples and conclude with a summary of the theory of *perceptual constancy*. Either approach is acceptable, but you should be sure to include both examples in your response (a plate may look round or oval depending on the angle from which we look at it, but we still recognize it as a plate; and the professor may appear smaller when viewed from the back of the room [instead of the front], but we still understand that the professor is the same person, and that he has not gotten smaller).

High-level Response: Listen to Track 163.

Rater Comments

This speaker's pronunciation is very clear, and her response is well-organized and easy for the listener to follow. She explains the examples from the lecture first, and defines the concept later. This is a different but effective approach to answering the prompt. Her word choice and expression is not always perfect. For example, when defining the concept of perceptual constancy she says, *"we know by distance and angle . . . it doesn't look the same."* This is a somewhat vague statement. She could have used a clearer and more complex sentence like, "Even though an object looks different when viewed from a different angle or distance, we know it is the same object." Nevertheless, her delivery is fluid, and she is able to construct long, clear phrases in the explanation of the examples *". . . a professor in a front row, he looks bigger than you see the professor in the back row, but . . . without even thinking, you know that it's the same professor, and the same guy who's lecturing."*

Mid-level Response: Listen to Track 164.

Rater Comments

This speaker covers most of the information required of the task, but his response is not as clear or efficient as that of the high-level speaker. His word choice is imprecise and at times causes difficulty for the listener. For instance, he says, *". . . perceptual constancy means* you may remain same ideas *when looking at something from different* aspects." The phrase *"You may remain same ideas"* is not grammatically correct and the use of the term "ideas" is rather vague in meaning. The speaker could have more accurately expressed the idea as "continue to recognize an object." Also, he uses the word *"aspect"* instead of "angle" or "perspective," which is confusing for the listener. The speaker's pronunciation is relatively clear, but he repeats words and phrases often, which is at times distracting and requires some effort from the listener to follow his response. Overall, there is some evidence that he understood the reading and lecture, but limitations in grammar and vocabulary prevent him from expressing some of the ideas clearly.

Question 5

Prompt

The speakers discuss two possible solutions to the man's problem. Briefly summarize the problem. Then state which solution you recommend and explain why.

Important Points

This question asks you to briefly summarize the problem being discussed (that the man, who is the president of the Anthropology Club, needs to transport the club members to the museum tomorrow, but the van he was planning on using has broken down) and recommend *one* of the solutions. Please note that it is not a requirement to summarize both solutions (renting a van or postponing the trip). After you state which solution you recommend, you should offer reasons and support for your opinion. For example, if you agree with the first solution, you could say that the club members will almost certainly help him pay for the van rental since they are his friends. You could add that the special exhibit might end before they could get to the museum at a later date, so if he postpones the trip, the club members could end up very disappointed.

High-level Response: Listen to Track 165.

Rater Comments

The speaker covers the problem thoroughly and accurately. Although she doesn't need to describe both solutions, she still mentions both, and goes into detail on the solution she is recommending. She offers a lot of support for her opinion—that he shouldn't disappoint the club members, and that as club president it is his responsibility to borrow and pay for the transportation. Her pronunciation is almost always clear, with the exception of the word *"exhibition."* She also has some grammatical inaccuracies, such as saying *"Man is the president"* instead of *"The man is the president,"* but they are minor and do not prevent the listener from understanding her points.

Mid-level Response: Listen to Track 166.

Rater Comments

The speaker's response is filled with many hesitations, which prevent her from completely finishing. She covers the problem accurately but runs out of time before she can finish explaining why she thinks the man should postpone the exhibit. In this case, she should not have tried to mention both solutions, because she used up needed time by doing so, and she is not quite fluent enough to cover that much information during the response time. Her grammar is generally accurate and her pronunciation of individual words is clear, but her frequent hesitations make her response somewhat difficult to follow.

Question 6

Prompt

Using the examples of the leafy sea dragon and the cuttlefish, describe two kinds of camouflage and the benefits they provide.

Important Points

When answering this question, you should provide a summary of the lecture in order to describe the two different kinds of camouflage the professor talks about and how the types of camouflage protect the animals that use them. You should explain that some sea animals have permanent camouflage (like their colors and shapes) that blend in with their specific environment, and describe the example of the leafy sea dragon, which is green and looks like the leaves it is surrounded by. You should also explain that other animals have camouflage that changes colors to match whatever environment the animals are in, so that they can move around and still be protected. For example, the cuttlefish can turn brown when it is swimming over the sea floor, and green when it is swimming near plants.

High-level Response: Listen to Track 167.

Rater Comments

This speaker provides a full, complete summary of the lecture. He describes the two types of camouflage, the examples of the sea creatures that use the types of camouflage and how the camouflage benefits them, as well as how the types of camouflage differ from each other. He makes use of complex structures, such as *"the cuttlefish is different from the sea dragon in that it doesn't have . . ."* and makes only minor errors. His pronunciation and delivery in general are very clear. His intonation is somewhat flat, which may cause some listener effort. Even though this is a high-level response, the speaker could benefit from increased attention to stress at the sentence level and using intonation more for emphasis. Overall, the response is complete and highly intelligible.

Mid-level Response: Listen to Track 168.

Rater Comments

This speaker provides a mostly complete response. It contains a description of what camouflage is and why it is useful, as well as explanations of the two sea creatures and how they use camouflage. The speaker could have provided a stronger response, however, if he had provided more information about the differences between the two types of camouflage (he mentioned that cuttlefish can change their color and shape, but didn't contrast this with the sea dragon's permanent camouflage). His hesitation between words and within words is at times distracting, but overall his message is clear. The speaker would likely benefit from working on agreement and more advanced vocabulary (to avoid confusing phrases such as "*two different method,*" "*the cuttlefish is another examples,*" and "*they shape any type any colors*").

Writing Section

Prompts, Topic Notes, and Sample Responses with Rater Comments

Use the sample Integrated and Independent Writing Rubrics in Appendix A to see how responses are scored.

This section includes topic notes that are guides to the kind of information raters expect to read in a high-level response.

This section also refers to sample responses, which can be found on the accompanying DVD. These responses were scored at the highest level. The responses are followed by comments from certified ETS raters.

Question 1

Prompt

Summarize the points made in the lecture, being sure to explain how they oppose specific points made in the reading passage.

Topic Notes

The reading discusses reasons why collecting and selling fossils for commercial purposes (for profit only), which now happens much more frequently than it did in the past, is a bad practice. The lecturer explains that these reasons are not convincing, and that the benefits from having more commercial operations collect fossils these days are worth the drawbacks.

Point made in the reading	Corresponding point from the lecture
When fossils are sold to private collectors, it means that museums will have fewer of them, and in turn the general public will have fewer chances to see them.	The general public will have more chances to see them; commercial fossil collecting is making more fossils available, so many more public institutions can now buy them.
It will also mean that scientists will lose opportunities to make discoveries from studying fossils, since they won't have access to really important ones.	Even if important fossils are sold to private collectors, scientists would still see the fossils because they have to be identified first by scientists.
Because most commercial fossil collectors are untrained, they will destroy important scientific evidence that scientists could have obtained had they been the ones to collect the fossils.	Even if some damage is done, it is better than having fossils go undiscovered, which was more likely to have been the case when only scientists were doing the collecting.

Responses with scores of 4 and 5 typically discuss all three points in the table.

Sample Response

Unlike the passage, which focuses on the negative sides of fossil trade, the lecture focuses on the benefits of having a fossil market.

First of all, the passage mentions that the fossils will be less exposed to the public's eye if they are owned by collectors, because they will not be donated to public museums. However, the professor argues that by letting all institutions to have the opportunity to purchase fossils, even the lower level public institutions such as libraries can purchase the fossils for display, which can be viewed by many people.

Secondly, the professor opposes to the passage's opinion that the scientists would miss out on the important information given by fossils possessed by wealthy collectors. The professor brings up a point that all fossils need to be scientifically identified and carefully investigated by certified scientists before going into the market.

Lastly, although it may be true that the collectors may damage the fossils, it is better to have them find it and damage it than to never find the fossils. There are not many fossil searching activities going on, and without the help of the collectors, many of the fossils probably would not have even been found. Taking that into consideration, it is certainly better to have some information from the fossils than to have none at all.

Rater Comments

This response earns a score of 5. It is a well-organized response that successfully explains the opposing relationship between the reading and the lecture. The three main points from the lecture are clearly identified, and the writer has provided relevant details or explanations for each of those main points. The writer's expression "There are not many fossil searching activities going on . . ." in the third point is somewhat vague, since the idea conveyed by the lecturer is actually that there are currently not that many fossil collecting efforts specifically by universities and scientific institutions. So the writer's idea here does not correspond to what the lecture is implying, which is that nowadays, because commercial operations started increasing their fossil hunting activities in recent years, between the large number of commercial operations and the limited activity of universities and scientific institutions, there is quite a lot of fossil searching activity going on. However, the lecturer's main idea, that without the commercial collectors, many fossils would go undiscovered, is conveyed. Overall, content from the lecture points is presented precisely, and the very few language errors in the response do not interfere with meaning.

Question 2

Prompt

Do you agree or disagree with the following statement?

The extended family (grandparents, cousins, aunts, and uncles) is less important now than it was in the past.

Use specific reasons and examples to support your answer.

Topic Notes

This topic asks you to compare the importance of extended family now and in the past. If you agree with the statement, you might want to discuss factors that have caused this to happen such as family members having to move far distances away from their hometown for their jobs. If you disagree with the statement, you might support your answer by explaining that in certain parts of the world, it is still very common for extended family members to play important roles in one another's day-to-day lives, and you might describe how this works. No matter which position you take, it is fine to include your personal opinion about the effects of changes over time to the importance of the extended family (for example, many writers comment that this change has generally been bad for society); that is appropriate for this task, as long as it is part of a well-developed response that includes sufficient explanation and details.

Sample Response

I agree with the statement that the extended family has become less important than it was before. In the past, there were the threats of bombings in the cold war or money depressions that place higher important on sticking and working together. However, there has been a change in the values of our world today that have severed many important relations between family members.

First, with new technology, older generations of grandparents and some aunts and uncles may be separated into a different world. One example is instant messaging and email; most young people use these ways to talk constantly with friends and other people, and consider this more exciting and important than talking with extended family members.

Also, students today are becoming more and more busy with school, after school activities, and homework. High achieving students take numerous advanced classes, overload on homework, and have little time to spend time with the other members of the family. Other children are constantly involved in after school sports and activities that take up most of their time. Because of the more importance placed on good grades, better test scores, and after school activities, the significance of the extended family has been decreasing.

Finally, families are becoming farther apart because of distance. Gone are the times in which families lived close together or in the same house, and have evenings with quality family times. In my case, I live halfway across the planet from the rest of my family and only get a few moments to talk on the phone with them every few months and a few weeks together during school vacation. Some other family members live so far away that I rarely get to talk to them, let alone meet them.

Therefore, the extended family has become less important because other values and factors have come into place. There is less communication going between them, less time to spend together, and more distance to travel to be with them. Extended family members have become quite separated from the rest of the family than in the past.

Rater Comments

The writer of this 5-level response agrees with the idea that extended family has become less important, and provides three reasons for this: widespread use of technology, busy lives of family members, and the distances separating family members. Each one of those points is well developed, and includes appropriate details and explanations; for the first point, specific types of technology and how people use them are referenced, for the second point, there is an explanation of how or in what ways children are busy these days, and for the third point, a personal example illustrates the idea that family members living far apart makes staying in touch harder. The organization is good and transitional sentences are used appropriately ("However, there has been a change . . ."). Throughout the response there are many examples of appropriate word choice, syntactic variety, and idiomaticity. Grammatical and lexical errors (for example, "families are becoming farther apart" instead of, perhaps, "families are *growing* farther apart") are very few and minor, and they do not interfere with meaning.

Appendix A

Speaking and Writing Scoring Rubrics

This section contains all the rubrics used by raters to score your Speaking and Writing section responses. There are two different rubrics used to score the Speaking section, and two used to score the Writing section.

Speaking questions 1 and 2 are scored using the Independent Speaking Rubric, while questions 3–6 are scored using the Integrated Speaking Rubric. Writing question 1 is scored using the Integrated Writing Rubric, while question 2 is scored using the Independent Writing Rubric.

The chart below shows the main features of your responses that must be considered when assigning a score.

Section	Question	Rubric	Main features considered when scoring
Speaking	1–2	Independent Speaking	**Delivery** • How clear is your speech? Good responses are fluid and clear, have good pronunciation, a natural pace, and natural-sounding intonation patterns. • Even at the highest level, there may be some minor problems; however, they do not cause difficulty for the listener. **Language use** • How effectively do you use grammar and vocabulary to convey ideas? In a good response, there is control of both basic and more complex language structures, and appropriate vocabulary is used. • Even at the highest level, some minor or systematic errors may be noticeable; however, they do not obscure meaning. **Topic development** • How fully do you answer the question, and how coherently do you present your ideas? In a good response, the relationship between ideas is clear and easy to follow, as is the progression from one idea to the next. Good responses generally use all or most of the time allotted.

Section	Question	Rubric	Main features considered when scoring
Speaking	3–6	Integrated Speaking	**Delivery** • How clear is your speech? Good responses are fluid and clear, have good pronunciation, a natural pace, and natural-sounding intonation patterns. • Even at the highest level, there may be some minor problems; however, they do not cause difficulty for the listener. **Language use** • How effectively do you use grammar and vocabulary to convey ideas? In a good response, there is control of both basic and more complex language structures, and appropriate vocabulary is used. • Even at the highest level, some minor or systematic errors may be noticeable; however, they do not obscure meaning. **Topic development** • How fully do you answer the question, and how coherently do you present your ideas? Are you able to synthesize and summarize the information that was presented? In a good response, the relationship between ideas is clear and easy to follow, as is the progression from one idea to the next. Good responses generally use all or most of the time allotted. • Even at the highest level, a response may have minor inaccuracies about details or minor omissions of relevant details.
Writing	1	Integrated Writing	**Quality of the writing** • A good response is well organized. Use of grammar and vocabulary is appropriate and precise. **Completeness and accuracy of the content** • In a good response, important information from the lecture has been successfully selected, and it is coherently and accurately presented in relation to relevant information from the reading. • Even at the highest level, a response may have occasional language errors; however, they do not result in inaccurate or imprecise presentation of content or connections.
Writing	2	Independent Writing	**Quality of the writing** • A good response effectively addresses the topic and task; it is well developed. It is also well organized. Use of grammar and vocabulary is appropriate and precise. • Even at the highest level, a response may have minor lexical or grammatical errors; however, they do not interfere with meaning.

TOEFL iBT® Speaking Scoring Rubric—Independent Tasks

Score	General Description	Delivery	Language Use	Topic Development
4	**The response fulfills the demands of the task, with at most minor lapses in completeness. It is highly intelligible and exhibits sustained, coherent discourse. A response at this level is characterized by all of the following:**	Generally well-paced flow (fluid expression). Speech is clear. It may include minor lapses, or minor difficulties with pronunciation or intonation patterns, which do not affect overall intelligibility.	The response demonstrates effective use of grammar and vocabulary. It exhibits a fairly high degree of automaticity with good control of basic and complex structures (as appropriate). Some minor (or systematic) errors are noticeable but do not obscure meaning.	Response is sustained and sufficient to the task. It is generally well developed and coherent; relationships between ideas are clear (or clear progression of ideas).
3	**The response addresses the task appropriately, but may fall short of being fully developed. It is generally intelligible and coherent, with some fluidity of expression, though it exhibits some noticeable lapses in the expression of ideas. A response at this level is characterized by at least two of the following:**	Speech is generally clear, with some fluidity of expression, though minor difficulties with pronunciation, intonation, or pacing are noticeable and may require listener effort at times (though overall intelligibility is not significantly affected).	The response demonstrates fairly automatic and effective use of grammar and vocabulary, and fairly coherent expression of relevant ideas. Response may exhibit some imprecise or inaccurate use of vocabulary or grammatical structures or be somewhat limited in the range of structures used. This may affect overall fluency, but it does not seriously interfere with the communication of the message.	Response is mostly coherent and sustained and conveys relevant ideas/ information. Overall development is somewhat limited, usually lacks elaboration or speci ficity. Relationships between ideas may at times not be immediately clear.

TOEFL iBT® Speaking Scoring Rubric—Independent Tasks, *continued*

Score	General Description	Delivery	Language Use	Topic Development
2	**The response addresses the task, but development of the topic is limited. It contains intelligible speech, although problems with delivery and/or overall coherence occur; meaning may be obscured in places. A response at this level is characterized by at least two of the following:**	Speech is basically intelligible, though listener effort is needed because of unclear articulation, awkward intonation, or choppy rhythm/pace; meaning may be obscured in places.	The response demonstrates limited range and control of grammar and vocabulary. These limitations often prevent full expression of ideas. For the most part, only basic sentence structures are used successfully and spoken with fluidity. Structures and vocabulary may express mainly simple (short) and/or general propositions, with simple or unclear connections made among them (serial listing, conjunction, juxtaposition).	The response is connected to the task, though the number of ideas presented or the development of ideas is limited. Mostly basic ideas are expressed with limited elaboration (details and support). At times relevant substance may be vaguely expressed or repetitious. Connections of ideas may be unclear.
1	**The response is very limited in content and/or coherence or is only minimally connected to the task, or speech is largely unintelligible. A response at this level is characterized by at least two of the following:**	Consistent pronunciation, stress, and intonation difficulties cause considerable listener effort; delivery is choppy, fragmented, or telegraphic; frequent pauses and hesitations.	Range and control of grammar and vocabulary severely limits (or prevents) expression of ideas and connections among ideas. Some low-level responses may rely heavily on practiced or formulaic expressions.	Limited relevant content is expressed. The response generally lacks substance beyond expression of very basic ideas. Speaker may be unable to sustain speech to complete task and may rely heavily on repetition of the prompt.
0	**Speaker makes no attempt to respond OR response is unrelated to the topic.**			

TOEFL iBT® Speaking Scoring Rubric—Integrated Tasks

Score	General Description	Delivery	Language Use	Topic Development
4	**The response fulfills the demands of the task, with at most minor lapses in completeness. It is highly intelligible and exhibits sustained, coherent discourse. A response at this level is characterized by all of the following:**	Speech is generally clear, fluid and sustained. It may include minor lapses or minor difficulties with pronunciation or intonation. Pace may vary at times as speaker attempts to recall information. Overall intelligibility remains high.	The response demonstrates good control of basic and complex grammatical structures that allow for coherent, efficient (automatic) expression of relevant ideas. Contains generally effective word choice. Though some minor (or systematic) errors or imprecise use may be noticeable, they do not require listener effort (or obscure meaning).	The response presents a clear progression of ideas and conveys the relevant information required by the task. It includes appropriate detail, though it may have minor errors or minor omissions.
3	**The response addresses the task appropriately, but may fall short of being fully developed. It is generally intelligible and coherent, with some fluidity of expression, though it exhibits some noticeable lapses in the expression of ideas. A response at this level is characterized by at least two of the following:**	Speech is generally clear, with some fluidity of expression, but it exhibits minor difficulties with pronunciation, intonation or pacing and may require some listener effort at times. Overall intelligibility remains good, however.	The response demonstrates fairly automatic and effective use of grammar and vocabulary, and fairly coherent expression of relevant ideas. Response may exhibit some imprecise or inaccurate use of vocabulary or grammatical structures or be somewhat limited in the range of structures used. Such limitations do not seriously interfere with the communication of the message.	The response is sustained and conveys relevant information required by the task. However, it exhibits some incompleteness, inaccuracy, lack of specificity with respect to content, or choppiness in the progression of ideas.

TOEFL iBT® Speaking Scoring Rubric—Integrated Tasks, *continued*

Score	General Description	Delivery	Language Use	Topic Development
2	**The response is connected to the task, though it may be missing some relevant information or contain inaccuracies. It contains some intelligible speech, but at times problems with intelligibility and/or overall coherence may obscure meaning. A response at this level is characterized by at least two of the following:**	Speech is clear at times, though it exhibits problems with pronunciation, intonation or pacing and so may require significant listener effort. Speech may not be sustained at a consistent level throughout. Problems with intelligibility may obscure meaning in places (but not throughout).	The response is limited in the range and control of vocabulary and grammar demonstrated (some complex structures may be used, but typically contain errors). This results in limited or vague expression of relevant ideas and imprecise or inaccurate connections. Automaticity of expression may only be evident at the phrasal level.	The response conveys some relevant information but is clearly incomplete or inaccurate. It is incomplete if it omits key ideas, makes vague reference to key ideas, or demonstrates limited development of important information. An inaccurate response demonstrates misunderstanding of key ideas from the stimulus. Typically, ideas expressed may not be well connected or cohesive so that familiarity with the stimulus is necessary in order to follow what is being discussed.
1	**The response is very limited in content or coherence or is only minimally connected to the task. Speech may be largely unintelligible. A response at this level is characterized by at least two of the following:**	Consistent pronunciation and intonation problems cause considerable listener effort and frequently obscure meaning. Delivery is choppy, fragmented, or telegraphic. Speech contains frequent pauses and hesitations.	Range and control of grammar and vocabulary severely limits (or prevents) expression of ideas and connections among ideas. Some very low-level responses may rely on isolated words or short utterances to communicate ideas.	The response fails to provide much relevant content. Ideas that are expressed are often inaccurate, limited to vague utterances, or repetitions (including repetition of prompt).
0	**Speaker makes no attempt to respond OR response is unrelated to the topic.**			

TOEFL iBT® Writing Scoring Rubric—Integrated Tasks

Score	Task Description
5	A response at this level successfully selects the important information from the lecture and coherently and accurately presents this information in relation to the relevant information presented in the reading. The response is well organized, and occasional language errors that are present do not result in inaccurate or imprecise presentation of content or connections.
4	A response at this level is generally good in selecting the important information from the lecture and in coherently and accurately presenting this information in relation to the relevant information in the reading, but it may have minor omission, inaccuracy, vagueness, or imprecision of some content from the lecture or in connection to points made in the reading. A response is also scored at this level if it has more frequent or noticeable minor language errors, as long as such usage and grammatical structures do not result in anything more than an occasional lapse of clarity or in the connection of ideas.
3	A response at this level contains some important information from the lecture and conveys some relevant connection to the reading, but it is marked by one or more of the following: • Although the overall response is definitely oriented to the task, it conveys only vague, global, unclear, or somewhat imprecise connection of the points made in the lecture to points made in the reading. • The response may omit one major key point made in the lecture. • Some key points made in the lecture or the reading, or connections between the two, may be incomplete, inaccurate, or imprecise. • Errors of usage and/or grammar may be more frequent or may result in noticeably vague expressions or obscured meanings in conveying ideas and connections.
2	A response at this level contains some relevant information from the lecture, but is marked by significant language difficulties or by significant omission or inaccuracy of important ideas from the lecture or in the connections between the lecture and the reading; a response at this level is marked by one or more of the following: • The response significantly misrepresents or completely omits the overall connection between the lecture and the reading. • The response significantly omits or significantly misrepresents important points made in the lecture. • The response contains language errors or expressions that largely obscure connections or meaning at key junctures, or that would likely obscure understanding of key ideas for a reader not already familiar with the reading and the lecture.
1	A response at this level is marked by one or more of the following: • The response provides little or no meaningful or relevant coherent content from the lecture. • The language level of the response is so low that it is difficult to derive meaning.
0	A response at this level merely copies sentences from the reading, rejects the topic or is otherwise not connected to the topic, is written in a foreign language, consists of keystroke characters, or is blank.

TOEFL iBT® Writing Scoring Rubric—Independent Tasks

Score	Task Description
5	**An essay at this level largely accomplishes all of the following:** • effectively addresses the topic and task • is well organized and well developed, using clearly appropriate explanations, exemplifications, and/or details • displays unity, progression, and coherence • displays consistent facility in the use of language, demonstrating syntactic variety, appropriate word choice, and idiomaticity, though it may have minor lexical or grammatical errors
4	**An essay at this level largely accomplishes all of the following:** • addresses the topic and task well, though some points may not be fully elaborated • is generally well organized and well developed, using appropriate and sufficient explanations, exemplifications, and/or details • displays unity, progression, and coherence, though it may contain occasional redundancy, digression, or unclear connections • displays facility in the use of language, demonstrating syntactic variety and range of vocabulary, though it will probably have occasional noticeable minor errors in structure, word form, or use of idiomatic language that do not interfere with meaning
3	**An essay at this level is marked by one or more of the following:** • addresses the topic and task using somewhat developed explanations, exemplifications, and/or details • displays unity, progression, and coherence, though connection of ideas may be occasionally obscured • may demonstrate inconsistent facility in sentence formation and word choice that may result in lack of clarity and occasionally obscure meaning • may display accurate but limited range of syntactic structures and vocabulary
2	**An essay at this level may reveal one or more of the following weaknesses:** • limited development in response to the topic and task • inadequate organization or connection of ideas • inappropriate or insufficient exemplifications, explanations, or details to support or illustrate generalizations in response to the task • a noticeably inappropriate choice of words or word forms • an accumulation of errors in sentence structure and/or usage
1	**An essay at this level is seriously flawed by one or more of the following weaknesses:** • serious disorganization or underdevelopment • little or no detail, or irrelevant specifies, or questionable responsiveness to the task • serious and frequent errors in sentence structure or usage
0	**An essay at this level** merely copies words from the topic, rejects the topic, or is otherwise not connected to the topic, is written in a foreign language, consists of keystroke characters, or is blank.

Appendix B

Audio Track Transcripts

TRACK 1 TRANSCRIPT

Narrator
Listen to a conversation between a student and her professor.

Professor
Before we get started, I . . . I just wanted to say I'm glad you chose food science for your major course of study.

Female student
Yeah, it seems like a great industry to get involved with. I mean, with a four-year degree in food science, I'll always be able to find a job.

Professor
You're absolutely right. Eh, before entering academia, I worked as a scientist for several food manufacturers and for the U.S. Food and Drug Administration. I even worked on a commercial fishing boat in *Alaska* a couple of summers while I was an undergraduate. We'd, we'd bring in the day's catch to a floating processor boat, where the fish got cleaned, packaged, and frozen—right at sea.

Female student
That's amazing. As a matter of fact, I'm sort of interested in food packaging.

Professor
Well, for that, you'll need a strong background in physics, math, and chemistry.

Female student
Those are my best subjects—for a long time I was leaning toward getting my degree in engineering.

Professor
Well, then you shouldn't have a, a problem. And fortunately, at this university, the Department of Food Science offers a program in food packaging. Elsewhere, you might have to hammer courses together on your own.

Female student
I guess I lucked out, then! Um, so since my appointment today's to discuss my, my term paper topic . . . I wanted to ask, could I write about food packaging? I realize we're supposed to research food-borne bacteria, but food packaging must play a role in all of that, right?

Professor
Absolutely. Maybe you should do some preliminary research on that . . .

Female student
I have! That's the problem. I'm overwhelmed!

Professor
Well, in your reading, did anything interest you in particular, I, I mean something you'd like to investigate?

Female student
Well, I was surprised about the different types of packaging used for milk. Y'know, clear plastic bottles, opaque bottles, cardboard containers . . .

Professor
True! In fact, the type of packaging has something to do with the way milk's treated against bacteria.

Female student
Yeah, and I read a study that showed how *light* can give milk a funny flavor and decrease its nutritional value. And yet, most milk bottles are clear. What's up with that?

Professor
Well, consumers like being able to visually examine the color of the milk. That might be *one* reason that opaque bottles haven't really caught on. But that study . . . I'm sure there're more studies on the subject . . . uh, you shouldn't base your paper on, on only one study.

Female student
Maybe I should write about those opaque plastic bottles . . . find out if there's any *scientific* reasons they aren't used more widely. Maybe opaque bottles aren't as good at keeping bacteria from *growing* in milk after the bottle's been opened or something. But where to begin researching this, I don't . . .

Professor
Y'know, there's a dairy not far from here, in Chelsea. It was one of the first dairies to bottle milk in *opaque* plastic, but now they're using *clear* plastic again . . . And they're always very supportive of the university and our students, so if you wanted . . .

Female student
Hmm . . . Yeah, I like that idea.

TRACK 2 TRANSCRIPT

Narrator
Listen again to part of the conversation. Then answer the question.

Professor
Maybe you should do some preliminary research on that . . .

Female student
I have! That's the problem. I'm overwhelmed!

Narrator
What does the woman mean when she says this:

Female student
I'm overwhelmed!

TRACK 3 TRANSCRIPT

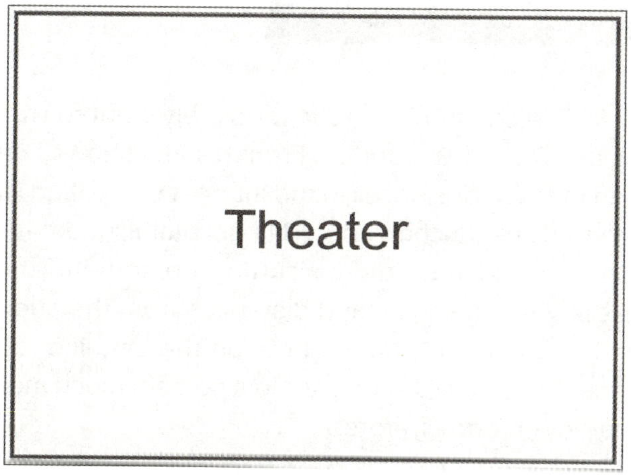

Narrator
Listen to part of a lecture in a theater class.

Professor
As we have seen, the second half of the eighteenth century was an exciting time in Europe. It was not only an age of great invention, but social changes also led to a rise in all sorts of entertainment, from reading to museums to travel. And finding himself in the middle of this excitement was an accomplished French painter named Philippe Jacques de Loutherbourg.

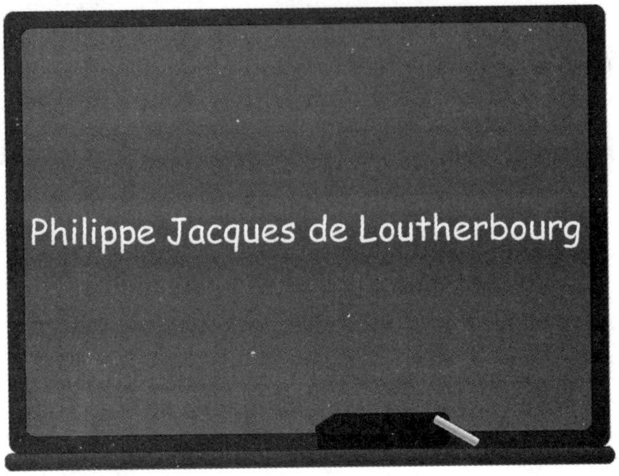

Loutherbourg arrived in England in 1771 and immediately went to work as a set designer at the famous Drury Lane Theatre in London. From his first shows Loutherbourg showed a knack for imagination in stage design, all in the interest of creating illusions that allowed the audience to suspend disbelief completely. He accomplished this by giving the stage a greater feeling of depth, which he did by cutting up some of the rigid background scenery and placing it at various angles and distances from the audience. Another realistic touch was using three-dimensional objects on the set, like rocks and bushes, as opposed to two-dimensional painted scenery. He also paid much more attention to lighting and sound than had been done before.

Now, these sets were so elaborate that many people attended the theater more for *them* than for the actors or the story. At the time people were wild for travel and for experiencing new places, but not everyone could afford it. Loutherbourg outdid himself, however, with a show that he set up in his own home. He called it the Eidophusikon.

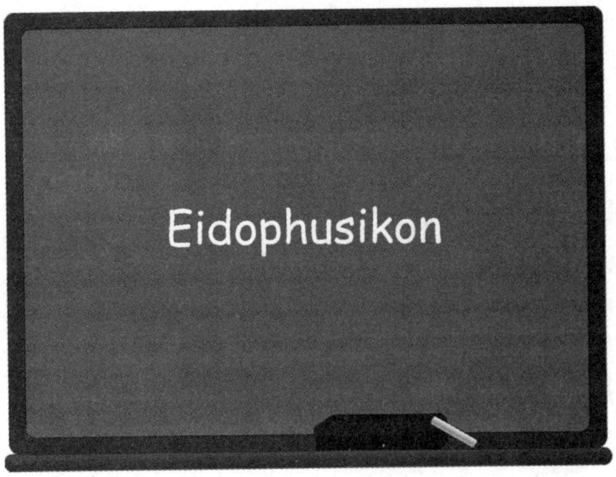

"Eidophusikon" means something like "representation of nature"—and that's exactly what he intended to do—create realistic, moving scenes that changed before the audience's eyes. In this he synthesized all his tricks from Drury Lane, mechanical motion, sound, light, other special effects to create, if you will, an early multi-media production.

The Eidophusikon was Loutherbourg's attempt to release painting from the constraints of the picture frame. After all, even the most action-filled, exciting painting can represent only one moment in time and any illusion of movement is gone after the first glance. But Loutherbourg, like other contemporary painters, wanted to add the dimension of time to his paintings. You know, the popular thinking is that Loutherbourg was influenced by landscape painting, but why can't we say that the Eidophusikon actually influenced the painters? At the very least we have to consider that it was more . . . it was more of a mutual thing . . . We know, for example, that the important English landscape painter Thomas Gainsborough attended almost all of the early performances, and his later paintings are notable for their increased color and dynamic use of light. Loutherbourg's influence on the theater, though . . . he was incredibly influential. The way he brought together design and lighting and sound as a unified feature of the stage can easily be seen in English theater's subsequent emphasis on lighting and motion.

Now, the Eidophusikon stage was actually a box, a few meters wide, a couple meters tall, and a couple meters deep; that is, the action took place within this box. This was much smaller of course than the usual stage, but it also allowed Loutherbourg to concentrate the lighting to better effect. Also, the audience was in the dark, which wouldn't be a common feature of the theater until 100 years later. The show consisted of a series of scenes, for example, a view of London from sunrise that changes as the day moves on. Mechanical figures, such as cattle, moved across the scene and ships sailed along the river. But what really got people was the attention to detail, much like his work at Drury Lane. So, for example, he painted very realistic ships and varied their size depending on their distance from the audience. Small boats moved more quickly across the foreground than larger ones did that were closer to the horizon. Other effects, like waves, were also very convincing—they reflected sunlight or moonlight depending on the time of day or night—even the colors changed as they would in nature.

Sound and light were important in making his productions realistic. He used a great number of lamps and he was able to change colors of light by using variously colored pieces of glass to create effects like passing clouds that subtly change in color. Furthermore, he used effects to make patterns of shadow and light rather than using the uniform lighting that was common at the time. And many of the sound effects he pioneered are still in use today, like creating thunder by pulling on one of the corners of a thin copper sheet. One of his most popular scenes was of a storm . . . And there's a story that on one occasion an actual storm passed overhead during the show, and some people went outside and they claimed Loutherbourg's thunder was actually better than the real thunder!

TRACK 4 TRANSCRIPT

Narrator

Listen to part of a lecture in an environmental science class.

Professor

So, since we're on the topic of global climate change and its effects . . . in Alaska, in the northern *arctic* part of Alaska, over the last, oh . . . 30 years or so, temperatures have increased about half a degree Celsius per decade. And, scientists have noticed that there's been a change in surface vegetation during this time—shrubs are increasing in the tundra.

Tundra is flat land, with very little vegetation. Just a few species of plants grow there because the temperature's very cold and there's not much precipitation. And because of the cold temperatures, the tundra has two layers. The top layer, which is called the active layer, is frozen in the winter and spring, but thaws in the summer. Beneath this active layer is a second layer called permafrost, which is frozen all year round and is impermeable to water.

Female student
So, because of the permafrost, none of the plants that grow there can have deep roots, can they?

Professor
No, and that's one of the reasons that shrubs survive in the arctic. Shrubs are little bushes; they're not tall, and being low to the ground protects them from the cold and wind. And their roots don't grow very deep, so the permafrost doesn't interfere with their growth. OK? Now, since the temperatures have been increasing in arctic Alaska, the growth of shrubs has increased. And this has presented climate scientists with a puzzle.

Male student
Um, I'm sorry, when you say the growth of shrubs has increased . . . um, do you mean that the shrubs are *bigger*, or that there are *more* shrubs?

Professor
Good question. And the answer is "both." The *size* of the shrubs has increased *and* shrub cover has spread to what was previously shrub-free tundra.

OK. So, what's the puzzle—warmer temperatures *should* lead to increased vegetation growth, right? Well, the connection's not so simple. The temperature increase has occurred during the winter and spring—not during the summer. But, the increase in shrubs has occurred in the *summer*. So, how can increased temperatures in the winter and spring result in increased shrub growth in the summer? Well, it may be biological processes that occur in the soil in the winter that cause increased shrub growth in the summer. And, here's how: there are microbes, microscopic organisms that live in the soil.

These microbes enable the soil to have more nitrogen, which plants need to live, and they remain quite active during the winter. There are two reasons for this. First, they live in the active layer which, remember, contains water that doesn't penetrate the permafrost. Second, most of the precipitation in the arctic is in the form of snow. And the snow which blankets the ground in the winter actually has an insulating effect on the soil beneath it . . . and it allows the temperature of the soil to remain warm enough for microbes to remain active.

So there's been increased nutrient production in the winter, and that's what's responsible for the growth of shrubs in the summer and their spread to new areas of the tundra. Areas with more nutrients are the areas with the largest increase in shrubs.

Female student
But what about runoff in the spring, when the snow finally melts? Won't the nutrients get washed away? Spring thaw always washes away soil, doesn't it?

Professor
Well, much of the soil is usually still frozen during peak runoff. And the nutrients are deep down in the active layer anyway—not high up, near the surface, which is the part of the active layer most affected by runoff. But, as I was about to say, there's more to the story. The tundra is windy, and as snow is blown across the tundra it's caught by shrubs . . . and deep snowdrifts often form around shrubs. And we've already mentioned the insulating effects of snow . . . So that extra warmth means even more microbial activity, which means even more food for the shrubs, which means even more shrubs—and more snow around them, etc. It's a circle, a loop. And because of this loop, which is promoted by warmer temperatures in the winter and spring . . . well, it looks like the tundra may be turning into shrubland.

Female student
But will it be long-term? I mean, maybe the shrubs will be abundant for a few years, and then it'll change back to tundra.

Professor
Well, shrub expansion has occurred in other environments, like semiarid grassland and tallgrass prairies. And shrub expansion in *these* environments does seem to persist . . . almost to the point of causing a shift. Once it's established, shrubland thrives. Particularly in the arctic, because arctic shrubs are good at taking advantage of increased nutrients in the soil—better than other arctic plants.

TRACK 5 TRANSCRIPT

Narrator
What does the professor imply when she says this:

Professor
So what's the puzzle? Warmer temperatures *should* lead to increased vegetation growth, right?

TRACK 6 TRANSCRIPT

Narrator
Listen to a conversation between a student and a library employee.

Student
Excuse me. Can you help me with something?

Librarian
I'll do my best. What do you need?

Student
Well, I received a letter in my mailbox saying that I'm supposed to return a book that I checked out back in January—uh, it's called *Modern Social Problems*—but because I'm writing my senior thesis, I'm supposed to be able to keep the book all semester.

Librarian
So you signed up for "Extended Borrowing Privileges?"

Student
Yeah.

Librarian
But we're still asking you to bring the book back?

Student
Uh-huh.

Librarian
Well, let me take a look and see what the computer says. The title was *Modern Social Problems*?

Student
Yeah.

Librarian
OK . . . Oh, I see. It's been recalled. You can keep it all semester as long as no one else requests it. But someone else has . . . it looks like one of the professors in the sociology

department has requested it, so you have to bring it back even though you've got "extended Borrowing Privileges." You can check out the book again when it's returned in a couple of weeks.

Student
But I really need this book right now.

Librarian
Do you need all of it, or is there a certain section or chapter you're working with?

Student
I guess there's one particular chapter I've been using lately for a section of my thesis. Why?

Librarian
Well, you can photocopy up to one chapter of the book. Why don't you do that for the chapter you're working on right now—and by the time you need the rest of the book, maybe it'll have been returned. We can even do the photocopying for you, because of the circumstances.

Student
Oh, well, that would be great.

Librarian
I see you've got some books there. Is that the one you were asked to return?

Student
Uh, no. I left it in my dorm room. These are books I need to check out today. Um, is it OK if I bring that one by in a couple of days?

Librarian
Uh, actually, you need to return it today, that is, if you want to check out those books today. That's our policy.

Student
Oh, I didn't know that.

Librarian
Yeah, not a lot of people realize that. In fact, every semester we get a few students who've had their borrowing privileges suspended completely because they haven't returned books. They're allowed to use books only in the library; they're not allowed to check anything out because of unreturned books.

Student
That's not good. I guess I should head back down to the dorm right now then.

Librarian
But before you go, what you should do is fill out a form requesting the book back in two weeks. You don't want to waste any time getting it back.

Student
Thanks a lot! Now I don't feel quite so bad about having to return the book.

TRACK 7 TRANSCRIPT

Narrator
Listen again to part of the conversation. Then answer the question.

Librarian
So you signed up for "Extended Borrowing Privileges?"

Student
Yeah.

Librarian
But we're still asking you to bring the book back?

Narrator
Why does the woman say this:

Librarian
But we're still asking you to bring the book back?

TRACK 8 TRANSCRIPT

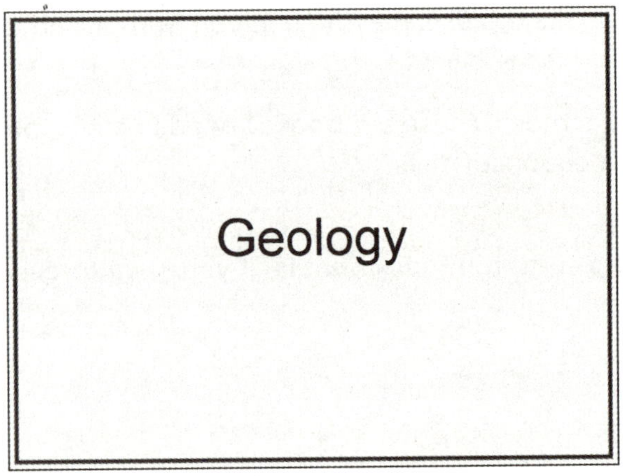

Narrator
Listen to part of a lecture in a geology class.

Professor
So, continuing our discussion of desert lakes, now I want to focus on what is known as the Empty Quarter.

The Empty Quarter is a huge area of sand that covers about a quarter of the Arabian Peninsula. Today it's pretty desolate . . . barren and *extremely* hot. But, there've been times in the past when monsoon rains soaked the Empty Quarter and turned it from a desert into grassland that was dotted with lakes and home to various animals. There were actually two periods of rain and lake formation . . . the first one began about 37,000 years ago. And the second one dates from about 10,000 years ago.

Female student
Excuse me, professor, but I'm confused. Why would lakes form in the desert? It's just sand, after all.

Professor
Good question. We know from modern day desert lakes . . . like Lake Eyre in South Australia . . . that under the right conditions, lakes **do** form in the desert. But the Empty Quarter lakes disappeared thousands of years ago. They left behind their beds, or basins, as *limestone formations* that we can still see today. They look like low-lying white or gray buttes . . . long, narrow hills with flat tops . . . barely a meter high. A recent study of some of the formations presents some new theories about the area's past. Keep in mind, though, that this study only looked at 19 formations . . . and about a thousand have been documented, so there's a lot more work to be done.

According to this study, two factors were important for lake formation in the Empty Quarter. Um, first, the rains that fell there were torrential. So it would have been impossible for all the water to soak into the ground. Second, as you know, sand dunes contain other types of particles besides sand . . . including clay and silt. Now, when the rain fell, water ran down the sides of the dunes, carrying clay and silt particles with it. And wherever these particles settled, they formed a pan . . . a layer that water couldn't penetrate. Once this pan formed, further runoff collected and formed a lake.

Now the older lakes . . . about half the formations, the ones that started forming 37,000 years ago, the limestone formations we see . . . they're up to a kilometer long but only a few meters wide . . . and they're scattered along the desert floor, in valleys between the dunes. So the theory is the lakes formed there . . . on the desert floor . . . in these long, narrow valleys. And we know, because of what we know about similar ancient desert lakes, we know that the lakes didn't last very long . . . from a few months to a few years on average.

As for the more recent lakes, the ones from 10,000 years ago . . . Well, they seem to have been smaller and so may have dried up more quickly . . . Another difference, very important today for distinguishing between older lake beds and newer ones . . . is the location of the limestone formations: the more *recent* beds are high up in the dunes.

Why these differences? Well, there are some ideas about that and they have to do with the shapes of the sand dunes when the lakes were formed. 37,000 years ago the dunes were probably nicely rounded at the top . . . so the water just ran right down their sides to the desert floor. But there were thousands of years of wind between the two rainy periods . . . reshaping the dunes. So, during the second rainy period, the dunes were kind of . . . chopped up at the top . . . full of hollows and ridges. And these hollows would have captured the rain right there on the top.

Now, in a grassland and lake ecosystem, we'd expect to find fossils from a variety of animals. And numerous fossils have been found, at least at these particular sites. But . . . where did these animals come from? Well, the theory that has been suggested is that they migrated in from nearby habitats where they were already living. Then, as the lakes dried up, they died out.

The study makes a couple of interesting points about the fossils . . . which I hope will be looked at in future studies. At older lake sites, there's fossil remains from hippopotamuses, water buffalo . . . uh, animals that spend much of their lives standing *in* water . . . and also, fossils of cattle. However, at the sites of the more recent lakes, there's only cattle fossils . . . additional evidence for geologists that these lakes were probably smaller, shallower . . . because cattle only use water for drinking, so they survive on much less.

Interestingly, there are clam and snail shells, but no fossils of fish. We're not sure why. Uh, maybe there was a problem with the water . . . maybe it was too salty. That's certainly true of other desert lakes.

TRACK 9 TRANSCRIPT

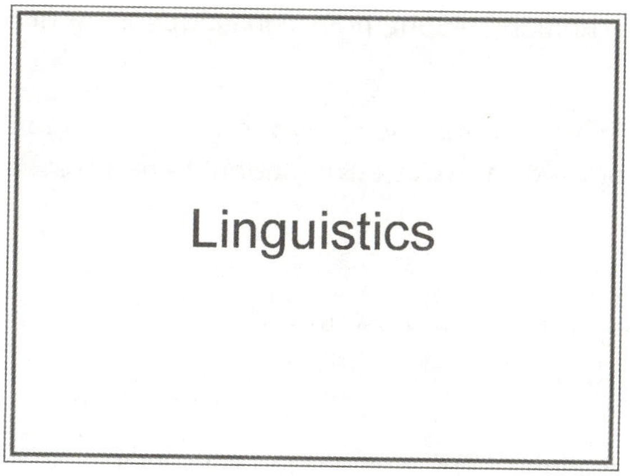

Narrator

Listen to part of a lecture in a linguistics class. The professor has been discussing animal communication systems.

Professor

OK, so last time we covered the dances honeybees do to indicate where food can be found, and the calls and songs of different types of birds . . . Today I'd like to look at-at some communication systems found in *mammals*—uh, particularly in *primates* such as, uh, orangutans, chimpanzees, gorillas . . . um, yes, Thomas?

Male student
Excuse me, professor, but . . . when you talk about *gorilla* language, do you mean, like, those experiments where humans taught them *sign* language, or-or a language like . . .

Professor
OK, OK, wait-wait-wait just a minute—now, who in this class heard me use the word "language"? No one, I hope—what we're talking about here are systems of *communication*, alright?

Male student
Oh, sorry, communication, right . . . uh, but could you maybe, like, clarify what the *difference* is?

Professor
Of course, that's a fair question . . . OK, well, to start with, let's make it clear that *language* is a *type* of communication, *not* the other way around. OK, so *all* communication systems, language included, have certain features in common. For example, the *signals* used to communicate—from the bees' dance movements to the words and sentences found in human language—all these signals convey *meaning*. And all communication systems serve a *purpose*—a, uh, *pragmatic function* of some sort—warning of danger, perhaps, or offering other needed information.

But there are several features peculiar to human language, that have, for the most part, never been found in the communication system of any other species. For one thing, *learnability*: Animals, uh, animals have instinctive communication systems; um, when a dog, a puppy gets to a certain age, it's able to bark. It barks without having to learn how from other dogs. It just . . . barks. But much of human language has to be learned, from other humans. What else makes human language unique? What makes it *different* from animal communication? Debra.

Female student
Uh, how about *grammar*? Like, having verbs, nouns, adjectives . . .

Professor
OK, that's another feature and it's a good examp—

Female student

. . . I mean, I mention this 'cause, like, in my biology class last year, I kinda remember talking about a study on *prairie dogs*, where . . .

I *think* . . . the researchers claimed that the warning cries of prairie dogs constitute *language* because they have these different parts of *speech*—you know, like *nouns* to name the type of predator they've spotted, uh, *adjectives* to describe its size and shape, *verbs*, um . . . but now it seems like—

Professor

Alright, hold on a moment . . . I'm familiar with the study you're talking about—and for those of you who don't know, *prairie* dogs are not actual *dogs*; they're a type of *rodent* who-who burrow in the ground in the grasslands of the western United States and Mexico.

And, uh—in this study, the researchers looked at the high-pitched *barks* a prairie dog makes when it spots a predator. And from this they made some pretty—well, they made some *claims* about these calls qualifying as an actual *language*, with its own "primitive" grammar. But actually these warning calls are no different from those found among certain types of monkeys. And—well, let's not even get *into* the question of whether concepts like "noun" and "verb" can be meaningfully applied to animal communication.

Another thing that distinguishes a *real* language is a property we call *discreteness*. In other words, messages are built up out of smaller parts—sentences out of words, words out of individual sounds, etc. Now maybe you could say that the prairie dog's message is built from smaller parts. Like, say for example our prairie dog spots a predator—a big coyote, approaching rapidly. So the prairie dog makes a call that means "coyote," then one that means "large," and then another one to indicate its speed. But do you really suppose it makes any difference what *order* these calls come in? No. *But* the discrete units that make up *language can* be put together in different ways . . . those smaller parts can be used to form an *infinite* number of messages—including messages that are completely novel, that've never been expressed before. For example, we can differentiate between "A large coyote moves fast" and, say, um, hmm . . . "Move the large coyote fast," or "Move fast, large coyote!"—and I truly doubt whether anyone has ever uttered *either* of these sentences before. Human language is *productive*—an open-ended communication system—whereas no other communication system has this property.

And another feature of language that's not displayed by any form of animal communication is what we call *displacement*—that is, language is *abstract* enough that we can talk about things that aren't present here and now—things like, "My friend Joe is not in the room," or "It'll probably rain next Thursday." Prairie dogs may be able to tell you about a hawk that's circling overhead right *now*, but they've never shown any inclination to describe the one they saw *last week*.

TRACK 10 TRANSCRIPT

Narrator
Listen again to part of the lecture. Then answer the question.

Male student
when you talk about *gorilla* language, do you mean, like, those experiments where humans taught them *sign* language, or-or a language like . . .

Professor
OK, wait-wait-wait just a minute—now, who in this class heard me use the word "language"?

Narrator
Why does the professor say this:

Professor
now, who in this class heard me use the word "language"?

TRACK 11 TRANSCRIPT

Narrator
Talk about an important experience that you recently had. Describe what happened and explain why it was important to you.

TRACK 12 TRANSCRIPT

Narrator
Some people think that family members are the most important influence on young adults. Others believe that friends are the most important influence. Which do you agree with? Explain why.

TRACK 13 TRANSCRIPT

Narrator
The business studies department at State University is creating a new requirement. You have 45 seconds to read the announcement. Begin reading now.

TRACK 14 TRANSCRIPT

Narrator
Now listen to two students discussing the announcement.

Male student
Did you read this announcement?

Female student
Yeah, and I disagree—I don't think it will actually help students.

Male student
Really? Why not?

Female student
Well, they talked about leadership . . . and organizational skills . . . but that's not really the kind of work you do. Like my older brother's had the kind of jobs they're talking about . . . and typically you're just there to do basic tasks like typing or filing stuff—nothing very meaningful

Male student
Oh, so you wouldn't actually learn anything new . . .

Female student
Exactly.

Male student
I guess I see what you mean—but what about the other point they make?

Female student
About this helping us after we graduate? I don't agree.

Male student
How come?

Female student
Well, the problem is that there are lots of other universities in our area that have the *same requirement* . . . so there are lots of other students at these positions.

Male student
Yeah, I guess I hadn't thought of that.

Female student
So even if you take a position like this in a company while you're still a student, once you graduate, the competition for permanent jobs will be impossible . . . I mean, there just won't be enough jobs available for all the business graduates in this city who will be looking for full-time work.

Male student
Hmm . . . I see what you're saying.

Narrator
The woman expresses her opinion of the university's new policy. State her opinion and explain the reasons she gives for holding that opinion.

TRACK 15 TRANSCRIPT

Narrator
Read the passage from a film studies textbook. You will have 50 seconds to read the passage. Begin reading now.

TRACK 16 TRANSCRIPT

Narrator
Now listen to part of a lecture on this topic in a film class.

Professor
So, the other day I went to this great new movie. And one of the scenes in particular, I thought, was really set up nicely. At the start of the scene . . . uh, before the action and talking and things started . . . you saw, on the movie screen, an image of a city. You could tell it was a big city . . . there were lots of buildings—tall ones, skyscrapers. And the cars and signs on the city streets looked old-fashioned—like they were from the past, like the 1940s.

The other thing I noticed right away, from this first image, just when the scene started, was that the city seemed, uh, gloomy. You couldn't see much because it was, well, there was mostly darkness rather than sunlight, and there was only just a little bit of light from the streetlamps. On top of that, it was raining, and kinda foggy. All of these details worked together to create a dark, gloomy, mysterious feeling.

So, then, when the action started, and it showed detectives talking to each other in an office, I already knew that the office was located in a tall building in a big city, sometime in the 1940s. And I, uh, had a good idea that the events that'd be taking place would be pretty dark and mysterious, because of the shot, the image, I saw at the beginning of the scene.

Narrator
Using the professor's example, explain what an establishing shot is and how it is used.

TRACK 17 TRANSCRIPT

Narrator
Listen to a conversation between two students.

Male student
Hey, Beth, how're things?

Female student
Not great . . .

Male student
Why? What's wrong?

Female student
I just found out I have to move out of my apartment . . . like, right away.

Male student
You're kidding? Why?

Female student
Well, my apartment . . . it's in a house . . . a kinda *old* house. And now something's wrong with the water pipes. I think some of the pipes burst or wore out or something. Anyway, we don't have any water in the house . . . and apparently it's gonna take about two weeks to fix the problem.

Male student
So you need to find a place to live for what . . . two weeks or so?

Female student
Yeah. Bad timing, huh? With midterm exams coming up and everything.

Male student
So have you figured out what you're going to do?

Female student
Well, some friends said I could stay at their place . . . they don't have an extra bedroom, but they said it'd be OK for me to sleep on their living room couch.

Male student
You could probably handle that for a couple of weeks, right?

Female student
I guess so. I mean it's really nice of them to offer . . . and it's free. The only problem is . . . they already have four people living there, so it could be a little crowded.

Male student
And not ideal for studying for midterms.

Female student
Yeah, too many distractions.

Male student
Hmmm . . . Any other options?

Female student
Well . . . I did find this place—it's a small hotel over on Third Street, right near campus . . .

Male student
Oh, right. A lot of kids' parents stay there when they come for a visit.

Female student
Right. So I could get a room *there*. They have a weekly rate . . . and it's pretty reasonable. But, I don't know . . .

Male student
At least at the hotel you'd have a space of your own, you know, so you could get more done.

Female student
That's definitely a plus . . . but I have to think about it . . . even though it's pretty cheap, it'll still end up costing me some money . . . and my budget's pretty tight right now.

Narrator
Briefly summarize the problem the speakers are discussing. Then state which solution you would recommend. Explain the reasons for your recommendation.

TRACK 18 TRANSCRIPT

Narrator
Listen to part of a lecture in a biology class.

Professor
We all know that insects like to eat plants. But some plants have been able to-to develop ways to protect themselves from insects. Today I'm gonna talk about some ways plants defend themselves.

Now, some plants have physical features that prevent insects from landing on them. Like the *passion plant*, for example. Its leaves have little spiky hairs all over them. They're like spikes . . . sticking out of the plant . . . that are so numerous and dense that they prevent insects from landing on the leaves. Basically, there's just no room for the insect to land. And since insects can't land on the leaves, they can't eat them. So, the little hairs serve as a physical feature that helps protect the passion plant from insects.

Alright, but other plants protect themselves using *chemical defenses*. Like the *potato plant*. The potato plant's able to release a chemical throughout its leaf system whenever an insect attacks it—starts eating the leaf. So, say an insect starts eating a potato plant's leaf. That will cause the plant to react by releasing a chemical throughout its leaf system. The insect swallows this chemical as it eats. And this chemical discourages the insect from wanting to eat any more of the plant. How? Well, the substance makes the insect feel full, like it's already had enough to eat. The insect no longer feels hungry. So it stops eating the plant. So, by emitting this chemical, the potato plant protects itself from insects.

Narrator
Using points from the lecture, explain how the passion plant and the potato plant defend themselves from insects.

TRACK 19 TRANSCRIPT

Narrator
Now listen to part of a lecture on the topic you just read about.

Professor
It's quite possible that *R. robustus* actively chased and hunted moving dinosaurs. It was not just a scavenger that ate eggs.

First, about *R. robustus* being too small to hunt dinosaurs. Sure, it would've been too small to have hunted a full-grown psittacosaur, but that doesn't mean it couldn't have hunted baby dinosaurs. *R. robustus* was considerably bigger than a baby psittacosaur would have been, which supports the idea that *R. robustus* was a hunter. Ya see, most predators have at least twice the mass of the animals they prey on, and *R. robustus* was more than twice the mass of the dinosaur in its stomach. Those size relations are exactly what we would expect to find if *R. robustus* hunted baby psittacosaurs and similarly sized dinosaurs.

Second, the length and position of *R. robustus's* legs. Well, there's a *modern* mammal known as the Tasmanian Devil.

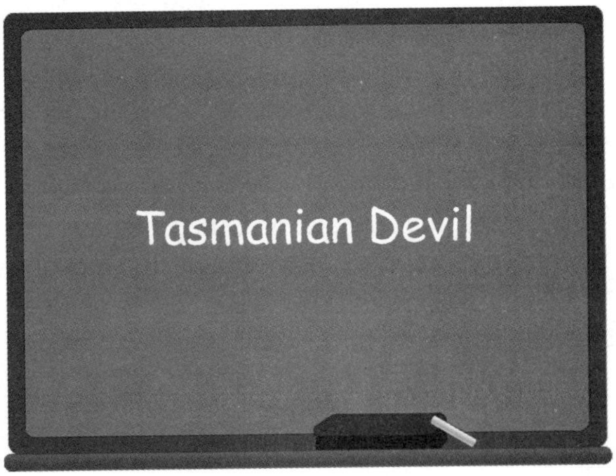

Like *R. robustus*, the Tasmanian Devil also has short legs positioned a little to the side, and yet the Tasmanian Devil can achieve speeds of up to 15 kilometers per hour and is an active and successful predator. Clearly, if the Tasmanian Devil can run fast enough to catch prey, an *ancient* mammal with similar legs probably could too.

Third, the absence of teeth marks on the psittacosaur's bones. The reading overlooks some important facts about *R. robustus*. While *R. robustus* had powerful jaws that it used for grabbing and holding onto prey, it didn't use its back teeth for chewing. We've concluded this because there isn't much wear on the back teeth of various *R. robustus* specimens. Given this evidence, it seems that *R. robustus* swallowed its prey whole or in big pieces. So, given the way *R. robustus* consumed meat, we shouldn't expect to find tooth marks on the bones of prey in its stomach.

TRACK 20 TRANSCRIPT

Narrator
Summarize the points made in the lecture, being sure to explain how they respond to the specific points made in the reading passage.

TRACK 33 TRANSCRIPT

Narrator
Listen to a conversation between a student and her photography professor.

Student
Professor Johnson, there's something that's been on my mind . . .

Professor
OK.

Student
Remember last week you told us that it's really important to get our photography into a show, basically as soon as we can?

Professor
Yup, it's a big step, no question.

Student
Thing is, I'm sitting here and I'm just not sure how I'd get there. I mean, I've got some work I like, but is it really what a gallery is looking for? How would I know? How do I make the right contacts to get into a show? I just really don't . . .

Professor
OK, hold on, slow down. Ah, these are questions that . . . well, that just about every young artist has to struggle with. OK, the first thing you should do is: you absolutely have to stay true to your artistic vision . . . uh, take the pictures you want to take. Don't start trying to catch the flavor of the month and be trendy because you think you'll get into a show. That never works, because you wind up creating something you don't really believe in, that's uninspired, and won't make any shows. I've seen it happen so many times. Uh, this doesn't mean that you should go into a cave. Uh, keep up with trends, even think about how your work might fit in with them, but don't mindlessly follow them.

Student
Well, yeah, I can see that. I think, though, that I've always been able to stay pretty true to what I want to create, not what others want me to create. I think that comes through in my work.

Professor
OK, just remember that it's one thing to create work that you really want to create when it's in the classroom—uh, the only thing at stake is your grade. But work created outside the classroom, that can be a different story. I'm not talking about technique, or things like that. It's just that there's so much more at stake when you're out there making art for a living–uh, there's a lot of pressure to become something you're not, and people often surrender to that pressure . . .

Student
But to get stuff exhibited . . .

Professor
Well, you need to be a bit of an opportunist—y'know, common sense things . . . like always having a sample of your work on hand to give to people. You won't believe the kind of contacts and opportunities you can get this way. And try to get your work seen in places like restaurants, bookstores. You'd be surprised how word gets around about photography in places like that.

Student
OK. It's just so hard to think about all of those practical things *and* make good work, you know?

TRACK 34 TRANSCRIPT

Narrator
Listen again to part of the conversation. Then answer the question.

Student
I think, though, that I've always been able to stay pretty true to what I want to create, not what others want me to create. I think that comes through in my work.

Narrator
Why does the student say this:

Student
I think that comes through in my work.

TRACK 35 TRANSCRIPT

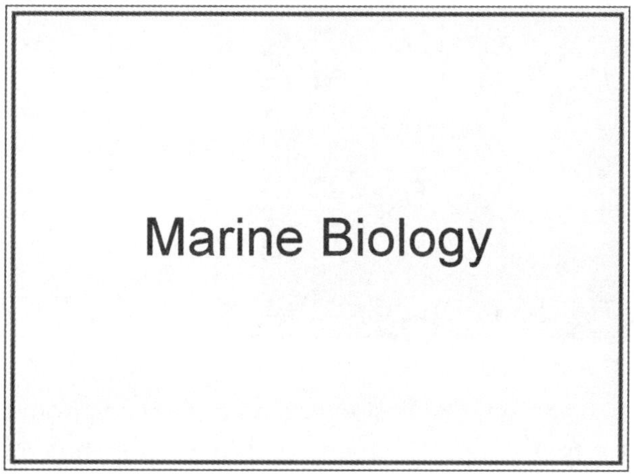

Narrator
Listen to part of a lecture in a marine biology class.

Professor

We know whales are mammals and that they evolved from land creatures. So the mystery is figuring out how they became ocean dwellers. Because, until recently, there was no fossil record of what we call "the missing link," that is, evidence of species that show the transition between land-dwelling mammals and today's whales.

Fortunately, some recent fossil discoveries have made the picture a little bit clearer. For example, a few years back, in Pakistan, they found the skull of a wolflike creature; it was about 50 million years old. Scientists'd seen this wolflike creature before, but this skull was different; the ear area of the skull had characteristics seen only in aquatic mammals, specifically whales. Uh, then—also in Pakistan—they found the fossil of another creature, which we call *Ambulocetus natans*.

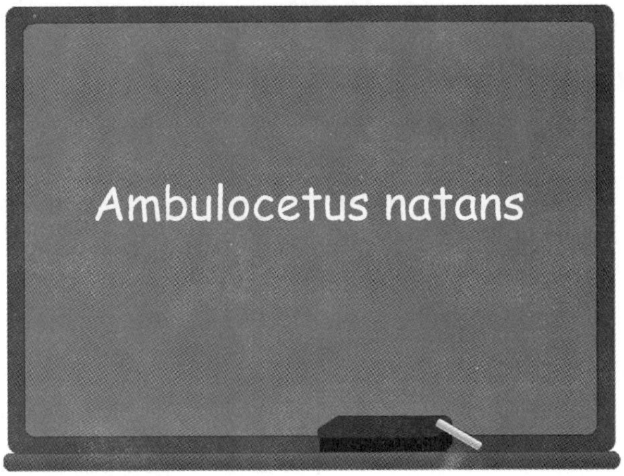

That's a mouthful, eh? The name Ambulocetus natans comes from Latin, of course, and means "walking whale that swims"; it clearly had four limbs that could have been used for walking. It also had a long, thin tail typical of mammals, something we don't see in today's whales. But: it also had a long skeletal structure, and that long skeletal structure suggests that it was aquatic . . .

And very recently, in Egypt, they found a skeleton of Basilosaurus.

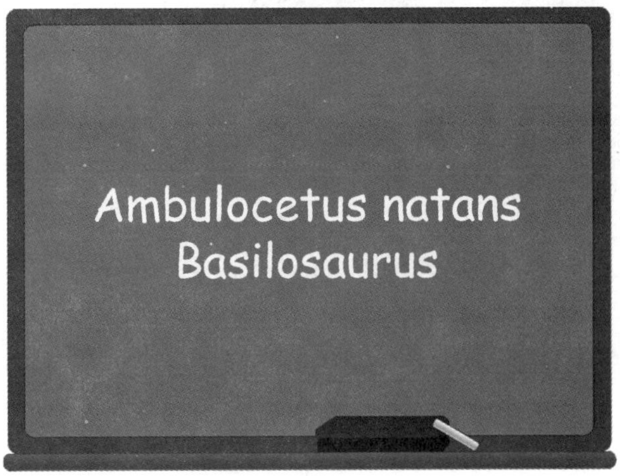

Basilosaurus was a creature that we had already known about for over 100 years, and it has been linked to modern whales because of its long whalelike body, but this new fossil find showed a full set of leg bones, something we didn't have before. The legs were too small to be useful—they weren't even connected to its pelvis and couldn't have supported its weight—but it clearly shows Basilosaurus' evolution from land creatures, so that's a giant step in the right direction. Even better, it establishes Ambulocetus as a clear link between the wolflike creature and Basilosaurus.

Now, these discoveries don't completely solve the mystery. I mean, Ambulocetus is a mammal that shows a sort of bridge between walking on land and swimming, but it also is very different from the whales we know today. So really, we are working with just a few pieces of a big puzzle.

Uh, a related debate involves some recent DNA studies. Remember, DNA is the genetic code for any organism, and when the DNA from two different species is similar, it suggests that those two species are related . . . And when we compared some *whale* DNA with DNA from some *other* species, we got quite a surprise: the DNA suggests that whales are descendants of the hippopotamus!

Yes, the hippopotamus! Well, that came as a bit of a shock, I mean, that a four-legged land and river dweller could be the evolutionary source of a completely aquatic creature up to 25 times its size? Unfortunately, this revelation about the hippopotamus apparently contradicts the *fossil* record, which suggests that the hippopotamus is only a very distant *relative* of the whale, not an *ancestor*, and, of course, as I mentioned, that whales are descended not from hippos but from that distant wolflike creature. So we have contradictory evidence. And more research might just raise more questions and create more controversies. At any rate, we have a choice: we can believe the molecular data, the DNA, or we can believe the skeleton trail, but, unfortunately, probably not both . . .

Uh, and there have been some other interesting findings from DNA research: For a long time, we assumed that all whales that had *teeth*, including *sperm* whales and *killer* whales, were closely related to one another. And the same for the *toothless* whales, like the blue whale and other baleen whales—we assumed that *they'd* be closely related. But recent DNA studies suggest that that's not the case at all; the *sperm* whale is actually closely related to the *baleen* whale, and it's only *distantly* related to the *toothed* whales. So that was a real surprise to all of us.

Note: The lecture above provides one professor's interpretation of evidence related to the evolution of whales. You might be interested to know that the evolution of whales is still being studied, and as new evidence becomes available, alternative interpretations may be more accurate.

TRACK 36 TRANSCRIPT

Narrator
Listen to part of a lecture in a European history class.

Professor
So would it surprise you to learn that many of the foods that we—uh, *today*—consider traditional European dishes—that their key ingredients were not even known in Europe until quite recently—until the Europeans started trading with the native peoples of North and South America? I mean, you're probably aware that the Americas provided Europe—uh, and Asia—with foods like squash . . . beans . . . turkey . . . peanuts . . . But what about all those Italian tomato sauces, Hungarian goulash or—my favorite—French fries—those yummy fried potatoes?

Male student
Wait—I mean, I knew *potatoes* were from—where, South America—?

Professor
South America, right—the Andes Mountains.

Male student
But you're saying . . . *tomatoes* too? I just assumed, since they're used in so many Italian dishes . . .

Professor
No, like potatoes, tomatoes grew wild in the Andes—although *un*like potatoes, they weren't originally *cultivated* there; that seems to have occurred first in *Central* America. And even *then* the tomato doesn't appear to have been very important as a food plant until the Europeans came on the scene. They took it back to Europe with them around 1550, and Italy was indeed the first place where it was widely grown as a food crop. So, in a sense, it really *is* more Italian than American. And another thing—and this is true of both the potato *and* the tomato—both of these plants are members of the nightshade family.

The nightshade family is a category of plants which also includes many that you *wouldn't* want to eat . . . like oh, uh, mandrake, belladonna, and, uh . . . and even tobacco! So it's no wonder that people once considered tomatoes and potatoes to be inedible too, even poisonous—and, in fact, the leaves of the potato plant *are* quite toxic. So it took both plants quite a while to catch on in Europe, and even *longer* before they made the return trip to North America and became popular food items here.

Female student
Yeah, you know, I remember . . . I-I remember my grandmother telling me that when *her* mother was a little girl, a lot of people still thought that tomatoes were poisonous.

Professor
Oh, sure—people didn't really start eating them here until the mid-1800s.

Female student
But, ah—seems like I heard . . . didn't Thomas Jefferson grow them or something?

Professor
Ah! Well, that's true . . . but, then, Jefferson is known not only as the third President of the United States, but also as a scholar who was way ahead of his time—in many ways! He didn't let the conventional thinking of his day restrain his ideas.

Now, potatoes went through a similar sort of, ah—of a rejection process, especially when they were first introduced in Europe—you know how potatoes can turn green if they're left in the light too long? And that greenish skin can make the potato taste bitter—even make you ill. So that was enough to put people off for over 200 years! Yes, Bill?

Male student
I-I'm sorry, Professor Jones, but—I mean, yeah, OK, American crops've probably contributed a lot to European *cooking* over the years, but . . .

Professor
But have they really played any kind of important role in European *history*? Well, as a matter of fact, yes, I was just coming to that. Let's, uh—let's start with North American *corn*, or *maize*, as it's often called. Now, before the Europeans made contact with the Americas, they subsisted mainly on grains—grains that often suffered from crop failures—and it's largely for this reason that political power in Europe was centered for centuries in the *south*—around the Mediterranean Sea, which was where they could grow these grains with more reliability. But when corn came to Europe from Mexico . . . well, now they had a

much heartier crop that could be grown easily in more *northerly* climates, and the centers of power began to shift accordingly.

And *then*—well, as I said, potatoes weren't really popular at first, but when they finally *did* catch on—which they did first in Ireland, around 1780—well, why do you suppose it happened? Because potatoes had the ability to provide an *abundant* and extremely *nutritious* food crop—no other crop grown in northern Europe at the time had anything like the number of vitamins contained in potatoes. Plus, potatoes grown on a single acre of land could feed many more people than say, uh, wheat grown on that same land. Potatoes soon spread to France and other northern European countries, and as a result, the nutrition of the general population improved tremendously, and populations soared in the early 1800s. And so the shift of power from *southern* to *northern* Europe continued.

TRACK 37 TRANSCRIPT

Narrator
Listen again to part of the lecture. Then answer the question.

Male student
I-I'm sorry, Professor Jones, but—I mean, yeah, OK, American crops've probably contributed a lot to European *cooking* over the years, but . . .

Professor
But have they really played any kind of important role in European *history*? Well, as a matter of fact, yes, I was just coming to that.

Narrator
What can be inferred about the professor when she says this:

Professor
But have they really played any kind of important role in European *history*?

TRACK 38 TRANSCRIPT

Narrator
Listen to a conversation between a student and an employee in the university bookstore.

Student
Hi, I bought this book at the beginning of the semester, but something's come up, and I'd like to return it.

Employee
Well, for a full refund, store policy is that you have to return merchandise two weeks from the time it was purchased, but for assigned textbooks or anything having to do with specific courses . . . wait, was it for a specific course?

Student
Yes, but, uh, actually . . .

Employee
Well, for course books, the deadline is four weeks after the beginning of the semester. So for this fall semester, the deadline was October first.

Student
Ouch! Then I missed it. But, uh, why October first?

Employee
I guess the reasoning is that by October first, the semester is in full gear and everyone kinda knows what courses they'll be taking that semester.

Student
I get it. So, it's mainly for people who decide to withdraw from . . . uh, to change to new courses early on . . .

Employee
Exactly. The books have to be in perfect condition of course; they can't be marked up or look used in any way. For the full refund, I mean.

Student
Well, but uh, see, my situation is a little different . . . I-I hoped you might be able to make an exception.

Employee
Well, the policies are generally pretty rigid—*and* the semester is almost over.

Student
OK—here's what happened . . . uh, I think my professor really miscalculated. Anyway, the syllabus was way too ambitious in my opinion. There are only two weeks of classes left in the semester, and there are, like, six books on the syllabus that we haven't even touched.

Employee
I see. So you were hoping to return this one.

Student
Yeah—the professor already announced that we won't be reading this one by Jane Bowles. And all the others I bought used.

Employee
Jane Bowles? Which book of hers?

Student
It's called *Two Serious Ladies*.

Employee
Oh! But you should keep that one! Are you interested in literature?

Student
Well, I am an English major . . .

Employee
You're lucky to have a professor who includes a lesser-known writer like her on the syllabus. You know, not the usual authors we've all read.

Student
So you really think, uh . . . ?

Employee
I do, and especially if you're into literature.

Student
Hmm, well, this I wasn't expecting. I mean, uh, wow!

Employee
I hope you don't think I'm being too pushy. If you prefer, you can return the book and arrange for a store credit. You don't qualify for a refund—policy is policy, after all—but you can make an exchange. And you can use the credit for your books for next semester. The credit carries over from one semester to the next.

Student
Hmm—that's good to know. But now I'm really intrigued. I guess that just because we ran out of time to read this book in class doesn't mean that I can't read it on my own time. You know, I think I'll give it a try.

TRACK 39 TRANSCRIPT

Narrator
What does the man mean when he says this:

Student
Hmm, well, *this* I wasn't expecting. I mean, uh, wow!

TRACK 40 TRANSCRIPT

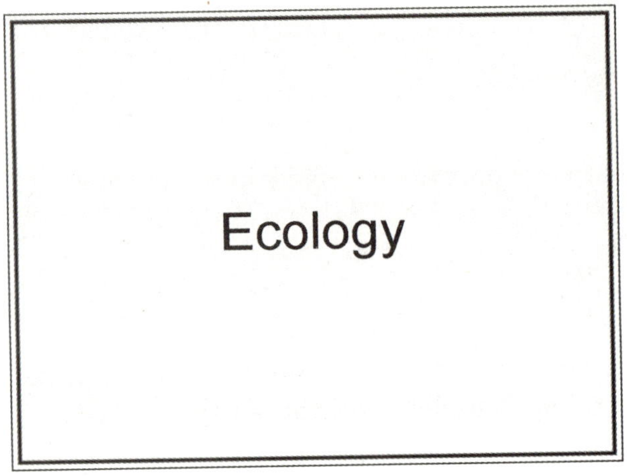

Narrator
Listen to part of a lecture in an ecology class.

Professor
So we've been talking about *nutrients*, the elements in the environment that are essential for living organisms to develop, live a healthy life, and reproduce. Some nutrients are quite scarce; there just isn't much of them in the environment, but fortunately, they get recycled. When nutrients are used over and over in the environment, we call that a *nutrient cycle*. Because of the importance of nutrients and their scarcity, nutrient recycling is one of the most significant ecosystem processes that we'll cover in this course.

The three most important nutrient cycles are the nitrogen cycle, the carbon cycle, and the one we're gonna talk about today, the phosphorus cycle.

So, the phosphorus cycle has been studied a lot by ecologists because, like I said, phosphorus is an important nutrient, and it's not so abundant. The largest quantities are found in rocks and at the bottom of the ocean. How does phosphorus get there? Well, let's start with the phosphorus in rocks. The rocks get broken down into smaller and smaller particles as they're weathered—they're weathered slowly by rain and wind over long periods of time. Phosphorus is slowly released as the rocks are broken down, and it gets spread around into the soil. Once it's in the soil, plants absorb it through their roots.

Female student
So that's the reason people mine rocks that contain a lot of phosphorus? To help with agriculture?

Professor
Uh-huh. They mine the rock, artificially break it down, and put the phosphorus into agricultural fertilizers. So humans can play a role in the first part of the phosphorus cycle—the breaking down of rocks and the spreading of phosphorus into the soil—by speeding up the rate at which this natural process occurs, you see?

Now . . . after the phosphorus is in the soil, plants grow, they use phosphorus from the soil to grow. And when they die, they decompose, and the phosphorus is recycled back into the soil. Same thing with the animals that eat those plants . . . or eat other animals that have eaten those plants. We call all of this the *land phase* of the phosphorus cycle.

But, a lot of the phosphorus in the soil gets washed away into rivers by rain and melting snow. And so begins another phase of the cycle. Can anyone guess what it's called? Nancy?

Female student
Uh, well, if the one is called the land phase, then this has to be called the *water* phase, right?

Professor
Yes. That's *such* a difficult point, isn't it? In a normal water phase, rivers eventually empty into oceans, and once in the oceans, the phosphorus gets absorbed by water plants like algae. Then fish eat the algae . . . or eat other fish that have eaten those plants.

But the water phase is sometimes affected by excessive fertilizers. If not all of the phosphorus gets used by the crops, and large amounts of phosphorus gets into the rivers, this could cause rapid growth of water plants in the river, which can lead to the waterways getting clogged with organisms, which can change the flow of the water . . . Several current studies are looking at these effects, and I really do hope we can find a way to deal with this issue before these ecosystems are adversely affected.

OK? Of course another way that humans can interrupt the normal process is fishing. The fishing industry helps bring phosphorus back to land. In the normal water phase, the remaining phosphorus makes its way—settles—to the bottom of the ocean and gets mixed into ocean sediments.

But remember, this is a cycle: the phosphorus at the bottom of the ocean has to somehow make its way back to the surface . . . to complete the cycle, to begin the cycle all over again. After millions of years, powerful geological forces, like underwater volcanoes, lift up the ocean sediments to form new land. When an underwater volcano pushes submerged rock to the surface, a new island is created. Then, over many more years, the phosphorus-rich rocks of the new land begin to erode . . . and the cycle continues.

Male student
What about . . . well, you said that the nitrogen cycle is also an important nutrient cycle. And there's a lot of nitrogen in the atmosphere, so I was wondering: Is there a lot of *phosphorus* in the atmosphere too?

Professor
Good question, George. You're right to guess that phosphorus can end up in Earth's atmosphere . . . it can move from the land or from the oceans to the atmosphere, and vice versa. However, there's just not a substantial amount of it there, like there is with nitrogen. It's a *very* minimal quantity.

TRACK 41 TRANSCRIPT

Narrator
Listen again to part of the lecture. Then answer the question.

Professor
Can anyone guess what it's called? Nancy?

Female student
Uh, well, if the one is called the land phase, then this has to be called the *water* phase, right?

Professor
Yes. That's *such* a difficult point, isn't it?

Narrator
What does the professor mean when she says this:

Professor
That's *such* a difficult point, isn't it?

TRACK 42 TRANSCRIPT

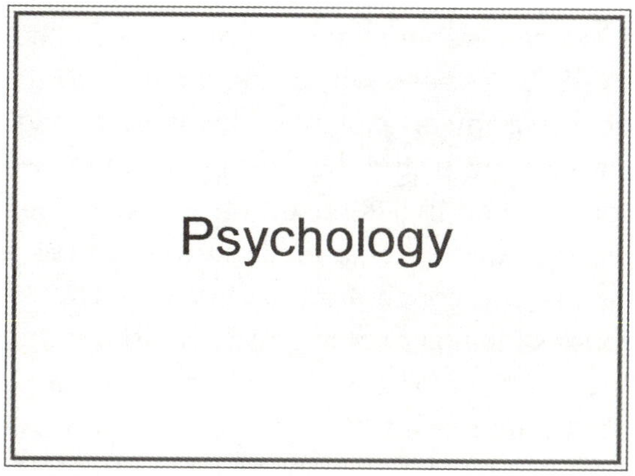

Narrator
Listen to part of a lecture in a psychology class.

Professor

OK, if I asked about the earliest thing you can remember, I'll bet for most of you, your earliest memory would be from about age 3, right? Well, that's true for *most* adults . . . we can't remember anything that happened before the age of 3. An-and this phenomenon is so widespread and well-documented it has a name. It's called childhood amnesia and was first documented in 1893.

As I said this phenomenon refers to *adults* not being able to remember childhood incidents. It's not *children* trying to remember events from last month or last year. Of course it follows that if you can't remember an incident as a child you probably won't remember it as an adult. OK? So–so–so why is this? What are the reasons for childhood amnesia . . . Well, *once* a popular explanation was that childhood memories are repressed . . . um, the memories are disturbing, so that as adults we keep them buried. And so we can't recall them . . . and this is based on . . . well—well it's *not* based on–on–on the the kind of solid research and lab testing I want to talk about today, so—so let's put that explanation aside and concentrate on just two. OK? It—it could be that as children we *do* form memories of things prior to age 3, but forget them as we grow older. That's one explanation. Another possibility is that children younger than 3 lack, um, lack some cognitive capacity for memory. And *that* idea . . . um, that children are unable to form memories, um . . . *that's* been the dominant belief in psychology for the past hundred years. And this idea is very much tied to two things: the theories of Jean Piaget and also to language development in children.

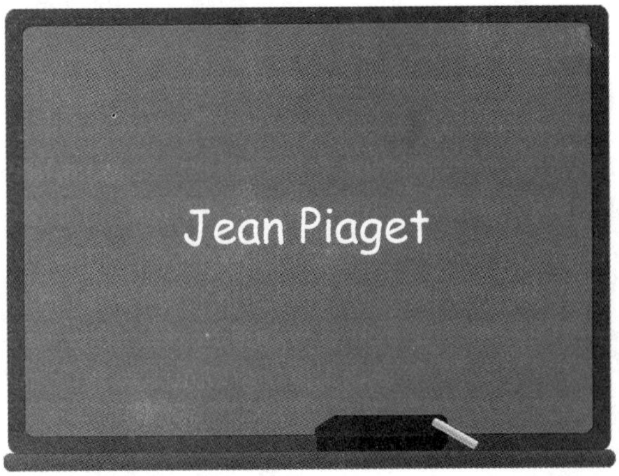

So . . . Piaget's theory of cognitive development. Piaget suggested that because they don't have language, children younger than 18-24 months live in the "here and now," that is, they lack the means to symbolically represent objects and events that are not physically present. Everybody get that? Piaget proposed that young children don't have a way to represent things that aren't right in front of them. That's what language does, right? Words represent things, ideas. Once language starts to develop, from about age 2, they *do* have a system for symbolic representation and can talk about things which aren't in their immediate environment, in—including the past. Of course, he didn't claim that infants don't have any sort of memory—uh, it's acknowledged that they can recognize some stimuli, like faces. And for many years, this model was very much in favor in psychology even though memory tests were never performed on young children.

Well, finally, in the 1980s, a study was done. And this study showed that very young children—under the age of two—*do* have the capacity for recall. Now, if the children can't talk, how was recall tested? Well, that's a good question, since the capacity for recall has always been linked with the ability to talk. So the researchers set up an experiment using imitation based tasks. Adults used props, um, toys or other objects, to demonstrate an action that had two steps. The children were asked to imitate the steps immediately, and then again after delays of 1 or more months. And, even after a delay, the children could-could recall, or replicate the action—the objects used, the steps involved and the order of the steps. Even children as young as 9 months! Now, tests showed that there was a faster rate of forgetting among the youngest children . . . but most importantly, it showed that the development of recall did not depend on language development. And that was an important finding. I guess I should add that the findings don't say that there was *no* connection, um no connection between the development of language and memory. There's some evidence that being able to talk about an event does lead to having a stronger memory of that event. But that doesn't seem to be the real issue here . . .

So, back to our question about the cause of childhood amnesia. Well, there is something called the "rate of forgetting." And childhood amnesia may reflect a high rate of forgetting. In other words, children under the age of 3 do form memories, and do so without language. But they forget the memories at a fast rate, probably faster than adults do. Researchers have set a standard . . . sort of an *expected* rate of forgetting. But that expected rate was set based on tests done on adults. So what is the rate of forgetting for children under the age of three? We expect it to be high but the tests to prove this really haven't been done yet.

TRACK 43 TRANSCRIPT

Narrator
Talk about a time when you accomplished something you did not think you could do. What did you accomplish? Why did you think you could not do it?

TRACK 44 TRANSCRIPT

Narrator
Do you agree or disagree with the following statement? Use details and examples to explain your answer.

All children should be required to learn a second language in school.

TRACK 45 TRANSCRIPT

Narrator
Read a student letter in the university newspaper. You have 45 seconds to read the letter. Begin reading now.

TRACK 46 TRANSCRIPT

Narrator
Now listen to two students discussing the letter.

Male student
Mary, *you're* an art student—what do you think of this letter?

Female student
I don't like the idea.

Male student
Why not?

Female student
Well, first of all . . . his first point, about a lot of people passing through the student center. That's true, but . . .

Male student
But?

Female student
But it's always really crowded with people coming and going, it's not good for showing artwork. Imagine you're standing there, trying to look at a painting . . . there's gonna be, like, a million people walking through . . . people walking in front of you, blocking your view, distracting you . . .

Male student
Hmm, yeah. I hadn't thought of that.

Female student
You won't be able to appreciate the artwork . . . or get a good look at anything, with so much going on, with so many people moving around.

Male student
Yeah, I see what you mean.

Female student
Plus, he's wrong about the windows.

Male student
But isn't it true that it's good for art to have lots of light?

Female student
In a sense, yeah. But *that* kinda light, all that *natural* light from windows, that's actually *not* good, because if it's really sunny out, it'll be way too bright, if it's cloudy it'll be way too dark.

Male student
Oh.

Female student
What you want is *controlled* light, *consistent* light—the kind you get from electric light bulbs. Think about in an art museum . . . in an art museum you've got electric lighting, and the light is always carefully controlled, always at the same level.

Narrator
Briefly summarize the proposal in the student's letter. Then state the woman's opinion about the proposal and explain the reasons she gives for holding that opinion.

TRACK 47 TRANSCRIPT

Narrator
Read a passage from a marketing textbook. You have 50 seconds to read the passage. Begin reading now.

TRACK 48 TRANSCRIPT

Narrator
Now listen to a lecture from a marketing class.

Professor
OK, so I've actually got a few different examples of this. You know, ah, when I was a kid a character named Action-hero was really popular with my friends and me. We would always watch the Action-hero program on television every week and, and play games pretending that we were as strong and powerful as he was. Then pretty soon we began seeing these small Action-hero figures in all the stores and . . . well . . . we all just had to have them. I mean, we'd been watching the television show for so long that it seemed only natural to want to own the toys too.

Well, I finally grew up and left the Action-hero television program and toys behind. Ah, but now I have a seven-year-old daughter who watches television a lot and also likes to play with her toys. And lately her favorite toy is a cute little baby doll with a big round face and lots of curly hair named Rosa. All my daughter's friends have Rosa dolls too, and they enjoy going to each other's houses to play with them. Then a few weeks ago my daughter came running up to me all excited because she had just heard there was going to be a new television program on every week with the doll—Rosa—as the main character. So naturally she and all her friends have begun watching the show, and it's already very popular—as popular as the toy doll.

Narrator
Using the examples from the lecture, explain the concept of entertainment merchandising.

TRACK 49 TRANSCRIPT

Narrator
Listen to a conversation between two students.

Female student
Is there a problem with the electricity?

Male student
Yeah. This storm has knocked out power all over the city, and they're saying it might be several hours before we have electricity again.

Female student
Oh, no, I have a history paper due tomorrow. And I've been writing it on my laptop computer, and the battery's running low. I'm going to need electricity—soon.

Male student
Well, you know, *Jefferson City* still has electricity. And there's a library there where you can plug in your laptop—you could go over there and work on your paper. It's only about a 20-minute drive.

Female student
That's a good idea . . . Of course, I'd have to pack up all of my stuff, and it is raining outside . . .

Male student
Yeah, that's true. Well, why don't you just ask the professor for an extension? You know, tomorrow when you go to class, just ask him if he'd give you an extra day to get the paper done. I'm pretty sure he'd agree, you know, with the storm and all.

Female student
Yeah, that'd sure be a lot easier. But then he did tell us when he gave us the assignment that he wouldn't grant any extensions.

Male student
You don't think he'd grant an exception in this case?

Female student
I'm not sure. It's a little risky. He might just say that we shouldn't have waited until the last minute.

Male student
Yeah, but maybe if other students have the same problem, you might be able to convince him.

Female student
Yeah, I mean it's not our fault the electricity went out. Hmmm.

Narrator
Briefly summarize the woman's problem. Then state which solution you would recommend. Explain the reasons for your recommendation.

TRACK 50 TRANSCRIPT

Narrator
Listen to part of a lecture in a psychology class.

Professor
OK, we generally assume that babies can feel only very basic emotions, like happiness, or anger. That is, that babies just react to things that happen directly to them. However, some new research is suggesting that babies may be able to feel concern for *others* . . . to have *empathy* for others. Now, empathy is a complex emotion—it involves a baby relating to someone else's emotions, not just reacting to things happening directly to them. Let's talk about an experiment that may show that babies could be capable of feeling empathy.

OK, for the first part of the experiment . . . Well, we've always known that babies start to cry when they hear other babies crying, right? One baby in a room starts crying, and all the rest join in. We've always assumed that the other babies cried because they were reacting to the *noise* of the crying, that the noise itself was distressing. So, in the experiment, researchers played a tape recording, a tape of babies crying, to another baby. And, sure enough, the baby started crying when he heard the sound of other babies crying. This was no surprise, of course, and the researchers assumed that the baby cried because of the noise.

But the next part of the experiment *was* surprising. The researchers played the baby a tape of his *own* crying. It was just as noisy, so the researchers expected him to cry. However, this time, the baby did *not* cry; he wasn't upset by the sound of his own crying. Why not? Well, maybe it wasn't the *noise* that had made him cry before, when he heard other babies crying. In fact, maybe noise had nothing to do with it. It could be that the baby felt empathy for the other babies, and that was why he got upset when he heard them crying. The researchers concluded that it's indeed possible that babies feel empathy, concern, for others.

Narrator
Using the points from the lecture, explain why researchers think that babies may feel empathy.

TRACK 51 TRANSCRIPT

Narrator
Now listen to part of a lecture on the topic you just read about.

Professor
Well, ongoing investigations have revealed that predation is the most likely cause of sea otter decline after all.

First, the pollution theory is weakened by the fact no one can really find any dead sea otters washing up on Alaskan beaches. That's not what you would expect if infections caused by pollution started killing a lot of otters. On the other hand, the fact that it's so hard to find dead otters is consistent with the predator hypothesis: if an otter is killed by a predator, it's eaten immediately so it can't wash up on shore.

Second, although orcas may *prefer* to hunt whales, whales have essentially disappeared from the area because of *human* hunters. That means that orcas have had to change their diet to survive, and since only smaller sea mammals are now available, orcas have probably started hunting those. So it probably *is* the orcas that are causing the decline of all the smaller sea mammals mentioned in the passage, the seals, the sea lions, and the sea otters.

And third, the uneven pattern of otter decline is better explained by the orca predation theory than by the pollution theory. What happens to otters seems to depend on whether the location where they live is accessible to orcas or not. In those locations that orcas can access easily, the number of sea otters has declined greatly. However, because orcas are so large, they can't access shallow or rocky locations. And shallow and rocky locations are precisely the types of locations where sea otter populations have *not* declined.

TRACK 52 TRANSCRIPT

Narrator
Summarize the points made in the lecture, being sure to explain how they respond to the specific points made in the reading passage.

TRACK 65 TRANSCRIPT

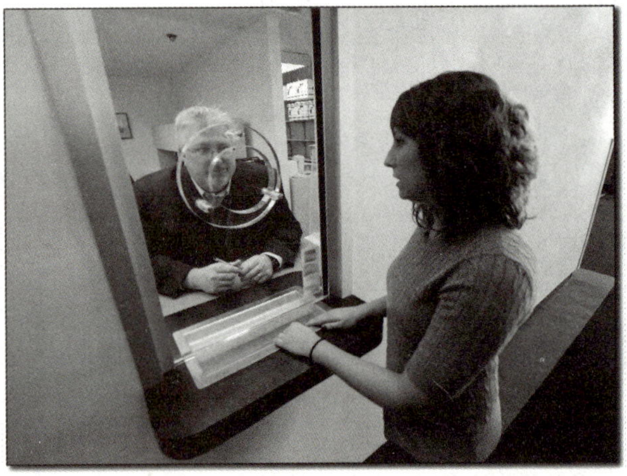

Narrator
Listen to a conversation between a student and a university employee.

Student
Hi, I need to pick up a gym pass.

Employee
OK, I'll need your name, year, and University I.D.

Student
Here's my I.D. card, and my name is Gina Kent and I'm first year.

Employee
OK, Gina, I'll type up a pass for you right away.

Student
Great. This is exciting. I can't wait to get started.

Employee
Oh, this is a wonderful gym.

Student
That's what everybody's been saying. Everyone is talking about the new pool and the new indoor courts, but what I love is all the classes.

Employee
The classes?

Student
Yeah, like the swimming and tennis classes and everything.

Employee
Oh yeah, but this pass doesn't entitle you to those.

Student
It doesn't?

Employee
No, the classes fall into a separate category.

Student
But that's my whole reason for getting a pass. I mean I was planning to take a swimming class.

Employee
But that's not how it works. This pass gives you access to the gym and to all the equipment, and to the pool and so forth, but not when the teams are practicing, so you'd have to check the schedule . . .

Student
But what do I have to do if I want to take a class?

Employee
You'll have to one, register, and two, pay the fee for the class.

Student
But that's not fair.

Employee
Well, I think if you think about it you'll see that it's fair.

Student
But people who play sports in the gym . . . they don't have to pay anything.

Employee
Yes, but they just come in and play or swim on their own. But taking a class, that's a different story. I mean someone has to pay the instructors.

Student
So . . . if I want to enroll in a class . . .

Employee
Then you have to pay extra. The fee isn't very high, but there is a fee. So, what class did you say you wanted to take?

Student
Swimming.

Employee
OK, swimming classes are $30 a semester.

Student
I guess I could swing that, but I'm still not convinced it's fair. So, do I pay you?

Employee
Well, first you need to talk to the instructor. They have to assess your level and steer you to the right class—you know, beginner, intermediate.

Student
You mean, I have to swim for them, show them what I can do?

Employee
No, no, you just tell them a little bit about your experience and skills, so they know what level you should be in.

Student
Oh. OK, so, I guess I'll need an appointment.

Employee
And I can make that for you right now. And then I'll type up your gym I.D. card, you'll need it to get into the building. Now, about that appointment, um, how does Wednesday at 3 sound?

Student
Fine.

Employee
OK, and you'll be meeting with Mark Giddis, he's the swimming instructor. He also coaches the swim team. And, here . . . I've jotted it all down for you.

Student
Great. Thanks.

TRACK 66 TRANSCRIPT

Narrator
Listen again to part of the conversation. Then answer the question.

Employee
Yes, but they just come in and play or swim on their own. But taking a class, that's a different story.

Narrator
What does the man imply when he says this:

Employee
But taking a class, that's a different story.

TRACK 67 TRANSCRIPT

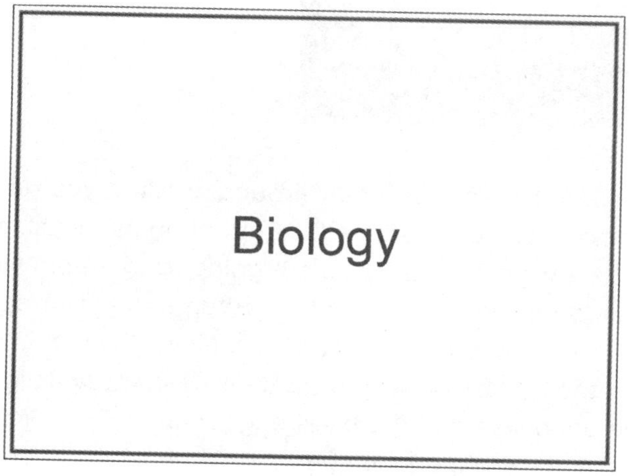

Narrator
Listen to part of a lecture in a biology class. The class has been learning about birds.

Professor
OK. Today we're going to continue our discussion of the *parenting* behaviors of birds . . . And we're going to start by talking about what are known as "distraction displays."

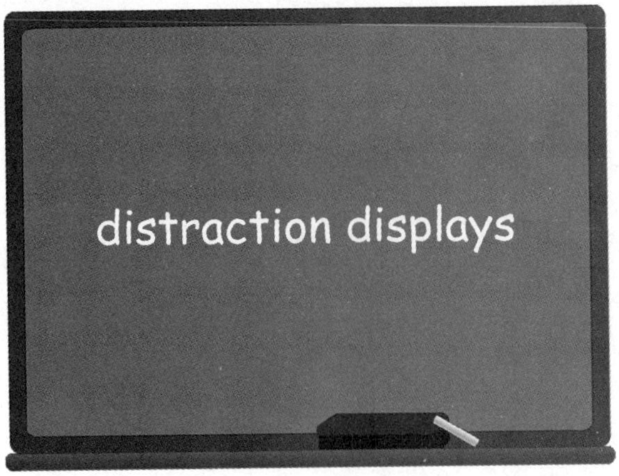

Now if you're a bird, and there's a predator around, what're you going to do? Well, for one thing, you're going to try to attract as *little* attention as possible, right? Because if the predator doesn't know you're *there*, it's not going to try to *eat* you. But sometimes, *certain species* of birds do the exact *opposite*: when a predator approaches, they do their best to *attract* the attention of that predator. Now why would they do that? Well, they do that to *draw* the predator *away* from their *nest*, away from their *eggs* or their *young birds*. And the *behaviors* that the birds engage in to *distract* predators are called "*distraction* displays," and there are a number of different kinds of distraction displays.

Most of the time, when birds are engaging in distraction displays, they're going to be pretending . . . either that they have an *injury* . . . or that they're *ill* . . . or that they're *exhausted* . . . You know, something that'll make the predator think, "Ah, *here's* an *easy* meal."

One pretty *common* distraction display is what's called the *broken-wing* display. And, uh, in a broken-wing display, the bird *spreads* and *drags* a wing or its tail. And while it does that, it slowly moves away from the nest. So it really looks like a bird with a broken wing. And these broken-wing displays can be pretty convincing.

Another version of this kind of distraction display is where the bird creates the impression of a mouse or some other small *animal* that's running along the ground. A good example of that kind of display is created by a bird called a "purple sandpiper."

Now what the purple sandpiper does is, when a predator approaches, it drags its wings—but *not* to give the impression that its wing's *broken*—but to create the illusion that it has a second pair of legs . . . and then it raises its feathers, so it looks like it's got a coat of fur . . . and then it runs along the ground, swerving left and right—you know, like it's running around little rocks and sticks . . . and as it, as it goes along, it makes this little squealing noise, so from a distance it really looks and sounds like a little animal running along the ground, trying to get away. Again, to the predator, it looks like an easy meal.

Now what's interesting is that birds have different levels of performance of these distraction displays. They don't give their top performance, their prime-time performance, every time. What they do is, they save their best performances, their most conspicuous and most risky displays, for the time just before the baby birds become able to take care of themselves. And they time it that way because that's when they'll've made the greatest investment in parenting their young. So they're not going to put on their best performance just after they've laid their eggs, because they haven't invested that much time or energy in parenting yet. The top performances are going to come later.

Now you have some birds that are quite mature, quite capable, almost as soon as they hatch. In that case, the parent will put on the most conspicuous distraction displays just before the babies hatch. Because once the babies are hatched, they can pretty much take care of themselves. And then you have other birds that're helpless when they hatch. In that case, the parent will save its best performances until just before the babies get their feathers.

TRACK 68 TRANSCRIPT

Narrator
Why does the professor say this?

Professor
But sometimes, *certain species* of birds do the exact *opposite*: when a predator approaches, they do their best to *attract* the attention of that predator. Now why would they do that?

TRACK 69 TRANSCRIPT

Narrator
Listen again to part of the lecture. Then answer the question.

Professor
Most of the time, when birds are engaging in distraction displays, they're going to be pretending . . . either that they have an *injury* . . . or that they're *ill* . . . or that they're *exhausted* . . . You know, something that'll make the predator think, "Ah, *here's* an *easy* meal."

Narrator
Why does the professor say this?

Professor
You know, something that'll make the predator think, "Ah, *here's* an *easy* meal."

TRACK 70 TRANSCRIPT

Narrator
Listen again to part of the lecture. Then answer the question.

Professor
Now what the purple sandpiper does is, when a predator approaches, it drags its wings—but not to give the impression that its wing's *broken*—but to create the illusion that it has a second pair of legs . . .

Narrator
Why does the professor say this?

Professor
but *not* to give the impression that its wing's *broken*

TRACK 71 TRANSCRIPT

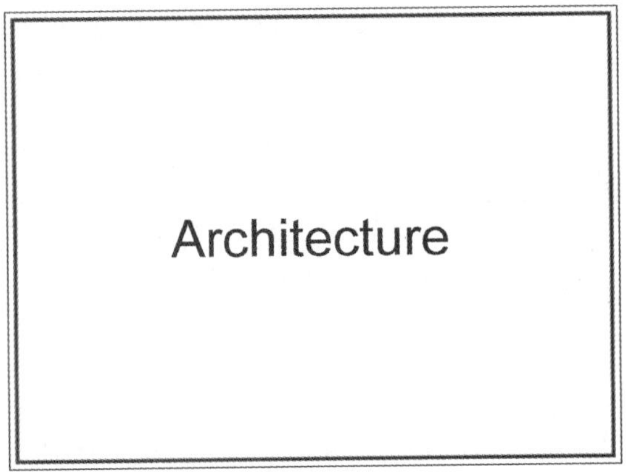

Narrator
Listen to part of a lecture in an architecture class.

Professor
Today we're taking, uh, a little detour from the grand styles of *public* architecture we've been studying . . . to, uh, look at *residential* architecture in the United States. Since this is something we can all identify with, I, I think it'll help us see the relationship between the *function* of a structure and its, uh, its style, or *form*; this has been an ongoing theme in our discussions, and we'll be getting back to it in just a moment.

Uh, but before we get started, I want you to take a moment to think: Does anyone know what the *single* most popular style for a house in the United States is today? Bob?

Male student
I bet it's the ranch-style house.

Professor
Well, in *this* area, probably—But are we typical? Yeah. Sue?

Female Student
How about the kind of house my grandparents live in? They call it, uh, a Cape Cod . . .

Professor
That's the one. Here's a drawing of a, of what we consider—of a classic Cape Cod house.

Cape Cod house

These days, you see this style all *over* the United States, . . . uh, but it **first** showed up in the U.S. northeast—in the New England region—around the late 1600s. Uh, for those of you who don't know the northeast coastal region—um, Cape Cod is a peninsula, a, a narrow strip of land that juts out into the Atlantic. And um . . . so, so *many* houses in this particular style were built on Cape Cod, that the name of the *place* became the name of the *style*. Uh, now, *why* did the Cape Cod-style house become so popular in the north-east? Well, *one* reason is that it's a great example of form following function. Uh, we've, we've talked about this design principle a lot . . . about form following function . . . and . . . what'd we say it meant? Someone give me an application of this principle. What does this concept, that form should follow function, how would it be applied to housing design?

Female student
Well . . . if it means that the *design* of a building should be based on the needs of the people who *use* it. Then . . . well . . . the architect has to be very practical—to think about . . . the people who'll actually be living in the house . . . or working in the office building—whatever . . . So, for the *architect*, it's all about the *users—not* about showing off how creative you can be.

Professor
Good! Of course, for a Cape Cod house, it might be even *more* accurate to say that, uh, form *also* follows *climate*.

Who knows what the climate's like on Cape Cod?

Male student
Cold in the winter!

Female student
And whenever I visit my grandparents, it's really wet—it's usually either raining or snowing or foggy . . . and windy, too. I guess because it's so exposed to the ocean?

Professor
That's right. So take another look at this drawing, and, uh, you can imagine how this design might be particularly helpful in that kind of climate.

Cape Cod house

Notice how the house sits fairly low to the ground. Uh, this relatively low, compact structure helps the house withstand the strong winds blowing off the ocean. An-and look at the slope of the roof. The steep angle helps keep off all that rain and snow that accumulates in the winter. A-another thing: Cape Cod houses usually face *south*, to take advantage of, of the sun's warmth through the windows—that's helpful in winter.

Now. What can you tell me about the chimney? A-about its location.

Female student
Well. It's in the middle . . . Because . . . Does that have something to do with heating the houses . . . I mean, since—the heat never has to travel very far.

Male student
That'd mean you can heat the house more efficiently, right?

Professor
Exactly. Now, see how the house has very little exterior decoration? Tha-That's also typical of early Cape Cod houses. The wind was one reason—nothing sticking out that might blow away in the harsh weather. Uh, but there was probably another reason—*not* related to the climate—um, more, um—more a reflection of rural New England *society* back then. You see, Cape Cod houses were not built in the big cities, where all the rich people lived back then. These were modest dwellings; the people who built them simply couldn't afford lots of expensive decorative details. But, it was *more* than just a matter of money. In these rural areas, people depended on each other for survival: uh, neighbors had to help and support each other in a difficult environment. So, you didn't want to appear to be showing off. You'd want to avoid anything that might set you apart from your neighbors—the same people you might need to help you some day. So, so, all this helped to create an attitude of *conformity* in the community . . . and you can see why a modest—a, a very plain style would have become so widely imitated throughout rural New England.

Female student
It *is* plain but, you know, it's nice looking.

Professor
Good point! And, in fact, it's precisely that aesthetic appeal—the um, uh, the purity . . . the nearly perfect proportions of the house—that's another reason for the Cape Cod's enduring popularity—even in places where the climate's so mild that its functional design doesn't matter.

TRACK 72 TRANSCRIPT

Narrator
Listen again to part of the lecture. Then answer the question.

Professor
Does anyone know what the *single* most popular style for a house in the United States is today? Bob?

Male student
I bet it's the ranch-style house.

Professor
Well, in *this* area, probably—But are we typical?

Narrator
Why does the professor say this:

Professor
Well, in *this* area, probably—But are we typical?

TRACK 73 TRANSCRIPT

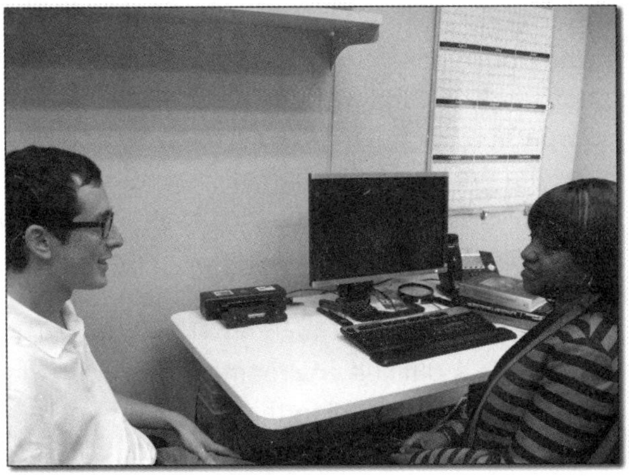

Narrator
Listen to a conversation between a student and a professor.

Student
Hi Professor Atkins, you wanted to see me?

Professor
Hi Bill, thanks for coming. I wanted to talk to you about . . .

Student
. . . Is there . . . is there something wrong with my research paper?

Professor
No, not at all. In fact, it's very good. That's why I wanted to talk to you.

Student
Oh . . . thanks.

Professor
I *think* you know the department is looking to hire a new professor. Are you familiar with our hiring process?

Student
No . . . but . . . what's that gotta do with me?

Professor
Well, Bill . . . we have several qualified applicants we're serious about. And as part of the interview process, we have them meet with a committee of professors and students in our department. They also have to give a talk.

Student
Do you mean . . . like a lecture?

Professor
Yes. Like a sample lecture on one of their academic interests.

Student
Oh . . . so you can see their teaching style?

Professor
Exactly.

Student
Uh-huh, makes sense.

Professor
So I'd like to know if you'd be willing to join as a student representative on the interview committee. It'd be a good experience for you. You could . . . uh . . . put it on your résumé.

Student
Oh! That'd look good for my grad school application, I guess. So what do I have to do?

Professor
The department secretary will give you a schedule of the applicants' visits. If you're free, we'd like you to attend their talks, and then later you can give us your opinion. Oh, and, we usually serve lunch or snacks, depending on what time the talk is.

Student
Cool! That's another good reason to do this. Um . . . when is the next talk?

Professor
We actually haven't had *any* yet. The first one is next Friday at 10:00 A.M. Then lunch and informal discussion with the applicant right after.

Student
Oh, well I'm free on Fridays. If all the talks are on Fridays, I'll be able to make it to all of them.

Professor
That's great! Now you should know that this job candidate is interested in the life cycles in the forest . . .

Student
That's . . . that's what my research is about!

Professor
Yes, I know. That's why I feel it necessary to point out that even though this applicant's research interests are similar to yours, we want you to tell us what you think about the

teaching of all these applicants. Your perspective as a student—how the applicant *teaches* in the classroom—that's what's important to us.

Student
I understand. So, how many applicants are there?

Professor
Let's see . . . we have . . . four—all very good candidates that we'll be looking at over the next few weeks. It's going to be a tough decision. But it'll be a good experience for you—especially if you're going to grad school.

Student
Thank you! It'll be cool to do this. I'll get a copy of the schedule from the secretary on my way out.

Professor
You're welcome! See ya in class this afternoon.

TRACK 74 TRANSCRIPT

Narrator
Listen again to part of the conversation. Then answer the question.

Professor
I *think* you know the department is looking to hire a new professor. Are you familiar with our hiring process?

Student
No . . . but . . . what's that gotta do with me?

Narrator
Why does the student say this:

Student
what's that gotta do with me?

TRACK 75 TRANSCRIPT

Environmental Science

Narrator
Listen to part of a lecture in an environmental science class.

Professor
When land gets developed for human use, the landscape changes . . . we don't see as many types of vegetation . . . trees . . . grasses . . . and so forth . . . this in turn leads to other losses . . . the loss of animals that once lived there . . . uh, but these are the *obvious* changes . . . But there are also *less* obvious changes, like the *climate*. One interesting case of this . . . uh . . . of changes in the local land use causing changes in climate, specifically the temperature, is in Florida. Now, what comes to mind when you think of the state of Florida?

Male student
Sunshine! Beaches . . .

Female student
Warm weather and oranges . . .

Professor
Yes, exactly. Florida has long had a great citrus industry—large groves of oranges, lemons, and the like. Florida's winter is very mild; the temperature doesn't often get below freezing. But there are some areas of Florida that do freeze, so in the early 1900's farmers moved even further south in Florida to areas that were even less likely to freeze. Obviously, freezing temperatures are a danger to the crops. A bad bout of cold weather . . . a long spell of frosts . . . could ruin a farmer's entire crop. Anyway, before the citrus growers moved south, much of the land in south Florida was what we call "wetlands."

Wetlands are areas of marshy . . . swampy land . . . areas where water covers the soil, or is present either at or near the surface of the soil, for a large part of the year.

Wetlands have their own unique ecosystems with plants and animals with special and interesting adaptations . . . very exciting, but it's not what we're talking about today . . . Ummm . . . where was I?

Male student
Farmers moved south?

Professor
Oh yes . . . farmers moved south, but the land was not suitable for farming . . . you can't grow oranges in wetlands . . . so farmers had to transform the wetlands into land suitable for farming. To do that, you have to drain the water from the land, move the water elsewhere, and divert the water sources, such as rivers. Hundreds of miles of drainage canals were built in the wetlands. Now these areas . . . the new areas the farmers moved to . . . used to be warm and unlikely to freeze, however, recently the area has become susceptible to freezes . . . and we are trying to understand why.

Female student
Is it some global temperature change or weather pattern . . . like El Niño or something?

Professor
Well, there are two theories. One idea, is as you suggest . . . that major weather patterns . . . something like El Niño . . . are responsible. But the *other* idea, and this is the one that I personally subscribe to, is that the changes in the temperature pattern have been brought about by the loss of the wetlands . . .

Male student
Well, how would loss of wetlands make a difference?

Professor
Well, think about what we've been studying so far. We've discussed the impact of landscapes on temperature right? What effects does a body of water have on an area?

Male student
Oh yeah, uh, bodies of water tend to absorb the heat during the day . . . and then they release the heat at night.

Professor
Yes, exactly! What you just said is what I want you all to understand. Bodies of water *release* heat—and moisture back into the environment. So places near large bodies of water are generally milder . . . uh, slightly warmer . . . than those without water. And what I . . . and others think is that the loss of the wetlands has created a situation where the local temperatures in the area are now slightly different, slightly *colder*, than they were a hundred years ago before the wetlands were drained.

Female student
Hmmm . . . do we know what the temperature was like back then?

Professor
Well, we were able to estimate this: We have data about south Florida's current landscape, uh, the plant cover, and we were able to *reconstruct* data about its landscape prior to 1900. Then we entered those data . . . information about what the landscape looked like before and after the wetlands were drained, we entered the data into a computer weather model. This model can predict temperatures . . . and when all of the data were entered . . . an overall *cooling* trend was predicted by the model.

Female student
How much colder does it get now?

Professor
Well, actually, the model shows a drop of only a few degrees Celsius . . . but this is enough to cause dramatic damage to crops. If temperatures overnight are already very *close* to the freezing point, then, this drop of just a few degrees can take the temperature below freezing . . . and freezing causes frosts, which kill crops. These damaging frosts wouldn't happen if the wetlands were still in existence. Just a tiny temperature difference can have major consequences.

TRACK 76 TRANSCRIPT

Narrator
Listen again to part of the lecture. Then answer the question.

Professor
Wetlands have their own unique ecosystems with plants and animals with special and interesting adaptations . . . very exciting, but it's not what we're talking about today . . . Ummm . . . where was I?

Male student
Farmers moved south?

Narrator
Why does the student say this:

Male student
Farmers moved south?

TRACK 77 TRANSCRIPT

Narrator
Listen to part of a lecture in a business class.

Professor

Let's get started. Last time we were talking about the *need* for advertising. Now let's look at how you can *successfully* call attention to the service or product you want to sell. To succeed, you've gotta develop a systematic approach. If you don't come up with a system . . . a plan . . . you risk making decisions that *waste money* . . . or even *drive away potential customers*.

But what does a systematic advertising plan look like? Well, it covers what we call *the four M's*.

The four M's . . . *market* . . . *media* . . . *money* . . . *message* . . . all are important areas to focus on when creating your advertising plan. We'll look at them one by one.

The first step is to look at your *market*. That's the people who might become *customers* . . . *buyers* of your service or product. You need to know all about your possible customers. Who are they? What age group are they? What do they like, or dislike? How do they shop? So . . . ya got that? A market is a *group of potential customers*.

Next, *media*. Obviously the major media are television, radio, newspapers, magazines, uh . . . billboards, and so forth. They're all avenues of communication. And you need to figure out *which* media you should advertise through . . . which media will reach your intended audience . . . your *market*. So you do *research*, trying to determine which media will reach the *most* potential customers for the *lowest cost*.

For instance, if you have a product that, oh, say, teachers would like, then teachers are your market . . . so you ask yourself: *What magazines* do the majority of teachers *read*? What *TV programs* do teachers *watch*? Do teachers listen to much *radio*? At what times of the day? Say . . . now, your *research* turns up two magazines that teachers read. And it also shows that the majority of teachers, say, ages 20 to 30 read the magazine about *classroom activities*, while most teachers *older than that* read the other magazine . . . the one about . . . oh, let's say *educational psychology*. You think your product will appeal most to teachers ages 20 to 30, so you decide to put your advertisement in *their* favorite magazine, the one about classroom activities. You *don't waste money* advertising in the . . . the educational psychology magazine . . . the one that the younger teachers generally *don't read*. And since you're reaching the *majority* of teachers in your *target* age group, you're probably spending your money well.

Which brings us to the *third* "M"—*money*. You have an advertising budget to spend, but how do you spend it wisely? Again, *research* is the key . . . good research gives you *facts*. Facts that can help you decide . . . well, as we already mentioned . . . decide the right market to target and the best media to use . . . but also *when* to advertise or how to get the best *rates*. Like, maybe you're advertising sports equipment, and you've been spending most of your budget during the holiday season when people buy gifts for each other. In theory, that . . . that would seem a great time to advertise. But maybe research shows that you're wrong . . . that the customers who buy sports equipment tend *not* to give it as a holiday gift, but want to use it themselves. In that case, advertising during a *different* season of the year might give you better results, and maybe, uh . . . even at lower, *non*-holiday rates, so you actually save money . . . .But you need to get the facts—facts that come from good research—to be certain . . . and know for sure you're getting your money's worth.

OK . . . finally, there's your *message* . . . what you want to say about your product—Why buying it'll make the customer's life easier, or safer, or better somehow. *Whatever* the message is, make sure you get it right.

Let me give you an example of *not* getting it right . . . and you're going to *love* this one! There was this soup shop. The soup was really tasty, but there weren't a lot of customers. The owners thought that maybe if they gave something away for free with each purchase, then more people would come buy soup. So they got some cheap socks and advertised to give a pair away with each bowl of soup. But then even *fewer* people came to the restaurant . . . well, you can imagine why. People started to *associate the soup with feet* . . . they began to *imagine the soup smelled like feet*. The advertising message—soup means free socks— was a bad choice. It was a waste of money, and *worse*, it caused a *loss* of customers!

Now, I want everyone to get into small groups and come up with some examples . . . not of *good* advertising messages, but of truly *disastrous* ones. Think of real examples or make some up, and, um, talk about the reasons those messages are *unsuccessful*. And then we'll get back together and share.

TRACK 78 TRANSCRIPT

Narrator
Listen again to part of the lecture. Then answer the question.

Professor
Let me give you an example of *not* getting it right . . . and you're going to *love* this one!

Narrator
What does the professor mean when she says this:

Professor
and you're going to *love* this one!

TRACK 79 TRANSCRIPT

Narrator
Talk about an interesting book you have read. Explain why you thought the book was interesting. Give specific details and examples to explain your answer.

TRACK 80 TRANSCRIPT

Narrator
Some people think that children should be allowed to watch whatever television programs they choose to. Others think that parents should exercise control over the television programs their children watch. Which do you agree with? Explain why.

TRACK 81 TRANSCRIPT

Narrator
Central College is planning to renovate its dormitories. Read the article in the college newspaper about the plan. You will have 45 seconds to read the article. Begin reading now.

TRACK 82 TRANSCRIPT

Narrator
Now listen to two students discussing the college's plan.

Female student
The college is making a mistake with this new plan.

Male student
What do you mean? I think it'll really help accomplish the college's goals.

Female student
Don't be so sure. All that construction—for *two* years—it's gonna create a lot of noise.

Male student
Oh you mean in the beginning, for students still living in the dorms . . .

Female student
Yeah, students who are trying to sleep or do work are constantly going to be disturbed. So people will try to get as far away as possible—probably by moving off campus. So they'll lose even more people.

Male student
Huh. I hadn't thought of that. But still, once all the construction's over, more people will probably want to live in the dorms, right? I mean, the living conditions will be so much better.

Female student
If they can afford to . . . Do you know how the college is planning on paying for this plan? By raising the cost of campus housing.

Male student
Oh, I didn't realize that.

Female student
Yeah. So if it's more expensive, why would people want to move back into the dorms if they can rent an apartment for less money?

Narrator
The woman expresses her opinion about the college's plan. State her opinion and explain the reasons she gives for holding that opinion.

TRACK 83 TRANSCRIPT

Narrator
Now read a passage about outsider art from a modern art textbook. You will have 45 seconds to read the passage. Begin reading now.

TRACK 84 TRANSCRIPT

Narrator
Now listen to part of a lecture in an art history class.

Professor
Alright, so let's consider the work of the outsider artist Henry Darger. Darger lived by himself in a tiny apartment in Chicago in the 1900s. He had no friends and spent all his spare time there alone, creating hundreds of paintings and drawings. He had never formally studied art and kept his work completely private, so no one ever saw it or responded to it during his lifetime.

And so when you see Darger's work, you notice how unique it is—it doesn't remind you of anything you've ever seen before—it's very much his own. For example, one piece—it's a watercolor painting . . . in this piece he illustrates a story . . . about the adventures of seven children. But see, Darger had a really hard time drawing human figures . . . yet he managed to come up with his own rather unique solution for the problem. He simply cut out pictures of children from newspapers and magazines and pasted them into his own painted illustration of trees, flowers, and grass. The results look . . . uh . . . a little strange. Darger's picture looks more cluttered . . . more crowded with details . . . than the pictures of other artists because its entire surface is painted and there are no spaces left empty. It's also a lot longer than the pictures of most other artists—about nine feet long.

Narrator
Explain why Henry Darger is considered an Outsider Artist.

TRACK 85 TRANSCRIPT

Narrator
Now listen to a conversation between two students.

Female student
By the way, Frank, I heard you got a summer research position with Professor Davis.

Male student
Uh-huh. But I've got a problem.

Female student
Oh?

Male student
Yeah, well, since I didn't hear from her for so long, I assumed I didn't get the position. So I didn't apply for a dorm room for the summer. I'm afraid it's too late for that now.

Female student
Yeah, the deadline for campus housing applications has already passed. So whadda you gonna do now?

Male student
Well, I can stay with my parents. They live two hours from here an' so I thought I could drive, uh, commute to campus every day. I know my mom and dad would be happy to have me over for a few weeks. And most of my old friends'll be home for the summer, so in a way it'd be fun.

Female student
Yeah, I understand. But you'd spend quite a bit of time on the road going back and forth. Won't you get tired?

Male student
Yeah, that thought *did* cross my mind. The other thing I could do is rent an apartment *off*-campus. Besides being much closer to work, I'd also save tons of money on gas.

Female student
Uh-huh, but then you'd have to pay rent.

Male student
I know. There's always something, isn't there.

Narrator
The students discuss a problem and two possible solutions. Briefly summarize the problem. Then state which of the two solutions you prefer and explain why.

TRACK 86 TRANSCRIPT

Narrator
Listen to part of a lecture in an interior design class.

Professor
So, we're talking about interior design, er, specifically the basic principles typically used in home and office decoration in the United States. Effective designs create a delicate balance between two things. You need unity *and* you also need contrast, which is essentially a break in unity. Now this might seem a little contradictory, but let me explain why we need both of these for an effective design.

So for the first principle . . . we need *unity* in our design . . . think of it as, hmm, *consistency*. Well, an easy and very effective way to do this is by bringing together similar elements—a common example is by matching colors. You pick a color and use it for different parts of the room. Say, you pick green, and then use a light shade of green for the walls, and maybe a somewhat darker shade for the fabric on the sofa, and finally complement that with a matching green in the rug. When elements match, the room is unified and gives its residents a sense of order and comfort.

OK, but there is such a thing as *too much* unity. Remember, you need a balance of unity and contrast. If all you do is focus on unity, the result will be a booooring room. So, what do you do? Well, you apply the second basic principle of design, which is *contrast*. Contrast serves to disrupt, or, er, break up, the unity in places, but in a careful, intentional way. Uhmmm . . . well let's continue using color as an example . . . to create contrast, color contrast, you need to abruptly change your color scheme once in a while. Ah let's see . . . you could um . . . throw bright red cushions on your dark green sofa, for example. Contrast makes things stand out: the green will look even greener next to the red. So, now your room is more interesting, not completely the same. But watch out, too much contrast is also dangerous, just like too much sameness is . . . too much contrast will make the room feel busy, chaotic.

Narrator
Using the points and examples from the lecture, explain what unity and contrast are, and how they make interior design more effective.

TRACK 87 TRANSCRIPT

Narrator
Now listen to part of a lecture on the topic you just read about.

Professor
It is often said that people are reading less literature today than they used to. What should we make of this?

Well, first, a book doesn't have to be *literature* to be intellectually stimulating. Science writing, history, political analysis, and so forth aren't literature, perhaps, but they're often of high quality. And these kinds of books can be *just* as creative and well-written as a novel or a play—they can stimulate the imagination. So don't assume that someone who isn't reading literature isn't reading a good book.

But let's say that people aren't just spending less time with literature, they're also spending less time with books in general. Does that mean that the culture is in decline? No. There's plenty of culturally valuable material that isn't written: music and movies, for example. Are people wasting their time when they listen to a brilliant song or watch a good movie? Do these non-literary activities lower cultural standards? Of *course* not. Culture has changed. In today's culture there are many forms of expression available other than novels and poems, and some of these creative forms speak more directly to contemporary concerns than literature does.

Finally, it's probably true that there's less support for literature today than in earlier generations. But don't be too quick to blame the *readers*. Sometimes it's the *author's* fault. Let's be honest: a lot of modern literature is *intended* to be difficult to understand. There's not much reason to suppose that *earlier* generations of readers would have read a lot of today's literature *either*.

TRACK 88 TRANSCRIPT

Narrator
Summarize the points made in the lecture, being sure to explain how they cast doubt on specific points made in the reading passage.

TRACK 101 TRANSCRIPT

Narrator
Listen to a conversation between a student and a professor.

Student
So, Professor Tibbits, your note said that you wanted to see me . . . about my Hemingway paper? I have to say, that grade wasn't what I was expecting. I thought I'd done a pretty good job.

Professor
Oh, you did. But do you really want to settle for *pretty* good when you can do something *very* good?

Student
You think it can be *very* good?

Professor
Absolutely.

Student
Would that mean you'd, I could get a better grade?

Professor
Oh sorry, it's not for your grade; it's . . . I think you could learn a lot by revising it.

Student
You mean rewrite the whole thing? I'm really swamped; there's deadlines wherever I turn, and . . . and I don't really know how much time I could give it.

Professor
Well, it *is* a busy time . . . with spring break coming up next week. It's your call, but I think that with a little extra effort you can really turn this into a fine essay.

Student
No, yeah, I mean, after I read your comments—I can see how it tries to do too much.

Professor
Yeah, it's just too ambitious for the scope of the assignment.

Student
So I should cut out the historical part.

Professor
Yes, I would just stick to the topic, anything unrelated to the use of nature imagery has no place in the paper; all that tangential material just distracts from the main argument.

Student
I never know how much to include, you know, where to draw the line.

Professor
Tell me about it. *All* writers struggle with that one. But it's something you can learn, that'll become more clear with practice. But I think if you just cut out the, uh . . .

Student
The stuff about the history . . . but, if I cut out those sections, won't it be too short?

Professor
Well, better a short, well–structured paper than a long paper that's poorly structured and wanders off topic.

Student
So, all I have to do is delete those sections?

Professor
Well, not so fast. After you cut out those sections you'll have to go back and revise the rest . . . to see how it all fits together. And of course, you'll have to revise the introduction, too, to accurately describe what you do in the body of the paper. But that shouldn't be too difficult; just remember to keep the discussion focused. Do you think you can get it to me by noon tomorrow?

Student
Wow . . . um, I have so much . . . uh, but I'll try.

Professor
OK, good, do try. But if you can't, we'll shoot for after spring break, OK?

TRACK 102 TRANSCRIPT

Narrator
Listen again to part of the conversation. Then answer the question.

Student
I never know how much to include, you know, where to draw the line.

Professor
Tell me about it.

Narrator
What does the professor mean when she says this:

Professor
Tell me about it.

TRACK 103 TRANSCRIPT

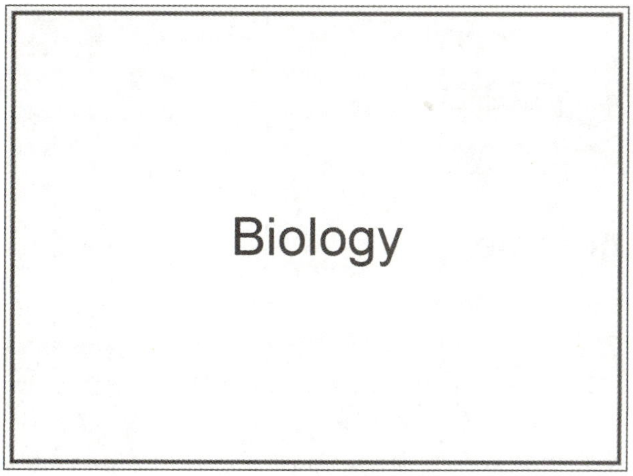

Narrator
Listen to part of a lecture in a biology class.

Professor
As we learn more about the DNA in human cells . . . and how it controls the *growth and development of cells* . . . then maybe we can explain a very important observation—that when we try to *grow* most human cells in a laboratory, they seem programmed to divide only a certain number of times before they die. Now this differs with the type of cell; some cells, like nerve cells, only divide seven to nine times in their total life. Others, like skin cells, will divide many, many more times. But finally the cells stop renewing themselves and they die. And in the cells of the human body itself, in the cells of every organ . . . of almost every type of tissue in the body, the same thing will happen eventually.

OK. You know that all of a person's genetic information is contained on very long pieces of DNA called chromosomes—46 of them in a *human* cell, that's 23 pairs of these chromosomes—of various lengths and sizes.

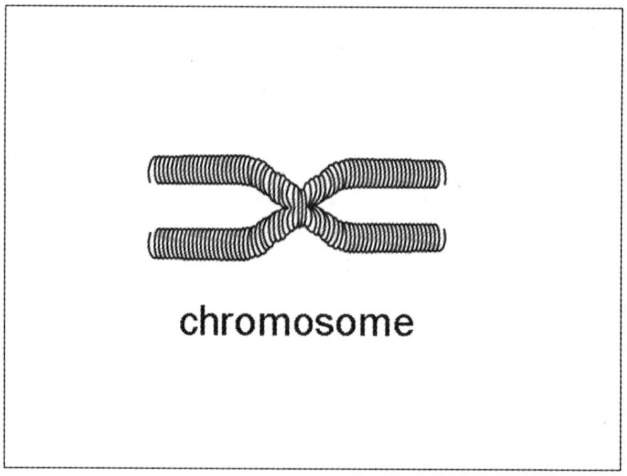

Now, um, if you'll look at this rough drawing of one of them—one chromosome about to divide into two—you'll see that it sort of looks like . . . well actually it's much more complex than this . . . but it reminds us of a couple of *springs* linked together . . . two coiled up pieces of DNA and, if you stretch them out, you'll find they contain certain genes, certain sequences of DNA that help determine how the cells of the body will develop. When researchers looked really carefully at the DNA in chromosomes, though, they were *amazed*—we *all* were—to find that only a fraction of it, maybe 20 to 30 percent, converts into meaningful genetic information. It's *incredible*, at least it was to *me*, but if you . . . if you took away all the DNA that codes for genes, you'd still have maybe 70 percent of the DNA left over . . . That's the so-called "*junk* DNA," though the word "junk" is used sort of tongue in cheek. The assumption is that, even if this DNA doesn't make up any of the *genes*, it must serve some other purpose. Anyway, . . . if we examine the *ends* of these coils of DNA . . . , we'll find a sequence of DNA at each end of every human chromosome . . . called a "telomere."

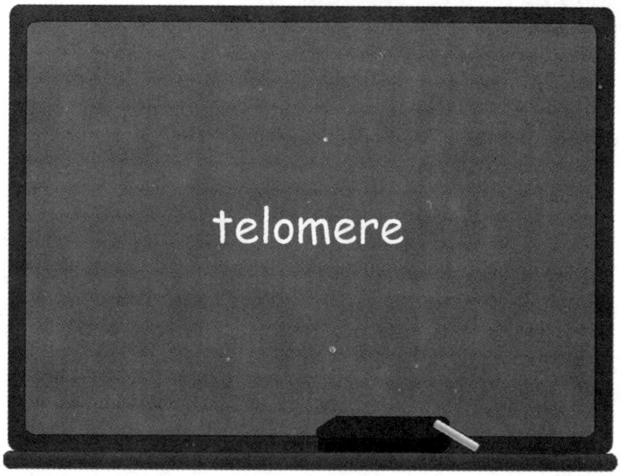

Now, a *telomere* is a highly *repetitious* . . . and genetically *meaningless* sequence of DNA, what we were calling "junk DNA." But it does have an important purpose. It's sort of like the plastic tip on each end of a shoelace. It may not help you tie your shoe, but that little plastic tip keeps the rest of the shoelace . . . the shoestring . . . from unraveling into weak and useless threads. Well, the telomeres at the ends of chromosomes seem to do about the same thing—protect the genes, the genetically *functional* parts of the chromosome, from being damaged.

Every time the chromosome divides—every time one cell divides into two—pieces of the ends of the chromosome, the telomeres, get broken off. So after each division, the telomeres get shorter; and one of the things that may happen after a while is that pieces of the genes themselves get broken off of the chromosomes . . . so the chromosome is now losing important genetic information and is no longer functional. But as long as the telomeres are a certain length they keep this from happening. So it seems that when the . . . by looking at the length of the telomeres on specific chromosomes, we can actually predict, pretty much . . . how long certain cells can successfully go on dividing.

Now there are *some* cells that just seem to keep on dividing, regardless . . . which may not always be a good thing if it gets out of control . . . , but when we analyze these cells chemically, we find something very interesting—a chemical in them, an enzyme called "*telomerase*."

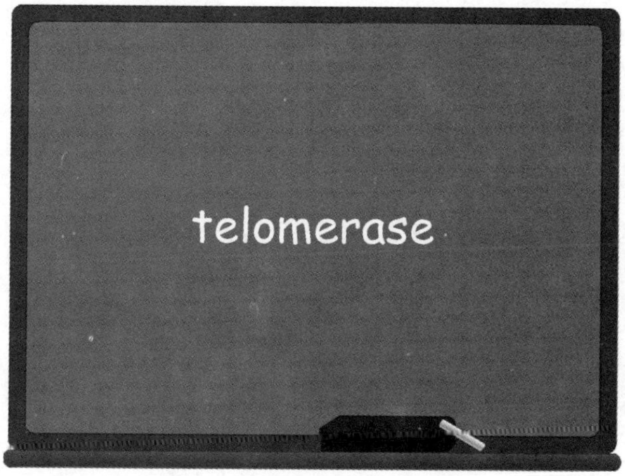

As bits of the *telomere* break off from the end of the chromosome, this chemical—this "*telomerase*"—can rebuild it . . . can help reassemble the protective DNA, the telomere, that the chromosome has lost. Someday, we may be able to take any cell and keep it alive, functioning and reproducing itself essentially forever, through the use of telomerase. And in the future we may have virtually immortal nerve cells and immortal skin cells or whatever, because this chemical, *telomerase*, can keep the *telomeres* on the ends of the chromosomes from getting any shorter.

TRACK 104 TRANSCRIPT

Narrator
Listen to part of a lecture in a business class.

Professor
OK, as we've talked about, a key aspect of running a successful business is knowing . . . um, getting a good sense of what the customer actually wants. And how they perceive your product. So with that in mind, I want to describe a very simple method of researching customer preference. And it's becoming increasingly common . . . and it's called MBWA, which stands for Managing By Wandering Around.

Professor

Now, MBWA, that's not the most technical-sounding name you've ever heard, but, ah, it describes the process pretty accurately. Here's how it works. Basically, um, the idea is that business owners or business managers just, just go out and actually talk to their customers and ah, to learn more about how well the business is serving their needs. And, and try to see what the customer experiences. Cause that's a great way to discover for yourself how your product is perceived, what its strengths and weaknesses are . . . you know, how you can improve it, that sort of thing. You know Dalton's, they make soup and canned vegetables and such? Well, the head of the company had Dalton's top executives walk around supermarkets, um, asking shoppers what they thought of Dalton's soups, and he used that data to make changes to the company's product. I mean, when Dalton's, of all companies, embraces something as radical as MBWA, it really shows you how popular the theory has become. Yes, Lisa?

Female student

But isn't it dangerous to base decisions on information from a small sample of people? Isn't large-scale market research safer, getting data on a lot of people?

Professor

That's a good question. And, ah, well I don't want to pretend that W, MBWA, uh, is some sort of replacement for other methods of customer research. Now, market research data definitely can give you a good idea of, ah . . . the big picture. But MBWA is, is really useful at kind of filling in the blanks, getting a good on-the-ground sense of how your products are used and how people respond to them. An-and yes, the numbers of opinions you get is small, so, yes, you need to be careful. But, good business managers will tell you that the biggest fear they have, and, and one of the most frequent problems they come across, is, well, becoming out of touch with what their customers really want and need. You know, surveys, and market research . . . stuff like that, they can only tell you so much about what the customers actually want in, in their day-to-day lives. Managing By Wandering Around, on the other hand, well that gets you in there and gives you a good sense of what customers need. So, so when used in combination, then, MBWA and market research, well, there're powerful tools. Oh, here's another example—senior executives for a clothing manufacturer, it was, um ah, Elkin . . . Elkin jeans, you know? They went and worked in a store for a few days selling Elkin's clothes. Now that gave them a very different idea about their product—they saw how people responded to it. They, they could go up to customers in the store and ask them questions about it. Ah, yes, Mike?

Male student
Well, I would think that a lot of customers would be bothered by, you know, if I'm shopping, I don't know if I'd want some business representative coming up to me and asking me questions. It's, it's like when I get phone calls at home from market researchers—I just hang up on them.

Professor
Well, it's certainly true that, well, no one likes getting calls at home from market researchers or, or people like that. But I'll tell you something—most customers have the exact opposite reaction when it comes to MBWA. Now, don't ask me why, because I, I really have no idea, but the fact is that customers tend to respond really well to MBWA, which is the key reason for its success. In fact, the techniques of MBWA work so well, they've actually been extended to all kinds of different contexts. Like politics, for instance. A few years back, the mayor of Baltimore . . . um, ah, I think his name was Schaefer, or something like that . . . anyway, he decided that the best way to serve the people of the city, of his city was to actually get out there and experience the things *they* experienced. So he'd ride around the city, and well, you know, in all parts of it, and he'd see all the potholes, he'd see how trash was sometimes, ah, not picked up off the side of the street, and he'd go back to his office write these memos. They were memos to his staff about the problems he'd seen and how they needed to be fixed, now, that sort of thing. But the thing is he got all this information just by going around, and seeing all the different Baltimore neighborhoods, and talking to people. He called it smart politics. We'd call it MBWA, or just plain good customer service!

TRACK 105 TRANSCRIPT

Narrator
What does the professor imply when she says this:

Professor
I mean, when Dalton's, of all companies, embraces something as radical as MBWA, it really shows you how popular the theory has become.

TRACK 106 TRANSCRIPT

Narrator
Listen to a conversation between a student and a department secretary.

Student
Hi, Miss Hendricks.

Secretary
Hi Brad. How are you?

Student
I'm fine except I have a question about my paycheck.

Secretary
Sure, what's up?

Student
Well, it's already been several weeks into the semester, and my paycheck was supposed to go directly into my bank account, but there haven't been any deposits.

Secretary
That's odd.

Student
Yeah, I thought graduate teaching assistants were automatically put on the payroll at the beginning of the semester.

Secretary
They *are* . . . let's see . . . did you complete all the forms for payroll?

Student
I filled in whatever they sent me, and . . . I returned it, like, at the end of August.

Secretary
Hmm. Well you definitely should've been paid by now. At least two pay periods have passed since then.

Student
I asked at the bank, and they didn't know anything. Who should I talk to about this? Payroll?

Secretary
I'm gonna contact them for you. There was a problem in processing some of the graduate student payroll paperwork, 'cause their computer program crashed after all the information was processed, and some people's information couldn't be retrieved.

Student
Oh . . . but . . . why didn't anyone let me know?

Secretary
I don't know how they work over there, cuz they couldn't even figure out whose information was missing. And this isn't the first time: Seems like something like this happens every semester.

Student
So . . . how do I find out if my information was lost?

Secretary
I'll contact them tomorrow morning to see if you're in the system, but you're probably not.

Student
Well, then what'll I need to do?

Secretary
Sorry, but you'll need to fill out all those forms again, and then I'll fax them over to the payroll office.

Student
And then what? . . . well . . . what I really need to know is . . . how long till I get some money? I'm already a month behind in my bills, and my tuition's due soon.

Secretary
They'll get you into the system the same day they receive your paperwork, so if you do that tomorrow, you'll get paid next Friday.

Student
That's a long time from now. Will that paycheck include all the money I'm owed?

Secretary
It should. I'll double-check with the payroll department.

Student
And another thing: Is there any way I could get paid sooner? I have been teaching all these weeks . . .

Secretary
I know it's not fair but . . . I don't think they can do anything. All the checks are computed automatically in the system. They can't just . . . write checks.

Student
But . . . they're the ones that made a mistake . . . and . . . they never told me.

Secretary
I understand how you feel. If I were you, I'd be upset too . . . I'll tell you what. When I call them, I'll explain the situation and ask if there's any way you could be paid sooner. But I have tell you that, based on past experience, you shouldn't count on it.

Student
I understand. Thanks. I know it's not your fault, and that you're doing everything you can.

Secretary
Well, what I *can* do is make sure that your first check is for the total amount that the university owes you.

Student
That'd be great. Thank you. I'll be on campus about ten tomorrow morning, and I'll come by to see you then.

TRACK 107 TRANSCRIPT

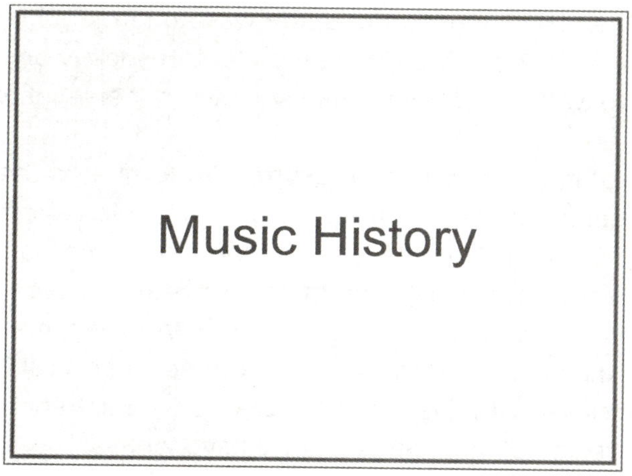

Narrator
Listen to part of a lecture in a music history class. The professor has been discussing opera.

Professor
The word opera means "work." Actually, it means "works." It's the plural of the word "*opus*" from the Latin. And in Italian it refers in general to works of art. "Opera lyrica," or lyric opera, refers to what we think of as opera, the musical drama.

Opera was commonplace in Italy for almost a thousand years *before* it became commercial as a venture. And during those years several things happened primarily *linguistic* or *thematic* and both involving secularization. Musical drama started in the churches. It was an educational tool. It was used primarily as a vehicle for teaching religion and was generally presented in Latin, the language of the Christian church, which had considerable influence in Italy at that time . . . But the language of everyday life was evolving in Europe, and at a certain point in the Middle Ages, it was really only merchants, aristocrats, and clergy who could deal with Latin. The, uh, the vast majority of the population used their own regional vernacular in all aspects of their lives, and so, in what is now Italy, operas quit being presented in Latin and started being presented in Italian.

And once that happened, the themes of the opera presentations also started to change, and musical drama moved from the church to the plaza right outside the church. And the themes, again, the themes changed, and opera was no longer about teaching religion as it was about satire, and about expressing the ideas of society or government without committing yourself to writing and risking imprisonment or persecution or what have you.

Opera, as we think of it, *is*, of course, a resurrected form. It is the melodious drama of ancient Greek theater. The term "melodious drama" being shortened eventually to "melodrama" because operas frequently are melodramatic, not to say unrealistic. And the group that put the first operas together that we have, today even, were . . . well it was a group of men that included Galileo's father, Vincenzo. And they met in Florence, he and a group of friends of the count of Bardi, and they formed what is called the Camerata dei Bardi. And they took classical theater and reproduced it in the Renaissance time. This . . . um . . . this produced some of the operas that we have today.

Now, what happened in the following centuries is very simple. Opera originated in Italy but was not confined to Italy any more than Italians were. And so, as Italians migrated across Europe, they carried theater with them and opera specifically because it was an Italian form.

What happened is that the major divide in opera that endures today took place. The French said opera ought to reflect the rhythm and cadence of dramatic literature, bearing in mind that we are talking about "the Golden Age" in French literature. And so the music was secondary, if you will, to the dramatic cadence of language–to the way the *rhythm* of language was used to express feeling and used to add drama–and of course as a result, *instead* of arias, or solos which would come to dominate *Italian* opera, the *French* relied on what the *Italians* called "recitativo" or "recitative" in English, the lyrics were *spoken* . . . frequently to the accompaniment of a harpsichord.

The French said, "You really can't talk about real people who lived, in opera." And they relied on mythology to give them their characters and their plots. Mythology, the pastoral traditions the . . . the . . . novels of chivalry, or the epics of chivalry out of the Middle Ages. The Italians said, "No, this is a great historical tool, and what better way to educate the public about Nero or Attila, or any number of people than to put them into a play they can see and listen to."

The English appropriated opera after the French. Opera came late to England because all theaters, public theaters were closed, of course, during their Civil War. And it wasn't until the restoration in 1660 that public theaters again opened and opera took off. The English made a major adjustment to opera and exported what they had done to opera back to Italy. So that you have this circle of musical influences.

The Italians invented opera. The French adapted it. The English adopted it. The Italians took it back. It came to America late and was considered too elitist for the general public, but Broadway musicals fulfilled a similar function for a great long while.

John J. Chapman wrote about opera, quote, "If an extraterrestrial being were to appear before us and say, 'What is your society like? What is this Earth thing all about?' you could do worse than take that creature to an opera," end quote. Because opera does, after all, begin with a man and a woman and an emotion.

TRACK 108 TRANSCRIPT

Narrator
Why does the professor say this:

Professor
The English made a major adjustment to opera and exported what they had done to opera back to Italy.

TRACK 109 TRANSCRIPT

Narrator
What does the professor imply when he says this:

Professor
John J. Chapman wrote about opera, quote, "If an extraterrestrial being were to appear before us and say, 'What is your society like? What is this Earth thing all about?' you could do worse than take that creature to an opera," end quote. Because opera does, after all, begin with a man and a woman and an emotion.

TRACK 110 TRANSCRIPT

Environmental Science

Narrator
Listen to part of a lecture in an environmental science class.

Professor
Alright folks, let's continue our discussion of alternative energy sources, and move on to what's probably the most well-known alternative energy source, umm, solar energy. The Sun basically provides Earth with a virtually unlimited source of energy every day, but the problem has always been, uhh, "How do we tap this source of energy?" Can anyone think of why it's so difficult to make use of solar energy?

Female student
Because it's hard to, ahh, gather it?

Professor
That's exactly it. Solar energy is everywhere, but it's also quite diffused. And the thing is, the dream of solar energy is not a new one. Humanity has been trying to use the Sun's light as a reliable source of energy for centuries. And, ahh, around the beginning of the twentieth century, there were actually some primitive solar water heaters on the consumer market, but they didn't sell very well. Any of you want to guess why?

Female student
Well, there were other energy choices, like oil and natural gas, right?

Professor
Yeah, and for better or for worse, we chose to go down that path as a society. When you consider economic factors, it's easy to see why . . . But then, in the 1970's, there was an interest in solar energy again. Why do you think that happened?

Male student
Because oil and natural gas were, uhh, became scarce?

Professor
Well, not exactly, the amount of oil and natural gas in the Earth was still plentiful, but there were other reasons, uhh, it's a political thing really, and I'm not gonna get into that now. So what happened in the 1970's was, oil and natural gas became very expensive very quickly, and that spurred people to start looking into alternative forms of energy—solar energy probably being the most popular. But then in the 80's, this trend, uhh, reversed itself when the price of oil and natural gas went down.

All right, let's shift our focus now to some of the technologies that have been invented to overcome the problem of gathering diffused solar energy. The most basic solution is simply to carefully place windows in a building so that the Sun shines into the building, and then it's absorbed and converted into heat. Can anyone think of where this is most commonly used?

Female student
Greenhouses.

Professor
Yup, greenhouses, where plants are kept warm and provided with sunlight because the walls of the building are made entirely of glass. But we do also have more *complex* systems that are used for space heating, and they fall into two categories, uhh, *passive* and *active* heating systems. *Passive* systems take advantage of the location or design of a house—for example, solar energy is gathered through large glass panels facing the Sun. The heat is then stored in water-filled tanks or concrete. No mechanical devices are used in passive heating systems. They operate with little or no mechanical assistance. With *active* systems, on the other hand, you collect the solar energy at one location, and then you use pumps and fans to move heat from the collectors through a plumbing system to a tank where it can be used to heat a home or to just provide hot water . . .

Male student
Excuse me, professor, but I've gotta ask. How can solar energy work at night or on cloudy days?

Professor
That's . . . well . . . that is a really good question. As a matter of fact, science is still working on it. Uh, trying to find ways of enhancing energy storage techniques so that the coming of night or cloudy days really wouldn't matter. That is the biggest drawback to solar energy, the problem of what do you do in cases where the Sun's light is weak or virtually nonpresent. So the storage of solar energy—lots of solar energy—is a really important aspect.

Female student
Does that mean that solar energy can only be used on a small scale . . . like heating a home?

Professor
Well actually, there have been some attempts to build solar energy power plants. The world's largest solar power plant is located in Kramer Junction, California. It can generate 194 megawatts of electric power, but that's just a drop in the bucket. Right now, the utility companies are interested in increasing the capacity of the Kramer Junction plant. But only time will tell if it will ever develop into a major source of power for that region . . . considering the economic and political factors involved.

TRACK 111 TRANSCRIPT

Narrator
Listen again to part of the lecture. Then answer the question.

Male student
Excuse me, professor, but I've gotta ask. How can solar energy work at night or on cloudy days?

Professor
That's . . . well . . . that is a really good question. As a matter of fact, science is still working on it.

Narrator
What does the professor mean when he says this:

Professor
That's . . . well . . . that is a really good question.

TRACK 112 TRANSCRIPT

Narrator
What is the most efficient type of transportation in your country? Explain why you think it is efficient. Include specific reasons or examples.

TRACK 113 TRANSCRIPT

Narrator
Some people believe it's essential for a person's education to learn to play a musical instrument. Others don't believe music education is important. Which view do you agree with? Explain why.

TRACK 114 TRANSCRIPT

Narrator
Read the article about a college radio station. You will have 45 seconds to read the article. Begin reading now.

TRACK 115 TRANSCRIPT

Narrator
Now listen to two students discussing the article.

Male student
What d' you think of the proposal?

Female student
I think it'll work. I mean, the range of the station now is basically limited to the campus and so it's basically just a few programs, mainly for students . . .

Male student
Yeah.

Female student
Well, if this proposal goes through, there will be more programs and it'll give the students more professional experience as they experiment with programming for a much larger . . . you know . . . "real-life" audience. And stuff like that'll give them a better shot at getting a job after they graduate.

Male student
Of course.

Female student
Besides, the whole university will benefit from it.

Male student
What d' you mean?

Female student
Well, you know my friend Tony, right? He told me that the radio station at his university did something like this about five years ago . . .

Male student
And . . .

Female student
Well. It's a success. They are making a lot of money out of commercials and they are using it to offer more scholarships and to help fund projects to renovate the facilities of other programs.

Male student
That sounds really good!

Narrator
The woman supports the proposal described in the article. Explain why she thinks it will achieve the university's goals.

TRACK 116 TRANSCRIPT

Narrator
Now read the passage about subliminal perception. You will have 50 seconds to read the passage. Begin reading now.

TRACK 117 TRANSCRIPT

Narrator
Now listen to part of a lecture on this topic in a psychology class.

Professor
Consider this experiment: two groups of people were asked to watch TV and while they were watching, a picture flashed on the screen, less than a second—very quickly, so it was barely noticeable.

The picture was of a boy with a birthday cake. Now, like I said, there were two groups and each group saw a slightly different version of the picture. One group got the boy looking angry; in fact, he was actually throwing the cake on the floor. The other group got a picture of the boy smiling, happy, holding out the cake like he was offering it. Same boy . . . same cake . . . but different emotions expressed in each picture.

Everyone was then asked to look at a different image—now this is a third image, right? Again it's the boy and the cake, but this time the image stayed on the screen. In this picture, the boy's just holding the cake, basically no emotion on his face—everything very neutral. Now remember, nobody knew they'd already seen a picture of this boy. After a minute, everyone was asked to describe the boy's personality. Those who'd been exposed to image of the angry boy, they generally described the boy's personality negatively. Those who'd earlier seen the happy boy described him, well, positively.

Narrator
Describe what subliminal perception is and explain how the experiment discussed by the professor illustrates this phenomenon.

TRACK 118 TRANSCRIPT

Narrator
Listen to a conversation between two students.

Male student
Hey, Madison. What's wrong?

Female student
Oh . . . I'm just struggling about what to do . . . I won an award from the Pacific Journalism Institute for an article I submitted, and . . .

Male student
Doesn't sound like anything's wrong!

Female student
Well, it's a huge honor to win, and there's an award ceremony they've invited me to attend—which I'm super excited about—but—and here's what's frustrating—I've got a philosophy exam that's scheduled to end right when the ceremony begins.

Male student
Uh-oh. You're saying you'd just be finishing up taking the exam right when the ceremony starts?

Female student
Exactly.

Male student
But those ceremonies never start on time. They give long introductions, ya'know, have a general speech or something before they ever get to handing out awards. I'm *sure* they won't be ready to hand out your award right at the beginning. Just go when you're done with the test. You won't miss anything important.

Female student
Maybe. But that's a bit risky. I don't want to miss being there when they announce my name.

Male student
Well, have you talked to your professor about this?

Female student
Dr. Forrester? No . . .

Male student
Maybe she'll let you take the exam some other time.

Female student
True. She lets people reschedule exams sometimes, but she always makes them take it a couple of days *early*. That would mean less studying time for me, which I'm not thrilled about.

Male student
Less time to study? Oh.

Female student
Like I said, I'm still struggling about what to do.

Narrator
The speakers discuss two possible solutions to the woman's problem. Briefly summarize the problem. Then state which of the solutions you recommend and explain why.

TRACK 119 TRANSCRIPT

Narrator
Listen to part of a lecture in an economics class.

Professor
So when we talk about the demand for a product, we're referring to *how much* consumers want to buy it, right? And often the demand for a product is influenced by its price—the more expensive it becomes, the less chance that people will want to buy it. OK. But that's not the whole story. Sometimes the *demand* for a product can also be influenced by the price of *other, related* products.

First, there are those products called *substitute goods*. If products can be *substituted* for one another, then, um, well, then they're called substitute goods. They're similar enough to be interchangeable. And, uh, an increase in the price of one means an increase in the demand for the other. Like, uh, like butter and margarine. They're pretty much used for the same purposes. Margarine's a butter substitute. And you can bake equally well with either. Well, when the price of butter goes up, it becomes less affordable, and so what do people do? They buy margarine instead, right? So, uh, you see, an increase in the price of *butter* increases the demand for *margarine*.

Now, another instance where the price of one product can influence the demand of another is, uh, is when you have two products that *can't* be *used* without each other. Those products we call *complement goods*. They complement, or, uh, complete, each other, if you will. Like compact discs and compact disc players. You need *both* products in order to use either. So if the price of either product increases, demand for *both* is likely to decrease. And if the price of CDs goes up, well, demand for them will go down, right? And because CDs and CD players complement each other, what'll *also* happen is that the demand for *CD players* will go down too.

Narrator
Using the points and examples from the talk, explain how substitute goods and complement goods influence demand for a particular product.

TRACK 120 TRANSCRIPT

Narrator
Now listen to part of a lecture on the topic you just read about.

Professor
The evidence linking this portrait to Jane Austen is not at all convincing. Sure, the painting has long been somewhat loosely connected to Austen's extended family and their descendants, but this hardly proves it's a portrait of Jane Austen as a teenager. The reading's arguments that the portrait is of Austen are questionable at best.

First, when the portrait was authorized for use in the 1882 publication of her letters, Jane Austen had been dead for almost *70* years. So the family members who asserted that the painting was Jane had never actually seen her themselves. They couldn't have known for certain if the portrait was of Austen or not.

Second, the portrait could very well be that of a *relative* of Austen's, a fact that would explain the resemblance between its subject and that of Cassandra's sketch. The extended Austen family was very large, and many of Jane Austen's female cousins were teenagers in the relevant period, or had children who were teenagers. And some of these teenage girls could have resembled Jane Austen. In fact, many experts believe that the true subject of the portrait *was* one of those relatives, Mary Ann Campion, who was a distant niece of Austen's.

Third, the painting has been attributed to Humphrey only because of the style, but other evidence points to a later date. A stamp on the back of the picture indicates that the blank canvas, you know, the actual piece of cloth on which the picture was painted, was sold by a man named William Legg. Records show that William Legg did not sell canvasses in London when Jane Austen was a teenager. He only started selling canvasses when she was 27 years old. So, it looks like the canvas was used for the painting at a time when Austen was clearly older than the girl in the portrait.

TRACK 121 TRANSCRIPT

Narrator
Summarize the points made in the lecture, being sure to explain how they respond to the specific arguments made in the reading passage.

TRACK 134 TRANSCRIPT

Narrator
Listen to a conversation between a student and his psychology professor.

Professor
Good afternoon, Alex. Can I help you with something?

Student
Well, I wanted to talk with you about the research project you assigned today. I, um, hoped you could clarify a few things for me.

Professor
I'll certainly try.

Student
OK, all we have to do is do two observations and take notes on them, right?

Professor
That's a start—but you'll need to do some research, too. Then you'll write a paper that's not so much about the *observations*, but a synthesis of what you've observed and read.

Student
OK . . . and what about the children I'm supposed to observe?

Professor
Not 'children'—a single child, observed twice.

Student
Oh! OK. So I should choose a child—with the permission of the child's parent, of course—and then observe that child a couple of times and take good notes. Then?

Professor
Actually, after your *first* observation, you'll go back and look through your textbook or go to the library and find a few sources concerning the stage of development this particular child is in. And then with *that knowledge*, you'll make a *second* observation of the same child to see if the expected developmental behaviors are exhibited.

Student
Can you give me an example?

Professor
Well, um, if you observed a four-year-old child—uh, for example, my daughter is four years old—you might read up on Piaget's stages of cognitive development. We covered those in class.

Student
Uh-huh.

Professor
Most likely, what stage would a child of that age be in?

Student
Um . . . the preoperational stage?

Professor
Exactly. If that's the case, her language use would be maturing, and her memory and imagination would be developed.

Student
So she might play pretend! Like, she can pretend when driving her toy car across the couch that the couch is actually a bridge or something.

Professor
That's right. In addition, her thinking would be primarily egocentric.

Student
So she'd be thinking mostly about herself and her own needs and might not be able to see things from anyone else's perspective.

Professor
Um hmm.

Student
But . . . what if she doesn't? I mean, what if she doesn't demonstrate those behaviors?

Professor
That's fine. You'll note that in your paper. See, your paper should compare what is expected of children at certain stages of development with what you actually observe.

Student
OK. I have one more question, though.

Professor
And what's that?

Student
Where can I find a child to observe?

Professor
Um, I'd suggest you contact the education department secretary. She has a list of contacts at various schools and with certain families who are somehow connected to the university. Sometimes they are willing to help out students with projects like yours.

Student
OK, I'll stop by the education department office this afternoon.

Professor
And if you have any trouble or any more questions, feel free to come by during my office hours.

TRACK 135 TRANSCRIPT

Narrator
Listen again to part of the conversation. Then answer the question.

Student
OK, all we have to do is do two observations and take notes on them, right?

Professor
That's a start.

Narrator
What does the professor mean when she says this:

Professor
That's a start.

TRACK 136 TRANSCRIPT

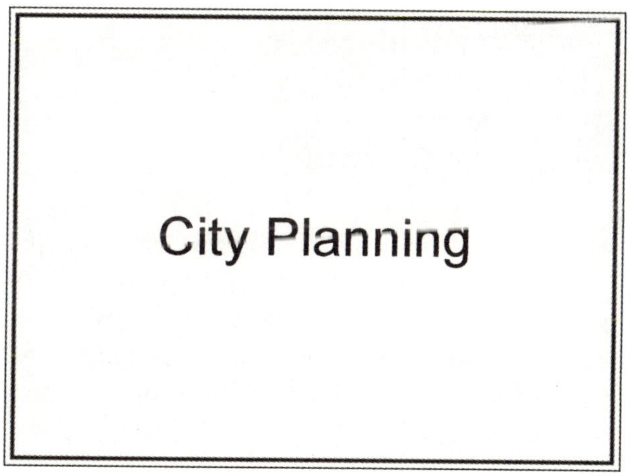

Narrator
Listen to part of a lecture in a city planning class.

Professor
In the last 50 years or so, many American cities have had difficulty in maintaining a successful retail environment. Business owners in the city centers, or, uh, the downtown areas, have experienced some financial losses because of a steady movement of people out of the cities and into the suburbs. In general, downtown areas just don't have that many residential areas; uh, not that many people *live* there. So, what have city planners decided to do about it? Well, one way they've come up with some ways to attract more people to shop downtown was by creating *pedestrian malls*.

Now, what *is* a pedestrian mall? It's a pretty simple concept, really. It's essentially, um, an outdoor shopping area designed just for people on foot. And—uh, well, unlike many other shopping malls that are built in the suburbs nowadays—these pedestrian malls are typically located in the downtown area of the city and, well, they have features like wide sidewalks, comfortable outdoor seating, and, uh, maybe even fountains and, you know, art.

Uh, there are variations on this model, of course, but the common denominator is always the idea of-of creating a shopping space that will get people to shop in the city without needing their cars. So I'm sure you can see how having an area that's off-limits to automobile traffic would be ideal for a heavily populated city, where, uh, well, the streets would otherwise be bustling with noisy, unpleasant traffic congestion.

Now, the concept, which originated in Europe, was adopted by American city planners in the late 1950's. And since then, a number of United States cities have created pedestrian malls, and many of them have been highly successful. So what have city planners learned about making these malls succeed? Well, there are two critical factors to consider when creating a pedestrian mall: *location* and *design*. Both of which are equally important.

Now, let's start with the location. In choosing a specific location for a pedestrian mall, there are, in fact, two considerations: proximity to potential customers—uh, that's we would call a "customer base"—and accessibility to public transportation, which we'll get to in just a moment. Now, for a customer base, eh, the most obvious example would be a large office building—since the employees could theoretically go shopping after work or during their lunch hour, right? Uh, another really good example is a convention center, which typically has a hotel and large meeting spaces to draw visitors to the city for-for major business conferences and events. Uh, but ideally, the pedestrian mall would be used by local residents, not just people working in the city or-or visiting the area. So that's where access to public transportation comes in. Either, um, either the designers plan to locate the mall near a central transportation hub—uh, like a bus terminal, a major train, or subway station *or* they work with city officials to create sufficient parking areas not too far from the mall. W-Which makes sense, because if people can't drive into the mall area, well, then they need to have easy access to it.

OK. So that's location, but-but what about design? Well, design doesn't necessarily include things like sculptures, or decorative walkways, or-or even eye-catching window displays—you-you know—art . . . Although, I'd be the first to admit those things are *aesthetically* appealing . . . However, visually pleasing sights, well, they're *not* a part of the pedestrian mall design that-that matter the most. The key consideration is *a compact and convenient layout*—uh, one which allows pedestrians to walk from-from one end of the mall to the other in just a few minutes . . . so they can get to the major stores, restaurants, and-and other central places, eh, without having to take more than one or two turns. Now, this takes careful and creative planning.

Eh, but, now, what if one ingredient to this planning recipe is missing? There could quite possibly be long-lasting effects. And, eh, I think a good example is the pedestrian mall in Louisville, Kentucky, for instance.

Now when the Louisville mall was built, oh, it had lots of visual appeal. It was attractively designed right in a small part of downtown, and it pretty much possessed all of the other design elements for success. But, uh, now here's where my point about location comes into play . . . there wasn't a convention center around to-to help draw in visitors, and, uh, well, the only nearby hotel eventually closed down for that same reason. Well, you can imagine how this must've affected local and pedestrian mall business owners. Sort of, what we call, a chain reaction. It wasn't until a convention center and a parking garage were built, uh, about decade later that the mall started to be successful.

TRACK 137 TRANSCRIPT

Narrator
What does the professor mean when she says this:

Professor
Well, design doesn't necessarily include things like sculptures, or decorative walkways, or-or even eye-catching window displays—you-you know—art . . . Although, I'd be the first to admit those things are *aesthetically* appealing . . .

TRACK 138 TRANSCRIPT

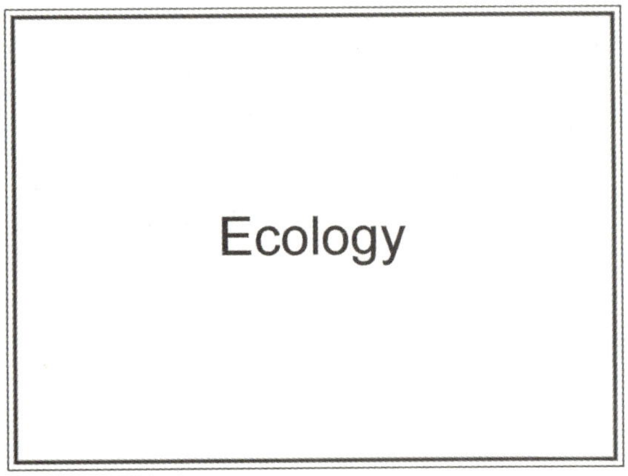

Narrator
Listen to part of a lecture in an ecology class.

Professor

So—uh, continuing our discussion of ecological systems, whole systems . . . the main thing to keep in mind here is the *interrelationships*. The species in a system, uh—and even the landscape itself—they're interdependent. Let's take what you read for this week, and see if we can't apply this interdependence idea. Mike?

Male student

Well, um, how about *beavers*—ecosystems with beavers and waterways.

Professor

Good, good. Go on.

Male student

Like—well, you can see how it's so important, 'cause if you go back before Europeans settled in North America, like before the 1600s, back when Native Americans were the only people living here—well, back then there were a lot of beavers. But later on, *after* Europeans—

Professor

OK, wait—I see where you're heading with this, but before we go into how European settlement affected the ecosystem, tell me this: what kind of environment do beavers live in? Think about what it was like *before* the European settlers came. We'll come back to where you were headed . . .

Female student

OK, well, beavers live near streams and rivers . . . And they *block up* the streams and rivers with, like, logs, and sticks, and mud, you know, they build *dams*, that really slow down the flow of the stream. So then the water *backs up* and creates, like, a pond that floods the nearby land.

Professor

And that creates *wetlands*. OK, tell me more.

Female student

Well, with wetlands it's like there's more *standing* water, more *still* water around. And that water's a lot *cleaner* than swiftly flowing water because the dirt and sediment and stuff has a chance to sink to the bottom.

Professor
More important for our discussion: Wetland areas support a lot more varieties of life than swiftly flowing water. For example, there are more varieties of fish, of insects, lots of frog species. And then species that rely on *those* species start to live near the wetlands, too.

Female student
Yes. Like birds and mammals that eat the fish and insects. And you get trees and plants that begin to grow near the standing water that can't grow near running water. Oh, and there's something about wetlands and groundwater, too . . .

Professor
OK. Good. Wetlands have a big effect on groundwater—the amount of water *below* the surface of the land. Think of wetlands as . . . um, like a giant sponge. The earth soaks up a lot of this water that's continually flooding the surface, which increases the amount of water below. So, where there are wetlands, you get a lot of groundwater. And *groundwater* happens to be a big source of our *own* drinking water today. All right. So back to the beavers. What if the beavers weren't there?

Male student
You'd just have a regular running stream, 'cause there's no dam. So the ecosystem would be completely different—there'd be fewer wetlands.

Professor
Exactly. So, now let's go back where you were headed before, Mike. Uh, you mentioned a change that occurred after Europeans came to North America . . .

Male student
Yeah—well, there used to be beavers all over the place . . . um, something like 200 million beavers, just in the continental United States. But when Europeans came, they started hunting the beavers for their fur . . . 'cause beaver fur, it's really warm—and it was really popular for making hats in Europe. So the beavers were hunted a lot, overhunted—they were almost extinct by the 1800s. So . . . that meant fewer wetlands—less standing water.

Professor
And what does that mean for the ecosystem? Kate.

Female student
Well, if there's *less standing* water, then the ecosystem can't support as many species, because a lot of insects and fish and frogs *can't live* in *running* water. And then the *birds and animals* that eat *them* lose *their* food supply.

Professor
Precisely. So the beaver, in this ecosystem, is what we call a *keystone species*.

The term "keystone" kind of explains itself: in architecture, a *keystone* in an archway or doorway is the stone that holds the whole thing together, and keeps it from collapsing. Well, that's what a keystone species does in an ecosystem—it's the crucial *species* that keeps the system going.

Now, beaver populations are on the rise again, but there's something to think about: consider humans as part of these ecosystems. You've probably heard about water shortages or, uh, restrictions on how much water you can use, especially in the summertime, in recent years. And remember what I said about groundwater. Imagine if we still had all those beavers around, all those wetlands. What would our water supply be like *then?*

TRACK 139 TRANSCRIPT

Narrator
Listen again to part of the lecture. Then answer the question.

Professor
So the beaver, in this ecosystem, is what we call a *keystone species.*

The term "keystone" kind of explains itself: in architecture, a *keystone* in an archway or doorway is the stone that holds the whole thing together, and keeps it from collapsing.

Narrator
Why does the professor say this:

Professor
The term "keystone" kind of explains itself: in architecture, a *keystone* in an archway or doorway is the stone that holds the whole thing together, and keeps it from collapsing.

TRACK 140 TRANSCRIPT

Narrator
What does the professor imply when she says this:

Professor
Imagine if we still had all those beavers around, all those wetlands. What would our water supply be like *then?*

TRACK 141 TRANSCRIPT

Narrator
Listen to a conversation between a student and the language lab manager.

Student
Hi. I'm not sure but . . . um, is this the Carter Language Lab?

Manager
Yes, it is. How can I help you?

Student
I'm taking first-year Spanish this semester. Our professor says we need to come here to view a series of videos. I think it's called *Spanish: Working on Your Accent.*

Manager
Yes, we have that . . . Um, they're on the wall behind you.

Student
OK, so . . . I can just take . . . can I take the whole series home? I think there are three of them . . .

Manager
I guess you haven't been here before . . .

Student
No, no I haven't.

Manager
OK, well, you have to watch the videos here. You need to sign in to reserve an open room, and sign out the video you need. Just start with the first one in the series—each video's half an hour long.

Student
So it's a video *library*, basically?

Manager
Yes, but unlike the library, you can't take any videos out of the lab.

Student
OK, so, how long can I use the video room for?

Manager
You can sign up for two hours at a time.

Student
Oh good. So I can watch more than one video when I come up here. Is the lab pretty busy all the time?

Manager
Well, rooms are usually full right after dinnertime. Uh, but you can sign up *the day before* to reserve a room if you want . . .

Student
Hmmm, *the day before* . . . But I can just *stop in* too . . . to see if there're any rooms open, right?

Manager
Sure. Stop in anytime.

Student
Um, what about copies of the videos? Is there just one copy of each in the series? I don't want to miss out if everyone comes in at once.

Manager
Oh, no. Uh, we have several copies of each tape in the Spanish accent series. We usually have multiple copies of everything for *each* video collection.

Student
Super. So, how many rooms are there in total in the lab?

Manager
Twenty. They're pretty small, so we normally get one person or no more than a small group of people in there watching a video together. Actually, someone else from your class just came in and took the first Spanish video in to watch. You could probably run in there and watch it with him. Of course, you're welcome to have your own room, but sometimes students like to watch with a classmate so they can review the material with each other afterwards . . . for example, if there was some content they didn't *really* understand.

Student
I guess I'd prefer my own room. I concentrate better by myself . . . and I don't want to miss anything . . . hmm, and he's probably already started watching it . . .

Manager
No problem—we've got a lot of rooms open right now. When you come in, you sign your name on the list and are assigned a room number. Or if you call in advance, the attendant will tell you your room number. If you forget, just come in and take a look at the list. The videos are over there.

Student
Great. Thanks.

TRACK 142 TRANSCRIPT

Narrator
Listen again to part of the conversation. Then answer the question.

Student
OK, so . . . I can just take . . . can I take the whole series home? I think there are three of them . . .

Manager
I guess you haven't been here before . . . ?

Narrator
What does the woman imply?

TRACK 143 TRANSCRIPT

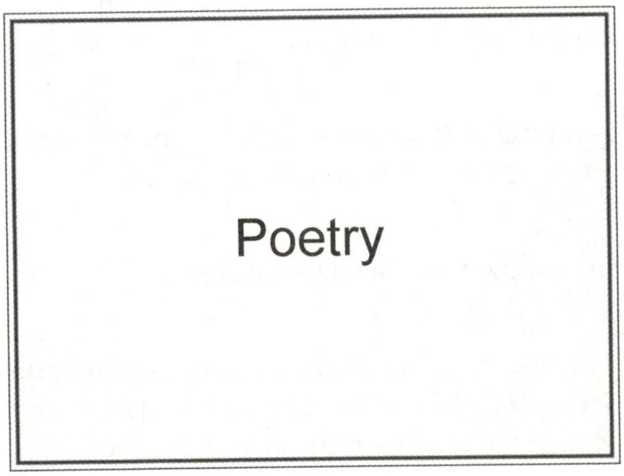

Narrator
Listen to part of a lecture in a poetry class. The professor is discussing medieval poetry.

Professor
OK, so, the two poems we're looking at today fall into the category of, uh, medieval times, which was how long ago?

Female student
Almost a thousand years ago, right?

Professor
Yes, that's right—

Female student
But professor, are you sure these are poems? I mean, I thought poems were shorter. These are more like long stories. I mean, one of 'em was all about love, but the other one, the chan—chan—whatever it's called, that other one, well, it was all about fighting and battles. I mean, can both of them be considered poems?

Professor
Well, think back to the very beginning of this course.

Female student
Uh-huh.

Professor
Remember how w-w-we defined poetry? In the very broadest sense, we said it's written to evoke, uh, to make *you*, the audience, have some kind of emotional experience through the use of imagery, uh, some kind of predictable rhythm, and-and usually, but not always, there's more than one meaning implied with the words that are used. Let's start with chanson poetry first. That's chanson.

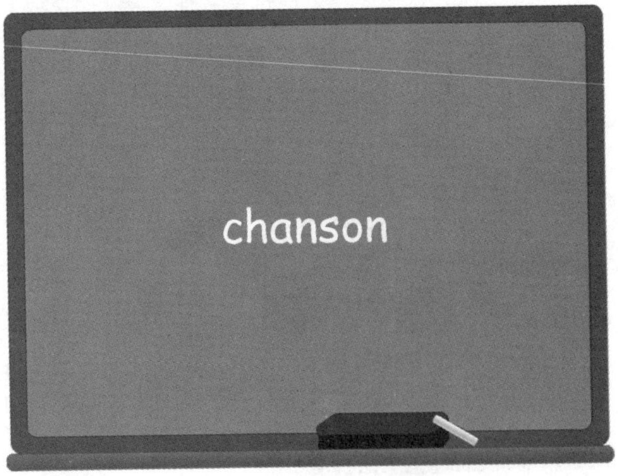

Chanson poems became popular in Europe, particularly in France, and the term is actually short for a longer French phrase that translates to, uh, *songs of deeds*. Ah, now, they were called songs of deeds because, strangely enough, they were written to describe the heroic deeds or actions of . . . of warriors, the knights during conflicts. We don't know a lot about the authors . . . it's still contested somewhat, but we're pretty sure about *who* the chanson poems were written *for*. That is, they were written for knights and the lords, the, uh, nobility that they served. The poems were sung, uh, performed by a minstrel, a singer who traveled from castle to castle, singing to the local lord and his knights . . . Well, would, uh, would someone summarize the main features of the chanson poem you read?

Male student
Well, there's a hero, a knight, who goes to battle, and he's admired for his courage, bravery, and loyalty, loyalty to the lord he serves, his country, and his fellow warriors in the field. He's—he has . . . uh, he's a, he's a skilled fighter willing to face the most extreme dangers, uh, sacrificial, uh, willing to sacrifice anything and everything to protect his king and country.

Professor
OK, now, given that the intended audience for these poems were knights and lords, what can we say about the purpose of chanson poetry? What kinds of feelings was it meant to provoke?

Female student
Well, I guess they must've been really appealing to those knights and lords who were listening to them, hearing the songs probably made 'em feel more patriotic, made 'em feel like it was a good and noble thing to serve their countries in whatever way they could.

Professor
Good. We've got a pretty good picture of what the chanson hero was like. Now let's compare that to the hero in the *other* poem. The other poem is an example of what's called romance poetry. And the hero in the romance poem was also a knight. But what made the knight in romance poetry different from the knight in chanson poetry?

Well, first, the *purpose* of the hero's actions was different. The hero in romance poetry is independent, purely solitary in a way, not like the chanson poet who was always surrounded by his fighting companions. He doesn't engage in conflict to protect his lord or country. He does it for the sake of adventure, to improve himself, to show he's worthy of respect and love from his lady. He's very conscious of the particular rules of social behavior he has to live up to somehow, and-and all of his actions are for the purpose of proving that he is an-an upright, moral, well-mannered . . . well-behaved individual. You may have noticed that in chanson poetry there isn't much about the hero's feelings . . . the focus is on the actions, the deeds. But the romance poetry describes a lot of the inner feelings, the motivations, uh, psychology, you could say, of a knight trying to improve himself, to better himself so that he's worthy of the love of a woman.

What explains this difference? Well, digging into the historical context tells us a lot. Um, romance poetry emerged a few generations after chanson and its roots were in geographic regions of France that were calmer, where conflict wasn't central to people's lives. More peaceful times meant there was more time for education, travel . . . more time for reflection. Another name for romance poetry that's often synonymous with it is *troubadour* poetry.

Troubadours were the authors of these new romance poems. And we know a lot more about the troubadours than we do about the chanson authors because they often had small biographical sketches added to their poems that gave pretty specific information about their social status, geographical location, and a small outline of their career. This information wasn't particularly reliable because they were sometimes based on fictitious stories of great adventure, or scrapped together from parts of different poems, *but* there is enough there to squeeze, mmm, *infer* some facts about their social class.

The political climate had settled down enough so that troubadours had the luxury of being able to spend most if not all of their time creating, crafting, or, uh, composing their love songs for their audiences. And yes, these poems were also sung. Many troubadours were able to make a living being full-time poets, which should tell you something about the value of that profession during medieval times.

TRACK 144 TRANSCRIPT

Narrator
Listen again to part of the lecture. Then answer the question.

Female student
But professor, are you sure these are poems? I mean, I thought poems were shorter. These are more like long stories. I mean, one of 'em was all about love, but the other one, the chan—chan—whatever it's called, that other one, well, it was all about fighting and battles. I mean, can both of them be considered poems?

Professor
Well, think back to the very beginning of this course.

Narrator
Why does the professor say this:

Professor
Well, think back to the very beginning of this course.

TRACK 145 TRANSCRIPT

Astronomy

Narrator
Listen to part of a lecture in an astronomy class.

Professor
OK, I want to go over the different types of meteorites . . . and what we've learned from them about the formation of Earth and the solar system. Uh, the thing is, what's especially interesting about meteorites is that they come from interplanetary space, but they consist of the same chemical elements that are in matter originating on Earth, just in different proportions. But that makes it easier to identify something *as* a meteorite, as opposed to, to just a terrestrial rock.

So, to talk about where meteorites come from, we need to talk about comets and asteroids, which basically, they're basically made up of debris left over from the origin of the solar system 4.6 billion years ago.

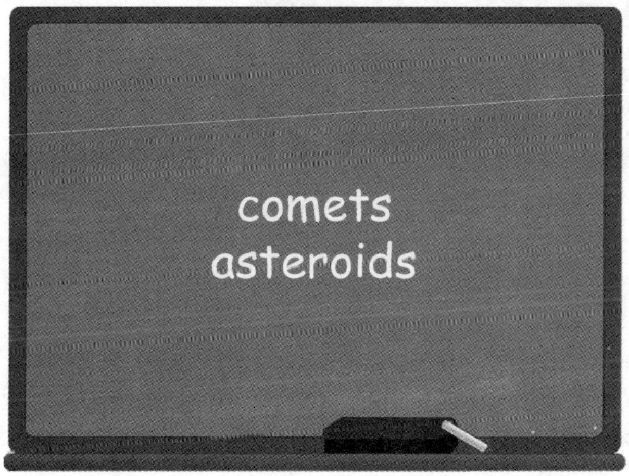

Now I'm going a bit out of order here, um, I'm not going to go into any depth on, uh, comets and asteroids now, but we'll come back later and do that. For now I'll just cover some basic info about them.

OK, comets and asteroids . . . it might help if you think of . . . Remember we talked about the two *classes* of *planets* in our solar system? And how they differ in composition . . . the terrestrial planets like Mars and Earth . . . composed largely of rocks and metals, and the large gas giants like Jupiter. Well, the solar system also has two analogous classes of objects *smaller* than planets . . . namely, asteroids and comets.

Relatively near the Sun, in the inner solar system, between Jupiter and Mars to be precise, we've got the asteroid belt, which contains about 90 percent of all asteroids orbiting the Sun. These asteroids are, uh, like the terrestrial planets, in that they're composed mostly of rocky material and metals.

Far from the sun . . . in the *outer* solar system, beyond Jupiter's orbit . . . temperatures are low enough to permit ices to form out of water and . . . and out of gases like, uh, methane and carbon dioxide. Loose collections of these ices and small rocky particles form into comets. So comets are similar in composition to the gas giants.

Both comets and asteroids are . . . typically are smaller than planets. An even smaller type of interplanetary debris is the meteoroid. And it's from meteoroids that we get meteors and meteorites.

Meteor*oids* are . . . for the most part, anyway . . . they're just smaller bits of asteroids and comets. When these bits enter Earth's atmosphere, well, that makes them so special that they get a special name. They are called "meteors." Most of them are very small and they burn up soon after entering Earth's atmosphere. The larger ones that make it through the atmosphere and hit the ground are called meteor*ites*. So meteor*ites* are the ones that actually make it through.

Now, we've been finding meteorites on Earth for thousands of years. And we've analyzed enough of them to learn a lot about their composition. Most come from asteroids . . . though a few may have come from comets . . . so essentially they're rocks, and like rocks they're mixtures of minerals. They're generally classified into three broad categories: stones, stony irons, and irons.

Stone meteorites, which we refer to simply as, uh, stones, are almost entirely rock material. They actually account for almost all of the meteorite material that falls to Earth. But even so, it's rare to ever find one. I mean, it's easier to find an iron meteorite or a stony iron. Anyone guess why? Look at their names. What do you think iron meteorites consist of?

Female student
Mostly iron?

Professor
Yeah, iron and some nickel, both of which are metals. And if you're trying to find metal?

Female student
Oh, metal detectors!

Professor
Right, thank you. At least that's part of it. Stone meteorites . . . if they lie around, exposed to the weather for a few years, well, they're made of rock so they end up looking almost indistinguishable from common terrestrial rocks . . . ones that originated on Earth. So it's hard to spot them by eye. But we can use metal detectors to help us find the others, and they're easier to spot by eye—so most of the meteorites in collections, uh, in museums, they'll be, they're iron meteorites or the stony-iron kind even though they only make up about 5 percent of the meteorite material on the ground.

TRACK 146 TRANSCRIPT

Narrator
Listen again to part of the lecture. Then answer the question.

Professor
Anyone guess why? Look at their names. What do you think iron meteorites consist of?

Female student
Mostly iron?

Professor
Yeah, iron and some nickel, both of which are metals. And if you're trying to find metal?

Narrator
Why does the professor say this:

Professor
And if you're trying to find metal?

TRACK 147 TRANSCRIPT

Narrator
Talk about a game, sport or other group activity that is played in your country. Explain why you think the activity is enjoyable.

TRACK 148 TRANSCRIPT

Narrator
When looking for information for a research project, some students prefer to get their information mainly from the Internet. Others prefer to mainly use printed materials such as books and academic journals. Which do you prefer, and why?

TRACK 149 TRANSCRIPT

Narrator
The university is considering building a new athletic stadium. Read the article in the student newspaper. You will have 45 seconds to read the article. Begin reading now.

TRACK 150 TRANSCRIPT

Narrator
Now listen to two students discussing the article.

Male student
So, what do you think of the university's new plan?

Female student
Oh, I don't know. I don't think it's gonna work.

Male student
No?

Female student
I mean, I can't imagine top students being too thrilled about some of the conditions on this campus.

Male student
What do you mean?

Female student
Like, the science laboratories having such old, outdated equipment, and the library needing more books, and the student center being so small. I think that the two million could be spent in better places if the university is really serious about achieving its goal.

Male student
OK. But what about the other reason for building the stadium? I mean, right now, we have so little contact with the town . . .

Female student
Yeah, but this won't help relations. Look, people from town hardly ever come to games because our teams always lose and they're not suddenly going to improve overnight. Besides, adding seats won't make a difference. I mean, if people from town didn't come before, they won't come now just because the place is bigger.

Narrator
The woman expresses her opinion about the university's plan. State her opinion and explain the reasons she gives for holding that opinion.

TRACK 151 TRANSCRIPT

Narrator
Now read the passage from a psychology textbook. You have 50 seconds to read the passage.

TRACK 152 TRANSCRIPT

Narrator
Now listen to part of a lecture on this topic in a psychology class.

Professor
Let's take an everyday example, an ordinary round plate like you'd find in a kitchen. If you hold the plate directly in front of your face and look at it, what shape do you see? A perfect circle, right? Suppose you tilt the plate to a different angle, to a horizontal position—like you're planning to put food on it. Still a perfect circle? No. The circle is now stretched out, flattened into an oval. Do you conclude the plate has actually changed shape? Or—that it's a different object, not the same plate? Of course not. It looks different, but we perceive it as still being the same.

Here's a different example. This classroom we're in . . . it's fairly large, right? Now, from up close, from the front row, I appear to be relatively big—bigger than if you were in the last row, right? But let's say you're sitting in the front row today, but tomorrow you're sitting in the back row. From back there I'm going to look smaller, but you don't think I've actually gotten smaller. You don't think you're seeing a different professor, a guy who looks like me except he's smaller. No matter where you are—up close or far away, you understand, without even thinking about it, that I'm the same size, the same person.

Narrator
Explain what is meant by perceptual constancy, using the examples provided by the professor.

TRACK 153 TRANSCRIPT

Narrator
Now listen to a conversation between two students.

Female student
Hey, Mark. How's it going?

Male student
Not too good.

Female student
What's wrong?

Male student
Well, you know how I'm president of the Anthropology club? Well, I'm supposed to drive everyone in the club to see a special exhibit at the museum tomorrow. My mom said I could borrow her van, you know, so everyone would fit, but unfortunately, it broke down and it's not going to be repaired in time for the trip.

Female student
Oh. So what are you going to do? Can you rent a van?

Male student
Yeah, that's a possibility. It's a little risky for me though. I've tried to get in touch with the club members, but only 4 have gotten back to me and said they'd contribute some money to the cost.

Female student
What about the other members?

Male student
I don't know. It'd probably be OK with them too. But that's the risk. I don't know for sure. I don't want to get stuck with having to pay for most of the bill.

Female student
Well, since not everyone's gotten back to you, why don't you just postpone the trip, you know, until your mom's van is repaired?

Male student
Yeah, I could do that. Though I'm sure everyone would be real disappointed if they show up tomorrow ready to go and find out that we're not going.

Narrator
The speakers discuss two possible solutions to the man's problem. Briefly summarize the problem. Then state which solution you recommend and explain why.

TRACK 154 TRANSCRIPT

Narrator
Now listen to part of a lecture in a biology class.

Professor
Now, many sea animals, in order to hide from predators, have over time, developed different kinds of *camouflage* to help them blend in with their environment and avoid detection by predators.

Picture the surface of the seafloor—it's as varied as the land we live on. It's got peaks and valleys, vegetation, rocky areas. And some sea animals have developed permanent colors or shapes to resemble these environmental features. This camouflage helps disguise them from predators by enabling them to blend into a-a *specific part* of the sea. For instance, take a kind of fish like the *leafy sea dragon*. Well, the name says it all: it resembles a small green dragon, with leaf-like protrusions sticking out like arms. Now, because of its color and shape, it blends in extremely well with green sea plants. So when the leafy sea dragon is swimming through these plants, predators have trouble seeing it. But when it enters other environments, without these green plants, its camouflage doesn't work anymore.

Now, other sea animals are difficult to spot *anywhere* in the sea because their type of camouflage enables them to change color. Take the cuttlefish, a fish that's closely related to the squid and octopus. Unlike leafy sea dragons, cuttlefish have not developed any particular shape to hide from predators, but, uh, they have a lot more mobility because their camouflage allows them to blend into any environment. Because cuttlefish have shifting pigments that allow them to change color in a matter of seconds. And so they can almost instantaneously match the color of their surroundings. If they're swimming by green sea plants, they'll turn green and if they're swimming over the brown seafloor, they'll turn brown.

Narrator
Using the examples of the leafy sea dragon and the cuttlefish, describe two kinds of camouflage and the benefits they provide.

TRACK 155 TRANSCRIPT

Narrator
Now listen to part of a lecture on the topic you just read about.

Professor
Of course there's some negative consequences of selling fossils in the commercial market, but they've been greatly exaggerated. The benefits of commercial fossil trade greatly outweigh the disadvantages.

First of all, the public is likely to have *greater* exposure to fossils as a result of commercial fossil trade, not *less* exposure. Commercial fossil hunting makes a *lotta* fossils available for purchase. And as a result, even low-level public institutions, like-like public schools and libraries, can now routinely buy interesting fossils and display them for the public.

As for the idea that scientists will lose access to really important fossils, that's not realistic either. Before anyone can put a value on a fossil, it needs to be scientifically identified. Right? Well, the only people who can identify fossils—who can really tell what a given fossil is or isn't—are *scientists*, by performing detailed examinations and tests on the fossils themselves. So, even if a fossil's destined to go to a private collector, it has to pass through the hands of scientific experts first. This way, the scientific community is not gonna miss out on anything important that's out there.

Finally, whatever damage commercial fossil collectors sometimes do, if it weren't for them, many fossils would simply go undiscovered, because there aren't that many fossil collecting operations that're run by universities and other scientific institutions. Isn't it better for science to at least have *more* fossils being found—even if we don't have all the scientific data we'd like to have about their location and surroundings—than it is to have many fossils go completely undiscovered?

TRACK 156 TRANSCRIPT

Narrator
Summarize the points made in the lecture, being sure to explain how they oppose specific points made in the reading passage.